Structural Prevention of Ethnic Violence

Structural Prevention of Ethnic Violence

Christian P. Scherrer

Ethnic Conflicts Research Project (ECOR)
The Netherlands

and

Hiroshima Peace Institute
Hiroshima City University
Japan

Foreword by Johan Galtung

First published 2002 by
PALGRAVE MACMILLAN
Houndmills, Basingstoke, Hampshire RG21 6XS and
175 Fifth Avenue, New York, N.Y. 10010
Companies and representatives throughout the world

PALGRAVE MACMILLAN is the global academic imprint of the Palgrave
Macmillan division of St. Martin's Press, LLC and of Palgrave Macmillan Ltd.
Macmillan® is a registered trademark in the United States, United Kingdom
and other countries. Palgrave is a registered trademark in the European
Union and other countries.

ISBN 0–333–75206–6

This book is printed on paper suitable for recycling and made from fully
managed and sustained forest sources.

A catalogue record for this book is available from the British Library.

Library of Congress Cataloging-in-Publication Data
Scherrer, Christian P.
     Structural prevention of ethnic violence / by Christian P. Scherrer.
         p. cm.
     'Ethnic Conflicts Research Project (ECOR), the Netherlands'.
     Includes bibliographical references and index.
     ISBN 0–333–75206–6 (cloth)
         1. Ethnic conflict–Prevention. 2. Political violence–Prevention.
     3. Conflict management. 4. Peace. I. Title

     GN496 .S37 2002
     305.8–dc21   2001053260

10   9   8   7   6   5   4   3   2   1
11   10   09   08   07   06   05   04   03   02

Printed and bound in Great Britain by
Antony Rowe Ltd, Chippenham and Eastbourne

To the threatened people and peoples of this world

Contents

List of Tables

Foreword

by Johan Galtung

This brilliantly conceived and very well researched book is a source of wisdom that will enhance your knowledge and compassion for the human condition. The amount of knowledge conveyed in its pages is amazing. Countless millions who have suffered – mainly but not exclusively at the hands of the West – are given a voice through its well-documented pages. They encounter so much almost endless violence, expressed either in direct violence as eradication or genocide; in structural violence as colonialism, manifest in today's reservations; or in cultural violence as an unbounded arrogance, bolstered by the sense of being chosen by God, by being socially at the peak of evolution and by being economically favoured by the Market. Nevertheless, a message of hope shines through, already expressed in the title: *Structural Prevention of Ethnic Violence*. The message carried by the word 'prevention' is very clear: act before violence breaks out, not afterward.

A nationality, as defined by Scherrer, is a 'nation without its own state but in search of statehood'. The United Nations should have been their trade union, if we take the name literally. As we know 'Members are States'; the UN is a trade union of states with one clear, common interest: do not touch our borders. With 200 states, at least 2000 nations but only 20 nation-states (to give some indication) there could be hundreds of wars to fight – some of which have taken place since 1945 – unless we learn to better handle the nationality question before hostilities break out.

Indeed, there may be nations within nations and so forth also seeking statehood. The term 'structural' carries another clear and important message: the arrangement must be solid, long lasting (although nothing is eternal), acceptable, self-sustaining – and as little dependent on outside 'guarantees' as possible. Again, act beforehand, pre-emptively, preventively, not as a cure after major violence has already struck.

A key instrument is 'self-determination', but, as Scherrer points out, it tends to 'protect states rather than peoples'. Moreover, there has been an unfortunate tendency on all sides to cast the struggle in terms of a (shameful) status quo versus independence where the broader term 'autonomy' may be more useful. As Scherrer says: 'Prevention through appropriate autonomy arrangements and generous nationality policies is not only cheaper than intervention, they are, in fact, the only real, ideal method when it comes to dealing constructively with the problem of ethno-national difference.' Adding: 'The development of concepts of structural prevention of genocide and mass violence are among the noblest tasks of peace research.' I could not agree more.

While the subject matter of medicine is to build health, avoid disease and specifically pandemics, the essence of peace research is to build peace, avoid violence and specifically genocide, defined as the extermination of people because they are identified as belonging to a certain category. One such category is 'nation', others categories are gender, class, race, citizen.

A generally accepted fact is that people want to be governed by their own kind, which is what autonomy is all about, from its lowest to its highest levels of articulation. Deny them that and there will be trouble. Our task now is to expand the spectrum of responses to that challenge. And Scherrer's book is indispensable in that search.

Preface

Prevention of destructive violence is a political imperative for the twenty-first century. Since World War II, more than 300 wars have taken place worldwide – most of them, until the end of the 1980s, in the Third World. Claims of a number of nation-states in regard to the nationalities, which they claim as their own citizens and in regard to ethnic minorities and indigenous peoples, seem to become increasingly aggressive in times of changes. On the view presented here, this state of affairs is, in empirical-cum-historical terms, the most dangerous potential and actual source of conflicts and wars both in the former Third World and, since 1989–90, in the former nominally socialist multinational states. Almost two-thirds of current wars are susceptible to 'ethnic' interpretation. It was only when the Janus-like countenance of nationalism reappeared in Europe that the media and broad sections of the public in the West became aware of this global trend towards ethno-nationalism, of which there had been evidence since the period of decolonization. This belated nationalism reviewed the situation left behind by the colonial world-order. Its duality has to do with an inherent dichotomy between liberation and oppression, between emancipation and barbarity.

The global trend towards an increase in intra-state conflicts and a decrease – if not near disappearance – of the classic Clausewitzean war between states has grown steadily over the last few decades. At the end of the millennium there was no interstate conflict, after the bloody war and *fratricide* between Ethiopia and Eritrea was stopped and UN peacekeepers deployed in December 2000, but – dependent on the criteria employed – there are several dozen other violent conflicts. Their main incompatabilities reflect intra-state conditions but the violence they produce does often spill-over borders. We witness a multiplicity of actors in some complex new conflicts (with the Congo and Sudan being the best examples). Different types of contemporary intra-state conflicts can be observed; their dominant characteristic being either anti-regime or ethno-nationalistic, followed by inter-ethnic wars – mostly without state actors being involved – and gang wars and warlordism, which were named 'postmodern wars' (despite the fact that this conflict type has a longer history). There are some decolonization conflicts; the last one to explode was East Timor. The list of conflict types would not be complete without the most deadly one: genocide and other forms of non-war mass violence. Terrorist conflicts, which in the form of international gang wars have gained much attention since 11 September 2001, are neither a new phenomenon nor a particularly deadly form of mass violence. The death toll is relatively low; in 2001 they might have caused 0.2 per cent of all conflict-related fatalities.

Those conflict types suited to ethnic interpretation – with ethnicity as the mobilizing force – seemed to grow fastest, although they have been prominent for quite some time. Increases in violent ethno-nationalist conflicts have been observed in the wake of a number of phases of decolonization. Ethno-national conflicts of a violent kind are both products and causes of colonial creation and of the inherent instability of *new states*. Thus, ethno-nationalism is a response to serious ongoing crises; its primary cause, the struggle against the neo-colonial state, has strong structural aspects and, therefore, a truly global spread. However, the level of conflict varies considerably in the different regions of the world. As the example of the CIS shows, the structure and dynamics of the process of fragmentation in the East followed its own rules and differed significantly from the situation in the South.

Any attempt to clarify or resolve sub-national conflicts must be preceded by the realization that existential questions relating to the survival of an ethnic group are not factors that are open to negotiation but essential prerequisites to dialogue. There are a number of highly destructive forms of interaction between states and nations/nationalities resulting in the exclusion and persecution of national groups that have not yet been subject to systematic investigation and for which the international community has not yet developed any consistent policy. This was demonstrated with devastating clarity in the case of the genocide in Rwanda in 1994. The crime of genocide not only calls for prevention but for its elimination. Genocide prevention requires different means other than the prevention of ethnic violence in general and ethno-nationalism in particular.

The political-cum-humanitarian concern to find ways of avoiding violent forms of ethno-nationalism from below and ethnicization from above leads on to the questions of (1) how ethnic and cultural difference can be understood and acknowledged; (2) how destructive forms of interaction between states and nations or nationalities can be prevented; and (3) which institutions, legal measures and policies are most appropriate for that purpose. At the beginning of 1993, former UN secretary-general Boutros-Ghali wrote, very appositely, that it was simpler and cheaper to tackle wars preventively than to try to put a stop to hostilities that had already broken out.

The main problems politicians face in promoting preventive measures and policies are three-fold: (1) the unspectacular and long-term character of many such measures makes them not very attractive if quick results are required; (2) the difficulty in measuring their effectiveness adds to confusion about the subject matter; and (3) a number of rather diverse institutions, measures and policies have preventive characteristics but often remain disengaged or partially implemented.

In preventing violence there are no 'easy solutions'. The great diversity of cultural and political characteristics exhibited by different types of society produce, correspondingly, different types of claims to autonomy and regulatory mechanisms, ranging from cultural autonomy through territorial self-governance to *de facto* sovereignty. Protection of ethnic and national minorities by means of a variety of arrangements for autonomy did not begin until the twentieth century, triggered by a worsening of the so-called 'minorities problem' as a result of revolutions and the regroupings that had occurred in the wake of the two world wars.

Too little account has been taken of the nationality policies of certain multinational states when it comes to looking for methods of prevention and dealing with protracted and bloody ethno-national conflicts. Many states have been able to pursue active and successful policies of prevention by making concessions and negotiation involving some element of nationality policy. Others have – often with limited success – used similar tactics to try to resolve armed conflicts that have already escalated. Nationality policies are generally not considered to be solutions to conflicts that are smouldering or have already erupted. Some procedures aim more at containment, or pose the nationality question in a purely socio-political context. But such policies are part of the problem. A detailed comparison ought to be made of the different approaches to nationality policy pursued by selected states such as Denmark, Canada, the USA, the CIS/Russian Federation, China, India, Australia, Brazil, Colombia, Panama, Nicaragua and Ethiopia.

During field research done in the 1980s and early 1990s in two deadly conflict areas (Nicaragua and Ethiopia), solutions – although not ideal ones, as in Nicaragua, or very partial ones, as in Ethiopia – were developed by the local actors themselves. This led me to think about forms of 'structural prevention' of violence, 'structural' in the sense that new frameworks and institutions are created to avert possible direct violence and reduce structural violence, such as discrimination against non-dominant groups. I am deeply indebted to Johan Galtung, who developed the concept of 'structural violence' in the 1970s, based on his path-breaking distinction between direct personal violence (massacres or war) and structural violence (that is, poverty kills). Galtung also reflected on cultural violence, for example values that promote and/or justify violence and superiority complexes that result in aggressive attitudes. Structural prevention aims at ending repression and injustice which is ingrained in state policies and underdevelopment and is also an inherent in the cultural attitudes of many dominant groups.

The contribution of systemic peace research is underestimated. The activities involved range from initiatives by popular local and regional movements to the elaboration of norms and legal instruments within the framework of international and universal organizations. Efforts to change a violence promoting framework through disarmament, controls and bans on arms production and trade, demobilization and the strengthening of civil society have often been neglected in the debate about how to deal with or prevent violent conflicts. Work on macro-themes seem to have little effect. Yet partial successes such as the ban on the production of anti-personnel landmines is a crucial step on the path to a more peaceful world.

The underdeveloped state of political and institutional consultancy in peaceful dispute settlement by third parties, or 'go-betweens' in the case of protracted 'ethnic' conflicts, is lamentable. Conflict mediation and facilitation in such conflicts undoubtedly can be successful as an instrument of international politics and should not be left solely to state and inter-state actors. But efforts at go-between mediation by civil actors and initiatives for transforming violent ethno-national and other ethnic conflicts are arduous and hold little attraction for the media.

Against the background of media discovery of the ethnic, and of the general inadequacy of research into the forgotten conflicts of the Third World, more studies should aim to outline and compare various regional and local attempts at conflict resolution within the framework of state policies on minorities and nationalities, to link these up with evolving provisions in international law and human rights and situate them within the international system. The role of multilateral regimes and of the international community in preventing and resolving violent conflicts should be discussed more systematically. Furthermore, more attempts should be made to give a thorough conceptual account of the phenomenon of ethnicity, to work out elements of a theory of modern genocides as well as of 'new wars' and ethno-nationalism, to investigate the latter's causes, to distinguish its many different manifestations, to highlight its political potential as an opposition force, to analyze its structural characteristics and the driving forces behind its militarization and to set the phenomenon of 'ethnic' conflict in a global context. These various aspects can be illustrated by means of examples from four different continents.

This can be read as a call for the reorientation of peace and conflict research towards the 'real existing' conflict formations and for the intensification of international attempts to find methods of preventing and resolving conflict. One factor that is of major importance in the prevention of ethnic and national conflicts is the extension not only of international norms and standards of protection for non-dominant minorities and indigenous peoples but also of the rights of these groups in regard to autonomy and self-governance. In the current debate, normative and structural dimensions of 'conflict prevention', (what is meant is the prevention of violence) are often neglected in favour of more activist and technical approaches. This contradicts the fact that techniques of preventive multi-track diplomacy (such as mediation, facilitation, good offices, arbitration and so on) and other forms of peaceful conflict settlement by go-betweens are – in regard to their overall effectiveness – of secondary importance when compared with a long-term policy for the prevention of violent inter-ethnic and other intra-state conflicts. Therefore, the proliferation of states since 1990 is seen by some observers as a form of 'conflict resolution' and by others as a dangerous fragmentation and a slide into chaos.

The account given here of applied forms of self-governance is the fruit of several years of field research in ethno-national war zones and of collaboration with representatives of indigenous and endangered nations/nationalities. To provide a global comparison of nationality policies based on a set of evaluative qualitative criteria for self-governance agreements is something that can only be attempted in outline here. For some of the cases mentioned, the author can call not only on a wealth of documentation, but also on first-hand information and personal on-the-spot observation.

A further study critically reviews the activities undertaken by international humanitarian organizations in ethnic conflicts and also the efforts of the UN Human Rights Commission to work out minimum standards for the rights of minorities and indigenous peoples. The observations on multilateral regimes are confined, for the most part, to the 'human dimension' – that is to say, to human rights mechanisms and minority rights issues. New paths in this direction have been embarked on within the framework convention of the Council of Europe, which laid great emphasis on the protection of national minorities and the creation of the institution of a High Commissioner for National Minorities within the OSCE. However, speculations about the transposability of such (limited) European 'models' must be viewed with scepticism. Legal instruments are not sufficient in themselves in promoting good relations between different communities on the ground. In addition to standard-setting activities (for example the Framework Convention for the Protection of National Minorities of Council of Europe), confidence-building and other measures at grassroot levels aimed at increasing tolerance and understanding between people belonging to different ethnic groups, are required. Reflection on increasing calls for the UN (or NATO) to become involved, or to intervene militarily, in war zones and areas of conflict since the early 1990s, makes clear the primary need for structural prevention and for an expansion in the choice of non-military options. To round off this part of the discussion, a few observations are made about a possible new role for the United Nations.

This choice of objectives necessitates moving far beyond a narrowly defined standpoint. As a field of study, ethno-nationalism embraces the disciplines of ethnology, sociology, folklore, the humanities, human geography, political science, international relations, and constitutional and international law. At present, the needs created by interdisciplinary co-operation have still only limited institutional possibilities corresponding to (or conflicting with) them. The use of various categories and concepts from other disciplines is a necessity in this area of study, but it does not in itself constitute interdisciplinarity.

Rigid subject-based division, with its differing perspectives and traditional areas of operation, has led to a fragmentation of the research-field and makes the prospect of any kind of understanding appear dim. The objective cannot be 'to know a little bit about everything'; what we need to do, rather, is to flesh out those issues and methods that have to do with current social problems or can be brought into some kind of relation with them. The separate disciplines can only be linked to current issues (such as intra-societal and cultural conflicts) when peace and conflict research has completed the process of reorientation that has been on the agenda since 1990. Peace research has to develop its communication skills before being able to promote issue-centred dialogue between the various disciplines involved. But establishing an interdisciplinary dialogue is a very demanding process. Where the networking indeed functions well, it does so only on a discrete basis. Up to now the peace research network has been a little too structured and very much tied to individuals. In terms of practical application, the outreach of peace research is almost completely restricted to conferences, workshops, the occasional public debate, and – a trend that is no doubt likely to greatly increase any attempt to link all continents in the near future – the internet. More influential to public awareness are mass media reports on wars or violence occurring in 'far-away places', which often include one-minute interviews with peace researchers who usually disagree with each other.

In the body of peace research there is still little regard to the fact that the distribution of wars has changed radically in the past twentieth century and that today almost all major conflicts are intra-state (civil wars and domestic genocides). Only a few institutions have programmes on intra-state conflicts, its causes and the peace strategies specifically designed to influence internal conflict. Systematic research on the various forms of prevention of violence, peaceful settlement of disputes and constructive transformation of latent and violent conflicts is still largely underdeveloped.

Surprisingly very few social anthropologists and sociologists are contributing to increase the competence of peace and conflict research – and, most importantly, its application by activists in peace-building and practitioners of conflict management – in regard to the types of civil wars driven by ethno-national, cultural and in some cases economic factors, or struggles for power. This lack of interest seems to prevail despite (or because?) of such research being a highly topical and fundamentally problem-oriented field. Its themes and methods overlap with similarly problem-oriented areas of research dealing with major contemporary issues such as migration, racism and multiculturalism. The preoccupation with such neglected topical problem areas nevertheless has become a new feature of studies, concepts and analyses of a growing body of research since the end of the cold war and more so since the mid 1990s.

The analytical framework of this study certainly cannot be constructed within the boundaries of a single discipline. While discipline based research in the humanities and social sciences continues to have an important task to do, the specializations of the individual disciplines must be linked up to themes and issues of general interest. It is in this area that peace and conflict research could exercise one of its most important functions within the academic enterprise. Because of its quasi-inherent orientation towards problems and topical events, it would be in a position to make a major contribution to the kind of reforming and innovatory thrust which is needed to respond to the new challenges of the present age and set the relationship of the sciences to society on an appropriate footing.

However, extending the frame of reference – for example, to include the political sciences and jurisprudence – also results in certain problems being 'imported'. As is demonstrated by the axiomatic presupposition of states as the primary political actors, this can become an obstacle. Such axioms tend towards exclusivity and towards the exclusion or neglect of the part played by other actors. In my view, an exclusively state-centred orientation is to be rejected. Nations without states look for a revision of international law that will secure them protection and guarantees within the community of nations. For indigenous peoples and for many endangered nationalities, the quest to secure an improvement in their legal status and recognition as political entities is a matter of survival. Not only has the concept of state sovereignty long since been undermined by the international enmeshment that has occurred in politics, the economy and communications. We live in the third era of globalization. The principle of non-intervention in internal affairs is now negated by the existence of international regimes and multilateral organizations: by the UN system; by powerful institutions (such as the IMF and World Bank); by the financial markets, the activities of international banks and multinational corporations and the omnipresence of the electronic media, with their disregard for national frontiers. The territorial integrity of the 195 states is increasingly being called into question by the existence of between 3000 and 10,000 ethnically distinct entities. Many nationalities aspire to separate statehood or respond to the particular configuration of power by seeking a free association with existing states; some already enjoy a form of autonomy or self-governance, others have fought for and secured a *de facto* autonomy based on arms.

For a long time, subjects such as 'the nation', 'nationalism', or 'ethnicity' were taboo in many parts of the world. As long as these ideas were being used in relation to the most remote areas of the Third World, the threshold of inhibition within the scientific community remained relatively low; but 'too bold' application of them to their own societies was regarded as well nigh outrageous. Not long ago, ideas such as 'ethnic conflict' or 'ethno-nationalism' were avoided as far as possible or, depending on the situation and area of the world, were replaced by misleading euphemistic (or demonizing) expressions such as 'miscellaneous conflicts', 'ethnic cleansing', or 'tribalism'. Because of the stigmatization of the subjects mentioned, there has been little incentive to try to fill the gaps in research on ethno-nationalism and on the ways of preventing or resolving such conflicts. This whole area has been left to the journalists, propagandists and bar-room politicians.

As a result of the frequently perverted depiction of the ethnic factor in the press and under the influence of the media's confused categorization of horrendous images of war, the scientific discourse on this subject is scarcely audible and remains largely ignored. The need to come up with new definitions and to make what may be unusual connections will place interested readers in the position of having to question well-established views. This study is part of an overdue attempt to address one of the major issues of our time from a multi-dimensional interdisciplinary perspective.

I should like to preface this work with some words of thanks to friends and colleagues. I am very grateful to Johan Galtung, Ted Robert Gurr, Kader Asmal, the late Bernard Nietschmann, the late Howard R. Berman, Judy Butler, Mohamed A. Teisir, Kumar Rupesinghe, Jannis Markakis, Mohamed Sahnoun, Julian Burger, Norbert Ropers, Michael van Walt, Matthias Stiefel, Joseph Nsengimana, Stephen Ryan, Hans Petter Buvollen, Willem J. Assies, Patricia van Nispen, Christoph Schwager, Alexander Sutter, Anton Ivanov, Regine Mehl, Martin Bondeli, Lorenz Löffler, Dieter Senghaas and Tobias Debiel for their comments and criticisms, and especially to Siglinde Gertschen and Sigi Szczepanski for suggestions and for reading through the manuscript, and to Margaret Clarke, for her careful and competent translation of large sections of my German texts.

I am particularly indebted, also, to all the representatives and champions of indigenous and endangered peoples whose acquaintance I have made over the last dozen years. They have opened my eyes to the profoundly desperate situations, the sufferings and the fighting spirit that exist on the periphery of the world's states and systems. Their resistance and their struggle for their historic rights and for the right to be different, deserve our sympathy and support.

CHRISTIAN P. SCHERRER

List of Abbreviations

ACP-EU	African, Caribbean, Pacific – European Union
ADF	Allied Democratic Forces (West Uganda, DRC)
AFB	Arbeitsgruppe Friedensforschung Bonn/Peace Research Information Unit Bonn (http://www.bonn.iz-soz.de/afb)
AFDL	Alliance des Forces Démocratiques de Libération (DRC)
AGKED	Arbeitsgemeinschaft Kirchlicher Entwicklungsdienste (FRG)
AGP	Assam Gana Parishad (India)
AI	Amnesty International (London)
AIM	American Indian Movement
AIPP	Asian Indigenous Peoples Pact (Bangkok)
AIS	Armée Islamique du Salut (Algeria, wing of FIS)
AJSU	All Jharkhand Students Union (India)
ANC	African National Congress (South Africa)
ANUC	Asociación Nacional de Usarios Campesinos
APEC	Asia Pacific Economic Co-operation
APPRA	Asia-Pacific Peace Research Association
ASEAN	Association of South-East Asian Nations
ASEN	Association for the Study of Ethnicity and Nationalism
ASSR	Autonomous Soviet Socialist Republic
Berghof	Center for Constructive Conflict Management (Berlin)
BIA	Bureau of Indian Affairs (USA)
BJP	Bharatiya Janata Party (India)
BRA	Bougainville Revolutionary Army (Papua New Guinea)
CARICOM	Caribbean Common Market
CCA	Carter Center, Atlanta (www.cc.emory.edu/)
CCM	Chama Cha Mapinduzi (Tanzania)
CDR	Coalition pour la Défense de la République (Rwanda)
CHSG	Conference of Heads of State and Government (OAU)
CIS	Commonwealth of Independent states (12 states, all former Soviet Republics except for the Baltic states www.cis.minsk.by)
CISA	Congreso Indígena del Sur de América
CMG	Conflict Management Group (Harvard)
CMM	Chattisgarh Mukti Morcha (India)
CoE	Council of Europe
COPRED	Consortium on Peace Research, Education & Development (http://www.igc.apc.org/copred/)
CORPI	Coordinación Regional de Pueblos Indígenas

CPB	Communist Party of Burma
CPC	Conflict Prevention Centre (OSCE)
CPSID	Convention on the Peaceful Settlement of International Disputes
CRP	Conflict Resolution Program (Carter Center, Atlanta, Georgia)
CSCE	Conference on Security and Co-operation in Europe (later OSCE)
CSE	Comunità di Sant'Egidio, Rome, Catholic INGO
CSO	Committee of Senior Officials (OSCE)
DAB	Democratic Alliance of Burma
DANIDA	Danish International Development Agency
Democide	website on Democide (www2.hawaii.edu/~rummel/)
DEZADDC	Swiss Agency for Development Cooperation, Berne
DGFK	Deutsche Gesellschaft für Friedens- und Konfliktforschung
doCIP	Documentation Centre for Indigenous Peoples (Geneva)
DRC	Democratic Republic of Congo
EBLUL	European Bureau of Lesser Used Languages
ECA	UN Economic Commission for Africa, Addis Ababa (www.uneca.org/)
ECOR	Ethnic Conflicts Research Project
ECOSOC	Economic and Social Council (UN)
ECOMOG	ECOWAS Cease-fire Monitoring Group I and II (in Liberia and Sierra Leone)
ECOWAS	Economic Community of West African States
EDF	European Development Fund (European Union; development fund)
ELN	Ejército de Liberación Nacional (Colombia)
EPCPT	European Platform for Conflict Prevention and Transformation (network of European NGOs, www.euconflict.org/)
EPLF	Eritrean People's Liberation Front
EPRDF	Ethiopian Peoples Revolutionary Democratic Front (gov. party, former liberation movement)
ESN	Ethnic Studies Network
EZLN	Ejército Zapatista de Liberación Nacional/Zapatista National Liberation Army (Mexico, Chiapas)
FARC	Fuerzas Armadas Revolucionarias de Colombia
FGN	Federal Government of Nagaland (India)
FIER	Foundation for Inter-ethnic Relations
FIS	Front islamique du Salut (Algeria)
FLEC	Frente de Libertação do Enclave de Cabinda (Angola)
FMLN	Frente Farabuno Martí para la Liberación Nacional (El Salvador)

FRELIMO	Frente de Libertacão de Moçambique/Liberation Front of Mozambique
FRETILIN	Frente Revolucionara de Timor Leste Independiente/ Revolutionary Front of Independent East Timor)
FSLN	Frente Sandinista de Liberación Nacional (Nicaragua)
FSO	foreign-state occupation
GfBV	Gesellschaft für bedrohte Völker (Göttingen, FRG)
GIA	Groupe Islamique Armé (Algeria)
GNLF	Gorkha National Liberation Front (India)
HCNM	High Commissioner on National Minorities (OSCE)
HDI	Human Development Index (UNDP, annual reports, http://www.undp.org/hdro/)
HRFOR	Human Rights Field Operation in Rwanda (1994–8, by UNHCHR)
HRW	Human Rights Watch (http://www.hrw.org/)
HSFK	Hessische Stiftung Friedens- und Konfliktforschung
IA	International Alert (http://www.international-alert.org)
IBRD	World Bank (http://www.worldbank.org/)
ICAR	Institute for Conflict Analysis and Resolution, George Mason University (Fairfax Virginia)
ICC	International Criminal Court (to be established)
ICC	Inuit Circumpolar Conference
ICCPR	International Covenant on Civil and Political Rights
ICESCR	International Covenant on Economic, Social and Cultural Rights
ICG	International Crisis Group (Brussels)
ICJ	International Court of Justice (The Hague)
ICON	Internal Conflicts and their Resolution (IPRA group)
ICRC\CICR	International Committee of the Red Cross/Comité International de la Croix-Rouge (Geneva, www.cicr.org)
ICTR	International Criminal Tribunal for Rwanda (Arusha, http://www.ictr.org/)
ICTY	International Criminal Tribunal for the Former Yugoslavia (The Hague, www.icty.or/)
IDP	internally displaced person
IFSH	Institut für Friedensforschung und Sicherheitspolitik (Hamburg)
IGCC	University of California Institute on Global Conflict and Co-operation (http://www-igcc.ucsd.edu)
IITC	International Indian Treaty Council (San Francisco)
IJC	International Court of Justice (The Hague)
ILO	International Labour Organization (Geneva)
ILRC	Indian Law Resource Center
IMEMO	Institute for World Economy (Moscow)

IMF	International Monetary Fund (http://www.imf.org/)
INCORE	Initiative on Conflict Resolution and Ethnicity (www.incore.ulst.ac.uk/)
INEF	Institut für Entwicklung und Frieden/Institute for Development and Peace (University of Duisburg)
INGOs	International Non-Governmental Organizations
INN	International Negotiation Network (Carter Center, Emory Univ., Atlanta, Georgia)
IPA	International Peace Academy (www.ipacademy.org/)
IPRA	International Peace Research Association
IRIPAZ	Instituto de Relaciones Internacionales y de Investigación para la Paz (Guatemala)
IUPIP	International University of Peoples' Initiative for Peace (http://www.unimondon.org/iupip)
IWGIA	International Work-Group for Indigenous Affairs
JEEAR	Joint Evaluation of Emergency Assistance to Rwanda (international consortium, coordinated by DANIDA)
KANU	Kenya African National Union
KIO/KIA	Kachin Independence Organization/Army (Burma)
KLA	Kosovo Liberation Army (Federal Republic of Yugoslavia, also known as UCK)
KNU	Karen National Union (Burma)
LLDC	least developed country
LNO	Lahu National Organization (Burma)
LRA	Lord's Resistance Army (North Uganda, Sudan)
LTTE	Liberation Tigers of Tamil Eelam (Sri Lanka)
MCAC	Mediation, Conciliation and Arbitration Committee (OAU)
MCC	Maoist Communist Centre (India)
MCTK	Movimiento Campesino Tupak Katari (Bolivia)
MFDC	Mouvement des Forces Démocratique de la Casamance (Senegal)
MIAND	Ministry for Indian Affairs and Northern Development
MINURSO	United Nations Mission for the Referendum in Western Sahara
MNF	Mwalimu Nyerere Foundation (Dar es Salaam)
MNRD	Mouvement National Républicain pour la Démocracie (Rwanda)
MONUC	Mission d'Observation des Nations Unies au Congo/UN Observer Mission to Congo-DR
MRTA	Movimiento Revolucionario Túpac Amaru (Peru)
MSF	Médecins Sans Frontières (humanitarian aid organization, emergency medical assistance; www.msf.org)
MTA	Mong Tai Army (Burma)
NAC	National Aboriginal Conference
NADECO	National Democratic Coalition (Nigeria)

NAFTA	North American Free Trade Agreement
NAILS	National Organization of Aboriginal and Islander Legal Services
NAM	Non-Aligned Movement
NCGUB	National Coalition Government of the Union of Burma
NCIV	Nederlands Center for Inheemse Volken
NNA	Neutral and Non-Aligned states
NNC	Naga National Council (India)
NSCN	National Socialist Council of Nagaland (India)
OAS	Organization of American States
OAU	Organization of African Unity (www.oau-oua.org/)
ODIHR	Office for Democratic Institutions and Human Rights (OSCE)
OECD	Organization for Economic Cooperation and Development (Paris)
OLF	Oromo Liberation Front (Ethiopia)
OSCE	Organization for Security and Co-operation in Europe (formerly CSCE)
ÖSFK	Österreichisches Studienzentrum für Frieden und Konfliktlösung
OW	One World (network, 250 NGOs www.oneworld.org/)
OXFAM	British development, advocacy and relief agency; http://www.oxfam.org
PBI	Peace Brigades International (www.igc.apc.org/pbi/)
PCA	Permanent Court of Arbitration (The Hague)
PGI	Prevent Genocide International www.preventgenocide.org
PHR	Physicians for Human Rights (medical forensic experts; http://www.phrusa.org/)
PIOOM	Interdisciplinary Research Programme on Causes of Human Rights Violations, Leiden, Netherlands (www.fsw.leidenuniv.nl/www/w3_liswo/pioom.htm)
PLA	Peoples Liberation Army (India)
PRIO	International Peace Research Institute Oslo (http://www.prio.no/)
PSLF	Palaung State Liberation Front (Burma)
RENAMO	Resistência Nacional Moçambicana
RGN	Revolutionary Government of Nagaland (India)
RPF	Rwandese Patriotic Front
RSS	Rashtriya Swayamsevak Sangh (India)
RUF	Revolutionary United Front (Sierra Leone)
SAARC	South Asian Association for Regional Co-operation
SADC	Southern African Development Community (Regional organization, 1992; 14 states from South Africa to Congo; http://www.sadcexpo.org/)
SADCC	Southern African Development Coordination Conference (Regional organization, 1980, frontline states against Apartheid South Africa, 1992 SADC)

SIDA	Swedish International Development Agency
SIPRI	Stockholm International Peace Research Institute
SLORC	State Law and Order Council (Burma)
SPLM/A	Sudanese People's Liberation Movement/Army
SSA	Shan State Army (Burma)
SSP	Shiv Sena Party (India)
SUA	Shan United Army (Burma)
TFF	Transnational Foundation for Future and Peace Research, Lund (www.transnational.org/sitemap.html)
TNC	transnational corporation
Transcend	Peace & Development Network (www.transcend.org)
TRC	Truth and Reconciliation Commission (South Africa)
UCK	Albanian name for Liberation Army of the Kosovo (Federal Republic of Yugoslavia)
ULFA	United Liberation Front of Assam (India)
UN DPI	UN Department of Public Information (various websites, e.g. http://www.reliefweb.int)
UN DPKO	United Nations Department for Peacekeeping Operations (http://www.un.org/Depts/dpko/)
UNAMIR	United Nations Assistance Mission for Rwanda (I, UN troops sent Oct. 1993, pulled out in April 1994, 2.500; II sent mid 1994, 5.500)
UNCTAD	United Nations Conference on Trade and Development
UNDP	United Nations Development Programme (http://www.undp.org/)
UNESCO	United Nations Educational, Scientific & Cultural Organization (http://www.unesco.org/)
UNHCHR	United Nations High Commissioner for Human Rights
UNHCR	United Nations High Commission for Refugees (http://www.unhcr.ch/)
UNICEF	United Nations Children's Fund (www.unicef.org/)
UNITA	Uniao Nacional para a Independencia Total de Angola/National Union for Total Independence of Angola
UNLF	United National Liberation Front (India)
UNPO	Unrepresented Nations and Peoples Organization (The Hague)
UNREO	United Nations Rwanda Emergency Office
UNRISD	United Nations Research Institute for Social Development (Geneva)
UNU	United Nations University (Tokyo; www.unu.edu/)
UNWGIP	United Nations Working Group on Indigenous Populations (Sub 2, UNCHR)
US-AID	Development agency of USA (http://198.76.84.1/)
USC	United Somali Congress (Somalia South)
USIP	United States Institute for Peace (www.usip.org/)

US-SD	US State Department, Bureau of African Affairs
UWSA	United Wa State Army (Burma)
WCIP	World Council of Indigenous Peoples
WF	State of the World Forum (www.worldforum.org/)
WNO	Wa National Organization (Burma)
WPI	World Policy Institute (www.worldpolicy.org/)
WSP	War-torn Societies Project (UNRISD, UN Geneva)
YATAMA	Yapti Tasbaya Masrika (Miskitu Indian movement, Eastern Nicaragua)

Introduction: Ethnos, Nations, Ethno-nationalism and Conflict

Often, those who pose the question of the ethnic basis of national identity find they have stirred up a hornet's nest. One largely unexamined presupposition underlying the idea of the nation-state in the European area was that a nation has a homogeneous basis – in other words, that ethnos and nation are one and the same. The terms 'ethnos' and 'ethnicity' – which have once again come into everyday use – are often devoid of content.

The state classes have sought to declare ethnicity to be a 'political pathology'. In political discourse, the term is mostly negatively charged, having connotations such as 'primitive', 'backward', or 'irrational'. Contrary to the prognoses of the political and social sciences in regard to the development of modern societies, ethnicity has lost none of its importance in recent years. On the contrary, the importance of the ethnic dimension and its politicization has grown into issues of status and categorization in violent conflicts, civilian disputes and instances of social demarcation and exclusion.

Different types of actors such as states, transnational companies, liberation movements, migrants' organizations, political parties, pressure groups, strategic groups, military leaders and populists, all seek to make political capital out of 'ethnic identity'. Some actors deliberately try to influence and manipulate the ethnic–identity set-up. In this study, the term 'ethnicity' is used to describe a variety of forms of mobilization, which ultimately relate to the autonomous existence of specifically ethnic forms of socialization, and which politicize these. No clear-cut distinction can, however, be made between struggles by social classes and struggles by ethnic groups.

The formation of ethnic identity cannot be taken as a given; it is the result (not an inevitable one) of processes of interaction within an ethnos, between one ethnos and another, and between one ethnos or more and a state or states. Of these three areas of conflict, only the second, the inter-ethnic, is generally taken into consideration – mostly in the form of supposedly tribal conflicts. In contrast, the conflictual relationship between ethnic groups and the state/states, which is of such significance precisely when it comes to ethno-nationalism, is frequently neglected.

Ethnic identity can, for example, be interpreted as the consciousness of cultural separateness or otherness. But this collective consciousness is not an intrinsic reflection of objective cultural characteristics in a particular ethnic entity of whatever kind. Nor is it a matter of 'free choice' resulting from subjective (individual or collective) identification with a specific ethnic group and its distinct character. It always exists within a conflictual context.

Following a long phase of avoidance and negation of the term, or of the reality it represents, 'ethnicity' has recently become a much-used byword. Reference to the supposedly ethnic character of a conflict often fulfils a purpose other than elucidation. Paradoxically, in those very conflicts that are described as 'ethnic' in the media, there is nothing, or almost nothing, typically ethnic to be found. The intention, rather – as in the coverage of the wars in Yugoslavia and the genocide in Rwanda – is to hamper the search for other causes. In extreme cases, the newly discovered byword 'ethnicity' is intended to divert attention from the true causal process. The ethnic discourse and its appeal to a particular community have, in each case and from the very outset, a political significance that is linked to the particular case and to the respective interests.

The concepts of 'minority' and 'ethnic group', which are often used in connection with ethno-national conflicts, are in need of elucidation. Similarly, the almost customary confusion of the concepts of 'nation', 'state', and 'nation-state' indicate a need for a thoroughgoing definition of terms. Colonial expansion put an end to the autonomous existence of a variety of social formations and political systems. 'Concepts' and reality were homogenized. The export of the nation-state model to the colonies ran into a host of difficulties, because no appropriate foundations for this kind of construct existed in the extra-European world.

Characteristics that define an ethnos or indigenous people as a nationality or as a nation without its own state continue to be a subject of dispute, for power-political (not analytical) reasons. Nowadays, however, stipulations are acquiring greater political relevance. The relationship between national minorities, nationalities and nations, on the one hand, and recognized states on the other, can no longer be declared to be solely an internal matter of states; it is increasingly being viewed as part of international relations.

Reference to ethnicity simplifies the search for the causes of conflict not one jot. Ethnicity is not an 'explanatory factor' in armed conflicts, nor should it be pressed into service as one because other explanations fail.[1] Often – as in the case of Yugoslavia – one can talk of a hybrid ethnicization of religious groups.[2] The violent conflict in Kosovo 1998/99 was the first war in the region showing a clear-cut ethnic component, with Serbian armed elements (army, police and paramilitary gangs) versus Albanian Kosovar civilians, and from May 1999 UCK or KLA elements versus Serbian and Roma civilians (after 78 days of NATO bombing of the Federal Republic of

Yugoslavia). The hope is that such practises will be stopped by an administration dominated by the party led by the veteran leader Ibrahim Rugova, which won the elections held in Kosovo in 2000.

To call for such 'ethnic conflicts' to be labelled blanket-fashion as 'identity conflicts' because there is nothing very ethnic about them is simply playing with words. Amnesia about historical developments, and a lack of understanding for the justified fears of non-dominant minorities, made comprehension of the wars in the Balkans impossible and encouraged the grotesquely distorted and more or less unquestioned coverage of them in the mass media.

Minority conflicts? an attempt at definition

Where ethno-nationalism is being discussed, there is often talk of minorities. This term seems in need of elucidation, and should only be used with reservations. The ideologies bound up with it range, in ascending order, from racial segregation, through unilateral assimilation and ideas about 'melting-pots' (racial amalgamation), to purely formally equal integration, then to the relativization of unitary-cum-homogenist ideas with the notion of 'diversity in unity', and, ultimately, to respect, protection and encouragement for otherness on an equal basis within the framework of a federal state. However, to place the content of ethnic conflicts on a par with that of minority conflicts or problems is, in many cases, mistaken. More far-reaching demands by many nations/nationalities point to structural differences between minority and nationality policy.

The concepts of minority, and the reality, in which minorities are created and obliged to live, point up a variety of facets that are often largely ignored in the debate about minority or ethno-national conflicts. The most important, however, seems to be that the concept of minority is essentially ascriptive in nature: as a rule, it is the state that decides what makes a minority and to which circle of people the term will apply. The state itself is dominated by, or in the ownership of, a particular ethnic group that defines itself as a majority but often is not one in demographic terms. National censuses and demographic statistics are just one more battlefield (for all the actors concerned). Statistics are usually presented according to predetermined political conditions.[3] In extreme cases, the ethnic group apostrophized as a minority is only a political minority, measured in terms of power, while demographically it constitutes the majority. This is the case, for example, with the Oromo in Ethiopia or the Mayan peoples in Guatemala.

The concept of minority requires elucidation for a variety of 'internal' reasons as well. Many nationalities that find their rights curtailed by the (new) states, or are harassed, threatened, or persecuted by them, do not regard themselves as minorities. They do not share the socio-psychological characteristics of minorities. On the contrary, some cultivate a robust nationalism: national minorities, which are mostly regarded by the dominant ethno-national group as subordinate segments of a (more) complex state society, have special phenotypical and cultural 'peculiarities' ascribed to them. These kinds of ascribed 'markers' are often looked down on by those segments of the state society that are dominant (either in terms of power or numerically). But traditional societies derive their distinctiveness and reproduce themselves on the basis of their non-integration into market economies; they have developed a whole series of autonomous, self-supporting modes of production.

The dual concept of the 'national minority' has come into increasing use in recent years in the discourse about the minority question and in international politics. This is a consequence of the increased attention that has been paid to the contentious minorities issue in post-cold war Europe; but it also means that a compromise formula has been found, ostensibly bridging or unifying the varying usages in eastern and western Europe.

The concept of the ethnos

The basic concept of the ethnos is not clearly defined. In ethnology it is delimited, but contentiously, within certain boundaries.[4] The variety and number of categorizations offered by the different ethnological schools is very great; but any combination of the more accessible definitions is not really possible, given the differing approaches and standards. The most frequently mentioned factors are shared origin and similar culture, religion, class and language.[5] However, two of these (class and religion) are not apposite.

The ethnic form of socialization must be distinguished from socialization into social classes. The extent and boundaries of the two are often congruent, but they can also overlap, as in more complex societies, or exclude one another, as in egalitarian societies. Religion must be rejected totally as a criterion, since it is an ideological domain, which, within the framework of colonialism, was mostly externally directed and fortuitously selected.

Imported religions and syncretistic variants are more common and/or more dominant than indigenous religions among the 2500 to 6500 ethnic groups world-wide.[6] The general supposition is that religions, like nationalisms, generate a transcendent identity-forming link, whereas ethnicity, though identity-forming, has a divisive effect. This supposition does not seem to be generalizable. Connections (or rather conflicts) between religion, nationalism and ethnicity ought not to be denied.[7]

One of several possible approaches to the subject focuses on attributes based on clusters of 'special features' or social specializations, which are both seen as constituting 'ethnic markers'. Such attributes are only relevant within the framework of inter-ethnic relations. Often they only become a major focus of perception when situations of conflict arise. The attributes of an ethnic community[8] include, as a minimum:

1. a historically generated or (in some cases) rediscovered community of people that largely reproduces itself
2. a distinct name, which often simply signifies 'person' or 'people' in the ethnic community's language
3. a specific, heterogeneous culture, including, particularly, a distinct language
4. a collective (ethnic) memory or historical remembrance, including community myths (myths of foundation or emergence relating to shared ancestry)
5. solidarity between members of the community, generating a feeling of belonging.[9]

These attributes by no means constitute a definitive checklist, rather, they are, an attempt to get closer to the problem of ethnicity, the individual elements of which need to be examined more closely and be defined in detail for each concrete instance. Maintaining ethnic borders – and thus also being able to delimit different ethnic groups – has its problems, for various reasons.[10] Overemphasizing individual elements, such as participation in a shared culture or the social dimension (which sees ethnic groups as a particular form of social organization), would appear to be problematic.[11]

From the point of view of those concerned, in their *emic* view as opposed to the *etic* view of the outsiders, most 'ethnic groups' – a technical term for scientific purpose – see themselves as a people or as a nation. Ethnic affinity is generally (*emically* speaking) not perceived in any way as ideologically generated or as 'primordial'.[12] But neither is it a quasi-organic process, produced by specific socialization as a member of a distinct social group (Schlichte 1994: 64). In contrast to the hypothesis of ideological construction, some authors talk of affinity based on traditional ethnic solidarity, as related to groups with high coherence and cohesion, such as clans and other tribal entities and which, say these authors, represents an almost naturally occurring form of 'unconditional ethnic solidarity'. The hypotheses on this subject are thus unusually far removed from one another. First of all, it is indispensable to state a frame of reference and to designate theoretical axioms. Statements about group affinity and personal identity can turn out differently depending on the terms of reference used. In modern societies, very different conditions of group affinity obtain than in traditional societies. The ethnic and socio-cultural identity of an individual varies according to the location or standpoint of the observer; identification of Other and Self can vary enormously; conflict situations can bring about fundamental changes in frames of reference.

In a situation of threat, individual elements of personal and collective identity can become enhanced or diminished in influence. The political instrumentalization of mechanisms of demarcation (for the purposes of exclusion) plays a role here, as does recourse (within the framework of peaceful coexistence) to socially unconscious elements of group identity. Identity constitutes itself via processes of demarcation that do not occur within a non-authoritarian space and whose modalities cannot be determined freely and independently. The abstract difference of others poses no problem; the experience of real threat from others, or a construed feeling of superiority *vis-á-vis* others, are, in contrast, results of processes of exclusion and polarization.

From an *emic* point of view, shared origin is crucial. The fact that this does not have to be 'real origin', and is usually putative-cum-mythical or fictitious in nature, is often overlooked. Other central elements that determine affinity to an ethnically constituted group – the capacity to reproduce as a group, for example, or common cultural configurations, or a so-called 'feeling of belonging' that implies group solidarity – may be regarded as too general to be able, ultimately, to provide precise empirical insights into the ethnic dimension of political processes in a conflict situation. Constant injury to central elements, either from within or from without, elicits specific forms of resistance in each particular case, ranging from withdrawal to armed rebellion.

The concept of nationality

Within the framework of socio-political or international legal categorization, an ethnos (or ethnic group) or an indigenous people may be viewed as a nationality. This conceptual shift should essentially be seen as the result of a political process, which, in most cases, has followed a conflictual course. Factors relating to political power play a decisive role here. As Zimmerman has observed, a structuralist semantic analysis of competing appellations (such as 'ethnos', 'people', 'nationality', 'nation') is not sufficient for ethnology, because it takes no account of social judgements, appropriateness, or the power question. The conquest and dominance aspect is of central importance. This constitutive aspect has been acknowledged, notably in the definition of indigenous peoples and in particular in the elaboration of new instruments of international law designed to protect them.[13]

In the concrete hostile conditions of internal or external colonization (with its unconditional claims of state sovereignty) an ethnos that does not reshape itself into a nation/nationality risks destruction as an independent unit. A cohesive non-dominant ethnic group reshaped in this way will be recognized as a nationality if it possesses certain other characteristics to some degree (to be verified in each individual case).

The following five characteristics of nations/nationalities represent a maximum definition – that is to say, the more clearly the named characteristics fit a particular nation/nationality, and the greater the number of them that apply, the nearer that nation/nationality comes to a hypothetical ideal type. An ethnos in the position of a non-dominant social group can, accordingly, be regarded as a nationality, despite the claims to dominance and sovereignty from outside if:

1. it constitutes a distinct space of communication and interaction, that is it is able to form or maintain a public sphere of its own
2. it has a particular mode of production and life identifiable with it, and is able to reproduce it
3. it has some form of political organization
4. it has settled an identifiable area of land or demarcated territory
5. it is distinctive, that is its members identify themselves or are identified by others as members of this particular community.

Ethnic characteristics are only relevant within the framework of inter-ethnic relations and it is primarily in conflict situations that they become a major focus of perception. The same characteristics – particular socio-cultural practices, for example – can (as has already been demonstrated with the example of cultural emblems) be totally unimportant in various inter-ethnic situations, but in a different context they can suddenly acquire huge significance. For example, skin colour and other phenotypic features are of secondary importance in many societies of the Third World; but in Western societies, physical characteristics are one of the main distinguishing features at home (in relation to migrants and asylum-seekers) and abroad (for example in holiday resorts).

The attempted definition consists of about half (inter-)subjective and half objective features. The disputed point with some of the named features is whether they can be described as 'objective'. Name-giving, certain cultural aspects (especially language), the association with a particular territory as a settlement area and site of economic activity (not with a mythical primeval homeland), the mode of production, and the degree of (present) political organization can, at least, be regarded as objective, empirically verifiable characteristics.[14]

An ethno-national community that possesses some crucial attributes, or all these attributes, develops a distinct collective identity; it could, in political contention, invoke the international legal principle of self-determination. This in no way implies a right to secession – something never acknowledged by the community of states. The creation of new states occurs in accordance with political opportuneness. International law speaks of 'nations' but actually means states; most states are multi-ethnic.

In actual political/legal practice, the right to self-determination is often not applied, even in the form of internal self-administration, because in these cases it is (allegedly) not linked to territoriality and because most peoples are generally not recognized as peoples but as minorities. The relevant legal basis is then human rights, which are generally individual rights.

As a consequence, the rights of ethno-national communities are located in a precarious 'grey area' between collective international law and individual human rights.

Politicization of the ethnic

Whether affiliation to an ethnic community becomes politicized and whether the right to self-determination is demanded depend on a large number of factors that will be analysed in the following chapters. It may be said, however, that the fundamental right to self-determination is generally in antagonistic relation to the 'inviolability of the borders' of existing state entities. In the Third World, state territory only rarely corresponds to ethnic territory. State borders, often traced out with a ruler at some official's desk, cut across natural ethnic borders.

The relationship between nationalities, nations and states is essentially part of politics and international relations. Nationalities are distinguished from nations by their degree of political organization, their readiness to fight and particular external circumstances. Part of the problem in most decolonized countries is that only very few new states (the same is applicable for many 'older' states) are genuine nation-states. But the definition of individual attributes of ethnicity and their relative weighting is contentious, as is that of the organization, *modus operandi*, tasks and manifestations of statehood. Different types of regimes have different approaches to what they perceive as the 'problem' of ethnicity.

The politicization of the ethnic (or ethnicity) is often seen as a precondition for conflictual processes between states and distinct ethnic groups. From the perspective of any ethno-national community, however, such politicization is, as a rule, not a precondition, but a *result* of conflictual processes. Politicization of the ethnic is one of several possible lines that may be followed by macro-social processes that may develop as a reaction, but not an automatic one, to changes in social surroundings.

Ethno-politicization is thus one possible (but not necessary) consequence of external interference. Such interference can either be destructive in its ultimate effects, as, for example, the preferential treatment of a particular ethnic group by colonial powers. Interference can be destructively structured from the outset, as a form of external aggression, like the invasion of an ethnic territory for the purposes of exploiting resources or of expelling an ethno-national community from its ancestral lands.

It was the creation of the nation-state in Europe that had momentous repercussions. Today, the official nationalism to which it gave rise in developing countries appears to have failed. The ambivalence and violence engendered by nationalism in the process of the creation of nations had manifested themselves early on in Europe as well. Europe has been the main theatre of war, on whose battlefields, between the years 1500 and

1990, almost two-thirds of the world-wide total of 150 million victims of war lost their lives 'in the cause of the nation'; the remaining third was accounted for in large measure by European colonial expansion, beginning in 1500. Historically, colonial expansion also put an end to the autonomous existence of a wide range of social formations and political systems. Attempts to export the idea of the European nation-state to the colonies came up against a host of additional ideological, structural and practical difficulties. There was no appropriate basis for this 'idea' outside Europe.

Since 1840, a whole series of alternatives to the European colonial legacy have bitten the dust. Projects for regional integration and self-determined development – including as a counterweight to ethno-nationally induced fragmentation – have foundered. The development-based nationalism of the new states was forced to recall its words, because it could not fulfil its promises in regard to development. Many states in the Third World fell deep into debt and forfeited their negotiating power. The crisis in regard to the legitimacy of peripheral states accelerated in parallel with economic decline. Advancing capitalist globalization appears to run counter to ethno-national fragmentation but in reality the two elements go together.

1
Contemporary Mass Violence

Compared to the tremendous increase of intra-state warfare and non-war types of mass violence such as genocide and mass murder the Clausewitzean type of inter-state conflict was in recent decades a rather exceptional phenomenon. In two-thirds of all contemporary conflicts the *ethnic factor* (for example ethnic nationalism) is a dominant or influential component. Hereafter, concentration will be on certain neglected relationships and issues.

The themes of intra-state conflict, its types, causes and possible peace strategies, are highly topical. However, research deficits prevail regarding abundant issues and problems in this vast field. Research on the causes of wars was mainly concerned with *classic* types of conflicts between states but does not easily apply to intra-state conflicts. The lacunas of global surveys on mass violence can be identified. Most present war registers overlook certain categories and types of violence such as genocide, mass murder, communal violence and postmodern types of conflicts that do not necessarily involve state actors, for example gang war. Most registers are constructing static entities instead of expressing the permanent mutation of conflicts in the real world. There are very few 'pure types'. Conflicts develop over time and may change in quality, with a new type becoming dominant over the other(s).

The question 'What to do in a particular situation?' is linked to the type of conflicts we are dealing with. The idea is that the results of systematic registers of mass violence point at priorities for action. The importance of timing in response to conflict will be stressed. Types of responses should be related to different types of conflicts and their underlying issues in order to be effective. The high frequency and huge potential of ethnic types of conflict is decisive with regard to the possibilities of structural prevention of violence, conflict management and transformation as well as with regard to the role of multi-lateralism in preventing violence. State failure and violent ethnic conflict are closely linked.

1.1   Ethnicity and mass violence

Ethnic and national groups' struggles for survival, rights, or recognition dominate contemporary warfare to an increasingly large extent and result in 'anarchy' in the state system. In the southern hemisphere of the so-called Third World a growing number of states can not claim to have an effective monopoly on violence. Depending on criteria employed about half of those states are *failed states* and have become *dangerous states*. Failed states potentially engage in repression, war and genocidal policy.

In the *grand design* the suggestion is to look at ethno-political conflict constellations as a structural feature of the *new world order*. Macro-trends have increasingly suggested since the 1980s that the world system is rapidly evolving into a complex multi-polar order.[1] Regional conflict scenarios make sense, even more so if they are determined not only by geographical but also by macro-cultural (*civilizational*) and political criteria. To give an illustrative exemplification: the collapse of the USSR and the subsequent outburst of ethnic conflicts on the periphery of that former 'empire' were closely linked. Some elements significantly differ from the situation in other world regions, particularly in the southern hemisphere. Ethno-nationalism in the East grew almost institutionally, resulting from a form of administrative *ethnicization*, which was one of the main constitutive elements of the Soviet experience.

A sort of 'Third World War' is in full swing. Warfare and mass violence are not going on between East and West, nor between North and South, but occurring this very moment inside some 50 states on four continents. The regional distribution of contemporary wars shows a clear global trend: warfare and mass violence is infrequent in the North and West but part of *normality* in the South and some areas of the East. Many wars in the South would not be fought without the involvement of the North.

According to the *Ethnic Conflicts Research Project* (ECOR) register, two thirds of the violent conflicts from 1985 to 1996 had a dominant or influential ethnic character. There were some disturbing changes of the general trend in recent years. Foreign military intervention has not at all been an exception and has lately increased significantly. Complex emergency cases led to an alarming increase in conflict-induced mortality. Warfare and mass violence are becoming increasingly chaotic at a conceptual and practical level, with inter-ethnic wars increasing at the cost of both inter-state and ethno-nationalist wars and gang wars nearly doubling in a ten-year period. State failure, warfare and mass violence are inextricably linked.

In view of the fairly recent discovery of the ethnic phenomenon by the mass media and considering a general research deficit concerning these 'forgotten wars' being fought in many Third World countries, research deficits prevail. The attempt here is ambitious: to propose an actor-oriented typology only indirectly related to root causes but directly linked with the main driving forces and manifestations of violent conflict world-wide.[2] One of the most dangerous sources of armed conflicts is the assertion of all powers by nation-states in their relations to what they call *minorities*.

1.1.1   Mapping conflict

Research deficits appear regarding all types of ethnic conflicts. In particular ethno-nationalist conflicts can still be called the *forgotten wars*, even though they account for a large number of violent conflicts. Analysis of the structural elements and dynamics of such conflicts is an inherently difficult task. A checklist of structural elements for mapping violent conflict is a basic requirement. Mapping conflicts begins with evaluating the warring parties' presentations – with reference to identifying:

- conflict type, causes, triggers, issues, etc.;
- antagonism or incompatibilities: different perception of security dilemma;
- groups/actors involved in particular conflict, their aims and objectives;
- leaders/population: objectives, interests and influence;
- communication structure or blockages between groups/actors.

The parties' version of a conflict map would be compared to other data. Mapping is based on different 'objective' sources, which are either involved in the conflict nor have vested interests. The second step, in-depth analytical mapping of violent conflicts, would result from analysis of the structural elements and dynamics of particular conflicts or conflict formations. Mapping of conflicts may typically look at the following elements:

1. conflict potential: on global, regional, local levels;
2. different actors: their motivation, interest, open and hidden agendas;
3. history: genesis/origins of destructive group interaction, colonial legacies and conflict causes (if applicable);
4. causes and driving forces of the conflict: root causes, immediate causes;
5. analysis of antagonism and incompatibilities (second step analyses);
6. dynamics of conflict: deeper/hidden conflict momentum, causes as opposed to triggers and escalators/de-escalators, conjunctures and essentials, degree of persistence and intensity;
7. objects and issues/threats of conflict: hierarchy of urgency regarding issues and perceived/real threats (needs, interests, grievances, vulnerabilities, memories of past disasters, threats, traumata, security dilemmas) (second step analyses);
8. formation of conflict and the process of militarization: the notion of protractedness, the role of ethnicity or identity, enemy images, background conditions, nation building;
9. essentials of the ideology of the warring parties (second step analyses);
10. aims/objectives of different actors: for example other national or

state-controlled political organizations, nationalists and civic movements, struggle for/against the state, incompatible declared goals;

11. leaders and masses: representation, the relationship between leadership and their political constituencies, the roles of leaders, legitimization of violence, legitimate leaders versus gang leaders and warlords;
12. mobilization of support and recruiting of activists, enigmas of clandestine organization, underground and permanent secrecy versus legal organization type (if applicable);
13. course of conflict: intensity, patterns of escalation/de-escalation;
14. phasing conflict: phases/periods distinguishing types or periods of time, different phases, paradigmatic changes in the course of warfare/violence: (a) different periods of a conflict, e.g. interrupted by period of peace; (b) changes of intensity: caused by changes of the course of violence, qualitative changes of strategies or availability of weapons; (c) paradigmatic change of character by which one component becomes dominant over an other: as a result of important political changes, change of objectives, new alliances, fall of regime, etc. (second step analyses);
15. resources, war economy, means of warfare: arms, equipment, strategies, sanctuaries, hinterland, international networks, diaspora;
16. question of outside parties: combat/non-combat involvement; possible foreign military intervention by neighbouring states as distinguished from out-of-area intervention by foreign states or by UN, role of foreign go-betweens, facilitators or mediators;
17. consequences of violence: polarization/despair, security concerns, transnational spillover effects, reinforcement of repression, structural violence, causalities, victims, refugees, prisoners, material damage, etc. (second step analyses);
18. possible policy options: shape and scope of options;
19. peaceful conflict settlement: conditions, form, criteria and 'musts';
20. sustainable solution: contours of conflict resolution and transformation, minimum requirements as measured at 'ideal model' solution;
21. cross-cultural comparison: for illustration purposes a number of comparative cases and examples could be given (second step optional analyses).

Distinguishing actors and their social base seems central. I take as a starting point that the conflict formation or conflict type I call 'ethno-nationalism' is the particular political form the struggle of a people, nationality or nation is organized. Typologies of nations and 'minorities at risk' (as coined by Gurr), or threatened non-dominant groups may differ but have to conceptualize types along the lines of nationality/ethnicity, indigenous/settlers, the question of size and prime characteristics.[3] Based on such concepts the view of the political struggles differs accordingly.[4] Societal structures of people(s) involved can have significant influence on their behaviour in conflict. One of the most striking observations in more than 15 years of research and field studies on ethno-nationalism were numerous signs of massive support of ethnic *liberation movements* among (formerly) stateless societies. Such actors and parties are not confined to small *tribal* communities. My hypothesis that the dichotomy between acephalous and centrally organised peoples is still very much alive can be verified by comparing series of case studies, whereby so-called transitional societies should also be included, showing tendencies to one or the other pole.[5]

1.1.2 The disappearance of interstate wars

According to the ECOR global survey nation states are exceptions to the rule: only a very small faction of the world's population lives in what could be called an ethnically homogenous state. Just 20 countries with a population average of 500,000 can be called nation states. Very few states with considerably more than 10 million citizens are homogenous nation states. In some cases minorities are a 'secret'.[6] Most states pretend to be nation states but in reality have a multi-ethnic and pluri-cultural composition. This fiction is maintained at high cost. For instance in the USSR, the very coining of the term 'titular nation' points at the fact that there was no single nation state in former Soviet space. In Africa, out of 50 states only five are relatively homogenous with regard to their ethno-national composition.

Since 1945 more than 300 major instances of mass violence have taken place mostly in the Third World and in the 1990s in the former Soviet Union and in Yugoslavia. Very few among the contemporary wars were inter-state conflicts. The last *classic* inter-state wars were fought for some weeks in 1995 between Perú and Ecuador, from March 1998 to December 2000 between Eritrea and Ethiopia, in 1999 for two months between India and Pakistan (about the 'line of control' in Kashmir) and for 78 days NATO versus Federal Republic of Yugoslavia (Kosovo). From October 2001 a US-led coalition launched a war against the Taleban regime and the terrorist network al-Qaeda in Afghanistan. In cases of *classic* interstate wars mediation is usually in place and hostilities rapidly cease or decrease.

Today, almost all wars are so-called *internal* conflicts, yet many are fought with outside assistance. Research to identify the root causes of the tremendous upsurge of ethno-nationalism in the global framework leads to questions linked with the nature of ethnicity and the ethnic base of nations. Often these categories are not adequately used. If we look underneath the structure of some 200 states there is an extraordinary multitude of perhaps between 6500 up to 10,000 nations and peoples as ethnic *entities* of diverse size. Groups rank from 900 Rama Indians in Nicaragua to 30 million Oromo at the Horn of Africa and up to 1.1 billion Han Chinese.

This diversity represents a tremendous richness of different cultures for most people, but a threat to others. Characteristics given to identify an ethnic group or a nationality are by no means an academic exercise but will gain more political relevance as relations between nationalities, nations and states are increasingly seen as an important element of *international relations*. While ethnic violence in the former Second World was a non-intentional result of Lenin's policy of administrative ethnicization (the *korenizatsiya*), the legacies of colonialism and other external conditions contributed in the former Third World to the separation of nations from nationalities. The *invention* of the nation state, its official nationalism and the false expectations raised by development ideologies in the former colonies are basic sources for past and future conflicts.

1.2 Non-Clausewitzean wars and mass violence

Practically all wars are nowadays intra-state wars. Since 1945 *internal* conflicts within the borderlines of a single state are by far more numerous than inter-state conflicts (international armed conflicts) between two or more states. Distinguishing *internal* and *external* conflicts – even thought to be politically as well as analytically relevant – tends to become invalid. The sacrosanct principle of non-interference in the *internal affairs* of states has always been a shaky rule as the high number of foreign state interventions shows: since 1945 states of the North were actively involved in over 390 wars fought by state actors in the South. Compilations concerning the period of 1945 to 1991 go as high as 690 foreign overt military interventions.[7]

The principle of non-interference was respected or violated according to the political or economic interests at stake. Interference traditionally takes place by supporting insurgents with arms and equipment and providing a safe haven (*hinterland*) for rebels in neighbouring states rather than through direct involvement of foreign states with combatant troops. Non-interference was never really applied to economic activities and contradicts fully with the trend of globalization. In the globalized economy the principle of autarchy is long obsolete.[8] Migration or ecological disruption does not stop at borders and could induce more conflict issues and threats in the near future. In the past non-interference was only exceptionally honoured, according to political preferences. The debate could best be linked with particular conflict issues and threats. The term *internal conflict* became invalid with regard to a number of issues and threats that can no longer be considered as falling under the competence of the state. Thus the scope of what are 'internal affairs' of states has to be redrawn.[9]

1.2.1 Definitions of mass violence, ethnicity and main actors

Wars and non-war types of mass violence, such as genocide or large-scale massacres, have to be clearly defined and distinguished.

Major wars and mass violence are distinguished from other armed conflicts or massacres by various degrees of medium or high intensity, claiming usually more than an estimated 1000 victims per annum or as an average during the course of the conflict (see, for instance, CoW, SIPRI and others). In many cases the numbers of victims are contested or otherwise questionable. Governments tend to reduce the number of victims while rebels usually inflate numbers. Additionally, in most wars the adversaries exaggerate enemy casualties. Verification of numbers of battle-related deaths and (even more so) of massacre-related deaths is an awesome task.

War is defined as a violent mass conflict involving two or more armed forces as combatants/actors in warfare. Not in all cases are regular state armed forces (such as military, police forces, militias and other paramilitary troops) involved. Not-state actors are mainly so-called liberation movements having regular guerrilla or partisan armies, often recruiting along ethnic, national or social class lines. Tribal militias, gangs and other irregular forces have different agendas; they have less or no centralized control or identifiable lines of command. In most types of contemporary warfare violent clashes and combat between the warring parties take place with some degree of continuity. Ethno-nationalist wars especially tend to become *protracted conflicts*.

Non-war types of mass violence are characterized by a separation of the perpetrators of mass murder and their victims. In most cases the victimization and aggression is organized, supported, or tolerated by state actors. Contrary to asymmetries in many types of wars (concerning quality of weaponry, use of resources and level of training) in non-war mass violence there is a clear difference to be made between armed perpetrators and the victimized non-armed civilians, which are by definition defenceless. The worst type of mass violence is genocide.

Genocide is defined as state organized mass murder (and crimes against humanity) and is characterized by the intention of the rulers to exterminate individuals because of their belonging to a particular national, ethnic, 'racial' or religious group. **Mass murder** committed against members of a particular political group (called *politicide* by Barbara Harff) or any social group (called *democide* by Rudolph Rummel) are equally horrifying but do not legally fall under the Anti-Genocide Convention of 1948. The **most deadly regimes** of the twentieth century have all committed total genocide against domestic groups, mainly in barbarian attempts to exterminate minorities.

Dominant groups acquire positions of command over the so-called monopoly of violence. Their assertive relationship toward ethnically distinct nationalities (*nations without their own state*) have become the most important, dangerous source of violent conflict since 1945 and increasingly so with each cycle of decolonization.

Ethnic communities can be defined as historically generated or (in some cases) rediscovered communities of people that largely reproduce themselves. An ethnic or **communal group** has a distinct name, which often simply signifies 'person' or 'people' in the ethnic community's language, a specific heterogeneous culture, particularly, a distinct language and a collective memory or historical remembrance, including community myths (myths of foundation or emergence relating to shared ancestry). This produces a degree of solidarity between members, generating a feeling of belonging.

Ethnicity as a term is used to describe a variety of forms of mobilization, which ultimately relate to the autonomous existence of specifically ethnic forms of socialization. However, no clear-cut distinction can be made between struggles by social classes and struggles by ethnic groups. To talk about the politicization of ethnicity seems tautological. Different types of actors such as states, transnational corporations, liberation movements, migrants' organizations, political parties, pressure groups, strategic groups, military leaders and populists all seek to make political capital out of 'ethnic identity'. Some actors deliberately try to influence and manipulate the ethnic-identity set-up.

1.2.2 Conflict causes, driving forces and colonial legacies

In over half of all contemporary conflicts the *ethnic factor* (ethnicity) is a dominant or influential component. Ethnicity is mostly negatively charged in political discourse, having connotations such as 'primitive', 'backward', or 'irrational'. Contrary to the prognoses of political and social sciences in regard to the development of modern societies, ethnicity has lost none of its importance in recent decades. On the contrary, the importance of the ethnic dimension and its politicization have increased – influencing issues of status and categorization in violent conflicts as well as processes of civilian disputes, social demarcation and exclusion.

Identification of the driving forces of ethnic nationalism in the global framework leads to questions linked with the nature of ethnicity and the ethnic base of nations. Often these categories are inadequately used. Underneath the structure of nearly 200 states there is an extraordinary multitude of perhaps between 6500 up to 10,000 ethnic entities of diverse size – from nations, nationalities and peoples to *minorities* and other distinct groups.[10]

The legacies of colonialism and other external conditions contributed to the separation of nations from nationalities. The *invention* of the nation state, its official nationalism and the false expectations raised by development ideologies in the former colonies are some of the basic sources for past and future conflicts. The European nation-state project created large-scale disorder after being exported to the colonies. The official nationalism failed to satisfy its own aspirations of achieving an acceptable degree of development. State failure to safeguard internal peace and security created most extreme problems.

1.3 Typology of violent conflicts

A comprehensive typology of violent conflicts is indispensable for any useful survey of conflicts. Surveys, indexes and registers are not a goal in itself but form the base for assessing possibilities for responses. In order to register violent conflict comprehensively the criteria and building blocks for constructing types of conflicts ought to be clear-cut. The combination of the dimensions of actor-orientation and driving forces, reflecting the basic incompatibility of a body of conflicts, is likely to achieve the best result regarding the elucidatory power and the logic of construing types. The (re-)evaluation of existing typologies and classifications can show that any other choice would be sub-optimal.

In order to register violent conflict comprehensively the next task was to develop a sophisticated methodology to codify conflicts in such a way that changes are indicated and become visible. There are abundant difficulties inherent in the subject matter. As a rule conflicts are extremely dynamic and can change their 'face' over time. Static models ought to fail to trace – not to mention anticipating – the changes and permutations in the appearance of violent conflicts, which are characterizing complex contemporary mass violence. ECOR first re-evaluated existing conflict indexes and subsequently developed methods and models which could cope with the changing nature of conflicts over longer periods. Credible work needs hard empirical data. The ECOR conflict typology and processual model to track down changes are the requisites of an inventory of conflict that is able to picture contemporary violence were elaborated step-wise and after intensive experience with armed conflicts and mass violence in the real world.[11]

1.3.1   Lacunae of global surveys on mass violence

Four main lacunae of global surveys on contemporary mass violence can be identified:

1. Present war registers 'overlook', deliberately ignore or even exclude certain categories and types of mass violence such as genocide (including the subtypes of *democide* (Rummel) and *politicide* (Harff), other state sponsored mass murder, communal violence and postmodern types of conflicts.
2. Some conflict types do not necessarily involve state actors, such as gang wars (warlordism) and most inter-ethnic conflicts, contrary to ethno-nationalist conflicts, which always include state actors versus ethnic rebels.
3. Most registers are constructing static entities instead of expressing the permanent mutation of conflicts in the real world, which develop over time and may change in quality, with a new type becoming dominant over the other(s).
4. External factors cannot be ignored, in fact, contrary to common belief, their importance increased in recent periods. Unfortunately there are just a few and no up-dated compilations of overt and covert foreign interventions.[12]

Such shortcomings and gaps have serious implications: the most critical limitation occurs if compilations exclude non-war types of mass violence. This necessarily results in limited explanatory power since the latter account for a higher number of casualties than wars in recent years. For instance the war that began in Rwanda in 1990 served only as a smoke-screen for a much larger crime, the extermination of an entire population group, killing twice as many people than all wars in the former Soviet Union and Eastern Europe since the end of the cold war.[13] For decades Rudolph Rummel compiled data on democide ('death by government'); he found out that for every period, governments have killed more of their citizens than foreign enemies (Rummel 1994, 1997); his estimates conclude that four times as many people were murdered by their own states than were killed in war (see Grimshaw 1999, 54 and 60, Table I and II).

Drawing on 15 years of fieldwork and conflict analysis, ECOR developed one of the conceptually most advanced surveys, based on a comprehensive typology and codifying conflict cases according to a dynamic model featuring multiple components, thus being a reflection of both complexity and change in contemporary mass violence. Analysis demonstrates that conflicts change over time and can have two or more different layers. The task is to anticipate developments and changes. Secondary and tertiary components have to be identified in order to understand changes and provide analytic insight for responses to conflict. This of course makes conflict analysis a complex task. In order to allow comparison with other compilations, the ECOR register somewhat follows (in types A–D) standards set by AKUF, corrected by Nietschmann's early works.[14]

1.3.2   Overcoming the exclusion of non-war mass violence

Regarding conflict actors the main criteria cannot be described adequately by the *ownership* of the state in all cases. The ECOR typology has been extended to include wars between non-state actors (E and F). Not only wars but also organized mass murder such as genocide (G) must be included. However, most present registers and 'war lists' (for example, AKUF, SIPRI, or CoW) exclude non-war types of violence. The major difference of the ECOR compilation with the Uppsala–SIPRI list is the issue to include rather then exclude non-war violence in a list of mass violence.

In an era characterized by non-Clausewitzean warfare, 'chaos power' and 'postmodern' mass violence, so-called lists of armed conflicts are of limited interest. Concerning the magnitude and salience of non-war mass violence it is hard to believe that excluding genocide and mass murder would be viable: many of those conflicts which are named 'armed conflicts' are in reality outright slaughter of civilians. Hence, a critical limitation occurs if compilations exclude non-war types of mass violence. This necessarily results in limited explanatory power. The most obvious reason for that would be that the latter account for a higher number of casualties than wars.

For instance, limited warfare that began in Rwanda in 1990 served as a smoke-screen for a much larger crime: the extermination of an entire population group, killing many more people than all wars in the former Soviet Union and Eastern Europe since the end of the cold war. My emphasis on inclusion of non-war types of mass violence is not an 'armchair idea'.[15]

1.3.3   Overcoming the exclusion of ethnicity

Another emphasis concerns ethnic conflict. The challenge is to introduce a clear-cut distinction for in different types of ethnic conflicts. Furthermore it has to be recalled that the newly discovered byword 'ethnicity' is in some cases (for example Rwanda or Yugoslavia) an utter misinterpretation of facts or might be deliberately used with the intent to divert attention away from 'real' causal processes and issues at stake. For many scholars 'ethnicity' is not an object of genuine attention but relegated as a sort of 'epiphenomenon' compared to the 'real' underlying issues or even referred as something that ought not to be. The problem is that *ethnicity* was seen in much of the academia as a taboo and this has only changed in recent years.[16] The virtual 'taboo' concerning ethnicity – never 'honoured' by some scholars but still held in good faith in much of the scientific community – has its consequences. The notion of ethnicity is largely missing in most indexes and 'war lists'.

A third emphasis concerns the notion of non-state actors. All registers and 'war lists' exclude the category of gang wars. It would be essential to elaborate: why exclude it and on what grounds? The phenomenon is of increasing importance, as can be seen from the findings based on the ECOR register. If violent conflict by non-state actors were to be excluded then according to the findings presented here, about one-fifth of contemporary mass violence (most of type E and all of F) would be excluded. The much discussed postmodern warfare and its various new actors such as war lords, gangs, mercenaries and commercial private armies (such as the *Executive Outcomes*) cannot be ignored.[17] Most scholars are still failing to grasp the essence of non-Clausewitzean warfare. ECOR's typology and conflict register constitute an improvement compared to most current typologies and 'war lists'. The PIOOM map of conflicts and the ECOR list of violent conflicts are nearly identical, even though elaborated in different ways. Self-reflection and re-evaluation of methods, models, concepts and theories are badly needed.

1.3.4   Typology of mass violence (A–G)

The resulting typology allows an analysis of global trends in warfare and non-war types of mass violence which is otherwise not visible. The methods and techniques applied to read the database of traditional registers would not detect the most disturbing trends and extreme problems the victims of conflict and the international community are facing today.

A   **Anti-regime wars or political and ideological conflicts**: State versus Insurrection (SvI). There are different forms: liberation movements versus colonial powers; popular movements and/or social-revolutionary movements versus authoritarian state; destabilization or re-establishing a *status quo ante*. The aim is to replace the government of the day or to change the socio-political system. Destabilization conflicts started in the framework of the cold war can be very violent and have long duration; exemplary cases are RENAMO in Mozambique or UNITA in Angola, the Mujahidin (until 1991) and Taliban in Afghanistan and Contras in Nicaragua. Although configured differently from ethno-nationalist conflicts some conflicts exhibit common dimensions. Today some former destabilization conflicts and proxy wars of the cold war period have mutated to become dominantly ethno-nationalist or ethnic-tribalist (for example in Afghanistan and Angola).

B   **Ethno-nationalist conflicts**: there are diverse forms, mostly as intra-state conflicts opposing states and national groups (State versus Nation, SvN); sometimes known as interstate conflicts (MSvN). Ethno-nationalist SvN conflicts are the most frequent type of contemporary armed conflicts and wars; such conflicts are generally of long duration (decades). The root causes of current incompatibilities are often perceived as 'ages-old'; there is a history of past threats, discrimination, targeted repression and violence. The aim is self-defence; in extreme cases as a struggle for survival against aggressive state policies and outright threats of extermination. Conflict resolution would only in a few cases afford to create new states. Possibilities for conflict resolution and preventive measures range from concessions regarding cultural autonomy and diverse degrees of autonomy and self-governance to (con)federal solutions and sovereign statehood.

C   **Interstate conflicts**: State versus State (SvS): earlier seen as the 'classic type' of warfare. Cases: war in the Persian Gulf between Iraq and Iran (1980–88), the 11 Days War between Mali and Burkina Faso (December 1985) or the invasion by the USA of Panamá (December 1989). The number is limited; according to the ECOR-Register during the decade 1985–94 there were only 12 cases (out of 102). In 1995 a brief border war occurred between Perú and Ecuador. The most recent cases were not minor: from March 1998 to mid 2000 an increasingly bloody war between Eritrea and Ethiopia was stopped by a disengagement plan signed in mid 2000,[18] and 1998/99 again between Pakistan and India in Kashmir. In all three cases the conflict was about (mutual) territorial claims. Coalitions or war alliances used to be rare; multi-state versus one state (MSvS); multi-state versus nation/nationality (MSvN); several states versus several other states (MSvMS). There were a few MSvS or MSvN cases since 1990, all opposing Western powers and smaller states or nations. The MSvMS subtype was the classic world war constellation. Since 1990 there have been five examples of the MSvS subtype: USA, UK, France and others versus Iraq 1990–91 (second Gulf war), the NATO intervention against Serbs in Bosnia 1995, new sustained bombardments of

Iraq by USA and UK as another attempt to destabilize Saddam Hussein, December 1998–2000, 75 weeks of NATO bombing raids against FR Yugoslavia in 1999 and the US-led coalition against Afghanistan, begun in October 2001. In type C the application of international law (for example, the Geneva Conventions) seems unproblematic but is often violated (such as massive bombardments of civilian targets in Yugoslavia 1999 and Iraq 1991–95). Contrary to common belief, since 1945, with the exceptions of the Chinese revolution (type A), the interstate wars in Korea, Vietnam and the Gulf (Iran versus Iraq), the mortality in B and G cases is generally higher than in C.

D   Decolonization wars or Foreign-State-Occupations (FSO): Eritrea became a sovereign state in 1991–92 and East Timor in 1999, after a UN peace-enforcement operation. There are still a number of Afro-Asiatic cases: Western Sahara, West Papua and Palestine; additionally, due to internal colonization by ethnocratic regimes, many ethno-nationalist movements claim that their case were a decolonization issue. Unsurprisingly, most examples of type D have a dominant ethno-national character. Because of its privileges in international law type D is different from type B; this is a decisive influence for possible conflict resolution. Essentially former European colonial territories were occupied or annexed by non-European regional powers; the occupied peoples have a good case if the United Nations adopts it and does not delay or mismanage the solution (as in Western Sahara).

E   Inter-ethnic conflicts: type E is, together with types B, D and most G cases, part of the 'ethnic' or ethnicized conflicts in a broad sense. Type E is different regarding actors and aims; the latter are characterized by particular collective (non-private) interests. The issues are narrowly defined: particular interests, *tribalism*, clan disputes, chauvinism and *narrow nationalism*. Economic aspects play a role but cultural and political aspects dominate. As in type B the militants use their own ethnic group as recruiting and support base (contrary to B, in most cases exclusively). E actors are not forced to develop a war economy above normal levels. Such conflicts are often fought without a state actor intervening directly in combat; foreign covert intervention can play a role.

F   Gang wars: non-state actors are mixed with criminal elements, especially in situations of state collapse. They act according to particular or even private interests. Economic aspects are dominant; a particular type of war economy is developed. Gang wars are fought over valuable resources (diamonds, gold, precious stones, drugs, etc.), land, or control of markets. Even 'modern' slavery is possible (for example, in Sudan). Type F developed a variety of characteristics. Actors can be rather diverse, such as village militias, demobilized soldiers, or mercenaries (*contras, re-contras, re-compas*), so-called 'dead squads', the Mafia, (drug) syndicates (for example, in Colombia or in the Golden Triangle of SE Asia), professional groups (for example, *Garimperos* versus Indians in the Amazon), private armies of warlords (for example, in

Afghanistan, Liberia, Sierra Leone and Somalia), terrorist groups or networks (such as al-Qaeda and Hamas), big landowners (in Latin America: *hacienderos* versus landless *campesiños*), or settlers or migrants versus indigenous peoples, for example, in mountain areas of Bangladesh, the NE Indian states of Tripura and Assam, the Kenyan Rift Valley and so on.[19]

G **Genocide**: state-organized mass murder and crimes against humanity characterized by the intention of the rulers to exterminate individuals belonging to a particular national, ethnic, 'racial', or religious group (genocide) as a whole or in parts. Genocide is the worst type of mass violence and has to be clearly distinguished from warfare. Targets and victims are civilians (non-combatants) including old people, children and even babies. Recent cases of large-scale genocide were exterminations committed by states. The Khmer Rouge regime in Cambodia, during 1975–79, exterminated Vietnamese, Cham Muslim and Chinese minorities; mass murder was also committed against ethnic Khmer (*auto-genocide*).[20] Rwanda's Hutu power regime overkilled almost the entire remaining Tutsi branch of the Banyarwanda in 100 days (from 7 April to 15 July 1994); massacres were repeatedly committed against Tutsi since 1959 (half of the Tutsi group had to flee to all neighbouring states) and against three other minorities (Gogwe, Mbo and Hima).[21] Sudan's NIF regime has committed genocide against the Nuba in Central Sudan and Dinka civilians in Southern Sudan since the early 1990s; this genocide continues to the present day.[22] Many of the 50 non-signatory states of the anti-genocide convention are potentially genocidal.[23] In a few other countries non-state actors are the culprits of genocidal acts, as for instance in Somalia, Sierra Leone and Tajikistan. Organized forms of communal violence can be genocidal.

A tentative attempt to introduce an eighth type (H for Homicide) was given up.[24] On the basis of these seven core-types of conflict diverse mixed forms can be identified.[25] Their characteristics and main impulses can be analysed, starting with their historical and regional backgrounds. The task of conflict research remains a Herculean one: to detect the roots, genesis and dynamics of intra-state conflicts. The aim is to give a survey of conflict potentials, to identify belligerent actors and their goals, to analyse characteristics of rebel forces and to research the course of a particular conflict and its means (domestic resources and external support) as well as possible foreign involvement. Furthermore, the task for peace research is to think about ways of structural prevention, transformation and peaceful conflict resolution.

1.4   Indexes of contemporary violent conflicts

Registers of contemporary warfare often blur the high proportion of ethnically determined or induced types of conflicts (including genocidal and communal violence). Such conflicts appear in combination with other types and forms of intra-state conflicts; this blurs a clear categorization.

Today the category of *ethnic conflict* has gained broad acceptance. A few years ago this category was generally avoided for different reasons: in many Third World countries it was because of its connotations with 'backwardness', 'primitive culture' and 'pre-modernity'; in Europe (especially in Germany) because of political implications or historical reasons. Somewhat 'value-neutral' official and camouflage terms were used instead. Usually the findings and results of a register have to be analysed and interpreted carefully, whereby the outcomes for the same period can show a high degree of divergence concerning the overall number of conflicts, the proportion of a particular type, for example, ethnic and ethnicized conflicts or substitute categories. Some authors underestimated the potential of ethnic intra-state conflicts. Today, most experts agree that their number is increasing; one of six individuals belongs to an 'at-risk minority'. The ECOR database suggests that this proportion could be even higher, depending on the criteria applied. These criteria would have to be compared to the non-dominant groups' perception of their own security risk.

1.4.1   Requirements for indexes of mass violence

Comprehensive registers of violent conflicts can either be structured according to levels of intensity or they deal only with major conflicts. Registers have to solve several problems:

1. Registering impure types and multiple components: combining the basic types can adequately solve the inherent difficulty of all the 'impure' types we find in the real world. That way we get closer to the 'mixed types' encountered in the field.
2. Expressing dynamics and change: contemporary wars do not resemble football games anymore. To illustrate the dynamics and the changing composition of contemporary wars different methods can be used. The diachronic development can be cut in phases of warfare. For a given phase the ECOR register shows the primary or dominant type followed (if necessary) by a secondary or tertiary characterization of a particular conflict, hence describing the heterogeneous and dynamic nature of most *modern* non-Clausewitzean types of conflicts.
3. Phasing conflict: phases shall be distinguished according to three instances: (1) different periods of a conflict, for example in some cases interrupted by a period of peace (autonomy in South Sudan 1972–93); (2) changes of intensity, caused by changes of the course of violence, qualitative changes of strategies by one or several actors, qualitative change in availability of weapons (for example the introduction of heavy artillery of

weapons of mass destruction); (3) paradigmatic change of character whereby one type or component becomes dominant over another, as a result of important political changes, change of objectives, new alliances, decay of the regime, fall of the government and so on.

1.4.2   Indexes of mass violence from 1985 to 2000

The heterogeneous dynamic character of contemporary violent conflicts has to be expressed adequately. In ECOR's *Indexes of Mass Violence* this has been solved as such: besides pointing at a dominant type secondary and tertiary components were also codified. In order to exclude multiple counting of particular components only the last phase of a war was considered relevant. In the register the composition of seven types of wars (A–G) is indicated for each conflict and for each phase of conflict (see Tables 1.1 and 1.4).

Types of Conflict Distinguished by the ECOR Index

A   Anti-regime-wars, political conflicts, state versus insurgents
B   Ethno-nationalist conflicts, mostly as intra-state conflicts (state versus nation), often cross-border or spill-over effects
C   Interstate conflicts, state versus state, seen as 'classic wars'
D   Decolonization wars or Foreign State Occupations
E   Inter-ethnic conflicts, mainly non-state actors
F   Gang wars, non-state actors (mixed with criminal and terrorist elements), especially in situations of state failure or state collapse
G   Genocide, state-organized, mass murder and major crimes.

Legend for Tables 1.1 and 1.4

Mixed types	AB, BA, BC, CA, BAD, etc.	first mentioned type in a given period is the dominant type, often with second or less influential component(s)
Foreign actors	+	direct participation of a foreign state or outside power deploying combatants
Phases	/	separating types or periods of time indicate different phases or paradigmatic changes
Period of time	–	conflict is continued after the registered period 31 Dec. 1994 or 31 Dec. 2000
Termination/ end	(?)	date or the termination of violence is unknown or questionable
Sources	ECOR, various	own data, evaluation of various compilations and conflict databases.[26]

Table 1.1   ECOR index of mass violence in the decade 1985–94

No.	Country	Groups/Actors	Conflict types	Period/Phases
Central-America and the Caribbean				
1.	Guatemala	Maya-Kiché, Ixil, EGP, others	B/GBA/BA	1954/1978–85/86–
2.	Guatemala	URNG	AB	1960/1980–
3.	Nicaragua	FDN-Contras/ Re-Contras	A+/AF	April 1981–1990/–
4.	Nicaragua	Miskitu factions, Sumu, Rama	B+/B	Feb. 1981–1987/ 1990
5.	El Salvador	FMLN, Pipiles	AB	1980/81–Feb. 1992 (?)
6.	USA	Panama (LD-RP)	C	20–24 Dec. 1989
7.	Haiti	Tonton Macoutes, FRAPH; US	FA/FA+	Sept. 91/Sept. 94–
South America				
8.	Brazil	Gold searchers vs. Yanomami	FE	1986 (?)–
9.	Colombia	FARC, EPL; ELN; M-19	AB; A; A	1964/65/Jan. 1974– March 1990/–
10.	Colombia	Drug syndicates, death squads.	AF	1970 (?)–
11.	Colombia	Guajiro	BA	1975 (?)–
12.	Suriname	Busi Nengee/ Kalinja, Lokono	BA/B	21 June 1986–7 June 89
13.	Peru	Sendero Luminoso, militias	ABF	May 1980–
14.	Peru	Aymara, Quichua, MRTA	BA	Nov. 1987–
North Africa				
15.	Morocco	West Sahara: Sahrawi	DB	18 Nov. 1975–1992 (?)
16.	Sudan	South Sudan: SPLA	BGA	Sept. 1983–
17.	Sudan	SPLA-Dinka, SPLA-Nuer	BE+	Aug. 1991–
18.	Algeria	GIA, AIS	AF	1991–
19.	Egypt	Islamic Jihad	A	1992–
West Africa				
20.	Senegal	Diola, MFDC	BA	April 1990–
21.	Liberia	NPFL, INPFL	EA/EA+	Dec. 1989/Aug. 90–
22.	Sierra Leone	RUF, NPFL, ULIMO	AEC	Jan. 1991–
23.	Mali	Burkina Faso	C	21–31 Dec. 1985
24.	Mali/Niger	Tuareg: MFUA, MPA, FIAA	BCE/BC	May 1990–92/June 1994–

Table 1.1 Continued

No.	Country	Groups/Actors	Conflict types	Period/Phases
Central Africa				
25.	Chad	FAN, FAP, MPS	E/BAC+/ BA+/B	June 1966/79/ 1990/1991–
26.	Rwanda	Hutu army, Tutsi rebels FPR/RPA	A+/BA+	Oct.1990/92–July 1994
27.	Rwanda	Interahamwe, CDR, GP, FAR vs. Tutsi	GEF+/G+	1990/96 Apr. 1994–15 July 94
28.	Burundi	Tutsi (army), Hutu militias FDD, FNL	G/GE/ EAC	1972/Oct. 1993/1993–
29.	Zaire	Luba; Hunde, Nyanga, Hutu	EA/GEA	Aug. 1992/ March 93–
East Africa/Horn of Africa				
30.	Ethiopia	Eritrea: ELF, EPLF	DB/DAB	1962/1976–May 1991
31.	Ethiopia	Tigrai, TLF, TPLF, EPRDF	B/BA	1975–May 1991
32.	Ethiopia	Oromo: OLF, IFLO, UOPL	BAD/BDA	1976/May 1991–
33.	Ethiopia	Gojjam, Gondar: EPRP, EDU	A/AB/BA	Mar 74/Dec. 75/May 91–
34.	Ethiopia	EPRDF: EPDM, OPDO, u.a.	AB	Jan 1989–May 1991
35.	Djibouti	Afar (FRUD, o/a)	BEA/BAE	1981/Oct. 91–
36.	Eritrea	ELF-Idriss, Jihad, ELF-GC	EA+	1993 (?)–
37.	Somalia	Somaliland: Isaaq, SNM	BA+/BA	1980/1990–May 1991
38.	Somalia	Marehan, SSDF, SDM, USC	EA/E/E+	1988/Jan. 91/Dec. 92–
39.	Uganda	NRM, Acholi, Langi, Bari	AB/EA	Feb. 1981/Feb. 1986/–
Southern Africa				
40.	Angola	MPLA; FLNA, UNITA	D/BAC+/ BAE	1961–75/20 June 1991–
41.	Namibia	SWAPO, Herero, !Khoi; TA	BD	1966–22 Dec. 1988
42.	Zimbabwe	ZANU, Ndebele-ZAPU	AB/EA	Jan. 1983/1987–May 1988
43.	Mozambique	FRELIMO; RENAMO	D/AC/AE+	1991/1975–Oct. 1992 (?)
44.	South Africa	ANC, PAC/ Inkatha, Boers	DA/DAE/ EAD	1962/1976/1990–

Table 1.1   Continued

No. Country	Groups/Actors	Conflict types	Period/Phases
Europe – West			
45. Spain	Euskadi, ETA, HB	BA	1937–
46. France	Corsica, FLNC	BA	1950–
47. Northern Ireland	IRA, UVF, UFF	DB/DEA/ EDA	1961–1969/1986–Oct. 1994
Europe – East			
48. Yugoslavia	Slovenia/Croatia	AB/CB	June 1991–July 91/ Oct. 91
49. Croatia	Serbs (Krajina, Slavonia)	G/BF+/EA	1940–44/mid 91–93/May 95
50. Bosnia	*Tshetniki*, Muslims, HOS, a/o	EFB+	March 1992–
51. Moldavia	Russians, Ukrainians, Kosaks	EF+	March–Aug. 1992
52. Romania	Securitate, Timisoara Magyar	AE	17–28 Dec. 1989
Europe – Southeast/CIS			
53. Georgia	Gamsachurdia rebels	A/AEF	Sept. 91/Jan. 92–Nov. 1993
54. Georgia	S-Ossetia	B	Dec. 1990–July 1992
55. Georgia	Abkhazia; alliance, Russians	BC/BC+	Aug. 92/July 93–Dec. 1993
56. Chechnya	Ingushi, North Ossetians	BE	Dec. 1991–March 1992
57. Azerbaijan	Nagorny-Karabach	BE/CBE	88–90/1992–May 1994 (?)
58. Armenia	SW-Azerbaijan	CBEF	March 1993–May 1994
59. Russia	Russian Army vs. Chechen rebels	BEAF	11 Dec. 1994–
West Asia/Middle East			
60. Lebanon	Maronites, Druses, Shiites/Hesb Allah	AE/CEA/ EAC	April 75/78/82–1993 (?)
61. Israel	Palestine: PLO/ Hamas; Druses	DB	1968–
62. S-Yemen	Tribes, clans, JSP	AEF	13–29 Jan. 1986
63. N-Yemen	South Yemen	ABC/BAC	Dec. 91/March 94–July 94
64. Turkey	Kurds, PKK, HRK	B/BADF	1970/1984–
West Asia/Persian Gulf			
65. Iran	Azeri, Kurds, Turkmen	BA	July 1979–1988/–(?)
66. Iraq	Kurds, PUK, KDP	BA/BAC/ BA+	1976/Feb. 91/March 91–

Table 1.1 Continued

No.	Country	Groups/Actors	Conflict types	Period/Phases
67.	Iraq	Iran (1st Gulf war), Kurds	CB	Sept. 1980–20 Aug. 1988
68.	Iraq	Kuwait	CD	2–4 Aug. 1990
69.	USA/GB and others	Iraq (2nd Gulf war)	C	17 Jan–27 Feb 1991/–
70.	Iraq	Shiites	AB/CAB	1990/March 1991–

Central Asia

No.	Country	Groups/Actors	Conflict types	Period/Phases
71.	Tajikistan	CP, clans, Russian troops	EAF+	Aug. 1992–June 1993 (?)
72.	Afghanistan	CP, Pathanen, Tajik, Uzbek, a.	ABE/BAE+/EB	1973/Oct. 78/Apr. 1992–
73.	Pakistan	Sindhi, SNA, Muhajir, Paschtun	BEF	Nov. 1986–

South Asia

No.	Country	Groups/Actors	Conflict types	Period/Phases
74.	India	Pakistan (Siachen glacier)	C	April 1984–1989 (?)
75.	India	Kashmir: Muslim/Jamu/Ladakh	BE/BAE	1986/1990–
76.	India	Punjab: Sikhs, KLF, KCF	BAE	July 1982–
77.	India	Bihar: Naxaliten	A	1988–(?)
78.	Sri Lanka	LTTE, EPRLF, Tamils, Muslims	B/BA+/BAE+	July 1983/Sept. 1987/March 90–
79.	Sri Lanka	JVP, Singhalese Youth	AE	July 87–Nov. 1989 (?)
80.	Bangladesh	CHT-Tribes, Chakma, SB, a.	BAF	1973–
81.	NE-India	Tai-Asom, ULFA, Boro/Bodo	BEA	1990–
82.	NE-India	West Begal/Himalaya: Gorkha	BA	1987–88 (?)

Southeast Asia

No.	Country	Groups/Actors	Conflict types	Period/Phases
83.	NE-India	Naga: RGN, NNC, NSCN	BD/BEA/AB/BA	1954/1963/1972/Nov. 1975–
84.	NE-India	Manipur: KNA, NSCN, Meitei	BA/BEA/BAE	1960/75/84/May 1992–
85.	NE-India	Mizo: MNF, u.a.	BAE	1966–June 1986
86.	Burma	Karen: KNDO, KNU	BEA/B/BA	1947/1950/1988–
87.	Burma	CPB (PVO, Red Flag), DPA	A/A+/AB	1948/1962/March 1989–
88.	Burma	KIO, Mon; NDF; Pa-O, KNPP	B/BAE/BA	1962/1976/Nov. 1988–

Table 1.1   Continued

No.	Country	Groups/Actors	Conflict types	Period/Phases
89.	Burma	Shan, Da'an, ALF, Wa, a, a.	EA/EBA	1970 (?)/1988–
90.	Burma	DAB: NDF, ABSDF, PPP, a.	AB	Nov. 1988–
91.	Burma	opium guerrilla: MTA, Wa	EA+/EFA/FE	1950/1976/March 1989–
92.	Thailand	Laos	C	Nov. 1987–Feb. 1988
93.	Laos	Hmong, LLA, drug wars	FEC+/FEA	1970/1975–
94.	Cambodia	Khmer Rouge, ANS, Sihanouk	A/CA/G/ AB+/A+	1968/70/1971–75/79/85–
95.	Vietnam	Montagnards, KPNLA, FULRO	B/BA+/B	1964/1970/75–Oct. 1992 (?)

East Asia

No.	Country	Groups/Actors	Conflict types	Period/Phases
96.	China	Vietnam	C	Feb./March 1979–88

Island Asia and Pacific

No.	Country	Groups/Actors	Conflict types	Period/Phases
97.	Philippines	NPA, Cordillera, CPA, Bontok	AB	1970–
98.	Philippines	Mindanao: Moro, MNLF, MILF	BA+/BA	1970/1989–
99.	Indonesia	Aceh, various groups	B	May 1990–
100.	Indonesia	East Timor: army vs. FRETILIN	DBA	Aug. 1975–
101.	Indonesia	West Papua, OPM	DGB	1965–
102.	Papua New Guinea	Bougainville: BRA vs. PNGDF army	BAE/BAD	1988/Feb. 1989–

Source: Scherrer / ECOR © 1995

Table 1.2   Frequency and dominance of seven types of conflicts in the decade 1985–94

World 1985–94	A	B	C	D	E	F	G	Cases
Latin America 13.7%	6-4-0	5-4-0	1-0-0	0-0-0	0-1-0	2-2-1		14
Central America	3-2-0	2-2-0	1-0-0			1-1-0		7
South America	3-2-0	3-2-0	0-0-0		0-1-0	1-1-1		7
Europe 14.7%	2-2-2	7-3-1	3-1-0	0-1-0	3-3-2	0-3-1		15
Western Europe	0-2-1	2-0-0	0-0-0	0-1-0	1-0-0			3

Table 1.2 Continued

World 1985–94	A	B	C	D	E	F	G	Cases
Eastern Europe	1-0-0	1-1-1	1-0-0	0-0-0	2-1-0	0-3-0		5
SE: Caucasus	1-0-1	4-2-0	2-1-0	0-0-0	0-2-2	0-0-1		7
Africa 29.4%	5-16-2	13-1-2	1-1-2	2-2-1	7-6-2	0-1-1	2-1-0	30
N-Africa	2-1-0	2-0-1	0-0-0	1-0-0	0-1-0	0-1-0	0-1-0	5
W-Africa	1-2-0	2-0-0	1-1-1	0-0-0	1-1-0			5
Central Africa	0-3-0	2-0-0	0-0-1	0-0-0	1-3-0	0-0-1	2-0-0	5
E-Africa	1-7-2	5-1-1	0-0-0	1-1-0	3-0-1			10
Southern Africa	1-3-0	2-0-0	0-0-0	0-1-1	2-1-1			5
Asia 42.2%	7-19-4	20-8-2	7-0-2	3-1-2	4-6-5	2-0-4	0-1-0	43
West Asia	1-6-0	4-2-1	4-0-2	1-1-1	1-1-0	0-0-1		11
Central Asia	0-1-0	1-1-0			2-1-0	0-0-2		3
S-Asia	2-4-0	4-0-0	1-0-0		0-1-3	0-0-1		7
SE-Asia	3-6-3	8-3-0	1-0-0		1-3-2	2-0-0		15
E-Asia	0-0-0	0-0-0	1-0-0					1
Island Asia/ Pacific	1-2-1	3-2-1	0-0-0	2-0-1			0-1-0	6
All conflicts 1985–1994	20-41-8	45-16-5	12-2-4	5-4-3	14-16-9	4-6-7	2-2-0	102 225
Types of conflict	A	B	C	D	E	F	G	
Dominance	20	45	12	5	14	4	2	102
Total appearances	69	66	18	12	39	17	4	225

Source: Scherrer / ECOR © 1995

Table 1.3 Frequency and dominance of conflict types in per cent during the decade from 1985 to 1994

Conflict types 1985–1994	A Anti-regime	B Ethno-nationalism	C inter-state	D decolonization wars
Dominance	19.6%	44.1%	11.8%	4.9%
mentioning	30.7%	29.3%	8.0%	5.3%

Conflict types 1985–1994	E inter-ethnic	F gang wars	G genocide	B+D+E+G ethnic conflicts
Dominance	13.7%	3.9%	2.0%	64.7%
mentioning	17.3%	7.6%	1.8%	53.7%

Result

Conflicts with a dominant ethnic-induced or ethnicized character (types B, D, E and G) account for nearly two third (64.7 per cent) of all contemporary conflicts. According to the number of appearances ethnic components made up 53.7 per cent. (For the same period, Gurr 1993, compiled 70 ethnic groups in armed struggle.)[27]

General observations

The number of conflicts remained high throughout the period 1985 to 2000. The absolute number of conflicts was not decreasing (or even sharply decreasing) as other sources suggest. There was a constant up and down of the annual number of indexed conflicts. Concerning the virulence of violent conflict in the South (especially in many regions of Africa and Asia) there is no evidence for a relaxation. Many *endless* civil wars are ongoing and many new ones have started. Some of the new conflicts are linked to older ones (Niger, India, DRC, Yugoslavia) while others are truly new.

Table 1.4   ECOR index of mass violence 1995–2000

No.	Country	Groups/Actors	Types	Period/Phases
Central America				
1.	Mexico	EZLN (Chiapas), Tzeltal, Tzotzil	BA/AB	Jan. 1994/2/ 1995–
2.	Mexico	EPR/ELN (Guerrero, Oaxaca)	BA	June 1996– (new)
3.	Guatemala	URNG	GAB/AB	1960/1980–Dec. 1996 (end)
4.	Haiti	Army/gangs, US force	FA+	Sept. 1994–95 (end)
South America				
5.	Brazil	settler, gold rush vs. indigenous peoples	GE/FE	1986 (?)/1989–
6.	Colombia South	FARC vs. army/ alliance with narco cartels	AB; A; A; A	1964/65/Jan. 1974– March 1990/1992–
7.	Colombia Northeast	ELN vs. army, TNC, paramilitaries; spill over to Venezuela	AB; A; AEC	1965/1974–96/ 1997–
8.	Colombia	drug syndicates, death squads	F	1970 (?)–
9.	Peru	Andes/Selva: Sendero Luminoso/Rojo; militias	AB/ABF/ AFB	1975/1980–March 1995/–
10.	Peru	MRTA; support among Aymara and Quichua low	AB/AB	Nov. 1987–92/Dec. 1996– Apr. 1997/1997–

Table 1.4   Continued

No.	Country	Groups/Actors	Types	Period/Phases
11.	Ecuador	Peru	C	Jan.–Feb. 1995 (end)
North Africa				
12.	Algeria	Islamists, MIA, AIS; (platform of Rome 95)	AF/AF	1991–94/Jan. 1995–Oct. 1997 (end)
13.	Algeria	GIA vs. army, civilians, intellectuals, France	AF/FAC/ FG	1992–94/1995–96/ 1996–
14.	Egypt	Muslim integrists/ al-djama'a al-islamiyya	AF/AF	1992–97/Nov. 1997–
15.	Morocco	W-Sahara; Polisario; MINURSO	DB	Nov. 1975–92/–(?)
16.	Sudan	South Sudan: SPLA vs. army	BA+/ BEA/BA	Sept. 1983–91/ 1991–91/1992–
17.	Sudan	SPLA vs. SPLA-U, SSIA, Nuer u.a.	F/BE+/ EF	Aug. 1991/–92/ Sep. 1992–
18.	Sudan	Arab militias vs. SPLA and civilians (slavery)	F/FE	1983/1991–
19.	Sudan	Central Sudan: Nuba genocide	BGA/ GBE/GE	1989/1991–98/1998–
20.	Sudan	NDA; North Sudanese + SPLA/M, from Eritrea	AB+/A+	Oct. 1989/1995–
West Africa				
21.	Liberia	NPFL, ULIMO (K+J), LPC/ ECOMOG (end of mission 1997)	EF/EA+/ EAC/EA	1989/1995/April 1996–97/2000–
22.	Senegal	Diola, MFDC, factions vs. Army; spill-over to Guinea Bissau	BAD/BA/ BDC	1990–July 93/Jan. 1995–Dec. 1995/ 1997–
23.	Sierra Leone	RUF, NPFL (Liberia), ULIMO/EO (SAR)/ RUF vs. Kamajors, gov., UN and British troops	EC/AE+/ EFA+	Jan. 1991–97/ 1998/1999–
24.	Sierra Leone	RUF and AFRC (army) vs. ECOMOG II (Nigerian)	FCG+	May 1997–98
25.	Mali	Tuareg: MPA, FIAA; militias	BAE/BCE	1990–92/1994–97 (?) (end)
26.	Niger	Tuareg: FLAA	BAE/ BCE/BC	May 1990–91/Oct. 1994–

Table 1.4   Continued

No. Country	Groups/Actors	Types	Period/Phases
27. Niger	Arabs, others; FDR	BE	1995–98 (new/end)
28. Ghana	Konkomba vs. Nanumba, Gonja	EA	Feb. 1994–96 (?) (end)
29. Nigeria South	Ogoni (MOSOP), others vs. army, TNCs/CHIKOKO	BA/ BAD	1990er/1997–99 (new/end)
30. Nigeria Delta	Ijaw (IYC) vs. Itsekiri, Ilaye, army, TNCs; NDVF	EA	1998–(?) (new)
31. Nigeria N/S	Islamists vs. migrants from South/Christians	EF	1998–(new)
32. Guinea-Bissau	coup d'état/intervention by Senegal and Guinea, later ECOWAS	AC+	June 1998–Nov. 1998/ Jan.–Nov. 1999/ 1999–(new)

Central Africa

No. Country	Groups/Actors	Types	Period/Phases
33. N-Chad	Frolinat, FNT; Libya; MDD, Frolinat-FAP, RAFAD	B/BAC+/ BA+/EC+/ EA	June 1966/1979–83/ 1983–90/1991–94/ 1995–
34. S-Chad	CSNPD, FARF	BA/BEA/ BA/BA	1985/1991/ Aug. 1994–97/1998–
35. Congo R	Ngesso militia vs. army	AE	1997–Oct. 97 (end)
36. Congo DR-South	Luba; Katangan Tigers; Lumumbist	EA/AE	Aug. 1992/1993–May 97 (end)
37. Congo DR Zaire-East	Rwandan Hutu, FAZ vs. Tutsi; a/o;/ RCD	GEF	mid 1994–Nov. 96/ Aug. 1998–
38. Zaire-East	AFDL, Banyamulenge vs. FAR, Rwanda Hutu	EA/A	Sept. 1996–May 97 (new/end)
39. Congo DR East-NE-South	RCD with RPA + UPDF vs. FAC+ FAA+ ZDF+ NDF+ Chad, Hutu, Maji-Maji, a/o	AC+	2 Aug. 1998–(new)
40. Congo DR North	MLC+UPDF vs. FAC+FAA+ZDF, SA	ACE+	2 Aug. 1998–(new)
41. Congo DR Northeast	Lendu+Hutu, ADF, Maji vs. Hema+UPDF	FEG+	1999–(new)
42. Rwanda	post-genocide destabilization by FAR-Interahamwe	EFC+/G/ EA+	Oct. 1990/1994/July 1994–98 (end)
43. Burundi	Tutsi/Hutu: Army vs. FDD/FNL+alliance, support by Kabila/ DRC	G/GF/ EAC/ EGC+	1972–/Oct. 1993/ 1993–96/Oct. 1999–

Table 1.4   Continued

No.	Country	Groups/Actors	Types	Period/Phases
Eastern Africa and Horn of Africa				
44.	Ethiopia Oromia	Oromo: OLF, IFLO,	BAD/ (UOPL)	1976–May 1991/ BDA April 1992–
45.	Ethiopia	Eritrea; spill-over to OLF, Somalia	C	March 1998–June 2000 (new/end)
46.	Ethiopia Ogaden	Somali, div.; al Ittihad; Somalia-South BC	B/BEA/	1974/1992–96/1997–
47.	Ethiopia	Gojjam, Gondar: EPRP, EDU	A/AB/ BA	March 1974/Dec. 1975–91/1991–95 (end)
48.	Djibouti	Afar (FRUD others.)	BEA/BAE	1981/Oct. 1991–
49.	Eritrea	ELF-Idriss, Jihad, ELF-GC	EA+	1993–97 (end)
50.	Somalia	clans; SNA, USC, RRA, UNOSOM/warlords/ EPRDF+SNF vs. various	EF/EA/ EF/EFC	1988–90/Jan. 1991/Dec. 1992–96/ 1997–2000
51.	Somalia	UNITAF (USA *et al.*)/ UNOSOM II vs. warlords	FC	Dec. 1992–May 93/ 1993–March 95 (end)
52.	Somaliland	Issa/other clans	EDC*/EF	May 1988–May 1991/1992–97(?) (end)
53.	Uganda NW	LRA, WNBF; a/o; support by Sudan vs. UPDF, SPLA	AB/EA+/ EAC+	Feb. 1981/Feb. 1986–96–/ 1996–
54.	Uganda North	MIR (Islamic), UDFM; support by Sudan	EA+	1995–(new)
55.	Uganda SW	ADF; alliance with Hutu, Maji-Maji, Lendu	ECA/FC	1991/1996–98/1998–
Southern Africa				
56.	Angola	UNITA vs. FAA army, supported by Sar, then Zaire; 'final offensive' by FAA late 1999	D/BAC+/ BAE+/ EAB/AE	1961–75/June 1991–94/ 1994–97/1997– Oct. 1999/Nov. 1999–
57.	Angola Cabinda	FLEC-FAC, FLEC II vs. FAA, TNCs	AE/AEF/ BAF	1975/1993–94/1997–
58.	South Africa	Kwa-Zulu: Inkatha IFA	EA	1990–
Western Europe				
59.	Spain	Euskadi, ETA, street kids	BA/ BAD	1937–Sept. 1998/ Nov. 1999–
60.	France	Corsica, FLNC a/o	BA/BA	1950–/1970–
61.	Northern Ireland	IRA, INLA vs. UK (RIR and RUC); UVF, UFF	DB/DEA/ EDA/ DA	1961–69/1986–Oct. 1994/ 1995–July 1997/ May 1998 (end)

Table 1.4 Continued

No.	Country	Groups/Actors	Types	Period/Phases
Eastern Europe				
62.	Croatia	Expulsion of Serbs Krajina/Eastern Slavonia	G/BF+/ EA	1940–44 mid 1991–93/ May 1995–(end)
63.	Bosnia	Chetniks, Muslims, HOS; NATO bombs against Serbs	ECB+	March 1992/Sept. 1995– Oct. 1995–(end)
64.	Russia	Chechen rebels vs. Dagestan; 2nd RF intervention	BEAF/ EF+	Dec. 1994– Aug. 1996/Oct. 1999–
65.	Yugoslavia Kosovo	UCK-KLA vs. Serbian Police, army, militias	BFE+/ FE+	mid 1999–March 1999/ May 1999–(new)
66.	Yugoslavia Kosovo	NATO bombardments vs. FRY (for 78 days)	C	March 1999–May 1999 (new/end)
67.	Serbia South/ Presevo Kosovo	UCK vs. Serb civilians, Roma, Egyptians, a/o/UCPMB vs. Serbs; in presence of KFOR	FE+ FEC+	May 1999–2000/ 2000–(new)
West Asia 7 Middle East				
68.	Lebanon South IDF Zone	Israel + SLA vs. Hisballah, Amal, PFLP, a/o supported by Syria/Iran	EC/EC+	1982–93/1993–2000 (end)
69.	Lebanon South	Israel IDF vs. Hisballah a/o supported by Syria/Iran	ECF+	2000 (new)
70.	Israel	Palestine: PLO/ Hamas/Jihad Islami, Intifada II (Sharon on Temple Mount)	DB/ DBA/ DBC	1968–May 1994/1994– Sept. 2000/28 Sept. 2000–
71.	Georgia	Abkhazia; army vs. Abkhaz militias + Kosaks + CIS troops/ UN; Georgian militias vs. Abkhas	B+/BE+	Aug. 1992–May 1994; 1998 (new/end)
72.	Turkey Southeast	Kurds, PKK-HRK vs. army, militias	B/BADF/ BAF/ BAFC	1970/Aug. 1984–91/ 1991–97/1997–
73.	Turkey	Iraq: Turkish Army + KDP vs. PKK + PUK in security zone (Kurdish proxy war)	BC	March 1997–May 1997/ Sept. 1997–Oct. 1997/ Dec. 1997–98 (new/end)
74.	Iran	Kurds, DPK/I; air raids vs. Kurds in Iraq security zone	BA/ BAD	July 1979–88/1988–

Table 1.4 Continued

No.	Country	Groups/Actors	Types	Period/Phases
75.	Iraq	Kurds, PUK, KDP; Republican Guards + KDP vs. PUK + supported by Iran	BA/BAG/ BAF+/ BF+	1976/–1988/March 1990–96/Aug. 1996–
76.	Iraq	Kurdish proxy war: PUK vs. KDP; Iraq RG + KDP vs. PUK + PKK	BFC+	Aug. 1996–Sept. 1996/1997 (new/end)
77.	Iraq	Shiites/Shia	AB/CAB/ AB	1990/March 1991/1991–
78.	Iraq	New sustained bombardments by USA and UK; new attempt at destabilizing Saddam	CA	Dec. 1998–2000 (new/end)

Central Asia

No.	Country	Groups/Actors	Types	Period/Phases
79.	Kirgistan Ferghana valley	Islamist Uzbeks IMU vs. Kirgys and Uzbek army; spill- over from Tajikistan/ Afghanistan	EAC+/ ECF*	Aug.–Oct. 1999/ Dec. 1999– (new/end)
80.	Tajikistan	Islamist UTO vs. communists, Clans, CIS/RF troops until 1997; Afghanistan spill- over; Uzbekistan	EAF+/ EA+/ EAF+	Aug. 1992–June 1993/ 1993–June 1997/Nov. 1998–2000 (end?)
81.	Afghanistan	CP, Pathans, Tajik, Uzbek; Taliban vs. alliance of the North	ABE/ BAE+/EB/ EBC/EC	1973/Oct. 1978–89/ 1989–92/Apr. 1992–96/ 1997–
82.	Kazakhstan South	Jihad extremists and mafia, Kazakh- Uzbek border; bomb raids by Hezb ut-Tahrir; Kazakh Russians at risk	FA	Aug. 2000–

South Asia

No.	Country	Groups/Actors	Types	Period/Phases
83.	Pakistan	India/Kashmir 'line of control'	C	1999 (new/end)
84.	Pakistan Sindh	Sindhi, MQM, Muhajir/Pashtun	BEF/EF	Nov. 1986–90/1990–
85.	India	Kashmir: Muslim JKLF, Hizbul a/o, /Jamu/Ladakh	BE/BAE	1986/1990–
86.	India	Bihar: Naxalits	A	1988–
87.	Sri Lanka	LTTE, Tamils	B/BA+/ BAE+	July 1983/Sept. 1987/ March 1990–

Table 1.4 Continued

No.	Country	Groups/Actors	Types	Period/Phases
88.	Bangladesh	Chittagong Hill Tracts: Chakma, Shanti Bahini	BAF	1973–97 (end)
89.	Nepal	UPF vs. special police forces	A	1998 (?)–(new)

Southeast Asia

No.	Country	Groups/Actors	Types	Period/Phases
90.	NE-India	Tai-Asom, ULFA; IBRF	FG/BEA	1983/1989–
91.	NE-India Assam	Boro; ABSU, BSF, BLTF	BEA/ BEF	1967; 1989–
92.	NE-India	Naga: RGN, NNC, NSCN; talks with GoI; ceasefire	BD/BEA/ AB/BA	1954/1963/1972/Nov. 1975–97 (end)
93.	NE-India	Manipur: Kuki KNA, Meitei vs. NSCN	BA/BEA/ BAE	1960/75/84/May 1992–
94.	Burma	Karen/Karenni: KNU, KNPP, DAB vs. Army and DKBA (quislings)	BEA/BD/ BAG	1947/1950–88/ 1988–
95.	Burma	Shan/Tai: SSPP-SSA, SURA, a/o	BAD/ BA/BAF	1950s; 1960s–1988/88–
96.	Burma	Mon, NMSP	B/BAE / BAG	1962/76/Nov. 88–June 95 (end)
97.	Burma	opium guerrilla: MTA, Wa, SSNA	EA+/ EFA/FE	1950/1976/ March 1989–
98.	Laos	Hmong, LLA, drug war lords	FEC+/FEA	1970/1975–(?)
99.	Cambodia	Khmer Rouge; ANS//// / Khmer Rouge+ FUNCINPEC vs. CPP	A/CA/G/ AB/A+/ AF+	1968/1970/1971–75/ 1979–97/Jun. 1997–

Island Asia Pacific

No.	Country	Groups/Actors	Types	Period/Phases
100.	Philippines	NPA, Cordillera, CPA, Bontok/RPP-ABB	AB/ABE	1970–96/1997–
101.	Philippines	Mindanao: Moro, MNLF, MILF; Abu Sayyaf, ICC	BA+/BA	1970/1989–Sept. 1996/1996–
102.	Indonesia Acheh	Acheh; GAM vs. Army and paramilitaries	BE/BE	May 1990–/1999–
103.	Indonesia Moluccas	Islamist vs. Christians; locals vs. settlers	FG	1998–(new)

Table 1.4 Continued

No.	Country	Groups/Actors	Types	Period/Phases
104.	Indonesia	East-Timor; 80% of vote in referendum; terror of Quisling militia; UN troops	DBA/ DG	Aug. 1975–/Aug. 1999–Oct. 2000 (new/end)
105.	Indonesia Irian Jaya	West-Papua, OPM vs. army, settlers and TNCs	DGBC/ DB	1965–1993/Nov. 1995–
106.	New Guinea	Bougainville, BRA, BTG, BIG vs. army, quislings, TNCs	BAD/ BAD+/ BAD	Feb. 1989–1990/1992– Dec. 1995/1996–Oct. 1997 (end)
107.	Solomon Islands	Guadalcanal; GLA-IFF militia vs. Malaitan migrants and police	EFA/EF	Dec. 1998–Dec. 1999/2000–(new)

Source: Scherrer/ECOR © 2001

1.5 Trends and perspectives

During the period 1995–2000 some 107 cases of mass violence occurred (1995–96: 80). Of these 107 conflicts 73 cases continued (1995–96: 75 of 80), 34 ended and 26 were new cases (1995–96: only five new conflicts were started). Contrary to other compilations ECOR found no significant decline in the number of the world's violent conflicts. This is partly due to the method of identifying and counting conflict: ECOR counts violent conflicts according to instances of organized mass violence between the mentioned conflict actors (including alliances) in a particular conflict and not according to countries/territories.

Due to the complexity of contemporary mass violence, several violent conflicts can occur in the same country during the period of observation. For instance in the six-year period 1995–2000 ECOR identified seven conflicts in the ex-Zaire/Democratic Republic of Congo and as many involving India on its territory, five conflicts in Sudan, four which involved Ethiopia, Burma, Indonesia or Iraq, three in Nigeria, Uganda, Somalia, Yugoslavia/Serbia and two conflicts in a larger number of states. Conflicts are identified and codified according to a dynamic model featuring multiple components, the base of which is a combination of the dimensions of actor-orientation and driving forces (reflecting the basic incompatibility) of a particular conflict. Actor and place is not counted the same way: for instance, USA and UK were directly involved respectively in four and three conflicts – not as a theatre of conflict but as actors elsewhere – in Somalia, Bosnia, Iraq and Serbia/FRY.

Some results are significant: the overall frequency of violent conflicts was higher in recent years (107 in the six years from 1995 to 2000 compared to 102 in the decade before) but their duration was shorter compared to the decade 1985–94. Regarding a conflict settlement the result shows that 61 violent conflicts were settled or ended otherwise within the 16-year-period since 1985 (1985–96: 27). However, in some of these conflicts the causes of the violence were resolved comprehensively while in a number of other cases the end or the ceasefire remain precarious and violent conflict may re-ignite in the future.

1.5.1   High frequency and dominance of ethno-nationalism

The results show some clear trends: in the 16-year period from 1985 to 2000 ethno-nationalist wars and inter-ethnic conflicts were more dominant than anti-regime wars, gang wars or inter-state wars. Dominance and frequency are roughly balanced regarding inter-state wars, decolonization wars and inter-ethnic wars. The Tables 1.5 and 1.6 show dominance and frequency of conflict types over the recent six-year period from 1995 to 2000.

Particularly significant is the result concerning the most frequent types A, B and E: the world's violent conflicts contain most frequently an anti-regime component, followed by inter-ethnic and ethno-nationalist components. According to dominance the ethno-nationalist conflicts (34 cases) are well ahead of inter-ethnic (25) and anti-regime wars (21). Most significant is the result that ethno-nationalist wars are much more frequently in a dominant position compared to anti-regime wars (31.8 per cent: 19.6 per cent); this

Table 1.5   Frequency of types and dominance 1995–2000

Type	A	B	C	D	E	F	G	Total
dominant	21	34	5	5	25	15	2	107
secondary	34	10	15	1	18	14	4	96
tertiary	4	1	8	4	6	8	4	35
Frequency	59	45	28	10	49	37	10	238

Table 1.6   Correlates of conflict frequency and dominance

Correlates	Dominance and frequency		Quotas	
Period	1985–94	1995–2000	1985–94	1995–2000
Anti-regime wars	19.2 : 30.7	19.6 : 24.8	0.63	0.79
Ethno-nationalism	44.1 : 29.3	31.8 : 18.9	1.51	1.68
Inter-ethnic wars	13.7 : 17.3	23.3 : 20.26	0.79	1.13

Source: Scherrer / ECOR © 2001

result is as a trend in line with the results from the decade 1985 to 1994 (44.1 per cent : 19.6 per cent) but ethno-nationalist conflicts – though still the most frequent dominant conflict type – lost ground to the inter-ethnic conflicts, which in recent years became the second most dominant type ahead of the anti-regime wars (1985–94 the second type).

Conclusion: the most frequently dominant conflict type continued to be the ethno-nationalist (31.8 per cent), followed by inter-ethnic wars (23.3 per cent), the latter with a strong increase, followed by anti-regime wars (19.6 per cent) and gang wars, including terrorism and organized crime (14 per cent, almost doubling compared to 1995–96), decolonization wars and interstate conflicts (4.7 per cent). Genocide (1.9) remains the most rare type of violent conflict but the one with the highest mortality. Those conflicts that acquired a dominant ethnic character (types B, D, E and G) account for 61.7 per cent (down from two-thirds or 66.25 per cent in the decade 1985–94) of all contemporary violent conflicts in recent years. According to the frequency per type of conflict the ethnic components appeared in 47.9 per cent of all cases (earlier above 50 per cent).

1.5.2 Reduction of inter-state wars; increase of interventions

Shocking for mainstream security studies and conflict research is the fact that the Clausewitzean type of inter-state conflict has practically disappeared. The most significant trend in recent years shows a decline of the absolute number (and proportion) of inter-state conflicts; according to dominance there are less than 1 in 20 conflicts. In the late 1990s there were only three cases of 'classic' inter-state conflicts (Eritrea versus Ethiopia 1998–2000; Pakistan versus India 1998; NATO versus Yugoslavia 1999).[28]

The provocative assessment is that inter-state conflict character may increasingly become a component of other types of conflicts. In the period of observation 1995–2000 we find only five classic inter-state conflicts. In 23 cases in the last six years the inter-state conflict character became a secondary component of intra-state types of conflict, most prominently in Africa.

The hypothesis is that today inter-state conflicts increasingly mutate into a sub-component or an extension of intra-state wars. In Africa this new pattern can be demonstrated in several recent cases occurring in the years 1996–1998.[29] The military involvement of eight African states and a dozen non-state actors in the new war in the Democratic Republic of Congo between the Kabila regime and the RCD-rebels since August 1998 is only the latest and most complex example.[30] Contrary to the *classic* type of inter-state conflict, different types of ethnic conflicts and disputes could be compared to rhizome plants growing for decades, nearly impossible to up-root, growing 'everywhere' and always surfacing where and when you would least expect.

Foreign state participation increased to 26 cases (of 107 conflicts) as for the most recent phases of current violent conflicts only (up from 17 of 80 conflict cases 1995–96).[31] In the decade of 1985–94 there had been 27 cases of foreign state intervention; in 15 of those 27 cases the intervention occurred in the last phase of the conflict, while in 12 cases the former state intervention took place in the 1980s. Hence recent foreign state intervention is extraordinarly high. A few interventions even occurred in types B and E.[32] The question of foreign state intervention is to be distinguished clearly from support by foreign states for one or more conflict actors (for example by providing safe hinterland or weapons).[33]

1.5.3   Decrease of conflicts in Asia; increase in Africa

The distribution of conflicts according to world regions shows the following picture. Today 45 per cent of all violent conflicts are taking place in Africa, which is more than 50 per cent more than during the decade 1985–1994 (Table 1.7). During the period of 1985 to 1996 the regional distribution of violent conflicts was largely modified. While the proportion of Latin America remained constant, those of Asia and Europe were declining. On the other side the proportion of violent conflicts in Africa was increasing dramatically.

In the mid 1990s the share of Africa in the world's conflicts became the largest. The threat of a further increase to about half of all conflicts was avoided by some increase in Asia. However, according to the number as well as the mortality of violent conflicts Africa has become the most war-torn

Table 1.7   Regional distribution of contemporary mass violence (percentage)

Distribution	1985–94 (decade)	(1995–96)	1995–2000 (six years)
Asia	42.2	(33.7)	37.4
Africa	**29.4**	**(45.0)**	**43.9**
Europe	14.7	(7.5)	8.4
Americas	13.7	(13.7)	10.3

Source: Scherrer / ECOR © 2001

Table 1.8   Regional distribution and change

Regional distribution and change	1985–94	%	1995–2000	%	Change
Latin America	14	13.7	11	10.3	–
Central America	7		4		–
South America	7		7		no
Europe	15	14.7	9	8.4	–
Western Europe	3		3		no
Eastern Europe	5		5		no
SE: Caucasus	7		1		–

Table 1.8 Continued

Regional Distribution Change	1985–94	%	1995–2000	%	Change
Africa	30	29.4	47	43.9	+
N-Africa	5		9		+
W-Africa	5		12		+
Central Africa	5		11		+
E-Africa	10		12		+
Southern Africa	5		3		−
Asia	43	42.2	40	37.4	−
West Asia	11		11		no
Central Asia	3		4		+
S-Asia	7		7		no
SE-Asia	15		10		−
E-Asia	1		0		−
Island Asia/Pacific	6		8		+
world's conflicts	102	100	107	100	−/+

continent in recent years, ahead of Asia (with West Asia and Southeast Asia accounting for over half of Asia's share), see Tables 1.7 and 1.8.

1.5.4 Changes in the regional distribution of conflicts

After 1990 Europe became once again one of the major theatres of war. The talk but 'Europe as an island of peace' in the midst of a war-torn world was abruptly silenced in 1991. The most peaceful world regions were East Asia and North America (the latter without taking into account high rates of urban violence and criminality). Six years later violent conflicts in Europe were reduced almost by half and conflicts in Asia decreased by some ten per cent. Only in Africa did conflict increase dramatically by almost 50 per cent.

1.5.5 Dramatic increase of most deadly conflicts in Africa

In Africa the civilian population suffered heavy losses by exterminatory mass violence, warfare and war-induced famine. Since the mid 1990s there are three macro trends regarding violent conflicts in Africa: (1) Africa's share of the world's conflicts is increasing; (2) inter-state conflicts are increasingly mutating into subcomponents or extensions of intra-state conflicts; and (3) the overall conflict situation in Africa has developed increasingly towards higher intensity conflicts – which means from armed conflict to major armed conflict (defined as claiming more than 1000 lives).[34] Especially the increase of major armed conflicts and mass slaughter in Africa is a matter of great concern.

The provisional compilation reviewing the world conflict situation in the years 1996–2000 with regard to conflict intensity exhibits a dramatic trend: since 1997 the number of such most deadly conflicts was generally higher in Africa then in the rest of the world.[35] Currently, the world's most deadly conflict, which has claimed an estimated number of two million victims within 30 months in the most complex of the African conflicts, is the one in the Democratic Republic of Congo.[36]

1.5.6 Increase of complex crisis situations and state collapse

Genocide and mass murder of defenceless victims account for around two per cent of all conflicts in the respective periods. This is an alarming sign and a matter of most serious concern. The number of victims of genocide and mass violence in the period from 1985 to 2000 is much higher than the frequency would suggest. The small numbers of genocidal mass violence show a higher mortality than those of all other conflicts combined. The state-organized genocide in Rwanda 1994 alone took one million lives in a period of 99 days. This incredible number of victims is more than twice the number of victims caused by all violent conflicts in the former Soviet Union and in the former Yugoslavia 1989–2000 combined. In the twentieth century the number of battle-related victims is much less than the number of victims of genocide and mass murder.[37] Genocide prevention is among the most urgent tasks for the new twenty-first century.

In the 1990s a dramatic increase of extreme crisis situations and complex emergency cases led to an alarming increase in conflict-induced mortality in cases of protracted conflicts. The most deadly contemporary case of mass violence – in a cumulative count since 1954 – ravages Sudan. An estimated 2.5–3 million people became the victims of genocide, war and famine, as a consequence of successive Sudanese regimes' onslaught in southern Sudan. At present this large-scale conflict is going on unabated.

1.5.7 Increase of gang wars and globally active terrorist gangs

Another matter of concern is the exponential growth of gang wars, first almost doubling from 3.9 per cent to 6.25 per cent in a period of less than ten years and then further rising to one out of seven conflicts (14 per cent of all recent conflicts). Until the mid 1990s 'chaos power' and warlordism characterized only a small number of all conflicts (one in 16), but gang wars increased even more, as predicted, based on data covering the period up to 1996 (see Scherrer 1999: 398). Evidence pointed to a higher proportion of cases of this type of postmodern conflict, indicating a trend toward further increases in dominance and frequency.

While in the 1970s this type of gang warfare was prominent in several world regions (Middle East, Western Europe and Japan), and some developed into transcontinental networks, it was not until the 1990s that this new type of terrorist network became a global threat. Growing out of US covert action against the Afghan leftist regimes of Taraki and Amin, and the subsequent Mujahiddin gang war against the Soviet military presence in Afghanistan 1979–89 – sponsored by the US, Saudi Arabia and Pakistan – an extremist Islamist movement emerged.

The al-Qaeda organization, trained and equipped by US special forces, became a multinational terror organization, built-up to destabilize the Central Asia republics of the USSR. Al-Qaeda was soon led by the charismatic Osama bin-Laden, who has worked closely with the CIA for more than a decade. After the Soviet retreat from Afghanistan, US support dwindled; former allies turned into enemies, provoked by the US military presence in Saudi Arabia since 1991 and the US policy in the Middle East. A series of terrorist attacks on US presence in eastern Africa and the Middle East culminated in the 11 September 2001 attack on the US itself.

1.5.8   Loss of hegemony of state actors: further fragmentation

In the case of most ethno-nationalist types of conflict the conspicuous silence of the Western mass media is even more suspicious; such conflicts account for about a third of all violent conflicts. The ethno-nationalist character is undoubtedly the dominant component of contemporary conflicts. Adding to that, the type of inter-ethnic conflict grew to be another quarter of all conflicts. One of the particularities of these conflict types is the relatively low chance for peaceful conflict settlement. This was one of the main causal reasons for the steady increase (up to 1995) of durable protracted conflicts, which again contributed significantly to the increase of the total number of wars since 1945. The related type of decolonization conflict is continuously accounting for 1 of 20 wars. Such conflicts received more attention from the Western media (for example, Palestine and East Timor).

Already in the mid 1990s conflicts between ethnic groups, mostly without the involvement of state actors, were a cause for alarm. Such conflicts, in most cases, take the form of 'communal violence' between warring ethnic groups, though this term tends to banalize rather sophisticated and extremely brutal forms of mass violence (for instance those occurring in parts of Central and West Africa). Comparing results in the most recent period of observation from 1995 to 2000 with those of the decade 1985–94, this conflict type increased by not less than 170 per cent, from 13.7 to 23.4 per cent of the world's violent conflicts and will – in all probability, taken its frequent appearance as secondary or tertiary component in many other ongoing violent conflicts – continue to grow in numbers. To sum up, current trends point toward a further fragmentation within existing states. In many countries of the southern hemisphere this results in a loss of hegemony of state actors. State failure, protracted warfare and other forms of mass violence are inextricably linked.

2
Approaches to Identifying and Dealing with Violent Conflicts

The weakness of many of the attempts made by peace and conflict research to respond to the ethno-national challenge is due to a variety of factors. The way in which, up to now, almost all research capacity has been geared to classical, inter-state situations of conflict, concentrating on the activities of the superpowers and big powers, has proved totally inadequate. Endogenous causes of conflict, most notably the virulence of the ethnic factor, have been systematically underestimated. The global phenomenon of violent intra-state conflicts has, it is true, assumed a higher profile in research terms since 1989–90, but there continue to be serious research-related deficiencies.

Considerable deficiencies exist in regard to: (1) diagnosis, especially of the causes and dynamics of various types of violent conflict; (2) anticipatory capacity – that is, the ability to identify and respond to signs of potential conflict with foresight, on the basis of a thoroughgoing knowledge of the major causes of dissension (early warning/early action); (3) the structural prevention of conflicts; (4) therapeutic measures, especially in the form of constructive conflict management and peaceful intervention; and, finally, (5) 'peace search' – in other words, influencing the macro-political framework conditions, ensuring certain weapons and weapons-systems are outlawed, and acting on the general imperative of disarmament and of the control of the international arms trade.

Only recently has there been an intensification of research efforts in regard to ethno-nationalism and other types of intra-state conflicts. The lack of political and institutional consultation in peaceful conflict settlement initiatives is particularly lamentable. The lacunae of research into the 'new' non-Clausewitzean types of mass violence as well as into activities in the field of peaceful conflict settlement perpetuate the lack of understanding for contemporary forms of mass violence and add to the difficulties go-between actors ('third parties') are facing in their quest for peace. A general lack of comparative studies can be identified. In the area of peace-building, externally directed, coercive mediation (power mediation) aims more at producing direct effects in ongoing violent conflicts – ceasefires, for example, or negotiations. Meanwhile medium-term 'go-between' actions or 'third-party' interventions work towards the broader transformation of such conflicts through a process of (re-)conciliation aimed at securing lasting peace. The tradition of arbitration exists in many societies.[1] Autochthonous or other long-established forms of peaceful conflict settlement offer a potential source of inspiration.[2] The political decision makers in Rwanda decided in 1999 to use the traditional participative jurisdiction of gachacha in order to address the horrific consequences of genocide in this country, to prevent further disaster and to reunite the Rwandans.[3] Genocide prevention requires a number of different measures, with the final goal of eliminating the crime of genocide, which is structurally different from preventing non-genocidal ethnic violence; the latter is chiefly building on acknowledging difference, promoting group rights and providing for autonomy or self-governance of non-dominant groups. In contrast, genocide prevention mainly builds on accountability, reforming criminal justice and early action, as one of the most urgent tasks for the twenty-first century.

The need to develop efficient and intelligent early-warning systems has long been recognized and yet one cannot talk of there being any fully fledged functioning schemes of rapid response. This is one of the major lessons to have emerged from the general failure in the face of the apocalyptic genocide in Rwanda.[4] Genocide scholars are working to develop an effective system of genocide alert; some projects have changes to be realized.[5]

Development aid should be suspended in cases of gross violations of human rights. Threats against groups of citizens must be dealt with immediately. Agencies of United Nations, regional organizations, donor states and NGOs shall impose conditionality on development aid in cases of organized forms of state criminality in weak states. Incentives shall promote democratization, respect for basic human rights and minority rights, rule of law, good governance and promotion of free media. Projects in these sectors should get priority funding.

Monitoring risk areas – particularly the evolving situation of minorities being threatened – is still largely underdeveloped. One of the key lessons to be learned from the Rwanda shock is the failure of early warning and the failure of the donor states, UN agencies and the established international human rights organizations to react promptly and monitor the situation. Generally, international and local non-governmental organizations as well as international governmental organizations should be more active in monitoring risk areas and minorities at risk. Averting genocide must become a main area of activity of all NGOs working in conflict areas.[6] Working up the history of a troubled region is the key for understanding complex situations. In cases of genocidal violence it is mandatory to explore the root causes, its ideology and the sequence of past traumatic experiences. Escalation processes can often be broken through permanent presence, monitoring and appropriate media coverage of the plight of minorities. A rapid and broad system of protection of possible victims should be organized by a NGO coalition in every conflict area. Civil actors shall intervene in addition to and as a correction to parallel efforts by the UN, IGOs and regional organizations. Much more attention should be given to non-spectacular silent work such as violence preventive and confidence-building measures; they should be compared and studied carefully. Civil actors should take the lead in fighting powerlessness and passive response on genocidal threats against vulnerable groups shown by many states and state organizations.

As *ultima ratio* the political will for military interventions – in situations of large crimes against defenceless civilians and humanitarian disasters – was recently raising again, after the total failure of the UN and the West in Rwanda had sent shockwaves through the international community. The two cases of military interventions in 1999 – made in the name of stopping human rights violations – have not only raised the question of utter selectivity but those of illegitimacy and abuse of the human rights discourse in pursuit of war aims. The case of Yugoslavia is particularly controversial: those who wanted to stop severe human rights violations themselves massively violated international law, the Geneva Conventions and its Protocols in particular. In the case of East Timor the intervention fulfils the provisions of international law and was generally seen as justified. But the intervention came too late to save thousands of lives; in fact, it came 25 years too late. A partial genocide unleashed by the Indonesian army had killed 200,000 Timorese since 1974.[7] The planned UN intervention in Congo DR did not materialize until March 2001, when less than 5,000 troops (MONUC) arrived in a country the size of Western Europe, although the Lusaka peace agreement of July 1999 and an impressive list of UN resolutions called for it. This again gave more weight to the argument that responses to crises made by the international community – chiefly the 'Northern' powers – are flawed.

There is little doubt that in some cases, for instance in situations of rapid escalation, averting gross violations of human rights can only be done by military intervention as *ultima ratio*. Future UN peace-enforcement missions in risk situations and in cases of genocide alert should be much better prepared and co-ordinated. Besides improving the early warning capacity of the United Nations, 'in particular its capacity to analyse and react to information' (Carlsson *et al.* 1999, IV.4.), the UN should enhance co-ordination with organizations in and outside the UN system, improve the flow of information and seek to protect civilians, local staff and its own personnel in conflict situations.[8]

However, the need for deterrence has finally been widely recognized. Deterrence in preventing genocide and crimes against humanity is largely dependent on progress being made in international law and the establishment of a permanent International Criminal Court in the first years of the twenty-first century.[9] The development of concepts of structural prevention of genocide and mass violence is among the noblest task of peace research. Charitable funds and scientific funding institutions should prioritize research projects in these fields. The prevention of violence against vulnerable groups should be written into the statutes of many more associations. Standardizing the prevention of genocide and mass violence internationally should become a key task for the UN Human Rights Commission in the twenty-first century. Genocide prevention should become part of domestic laws and national constitutions as well as of relevant international conventions and pacts.

2.1 Legitimate opposition in the unequal struggle for survival

The new states that are emerging are often of multi-ethnic character; so-called new ethno-states have so far been the exception in the Third World. Since decolonization, however, ethnocracies – that is to say, multi-ethnic states ruled by a dominant ethnic group – have been the norm, particularly in the Third World (and recently also in the CIS). They may be divided into minority and majority dictatorships, and into stable and unstable regimes.[10] In the conflict regions of the Middle East and the Horn of Africa, minority ethnocracies are particularly common, whereas in the Far East, the more stable majority ethnocracies predominate. The stability that is claimed to exist is relative and cannot obscure the fact that, as a regime type, ethnocracy is merely the political expression of the dividedness or scission of the societies in question. And dividedness is essentially a potentially conflictual, destabilizing factor.

Second World ethno-chauvinist movements, which are pursuing the creation of (additional) ethno-states, do not owe the conditions that have made their 'success' possible primarily to their status as oppressed minorities invoking a legitimate claim to resistance. Nor is their 'success' a result of their capacity to mobilize or persuade. Rather, it is due to the favourable climate engendered by the upheavals in world politics and to the peculiarities of the ethnicized political structures in the now-defunct Soviet Union.

Contrary to journalistic myths and commonplace notions of 'backward-looking tribalistic feuds' and so-called 'ethno-political protest-movements',[11] many oppressed nationalities and non-dominant ethnic groups, particularly in the Third World, find themselves in a desperate plight, or indeed in an unequal struggle for survival against aggressive, militaristic state classes. A number of methods of categorizing ethno-national conflicts seem to be aimed at denying the particular rebel movements the legitimacy for their resistance.

The terminological embodiment of double standards for states and ethnic groups is particularly disquieting in those cases where regimes are prepared to use almost any means to break opposition. The ruling élites often seek to make use of superior resources to settle old scores and to appropriate the land and resources of minority nationalities. Many regimes talk of a threat to territorial integrity and national sovereignty. They justify their use of repressive agencies to quell the rebels – agencies whose activities may range from the mere waging of propaganda wars to various forms of (state) terrorism – by invoking reasons of state and ideological bogeymen.

2.1.1   Proposals for a secession regime

Up to now, public international law in general and the law of the nations in particular have, as a rule, set the right of existence of already constituted states above the right to self-determination, with its implied claim to secession. Under the protection of the UN Charter, realization of the right to self-determination proceeded relatively smoothly for inhabitants of colonial territories in the colonial age, as long as they comported themselves as united 'state peoples'.

However, remnants from the decolonization period, and also former colonial territories annexed by regional powers (for example Eritrea, East Timor, Tibet, Hong Kong) continue to cause problems even now. In view of the lamentable brutalization of many ethno-national conflicts and the shameless propping-up of unitary state structures by violence in many Third World countries, thought should be given to alternatives, including 'real secession regimes'. Using the bloody conflicts in Yugoslavia and the Caucasus as a basis, Ropers and Schlotter have mooted various alternative methods of conflict resolution in this connection.[12] Instead of tacitly conceding existing states the *de facto* right to use violence against non-dominant minorities, the OSCE should agree rules of conduct for legitimate secession.

Secession would be justified in three cases:

- where there is 'massive and prolonged violation' of human rights, with no prospect of change;
- where there are gross structural inequalities in living-standards based on ethnic/national discrimination;
- where one state has been annexed by another and this is to be reversed – in other words, in the case of a decolonization conflict (as in Eritrea).

As regards the last point, legal guarantees already exist in the international system, within the framework of self-determination for colonized peoples. The other two grounds for legitimate secession – namely, massive violations of human rights and gross socio-economic asymmetries – apply to many ethno-national trouble spots in the Third World.

2.1.2 Recognition regimes: the case of Yugoslavia

In an analogous process, recognition regimes for new states should be developed, containing the same sorts of stipulations as those listed above. The effective protection of (new) minorities should be guaranteed and made an 'indispensable condition' (Hofmann 1992) of awarding new states recognition. In the case of the Soviet and Yugoslavian successor states, this opportunity was squandered.

At the end of 1991, the foreign ministers of the European Union approved a recognition regime for the Yugoslavian constituent republics. The EU stipulated that there must be respect for the rule of law, democracy and human rights (as laid down in the UN Charter, the Helsinki Final Acts and the Paris Charter) and for the rights of minorities, in line with the obligations entered into within the framework of the C/OSCE. In practice, however, the approved stipulations relating to the recognition of independent statehood had no impact.[13] Recognition of Croatia and Slovenia had been pushed through hastily as early as January 1992, under pressure from the German government, and in that process the Badinter Commission had (only a month before this date) declared Croatia 'whiter than white'. Unfortunately, there was nothing at all to guarantee the rights of the 600,000-strong Serb minority, survivors of Ustacha terror.[14]

The recollection of the genocide by the Croatian vassal state is part of the collective memory of all those involved in it; in a situation of threat, traumatic memories are reactivated. Extreme collective experiences, such as genocide and expulsion, have a traumatizing effect that reaches beyond the generations directly affected by them. The mass murder perpetrated on the Serbs is scarcely two generations old.[15] Every new threat rings alarm bells.

Because of the reactivation of feelings of threat, the ethnicization of the conflicts in former Yugoslavia acquired a new credibility. This is the only possible explanation for the success of the ethno-political mobilization launched by the old state and party élites, who found themselves in danger of losing their power. In 1991–92, the UN had to set up buffer zones between the Croatians and the self-proclaimed independent republic of Krajina, and also in Slavonia. The UN troops stationed there were present on the ground until the Croatian forces – numerically three times as strong – took possession of Krajina, and almost the whole Serb population (300,000 people) fled in panic or were driven out. The same happened in September 1995 in Bosnia, where Muslims and Croats, screened by massive NATO bombardments of Serb positions, proudly declared that they had 'liberated' whole areas of Bosnia – an ethnically cleansed state! The ethnicization of the conflicts in ex-Yugoslavia also shaped the Dayton/Paris framework-accord for Bosnia and Herzegovina (November–December 1995);[16] tens of thousands once again abandoned their homes. Sarajevo's suburbs are now 'Serb-free'; a multi-ethnic society that had coexisted for centuries has disintegrated.[17]

The dangerous chimeras of a Greater Serbia (something of which the Serb Chetniki dream) and a Greater Croatia are both still being officially kept alive (the latter by, among others, the late head of state Tudjman and the HOS), and they form the basis for latent threats of war. Croatia repeatedly threatened that it would reconquer or 'liberate' Serb settlement-areas. Krajina has now been 'liberated' and 'ethnically cleansed', and Tudjman's regime has threatened the same for Slavonia if the Serbs do not knuckle under. Croatia also lays claim to territories in Slovenia and Bosnia.[18] The war that eventually broke out in Bosnia as well, a few months after the international recognition of the Croatian state, was regarded by many observers[19] as a consequence of the historical amnesia of the Europeans, and, above all, of the lead which Germany took in granting over-hasty and ultimately catastrophic recognition to the by-products of the collapse of Yugoslavia.

A step further is the *de facto* recognition of an armed group as the legitimate representative of a minority. Not only recognition but massive military support for the Kosovo Liberation Army (KLA, UCK) was the response of NATO in the latest crisis in the Former Yugoslavia. Unfortunately, the enforcement of international law became an argument to launch military interventions – in outright breach of international law – as in Kosovo.[20] A Human Rights organization finds that the most dramatic developments in 1999 were that twice, in Kosovo and in East Timor, 'members of the international community deployed troops to halt crimes against humanity', although these crimes very much continue – this time in a contrary way.[21] The price to pay for the Kosovo intervention targeting of civilians was utterly disproportionate.[22] The damage and death toll caused by NATO was kept under seal.[23] The war aim, the toppling of the Milosevic regime, was not achieved by NATO in 1999 but by democratic elections in 2000 and the Serbian people's determination to honour its result.

2.1.3 Preconditions for and methods of recognizing secession

International law recognizes the right to self-determination but not, as a rule, the right to secession. The three remaining alternatives, distinct in status and structure, are: (1) substituting (partial) self-governance for separate statehood – that is federation as a constituent state (as the Mizo and some Naga have done in India); (2) regional autonomy (like that of the Autonomous Soviet Socialist Republics (ASSRs) within the USSR, or the Yapti Tasba in Nicaragua, or China's autonomous regions); and (3) protection of minorities (as with the Sorbs in eastern Germany).[24]

In Europe, the prospects for nationalities defined by states as minorities are relatively good as long as it is autonomy (and not independence) they are seeking, because a network of relevant international agreements and consultation mechanisms exists (as in the OSCE). States can no longer simply cite the principles of sovereignty and non-intervention when they deprive their minorities of rights. In Third World conflict regions, however, minority nationalities mostly have only the UN system to call on – the forums of the powerless Human Rights Commission, for example. Many Third World élites do little to render their states capable of integration through minority protection, autonomy/nationality policy, or increased democratization; furthermore, they do not have the resources to ensure minimum social security for their citizens or to develop backward areas. Under certain conditions – where the political system is repressive, inflexible and discriminatory, and where ethnically motivated attacks are a 'normal occurrence' – secession is the only option.

One precondition for the recognition of a state is that it should already 'exist' *de facto* – in other words, secession already must be virtually complete. The point at which recognition takes place is then a question of political opportuneness. In order that the process of recognition can begin in practical political terms, there must already be a demarcated state territory, a state people and a state executive. There are two variants here: (1) a secession movement that is already administering 'liberated' territories, and (2) a provincial government that will promote its province to the rank of a state – in other words, secession through upgrading. It is rightly objected that the underlying tendency of this is to encourage the seizure of territory and the declaration of sovereignty (mostly with violent consequences) as a means of lending substance to the sought-after statehood. In the case of many indigenous peoples and minority nationalities, the first requirement (territory) would be a contentious one, in that the actual size would have to be determined if there were no mutually recognized borders that could be adopted. The second requirement (a people) is not likely to be an issue. The problem lies in the executive.

A self-governed, 'liberated' territory whose freedom has been secured by a nationalist liberation movement is unlikely to be recognized as a regularly governed state by other states. This would be tantamount to breaking off diplomatic relations with the state from which the new state has broken or is to break away. In international diplomacy, however, there are gradations or interim forms of recognition. The Norwegian government, for example, recognized the opposition provisional National Coalition Government of the Union of Burma (NCGUB) as legitimate, but without as yet having broken off relations with the military junta.[25]

The path of secession via upgrading – the upgrading of constituent republics or autonomous territories, for example – has generally followed a peaceful course in recent times. This option was used successfully in the case of the 15 Soviet and seven Yugoslavian constituent republics. However, in the case of former Autonomous Soviet Socialist Republics in the Russian Federation or other CIS countries, upgrading would appear to be of internal relevance only. The example of the CIS does, however, reveal an extremely broad spectrum of internal and international types of (non)recognition of *de facto* secessions or of (non)recognition of spurious secessions/declarations of sovereignty, the consequence of which, though not necessarily, may be war.

2.1.4   Recent secessions and declarations of sovereignty

In the case of the three autonomous republics within Georgia, the new Georgian rulers unilaterally revoked their autonomous status. War resulted in two cases (Abkhazia and South Ossetia). Abkhazia secured secession without international recognition. In former Yugoslavia, the same process of abrogation of autonomy in the formerly autonomous areas of Serbia (Vojvodina and Kosovo) did not result in war. Abrogation of autonomy was the chief trigger to four wars in the former USSR and two wars in Yugoslavia.[26] Unilateral upgrading to sovereign republics was demanded by five previously not fully self-governing nationalities in Russia; the new status was recognized by the Russian Federation. For territorial units that have exportable natural resources, declaring sovereignty is a great temptation: an increase in status generally means a greater share of export revenues. As is shown by the example of the Republic of Sakha-Yakutia (which is the size of Western Europe and has a population of one million), this can produce the oddest of effects.[27]

Conversely, the new Russian minorities in the Ukrainian-owned Crimea and in Moldova's Dniester Republic declared themselves 'sovereign republics' (in the first case peacefully and in the second after armed contention) but were not recognized by any state. In the case of the Dniester Republic, independence existed in principle but, after negotiations between Russia and the OSCE, was withdrawn to the extent that secession entailing separate statehood was excluded. In contrast, minorities in other CIS states and in Serbia (for example the Kosovo Albanians) have – with good grounds – shied away from any armed declaration of sovereignty, because this would entail war.

The Abkhaz only managed to gain *de facto* independence from Georgia by resorting to armed violence, but have not, up to now, secured international recognition. Since 1991 they have been members of the Unrepresented Nations and Peoples Organization (UNPO), which also acted as a third party in the war of secession against Georgia (UNPO 1992*c* and 1994*a*). Similarly, Chechnya's armed declaration of sovereignty had little chance of being acknowledged, even by a few states. It was the first time the 'rules of the game' had been broken unilaterally by a minority leadership within the framework of the Russian Federation.[28]

2.1.5   Ethno-nationalism as a response to serious crises

Ethno-nationalism is a response to serious ongoing crises. In this connection, there are certain differences between the Second and Third World, due to differing structural characteristics. In eastern Europe and the CIS, the course of the crises has been shaped by the collapse of old world-orders, triggered by the democratization of a repressive but secure social set-up – a democratization that ultimately does away both with the repression (albeit often only temporarily) and with social and economic security. In the previously nominally socialist Second World, nationalism becomes a kind of quest for identity, and a vehicle exploited by new élites to gain positional advantage.

In the Third World, on the other hand, the course of crises is often shaped by real threats to the existence of non-dominant groups on the part of the nation-state (sometimes several states) or on the part of the dominant group that is using the state to further its own interests. Single, multiple, or systematic aggressive measures taken by the state classes against non-dominant ethnic groups often have the effect of escalating the conflict. Such measures include: repression on the grounds of affiliation to a particular ethnic, racial, linguistic, or religious group; the invasion and occupation of minority areas; the rape of minority lands and resources; expulsion through acts of terror – up to and including genocidal actions – by the army or armed settlers.

In repressive ethnocracies in particular, nationalist movements that do their mobilizing along ethnic lines often find themselves in situations where they are forced to act in self-defence. The use of armed force (often of a terrorist kind) by the state classes constrains them to armed resistance. Ethno-nationalism becomes a matter of survival; it involves necessary resistance to existential threat.

2.2 Reorientation of peace and conflict research

Present-day European peace and conflict research was essentially born out of East–West conflict.[29] With the de-escalation of this 'major conflict', at least in Europe – but not by any means yet in East Asia – whole swathes of this research became obsolete or were refocused on arms conversion, peace education and many other previously neglected, areas. The end of the cold war in much of Europe imposed new preoccupations and offered an opportunity to reflect on beginnings and to effect a comprehensive reorientation.

One section of peace research, notably the Scandinavian school – chiefly represented by Johan Galtung, one of its founding fathers – and one section of the West German variant, had begun to distance themselves from older, American research conducted during the 1960s. Critical peace research introduced global-cum-structuralist approaches and viewed global economic relations based on violence and exploitation as constituting conflictual relations. The postulate of structural violence reached far beyond the narrow confines of peace and conflict research in its potential capacity as an integral part of military science. Structural conflict linked in with the new critical theory that was making in-roads into various schools of economic and social thought and which tied into classical twentieth-century theory on imperialism.[30] At the end of the 1960s, theories critical of the established order experienced a huge upswing, especially in France, with the structural Marxist school and *Tiers-Mondisme*, but also in Latin America, with the *dependencia* school.

Even though the political half-lives of critical theories of unequal exchange/unequal development, or of periphery–centre models and dependency paradigms, are apparently spent (which has a good deal less to do with their quality than with the spirit of the times), it remains true that their influence not only opened up a window onto the Third World for peace and conflict research, but also challenged some of the latter's premisses and models. A return to that period of renewal would seem to be urgently required but would not accord with present trends.

As early as 1964, in the very first issue of the *Journal of Peace Research*, Galtung had called for attention to be paid to intra-state group conflicts, had warned against fixation on the 'transitory phenomenon' of the nation-state and exclusion of cross-cutting themes and had called for a broad geographic and disciplinary distribution of themes and of research-establishments.[31] Only now has research into intra-state conflicts begun to acquire a higher profile. Since the end of the cold war, there has been an enforced reorientation, because the sterile and distorting antagonism between East and West has dissolved, and thus has cleared the view on the real conflict situations and the global phenomenon of violent intra-state conflicts.

Only 12 out of a total of 102 wars between 1985 and 1994 were of a (primarily) inter-state nature.[32] Yet until recently, this type of war commanded almost all the attention of researchers – though for decades this had had more to do with inherently research-related and ideological constraints than with actual conditions. In terms of research attention, 'anti-regime' war (rebel movements) was next on the list. Up to now, when investigating intra-state conflicts, research has accorded much greater attention to this type of war than to ethno-national wars, even though this, too, does not reflect reality.[33]

At the end of the cold war era, at the conference held by the International Peace Research Association (IPRA) in Groningen in 1990, some peace and conflict researchers seemed not just surprised by the rush of events, but baffled and disoriented. The totting-up of missile batteries on either side had suddenly become meaningless. The majority of peace researchers had been caught 'on the hop'.[34] The sudden dearth of supposedly 'major' conflicts had an adverse effect on peace and conflict research: its funding was curtailed. Faced with irregular wars, some researchers began to relapse into *realpolitik* or traditional power politics. Under the influence of media coverage of the barbaric events in nearby Bosnia, some well-known peace researchers declared themselves in favour of 'peace enforcement' – as if peace could ever be enforced. Reduced funding forced other researchers back into the established political sciences.

Analysis of structural violence in the international system already had been largely abandoned. In Germany, some of its former protagonists have called for 'peace keeping action' by NATO; some maintained that this should be carried out under UN supervision. As far back as in the 1991 edition of the *Friedensgutachten* (Peace Report), produced by representative German research organizations HSFK, IFSH and FEST, there was support for the idea of out-of-area operations by the German army.[35] While the existence of the Bosnian war 'in their own backyard', heard some *peace* researchers voicing support for violence.

2.2.1   Farewell to conflict research as military sociology

Up to now, almost all the capacities of established peace research have been concentrated on the classical situation of war and conflict between states, with a fixation on the North and the activities of the superpowers and big powers. This approach has proved totally inadequate.[36] Military and political/ideological aspects were overemphasized, and economic, ecological and cultural factors neglected. Proxy wars were identified even in the furthest removed 'corners' of the earth in the otherwise scarcely heeded Third World. Endogenous causes of conflict and the virulent nature of ethnic/cultural factors were systematically underestimated. Many did not yet recognize ecological destruction as a conflictual factor.

There were a number of reasons for these fatal misjudgements. They had to do, first, with the way in which most peace research facilities were concentrated in and on Europe and North America (and not on the major areas of conflict[37] and), second, with the fact that in many countries peace and conflict research was subsumed under military sociology. There was talk of the emergent 'small-scale and regional conflicts' (*AFB-INFO* 1992, 1: 1) presenting conflict research with new challenges – which, however, were not so new.

The allegedly small-scale conflicts are only small-scale when viewed through the spectacles of the 'large-scale conflict between East and West'. In reality, they have claimed millions of victims, far more than the 'regional conflicts' supposedly triggered by the East–West clash. A radical reorientation was overdue. As early as 1990, in Groningen, there were unmistakable signs of the shifting trend: the work-group which did the briskest business was the one on *internal* conflicts and options for dealing with them. To talk of ethnic or ethno-national conflicts in the German-speaking area at that time (unlike in the Anglo-Saxon area) was still considered 'bad form'.

2.2.2   New research priorities

Only a few institutes in Western countries had began to reorganize their research priorities before 1989–90.[38] Until recently, the United Nations University and its regional branches had contributed little to research into ethnicity. Once it began to become more and more obvious that ethnic/ national conflicts had the greatest explosive potential, and constituted a threat to the existence of the former USSR, research such conflicts was given a massive boost within the Russian Federation.[39]

What practical effects international research on intra-state conflicts may have on the conduct of repressive states is largely unknown, since its influence is indirect and still new. Action research is hardly represented in this area in Europe; it currently functions to some extent via intermediate UN bodies. Although the need for research has been recognized. In 1993, the then UN Secretary-General Boutros-Ghali wrote very appositely, that it was simpler and cheaper to tackle wars preventively and thus avoid them than to try to put a stop to hostilities that had already broken out. The capacity for prevention, he said, depended precisely on research and access to information that would enable conflicts to be anticipated. For this reason a programme concerned with conflict resolution in ethnically divided societies (INCORE) was to be instigated forthwith, under the aegis of the United Nations University.[40] This belated enhanced involvement by the UN University reflected the realization that 'ethnic violence' no longer represents a second-rank threat to the international order.[41] In his *Agenda for Peace*, Boutros-Ghali had talked ambiguously of a new threat – namely, that which ethnic groups pose to states.[42]

Intra-state conflicts, particularly ethnic ones, are still regarded in most research institutes as a special kind of problem, not as the major conflict type.[43] Until the mid 1990s the specialist literature on ethnic conflicts was still modest in volume measured against the importance of the topic. Remarkably, it seemed only to be political scientists, sociologists and economists who concerned themselves with ethnicity as a conflictual factor, rather than ethnologists and social anthropologists.[44] Some of the research approaches have, so far, baffled than more enlightened.

2.2.3 Critique of some approaches to conflict research

North American approaches that seek to explain ethnic or ethno-political conflict exclusively and one-dimensionally as a consequence of strategic groups' lack of success in the competition for resources (a failure brought about by the state's lack of flexibility and inability to resolve conflict) do not seem very convincing.[45] Other approaches stress the weaknesses from which peripheral states suffer on account of their lack of resources, or of their social and ethnic incoherence, or of their insufficient power to enforce decisions or maintain cohesion. They highlight the top-heavy bureaucracy and lack of legitimacy of such states, but they often take insufficient account of the fact that it is precisely these weaknesses that make the rulers of Third World states, and the forces of repression under them, dangerous to the civilian population.

It is true that the administrative, managerial and economic capacities of peripheral states are, as a rule, limited; but this does not prevent most of these regimes from using their meagre resources and manpower for repressive purposes. Even with limited means, a great deal of suffering can be caused. Often, the resources that do exist are employed in a brutal and cynical way as part of a policy of organized state terrorism. As a result, armed ethno-national and other movements of opposition to repressive regimes claim the right to resistance. The contrary trends of, on the one hand, the 'civilization' of states through the creation of an appropriate social and political environment (embracing the international level also) and, on the other, the 'brutalization' of societies by state organs, should be brought more into the field of vision of peace and conflict research. This would also have consequences in regard to how regime-types are defined.[46]

The 'resource-competition' approach has provided a plausible explanation for some instances of escalation to ethno-national conflict. But the two obvious weaknesses of all theories connected with it (pluralist societies, 'consociation', hegemonial exchange) in their respective permutations are, as Stephen Ryan has already critically observed, over-emphasis on élite interaction/neglect of popular movements and the blocking-out of the international, global and regional context (Ryan 1990: 21). My experience in areas of ethno-national conflict indicate that the range of instruments used by the resource–competition school cannot, or can only inadequately, describe certain important aspects relevant to a conflict. The school's central thesis is that – assuming an ethnicized state-apparatus – the distribution of resources or the burden of costs (felt to be unfair by the élites and a sufficient number of members of an identifiable ethnic community) will cause an escalation in ethnic tensions and will lead to conflicts that have a tendency towards violence (Wimmer 1994: 532). This thesis turned out to be false, for most conflicts in the South (where more important issues are at stake), or is of secondary importance, for example, for most of the conflicts that took place in the period 1989–94 in the former USSR, with the possible exception of the second war in Chechnya (Scherrer 1997: 306–8); abrogation of autonomy was a much more important direct cause of conflict in the former Soviet Union.

The general preconditions in a model of escalation are in reality more multi-layered than the economic/socio-psychological approach will acknowledge. Some authors introduce nuances based on psychological–symbolic aspects of conflict inducing factors – such as fear of having the rules of the game for a particular regime revised (a fear that was very real, for example, after the collapse of the USSR), or the effects of negative collective memories and ideas in ethno-social groups (sensitivity to danger because of experiences of genocide, for example), or the resolve to oppose the policies of cultural assimilation pursued by dominant groups if the latter is not ready to give way. Rothchild has rightly lamented researchers' lack of interest in non-'externalist' conflict inducing demands (and counter-demands) that do not threaten to break the bounds of the system (Rothchild 1991: 194, 198).

A number of questions remain open: of what relevance are social–psychological factors outside the domain of traumatic experiences? What context, what structures and alliances, what breaches in the history of repressive regimes incite oppressed groups to rebel? Why should the expropriation of resources not be as open to discussion as their distribution?

2.2.4 Increasing awareness of the problems associated with ethnic conflicts

Generally speaking, increased activity by internationally active human-rights and indigenous organizations in the first part of the 1990s, the work of some high-profile peace researchers and the turning of the media-spotlight onto selected conflicts, contributed to a growing awareness of problems associated with intra-state conflicts and ethnicity. The prime concerns, within the framework of interdisciplinary conflict research (earlier co-ordinated by IPRA's ICON group and the ESN)[47] ought to be to prepare and compare rules, laws, conventions and concepts which envisage sanctions for enforcing a 'humanitarian minimum', and to discuss options for settling ethnic conflicts on the basis of international or human-rights-related law.

Given the prevailing inadequacy of research in the area of intra-state and ethno-national conflicts, there are a number of factors that will probably help in bringing about a reorientation of conflict research and a more intensive study of areas of activity that have so far been neglected. Some factors that might be mentioned here are:

- increasing awareness of the conflict-inducing problems associated with ethnicity, ethno-nationalism and its claims for the self-determination of non-dominant groups;
- fear of the large-scale influx of refugees from the Third World, Eastern Europe and the FSU states;[48]
- the political debate about the new role of the United Nations, prompted by dramatic events in the first part of the 1990s – Bosnia (1992), Somalia (December 1992–February 1995) and Rwanda (1994) – continued with the Yugoslavia–Kosovo crisis, with a NATO war and the UN civilian take-over mid 1999 and the spread of violence – despite the presence of NATO forces – into Macedonia 2000–01.

There is a gradual realization that the UN, NATO and the OSCE are largely unable to exercise long-term impact on intra-state or ethnic conflicts. The activities of international and humanitarian organizations, particularly the non-governmental organizations, in areas of conflict are being influenced by the increasing awareness of the problems associated with ethnic conflict situations (NGO fundraising is directly dependent on public opinion in the metropolises),[49] while the embarrassing blunders resulting from the ill-thought-out humanitarianism of many NGOs in Rwandan refugee camps in Congo–Zaire remain in the memory.

2.3 Current state of peace research and search for peace: deficiencies and developments

The number of theoretical studies on concepts of conflict mediation (and the number of detailed case-studies) has recently begun to rise, with no indication that there is to be any standardization of the instruments used or of the methods applied. Two things that might encourage such a trend are, on the one hand, the linking together of different data-banks and strands of information, and on the other, the resolution (or at least exposure and systematization) of terminological problems. But the real problem in both cases lies 'deeper down'. There are serious deficiencies with regard to:

- diagnosis – in respect of knowledge about the causes and dynamics of violent conflicts and of the capacity for anticipation, that is foresighted preventive identification of the signs of potential conflict; in this connection, the need for early-warning systems has now become a matter for common sense; and
- treatment – especially in respect of the ability to take early action, of guiding concepts and of the practical implementation of ideas and strategies of preventive and constructive conflict resolution.

In the domain of civilian conflict transformation, Christine Merkel identified the inability to act (despite early warnings) and poor theoretical grounding as the chief weaknesses of both state-sponsored and civilian peace-workers.[50] Some intergovernmental organizations (such as the UN, the OSCE, the OAU and the Council of Europe), the EU since the mid 1990s and some governments have begun to work along violence-prevention lines, which indicates an opening-up to the modes of working used by civilian actors which in turn demonstrates that established institutions are capable of learning under the pressure of changed requirements.[51]

As a general trend, greater emphasis is being placed on strategies for containing violence that are based on de-escalation achieved through mediation rather than through the classical policy of hegemonial containment. However, the involvement of so-called neutral outsiders in peace-building often remain unsuccessful; one solution would be to support local capacity building and efforts which 'involved insiders' (Lederach) make to create enough negotiating space on the ground so that conflicts over identity or power can be settled non-violently. 'Outside parties' (Galtung) play a secondary role; the crucial figures as far as mediating activities are concerned, are local go-betweens. In practice, this requires both integrated, long-term co-operation between international NGOs (INGOs) and research institutions on the one hand and local go-betweens on the other, and also co-ordinated modes of operation by actors from civil society and governmental or intergovernmental actors. In reality we saw a reluctance to act in a foresighted informed way, in close collaboration with the actors on the ground. Many

NGOs prefer high-impact 'fire-fighting exercises' and the kind of mediation that brings spectacular success, which they think they need for fundraising reasons. The practical benefit to those affected, meanwhile, is often minimal. This highlights a structural conflict of objectives that is not easy to overcome, even with a great deal of 'good will'.

Deficiencies with regard to information and organization can be eliminated once they have been located and identified, and this process would undoubtedly be aided by an improved supply of information and a systematic method of exchange (networking). However, the problem with ever-greater networking is not just having to make data on conflict accessible; what is much more important is the introduction of quality control. The internet, which is now being used more and more often for the exchange of data, is open not only to researchers and peace workers, but to propagandists and manipulators as well.

Behind terminological problems there lurk, as ever, ideological attitudes, solid interests and specific cultural-cum-cognitive features, and this implies a danger that certain ways of thinking will be inappropriately imposed (for example the Western Christian paradigm of guilt, expiation and atonement within the framework of conflict mediation). As a first step, INCORE has proposed the compilation of a kind of thesaurus listing and comparing the schemes of categorization used and their key concepts such as 'conflict', 'ethnicity' and 'the right to self-determination'. (Such an attempt for standard-setting in the field of terminology would certainly not succeed.)[52] A second step could then be to chisel away at dogmas and call particular terms and concepts into question – as Galtung has in critical peace research since 1960.

The dire lack of information on intra-state conflicts in general and of those susceptible to 'ethnic' interpretation – currently the major type of conflict – in particular is disquieting. The lack of data affects almost all the aspects and elements of contemporary violent conflicts. As a result, options for conflict prevention or for whatever treatment of conflict may be necessary, from mediation to negotiated agreement and resolution, are rendered null and void, or are diminished in quality.[53] Successful dispute settlement and the much-sought-after success stories are thwarted.

The lack of information, flawed concepts, weak methods and lacunae in present 'war lists' and indexes affect the comprehensive understanding of contemporary mass violence:

- series of lacunae of global surveys on mass violence can be identified, for example the flawed construction of conflict types and inadequate methodology
- static models result in a lack of capacity to anticipate change
- exclusion of important types, due to flawed concepts/theories, sometimes because stumbling blocks are put in the way of an adequate understanding of the driving forces

- exclusion of a non-war types of mass violence in most indexes necessarily results in reduced explanatory power
- inadequacies due to ideological fixations and a state-centred view
- errors in the actual data collected, for example, with regard to ethno-demographic structure due to bias or to exclusive dependence on government statistics[54]
- weak theoretical instruments affect the ability to detect important elements or result in misinterpretation, for example hidden causes of conflict, with root causes being different from immediate causes (incompatibilities), triggers for violence and de/escalators
- lack of knowledge, for example, about the actors directly and indirectly involved, the means used, the nature of conflict, the course of the conflict, the demands of the opposition, the nature of the regime, possible interference from outside, foreign actors and so on
- inability of many scholars to distinguish 'ethnic' or ethnicized conflicts and to identify such types according to causes, disputants, gravity/size, region, macro-political framework-conditions and a sound method of classification
- inability to trace the implications of ethnic and ethnicized politics, which are dangerous devices that need to be thoroughly investigated
- serious limitations to effective intervention, successful conflict management, transformation and possible solutions resulting from a lack of understanding of contemporary conflict.

It became common knowledge that intermediary activities in intra-state conflicts in general and 'ethnic' conflicts in particular have so far only exceptionally been crowned with success. The great complexity and 'inaccessibility' of violent ethno-national or inter-ethnic disputes, the strong emotions tied up with threats to identity, the persistence of such conflicts, and the highly uncompromising attitude of militant ethno-nationalist resistance movements and militarized states alike, diminish the options for peaceful as well as military intervention and reduce the prospects for success.

2.4   The tasks of peace research in the twenty-first century

Aspects of great significance for the peace and conflict research of the future are: inspection of its own role according to non-research criteria; continuation of the comprehensive reorientation that is already underway; and increased activity in certain previously neglected fields. Part of the self-inspection is reflective on some of the open debates of the early days of peace research, including the question of the normative bases of the international political system and the globalizing world economy.

Calling Western universalisms into question implies a criticism of individual human rights, the utilitarian application of which (as critical philosophers long ago noted) is the right to private property. These kinds of ideas are not shared by most extra-European societies nor by the majority of indigenous peoples.[55] The universality of human rights is dependent on the benevolence of state power-élites; this fact emerges clearly from every yearbook of human rights organizations such as Amnesty International. Yet international law – in general, and the law of the nations in particular – and human rights are linked to one another as 'ideas', and both had emerged in a Euro-centric context before they were declared part of the global ethic.

2.4.1 Global ethic, normative bases and human rights

The twofold 'original sin' of which universalist human rights are guilty stems from the fact that they were born of 'national liberation struggles' and of the establishment of the bourgeoisie as the new ruling class.[56] On the one hand, millions of people lost their lives in the name of the nation, and the dying goes on even now and, on the other, the utilitarian application of the right to freedom was the right to property – or, more precisely, private property. With advancing globalization and the increasing concentration of economic power, this results in freedoms and advantages for possessors but not for the dispossessed. The foundations of bourgeois–democratic society, in which free individuals interact with one another as property owners, in which society is organized along democratic–republican lines, and in which human rights are combined with free trade, a free market and freedom to enter into contracts, collapse when democratic control fails and the market develops in an unregulated way and deprives the mass of people of the bases for life.[57]

A global ethic[58] ought to combine the idea of freedom with that of equality. In order to satisfy the demand of the majority of the world's population in the Third World for justice in the international system, measures such as the institution of mechanisms of fair exchange, for the purposes of ensuring equality of opportunity on the world market, should be promoted on the basis of a global ethic. Reparation and compensation by the former colonial powers, affirmative action for the poorest and joint efforts at co-operation by the community of nations, would be further macro-political requirements.

2.4.2 Putting the world of states in its place

One decisive question that peace research will have to pose itself in future has to do with putting states into proper perspective. The question is whether, given the increasing restrictions on nation-states' and territorial states' scope for action (as a result of internationalization, the power of the financial markets, 'internal' politicization, or the propensity to conflict), it still makes sense to proceed from the notion of the state as the central actor.

The core question is whether the nation-state has not already become a variable quantity, dependent on the regional environment and internal power-relations.[59] Despite the restricted applicability of these kind of observations, they make it clear that the collapse of state structures (as in the USSR and Yugoslavia) have long since ceased to be capable of being interpreted using categories of established research such as 'nation-building', 'integration' and so on.

And even though it appears that bi-polar thinking, with its notorious overemphasis on state sovereignty – to the detriment of the sovereignty of peoples – is long out of date, there is as yet no interpretation that matches up to the multi-polar world as it really is.[60] In particular, there is a lack of willingness to learn from the experiences of culturally distinct people or foreigners, or to question one's own dogmas.[61]

2.4.3 Urgent tasks of peace and conflict research

Some of the urgent tasks facing a newly configured version of peace research would be:

- to rid research into the causes of war of all ideological ballast from the cold war
- to promote non-Eurocentric and global perspectives
- to rethink the premisses, models and concepts currently in use, in the light of the actual multi-polar nature of the international system, the relativity and conflictual nature of the nation-state concept, and the increasing importance of non-state actors
- to review the normative, ethical-cum-moral bases of international politics, and to question the universal validity of Western conceptions[62]
- to return to the study of the causes of war and positive peace[63]
- to realign and redouble research into the ethnic factor and into both challenges, the one which ethnicization by genocidal states presents to non-dominant groups and the other one which ethno-nationalism presents to the *old* neo-colonial world order[64]
- to expand knowledge and capacities of peace research on preventive measures, processes and institutions, on conflict-resolving and on peace-building in general.

Comparative investigation into global and regional conflict constellations should systematically be pushed forward. The way in which the 'overall climate' affected local political events in areas of tension was previously thought of solely as deriving from the confrontation between the Eastern and Western blocs. Nowadays, however, regionalization and formation into world regions take place according to quite different co-ordinates.

2.5 General heuristic maxims for research into ethnicity and conflict

As a general guide as to how to approach the complex area of 'politicized ethnicity', I shall here make one or two supplementary observations of a general kind. The first group are of a negative kind: first and foremost, modes of investigation that distort or hamper access to the issues must be avoided. The call for research to be objective, unprejudiced and impartial is particularly important in highly emotional or alien situations. Yet in part of the literature on this topic, denunciation rather than analysis has been the dominant feature up to now.

- Accusations of manipulation against the leaderships of ethno-national movements and the imputation of particularistic economic interests are two of the commonest 'explanatory models' in use; but they almost always do not go far enough. In many cases, such accounts are merely an attempt to deflect attention from the real situation.
- 'Enemy traps' must be avoided – that is to say, the deliberate attempt to mislead in regard to what triggers or shapes ethnic conflicts. Where there is conflict, there are at least two sides and always completely divergent accounts of the situation.
- A distinction must be drawn between ethno-nationalism from below and ethnicization from above; confusion of these two phenomena, or failure to distinguish clearly between them, hampers understanding of ethno-national opposition and casts legitimate ethnic demands in a pathological light.
- The 'confusion' about the major objects, causes and triggers of ethnic conflicts is generally due not so much to the allegedly 'intangible' or 'irrational' quality of such conflicts, but to deliberate directed attempts to mislead on the part of state and other actors.
- Attempting to fathom complex realities by having recourse to 'purified forms' of ethnic conflict is doomed to failure. This kind of approach often has a lot in common with the obfuscating strategies employed by individual actors in conflicts.
- Highlighting resistance and preservation as motives of ethno-nationalism attempts to taint such movements as 'backward-looking' and as resisting 'inexorable' modernization.
- It is not only active denial of the true driving forces of ethno-national movements that distorts access to an understanding of them. Abstracting the basic asymmetry present in most ethnic conflicts and blocking out relationships of power and dominance also distort findings.
- Adopting a state-centred interpretation results in many models of, and findings on, ethnicity being one-sided, incomplete and 'false', and leads to a distorted account of illustrative cases.

Some theoretical approaches lack empirical foundation; others continue to be applied without regard to empirical findings. What dominate the attempts to tackle the ethno-national phenomenon is not understanding or the desire to understand but prejudice, myths and artificially constructed approaches.

Ethno-nationalist conflicts of a violent kind are a response to deeply rooted crises and dislocations – and not only in the decolonized states of the Third World and former Eastern bloc. Such conflicts become comprehensible when they are seen as processes of resistance and self-identification. Their social, cultural and economic aspects must be investigated from both horizontal and vertical perspectives, and from the point of view of their depth or intensity. Studies of ethno-nationalism will in future make an important contribution to the general theory of social transformation.

The most important prerequisites if research into ethnicity in general and the analysis of ethno-nationalism in particular are to be made fruitful in terms of the theory of social transformation are:

- a process-based and empirical (rather than an aetiological and theoretically predefined) approach, in which violence does not appear as anomie, ethnicity does not appear as 'primitive' and ethno-nationalism does not appear as a pathological condition[65]
- a dynamic type of analysis rather than a static and isolating mode of observation
- situating the analysis – in other words exploring violent conflicts in their historical and regional contexts
- a comprehending, critical (not denunciatory) purpose, operating as a dialectic between the *emic* and *etic* perspective which, rather than denying differences, discusses them.

A dynamic analysis would embrace the causes and objects of ethno-national conflict formations and would cover all the actors involved, along with their interests, divergent discourses, goals, resources and so on. Such analysis would distinguish between the various phases of escalation, would acknowledge outside elements and external factors (including macro-political ones), and would be able to point up options for de-escalation and peaceful resolution.

Conflict researchers, political scientists and development sociologists cannot come to terms with the fact that peace research has not as yet developed any heuristics worthy of this name. At the level of international politics, it would be particularly useful in terms of actual practice, if a framework of recognized structural analysis was established, that could act as a guide in defining properly planned, reflective and responsible conduct in political decision-making processes. This kind of recognized unitary framework does not exist today even in a rudimentary form. Questions of the most crucial nature remain unclarified.

Dividing off causes of conflict and processes is wrong, because then the antinomy between social science and historiographical modes of research and thought that we want to eliminate just waltzes back in 'through a different door'. Past causes, whose histories often stretch back over decades or even longer periods of time, may be difficult to identify in terms of their bearing on current processes of violence, or may have 'only' an indirect effect – compared to manifest triggers to conflict; but they are ultimately crucial to the (re)cognition and understanding of conflictual processes. The historical amnesia not only of Western European politicians but also of political scientists in regard to the Yugoslavian conflict is only the most recent of many examples.

Division of the totality of a conflict into neat analytical compartments of structural and other causes, economic and political (power) structures, and socio-cultural processes is also to be rejected. Western-style terms and concepts can often be traced back to long-lived nineteenth-century paradigms.[66] In this connection, concepts such as those popular export-items the 'nation-state', 'development' and 'sovereignty' must be critically put into perspective, adapted, or, if that is not possible, rejected.

The seemingly permanent establishment and globalization of ethno-nationalism in the last 50 years dictates that research efforts ought to be multiplied. But there is a real cognitive problem here, in that many sociologists, ethnologists and conflict researchers 'have never experienced (the horror of war or of mass violence) at close quarters and have no realistic prospect at all of going through a trauma of this kind'.[67] The overstated contrast between modern and non-modern societies implies different potentials for violence. It was the modern societies who waged the most violent of wars against one another and in the colonies.[68] Only detailed, empirical-cum-practical knowledge of the causes of war, its structural characteristics and the forces that drive it – ideally first-hand information combined with personal experience – will turn up the kind of solid findings that are a prerequisite for practical action in concrete instances. Otherwise, well-meaning attempts at prevention, containment, or peaceful intervention by multiple actors risk failure.

That said, it would be naïve to believe that the series of recent cases in which the spectacular failure of the international community was repeatedly and amply demonstrated were due 'only' to deficiencies in fact-finding and poor implementation. Knowledge and interests are seldom compatible in international politics. But ignorance and inadequacy did contribute to the political failure. The threat to the world order emanating from ethno-nationalism will increase efforts to identify and deal with the underlying, unavoidable wrongs – within the limitations imposed by practical politics, big-power interests and the crumbling principles of non-intervention in the 'internal affairs' of sovereign nation-states. The success of attempts at solution depends on whether states can be civilized – that is to say, whether states, which up to now have been the universally privileged protagonists, can be forced to share the sovereignty to which they lay claim with 'their' peoples. Ethno-national conflicts can only be resolved politically, not militarily.

2.6 The need for applied research methods

Fieldwork is indispensable for comprehensive analysis of a particular conflict. Existing and intensive contacts in a particular conflict area will prove productive in due course. Field research is essentially 'listening to the people'; it includes all forms of data collection. It can be carried out mainly by interviewing different types of informers: on one side key conflict actors of all sides, medium/mediate actors, civil society leaders, and on the other side, distinguished experts and observers. For the first category of informers interviews might be conducted with members of nationalist organizations, political parties and other relevant political actors (a list of interviewees should be kept open for possible amendment and revision over time). Information should be crosschecked with other interviewees; the second category of interviews is the ones with local and international experts. Ongoing evaluation may point at gaps to be closed. Field research or fact-finding missions may typically combine the following three steps:

1. Interviews with top and middle-level leaders of all sections of the civil society, especially representatives of new social movements for a double purpose of discourse analysis and investigation of facts and relationships (social relations and internal life of organizations) will be conducted and carefully evaluated.
2. Participating observation is the second main method to be employed; it is indispensable for a comprehensive approach to understanding conflict and contains elements of Participative Action Research (PAR) in order to gain a direct on-the-spot view, for instance following lists of exemplary groups, sectors, areas, and so on.
3. Collection of documentation on the spot and abroad is also indispensable, especially concerning historic background (in its conflicting versions). Task: archives investigation, libraries, reviewing literature and collection of a list of items indispensable to understanding the basic rationale of disputes in a particular area.

Working with non-structured or structured interviews is one of the main methods of data gathering developed in field research. Usually conversations are taped and transcriptions are produced. The idea is that the interviewed will be able to scrutinise the draft transcriptions. Such transcriptions will be kept in original tone, edited later on (o-tone, with titles and possibly including explanatory footnote) and put together, in order to obtain a full picture of certain processes. Often it is preferable to have talks and interviews with members of political and civic organizations in as much as an improvised way as possible, following a checklist of items provided in advance and agreed upon. No interview and no sensitive information shall be published without the informed consent of the interviewed – in order not to impair peace initiatives.

2.7   Development of appropriate concepts and instruments

Regional scenarios, phase models, early warning/early action systems and other, new, yet to be developed instruments, can help increase the capacity of peace research to prevent and resolve violent conflicts. The strengthening of these capacities is of special practical political significance. The development of appropriate 'strategic instruments' should focus on: the elaboration of regional scenarios based on compatible criteria; the evaluation of an integrated model of conflict escalation and of the different phases of conflict; development of early-warning and early-response systems and of an international response to complex emergencies.

Within the framework of a comprehensive understanding of conflict prevention, there is an especially urgent need for practical proposals as to how the highly conflictual concept of the nation-state (territorial state) may be put into some kind of perspective and overhauled. But the idea of departure from the concept of the state as a central actor is highly contentious. Important aspects in this connection are:

- the drawing-up of a list of criteria for evaluating demands for self-determination by opposition actors (ethnic-national minorities or indigenous peoples)
- intensive research into autonomy regulations and systems of self-governance as instruments of preventive conflict management (or peaceful dispute settlement)
- comparative study of examples of successful prophylaxis against conflict
- elaboration of standards of quality for self-governance
- standard-setting for all forms of 'internal' self-determination
- elaboration of legally binding instruments for the protection of national minorities (within the framework of the UN, ILO, OAU, OSCE, CoE and so on) and their verification
- reflection on a range of democratic mechanisms, popular referenda and other regimes for regulated 'international divorce' and bloodless secession.

The end of the cold war made reflection on, and study of, the new role of civil society actors possible. The development that has now begun of multilateral regional regimes for regulating minority rights is an outstanding new feature of international politics and must be monitored by back-up research. Of equal importance is a critical consideration of new UN policy within the framework of the treatment of internal conflicts. There should be a systematic analytical examination of ongoing and projected UN interventions aimed at peace enforcement or peace building – in other words, aimed at the creation, preservation and consolidation of peace on the ground.

The ideal method of dealing with conflicts consists in measures that will ensure an interactive resolution that is fruitful and peaceful for all concerned. Avoidance and anticipatory containment are applicable to all potentially destructive forms of conflict resolution, not just the spectacular and violent ones. Preventive measures against destructive interaction in the inter-ethnic context include the protection of non-dominant groups and respect for the rights of all linguistic–cultural, ethnic and national groups. Structural prevention should not just be talked about. The need is now almost universally recognized, but the disproportion between the resources expended on military peace keeping and peace enforcement and those expended on preventive care and civilian conflict transformation could not be greater.

2.8   The challenges of building peace

Challenges and tasks for internal and external go-between parties vary greatly in times of peace or in times of a lapse in to higher tensions. Usually one will witness a difficult starting phase. Among the main tasks of the local go-between (such as peace groups and civic organizations) would be the task to cope with the dynamics of developments, to mobilize support for dialogue among political and social organizations, and to mobilize support for dialogue from local, regional and other organizations and from the International Community at large.

Some of the main problems and practical questions are:

- the analysis of the right time for intervention with a view of the issues at stake is of crucial importance
- the roles and functions of the go-between, and their constant change during the process of peaceful intervention (see 3.1.2)
- the categories of negotiators or informers and the definition of functional roles: parties (soft/hard-liners), top-level, middle-range and grass-roots leadership; groups at risk; competitors; drop-outs; users; partial insiders/neutral outsiders and so on
- the role of the media.

The media can critically affect the process and the outcome of any peace initiative and beg the question: how to control the relationship with the media during initiatives or talks? Media coverage can be used as an excuse for the breaking down of talks. Leaking of information will increase distrust. Indeed, the struggle for trust is at the core of the whole peace process of dialogue, talks or formal negotiations. There are several ways of looking at the result of peace processes:

- outcome and process: focusing on the outcome or alternatively on the process that may lead to peaceful conflict resolution
- type of agreements: the definition of the outcome is particularly critical. Attention should be paid to the full versus partial agreements or to lasting

versus temporary agreements. What key issues were left unresolved in a partial solution/partial implementation? What potential have dissident groups/militant factions to jeopardize the implementation of peace agreements?

Unfortunately, not only dissident groups can jeopardize the implementation of peace agreements. Sometimes the weak elements are those who were chosen to supervise the implementation, usually international organizations (UN, OAS, OAU, SADC and so on) or government representatives from neighbouring states (often regional powers have vested interests). For a more in-depth elaboration of the issues raised here see section 3.1.

2.8.1 Outside/inside views. Motivation and entry points in peace building

In order to raise the impact of peace building a series of research questions regarding the relationship between outsiders and actors should be asked. Many practitioners of conflict resolution agree that the ideal case would be if no outsiders would be necessary, as a result of the empowerment of local actors. The problem of Cultural Clash between outsiders and insiders is just one of the pertinent questions which addresses the main structural problem areas between outsiders and insiders. The problem of cultural clash and conflicting identities may also arise among the Warring Parties themselves. These reflections get down to the main question 'Who is likely to be successful?' More questions to be asked about the go-betweens are:

- the question of the difference/similarity of culture between the parties involved are a permanent challenge in the quest for understanding
- who is representing what kind of cultural background, for example 'neutral outsiders', local 'partial insiders', eminent personalities (elder statesmen, wise men and so on)? What status questions could be evoked (for example indigenous versus settlers/migrants)?
- motivation to stop the hostilities: altruism or hidden agenda? Motivation behind go-between activities? What was the role of individuals in the process leading to conflict transformation (for instance a ceasefire)? What is the role of outsiders in following-up an agreement?

General problems to be addressed and questions to be asked: what is the conflict actors' choice; who is acceptable for the parties? What could be the entry points and stepping-stones for a peace initiative in a particular conflict? An inquiry into the approaches chosen by the go-betweens is necessary but difficult to carry out.

Agreement on the 'terms of reference' for dialogue: for example earlier agreement between the actors would provide for terms of reference or provisional agendas made by different actors. An inquiry will look for specifications on where, when, in what form, with whom (parties, go-betweens, 'observers', others), and under what conditions (for example media attendance or complete secret?) round table talks shall be held in the future. Essentially, dialogue must be conducted in an all-inclusive manner.

2.8.2 Processual definition of outcomes in peace initiatives

A holistic analysis of the question of success or failure of go-between initiatives will not only explore the outcome of the negotiation process as such but also how it was followed-up: to what extend was an agreement implemented? For whom? Who are the beneficiaries of an implemented peaceful settlement? What is the extent of their satisfaction with the settlement in practice?

The formal possibilities when perceiving what talks were good for, is to focus on the outcome or alternatively on the process that may lead to peaceful conflict settlement. Usually most mediator–facilitators and the general public are outcome oriented. But the problem of perception is more complex. Starting with the question 'What kind of agreement has been made?' it becomes clear that the definition of the outcome is particularly critical. Attention could be paid to differentiate between full versus partial agreements or lasting versus temporary agreements. Other questions are 'what key issues were left unresolved in a partial agreement?' and 'what potential have dissident political groups and military factions to jeopardize the implementation of agreements?'

After negotiations the work of the mediator–facilitator(s) very much continues. Now his/their role is to persuade the warring parties to comply. Other roles such as monitor/verifier and peace keeper/observer become crucial. The go-between has to gain support from the international community. The UN or regional organizations might hesitate to become active and monitor the outcome. International NGOs might be more ready to monitor work. But UN and regional organizations have many more possibilities for the enforcement and implementation of the agreement, to deploy watchdogs to monitor the implementation, and to ask for reasons in case of noncompliance. In the phase of post-conflict rehabilitation, the role of the rehabilitators and developers in taking-up middle and long-term measures now attract state development agencies as well as NGOs. Given their respective competence base, NGOs might concentrate on less cost-intensive tasks, such as reconciliation and the building of a new set of relationships between the warring parties.

Concerning the assessment of success or failure of go-between activities there are a number of questions to be asked. A dynamic definition of success/ failure seems to be almost 'self-evident' when looking at go-between processes. Despite such apparent evidence a number of precise research questions shall be asked: what are the criteria for success? Can the agreement be separated from its implementation? Who is defining success or failure? Are the parties to the negotiation defining success or failure? What about the users/beneficiaries? How can success/failure be objectively assessed? How can failure be verified? accused? sanctioned? How can success or partial success be measured? observed? monitored? assured? maintained? What are the benchmarks of such measurement? Is success externally observable? Can the behaviour of the warring parties be easily observed? Are there obstacles such as a dangerous security situation, no-go areas? Are there differences between urban and rural areas? Questions about the parameters for comprehensive verification are particularly complicated: what obstacles are identifiable? What juridical problems of interpreting an agreement exist? What political will to achieve adequate verification mechanisms? What are the regulations for the implementation of an agreement, if any?

There are a number of areas of special interest, which go beyond a case-study analysis. For instance, focusing on inter-linkages between negotiations and reconciliation efforts, the dynamic interplay of levels (top/middle levels and middle/local levels), and the identification of key players, middle-level leaders and facilitators are general issues. The same is true for possible clashes of perceptions of the mediators, the parties to the conflict and the users and beneficiaries.

2.8.3   From conflict research to peace research

Realization of the need for a shift of perspective, from conflict research to peace research, was almost 'forced' upon me between 1987 and 1992 by the historical process attendant on dramatic changes in two areas of acute conflict in the South. This happened when I was carrying out empirical investigations into ethno-nationalism – out in the field. Regional and local schemes for the structural prevention of future conflicts were developed on the ground and went far beyond so-called peace talks (involving local and Western mediators). Demands made by the parties to the conflict were worked into a politically viable shape and then implemented within the framework of a reform of the constitution and of state structures. But scientific interest in this process was relatively meagre, as was clear from two examples.

Once hostilities in Nicaragua had died down, almost no one seemed interested in the promising new beginnings that had been made in the 'other half' of the country. The war was over, or 'in its last throes' and, compared with the spectacular armed hostilities and subsequent peace negotiations conducted at the highest levels, peace soon came to appear not particularly attractive, indeed 'run of the mill'. The change in the peace and war situation in Ethiopia in March 1991 was even more unexpected and dramatic.[69] I was witness, during this initial period, to the start of the 'struggle over the postwar order' that was waged over the next few months, admittedly not with arms, but definitely 'with gloves off'. The Ethiopian charter, a transitional government and the planned new order were elements of a unique experiment in Africa. For the first time, the ethnic-national question was brought out 'onto the table' – almost, as it were, from the bottom of the pile. The conflict between the Abyssinians and Oromo that is of such crucial significance for Ethiopia has remained unresolved; to many observers it seems unfounded and it fails to attract the attention it deserves in EU diplomacy and foreign policy.

The major regulations aimed at preventing violence affect the rights of the various non-dominant ethnic groups, particularly their rights in regard to autonomy and participation, and also the distribution of public goods. The aim is to seek out an equitable arrangement among the ethno-social groups involved. This necessitates getting rid of the dominant groups' monopolies and channels of influence. Power-sharing and respect for distinct cultures are among the core elements of any policy for preventing violence. Through bilateral negotiations between states and nations, preferably with the involvement of a go-between or a third party, possible solutions can be discussed in a mutually acceptable fashion. With the Permanent Court of Arbitration in The Hague, there is an independent institution available that could be mandated to deal with 'intra-state' disputes and whose rulings the parties can accept without loss of face.

I estimate that up to 80 per cent of ethno-national conflicts solutions could be found through sincere (or facilitated) negotiations, provided the political will exists. 'Minority rights', affirmative action, autonomy arrangements, nationality policies, self-administration and free association are some of the possible concrete solutions on offer (see Table 3.2). Only 20 per cent of such conflicts require federated schemes or independent statehood.

Frequently, there is a lack of will on the part of states to prevent conflict or settle a dispute peacefully, for example, by granting autonomy rights, power sharing, self-governance, or federal solutions. In some cases, the end result has been the formation of new states. Where this happens, it does so in two forms: (1) *de jure*, in the sense of a true secession regime or as an upgrading of status within the framework of existing nationality policy structures; this was the case with the successor states of the USSR (15 former Soviet republics became sovereign states) and with Yugoslavia (five new states so far); (2) in the South, as a belated decolonization, as was the case in Namibia and Eritrea (type D). Somaliland (type BA) and 'liberated areas' in Colombia (type A) provide examples of *de facto* state formation.

According to UN resolutions, a referendum is to be held in Western Sahara (type D). In a major regional conflict (Middle East 1993), mediation by a third party (Norway) has produced an agenda for peace, which has faced too many obstacles since. In Palestine (type D), the promise of autonomy (Oslo peace accords between the Israeli government and the PLO) seemed to prepare the way to a partial solution. The United Nations ought to play a more active part – in the sense of peaceful intervention – among others in Palestine, West Papua, Western Sahara, Kurdistan and Kanaky/Nouvelle Caledonie.

2.8.4   Positive peace: between past, present and utopia

According to Kant, positive peace requires constant effort. For every society the understanding of peace has its own meaning and its own taste. Today Kant's thoughts seem very modern: he mentioned the central problem, which is the nation states' claims for absolute sovereignty, and resulting from that the permanent threat of war. Kant proposed in 1795 to establish a League of Nations to end war and that reason shall triumph over the anarchy of warfare. He wrote that at the place of the positive idea of a veritable world republic only the negative surrogate of a league of all peoples could prevent war and contain lawless hostility. Galtung rediscovered Kant for the purposes of international peace research.

While negative peace would only mean the absence of violence or war, *positive peace* would exist in its own right and represent a new quality of social interaction. Positive peace only exists as an incessant effort to approach it. Negative peace could be seen as corresponding to the stage 1 of *dormant conflict*.

Peace researchers have been busy elaborating typology of wars. Implicitly they deal with peace as a mere *normal situation*. Almost nobody thought of the advantage of elaborating a typology of peace. In an attempt to do so I identified 21 such types, cases or transitional stages of peace by their scope, key principle, their time frame or period, their characteristics and aims (see Table 2.1).

Any typology of peaceful coexistence will probably be considered as far from being complete but might well be a source of inspiration. I tried to include social-historic types of peace taken from different periods of history and regions of the world; two types belong to utopia. At present most of these types have their place in reality in somewhat modified form. For instance, one could relate traditional societies of a less 'extreme kind' as in the case of the !Khoi to (post)modern sub-cultures. Through the course of human history different forms and ways of peaceful coexistence of peoples, nations, cultures and civilizations have been experienced.

Up to now, the *irenological* perspective has only been dealt with in passing. Just as for polemology, irenology must be systematically pursued as a necessary complement to what has so far been the exclusively polemological orientation of research.[70] Peace itself, and different forms of peaceful coexistence, must be subjected to a greater degree of systematic documentation and analysis. The positive effect of references to functioning models (even if incomplete) and to (partial) successes in resolving conflicts should not be underestimated.

Table 2.1 Social–historical typology of peace

Type of peace	Scope, world	Key principle	Period	Characteristics/phenomena/aims
1. **original positive peace**	society	stable in itself	very long periods	small(er) communities, intra-focus, harmony
2. tranquil/silent peace by retreat/fleeing **!Khoi type peace**	*civitas* traditional societies	dissociation; stable in itself, internal, extremely peaceable	long and very long periods	small(er) communities; conflict prevention by retreat/flight to remote uninhabited or ecologically difficult areas; cases: hunters and gatherers in deserts (!Khoi, Zhu Twasi), rain forests (Aka and Mbuti pygmies, Efe, Amazon tribes), mountain areas (Orang Asli, Aita, Papua tribes), bush land (Hadza), islands (Onge, Negritos)
3. peace through isolation **case of traditional societies or modern sub-cultures**	society world traditional communities; modern subcultures	dissociation; stable in itself, internal, peaceful	longer periods	limited-size societies; conflict prevention through isolation in geographically hidden areas/up-country, also areas with difficult communication and access; traditional societies; adaption to nature; contemporary cases: many traditional societies, modern alternative land communities; aim: survival+/original life-style
4. dynamic negative peace (peaceful coexistence broken by raiding) through high mobility and vigilance **acephality case**	society world traditional communities clans/lineages	dissociation; self-centred, internal, acephalous–segmentary	longer and fairly long periods	bigger-sized decentral (acephalous) tribal societies based on descent; conflict prevention through high mobility/vigilance in open areas (savannah, mountain tracts); some zones unsuitable for farming; traditional (semi-)nomadic communities; contemporary cases: pastoralists (Nilotic peoples, Somali), hill tribes in SE-Asia, Amerindians, etc.; aim: survival in pride/autonomy
5. Peace as refuge **acculturation type**	sub-societies/ traditional communities	dissociation; self-centred, internal; not closed, adaptable	medium to longer periods	bigger-sized decentralized ethnic groups; conflict prevention through self-defence by refuge to areas with indigenous people; adaption/acculturation to other societies; simple mode of production; aim: autonomous survival, option for later return to homeland

Table 2.1 Continued

Type of peace	Scope, world	Key principle	Period	Characteristics/phenomena/aims
6. silent peace by selective isolation and self-centred culture *irrigation-based society type*	hydraulic societies and states	dissociation; self-centred, internal; not closed	very long periods, cycles	large societies, 'high cultures' (behind 'Chinese walls'), save from alien intruders, barbarians; conflict prevention by establishing safe areas; sophisticated work intensive production (irrigation, AMP); high degree of organization; aim: peace, security and order
7. peace by civilizational cultural development *great tradition type*	irrigation-based (hydraulic) societies and empires	more dissociative as associative; not expansive, self-centred; receptive	medium and long periods; dynastic	large class societies, 'high cultures' behind walls, standing armies against barbarians; conflict prevention by self-centred development incl. foreign exchange and trade; sophisticated production (AMP+); high geared organization; aim: security and prosperity
8. coexistence through (peace) treaties, agreements, alliances *colonial peace*	state/corporate economy primary scope; societal scope	expansive, aggressive (internal/external)	medium or longer periods; boom–bust	class societies/metropolitan states; conflict regulation through agreements with other powers; ceasefire agreements if wars become costly; (arms-) production; security through deterrence; higher degree of organization; aims: prosperity through resource exploitation and dominance
9. coexistence through development and trade, negative peace capitalist economy type *imperial coexistence*	societies and economies	associative; external expansion	medium or longer periods; intended linearity	class societies, stable state structure; rule of law, elites; conflict avoidance, social containment and normalization (internal); prevention case by case, conflict avoidance through trade and 'interdependency' (external); industrial goods; higher degree of organization; power, profit and influence (for a few); aim: securing growth/prosperity
10. dynamic negative peace and coexistence through development and trade modern	societies and states	associative–dissociative; tends to expansionism;	medium periods linearity	class societies/'consumer cultures'; conflict containment, dynamic social normalization and integration (internal); conflict prevention by foreign exchange, trade (external); migrants for cheap labour followed by walls against

society type	scope	character	time	
peace of the rich		some receptiveness		migrants; solid production, innovation; high degree of organization; aim: security for all, prosperity for the upper class
11. negative peace and coexistence through self-centred development and selective trade **Indian coexistence**	poor states and heterogeneous societies	associative-dissociative; tends to isolationism; some receptiveness	medium /longer periods; political cycles; intended continuity	multi-ethnic pluri-cultural class (or caste) societies, heterogeneous states (often former civilizations); conflict prevention mechanisms, regulation through creation of new union states, cultural or religious rights for non-dominant groups, self-governance; quota system; degree of organization; agriculture, emerging industry; aim: security based on respect of multiplicity (internal) and negative peace through strength (external), prosperity for middle and upper classes
12. military coexistence through alliances, negative peace broken by wars; settler state type **pax Americana**	state of TNC-dominated economy primary scope; societal scope	expansive, interventionist; aggressive (internal/external)	medium and longer periods; linearity; intended continuity	mainstream settler society, strong state structure; (formal) rule of law; regulation through social segregation, welfare programmes; ideology of melting pot, schemes for indigenous minorities (internal), agreements with other powers (external); major wars possible; security through strength and dominance; high degree of organization; sophisticated capitalist mode of production; aims: securing prosperity, free resource exploitation, military strength
13. peace and coexistence through autonomization of nationalities (internal) and alliance (external), case of USSR/FSU* **pax sovietica**	state scope primary; societal scope secondary	non-expansionist, self-centred; active/interactive (internal, external)	medium and longer periods; political cycles; stagnation	multi-ethnic pluri-cultural societies/heterogeneous states; structural conflict prevention institutionalized, regulation through dispute resolution with/cultural rights for non-dominant ethno-national entities, autonomous territories/self-governance according to the *Korenisazia*-model; high degree of organization; aim: security based on respect of others (internal) and negative peace through deterrence (external), some prosperity for many

80

Table 2.1 Continued

Type of peace	Scope, world	Key principle	Period	Characteristics/phenomena/aims
14. positive peace and coexistence through sociability and pragmatism, African society type ***pax Africana***	societal scope primary; state scope secondary	peaceful non-expansive pattern; local/regional setting	longer periods; no intention of linearity	many diverse societies/weak dependent periphery states; internal societal regulations by hospitality, neo-traditions (rituals, myths), respect for *otherness*, palaver-democracy; peaceful settlement of disputes with neighbours; agrarian production (security by subsistence), industry disconnected; lower degree of organization; aim: securing survival+
15. peace and coexistence through integration into the world market; dependent state type ***neocolonial coexistence***	state scope primary; societal scope secondary	non-expansive (internal/external)	medium periods not much linearity	weak dependent states at the periphery/many societies; internal state-based regulations (political ceremonies, elite co-option and bargaining), lobbying with metropolitan powers; agriculture (subsistence+/export sector) and industrialization (weak); low degree of organization; aim: preservation of *status-quo*, development
16. peace and coexistence through vertical integration (foreign dominated) and cultural assimilation despotic static type ***repressive coexistence***	state scope primary; societal scope restrained and repressed	forced association; expansive state structure internally	shorter/ medium periods; pretension of linearity	manifold multi-ethnic societies/military and despotic periphery states; weak internal state-dominated regulations lobbying with metropolitan colonial powers or new regional powers; agriculture (subsistence+/export sector) and weak dissociated industry; aim: preservation of *status-quo* and elite power
17. coexistence through autonomy or conservation for indigenous nations as well as regional co-operation	state scope (primary); catholic clergy, civil society (secondary only)	state-centred; internal colonialism by less repressive means	shorter and longer periods	periphery states; *mestizo* societies searching for identity vs. indigenous communities; autonomy types: *comarca* (Kuna since 1920s), *resguardo* (Colombia), self-rule (Nicaragua 1990); weak economic base for autonomy; non-integration in most states broken by attempts to assimilation; neglect/ paternalism; traditional institutions rarely honoured

	state scope	scope type	time period	description
Latin American neo-liberal type **neoliberal coexistence**				(*caciques/congreso*-system); Mexico to avoid armed conflict by autonomy in Chiapas (?); aim: control by concessions
18. peace/coexistence by new autonomy concessions (internal) and joining EU/ NATO (external) *case of Eastern Europe and former FSU states*	state scope primary; civil societal scope still underdeveloped	non-expansive, West-oriented; reactive (internal), subactive (external)	medium/ longer periods; political decline and stagnation/ regression	multi-ethnic pluri-cultural societies with (new) minorities/ heterogeneous (partly) new states; structural conflict prevention formerly institutionalized, cultural rights for non-dominant ethno-national entities and autonomy regulations in ethno-nationalist frenzy often unilaterally cancelled/revoked after 1990 (loss of autonomy led to several wars); underdeveloped dispute resolution (exception: *Korenisazia*-model still valid in Russian Federation); declining degree of organization; some prosperity for a few; aim: security based on control of others (internal) and go-West (external)
19. peaceful coexistence through autonomy for minorities (internal) and alliance/treaties (external); liberal welfare state type *pax helveto-scandinavica*	state scope and societal scope	non-expansive; active/ inter-active (internal)	medium/ longer periods; intention of linearity	plural societies/welfare states; structural conflict prevention institutionalized, regulation through democratic dispute and affirmative action/rights for non-dominant ethno-national entities; political concessions in case of antagonizing dispute; autonomy/self-governance/home rule for so-called minorities (Åland-model); high degree of organization; aim: security based on respect of others (internal) and negative peace through neutrality (external), 'prosperity for all' (if funds available)
20. negative peace through global governance (*Weltinnenpolitik*) with key objective to prevent and outlaw violent conflict on global scale *'eternal peace' (Kant)*	state scope reduced to global state (*Weltstaat*); societal scope to be fully developed	utopia establishing one single *world state* with manifold societies	medium/ long period; some linear thinking	resolving the central problems (nation states' claims of sovereignty and permanent threat of war) by establishing a *world state*; objective: preventing war (containing lawless hostility), thus *reason* will triumph over anarchy and warfare; base for development of positive peace; every society has its own understanding of peace, no limits to multi-facet peace and the positive idea of a *world republic*; aim: sustainable peace by banning wars on a global scale 'for all times'

Table 2.1 Continued

Type of peace	Scope, world	Key principle	Period	Characteristics/phenomena/aims
21. positive peace through disappearance of statehood and borderless freedom; full emancipation of humanity '*positive peace*'	state scope disappeared; societal and individual scope fully developed	utopia emancipation; egalitarian society	long period; linear thinking to be abolished	*positive peace* would represent a new quality of social interaction; proactive; need for constant efforts by humanity on individual/group base; to reproduce as a free and emancipated individual everyone shall as a free associated member of a chosen group by respect the freedom and space for personal development of others; aim: positive anarchy; full emancipation and satisfaction for all and everyone
Back to (1)				full cycle forward to original positive peace (type 1)

3
Peaceful Conflict Settlement, Go-between Facilitation and the Timing of Responses to Conflict

There is a general lack of systematic analysis and comparative studies in the field of peaceful conflict settlement. This contrasts with the many competing approaches to conflict resolution and theoretical works covering the field. Different types of responses to conflict are rarely compared. What can be achieved with different responses remains a largely under-researched area of peace studies. This chapter aims at filling some gaps and tries to contribute to expand the competence base needed for go-between conflict mediation and facilitation. Here, the latter two terms are defined according to the degree of intrusiveness,[1] while the term of 'go-between parties' is preferred to the misleading term of 'third party', for which Galtung has given good reason.[2]

The possibilities for transforming a conflict depend largely on the willingness of initiating and institutionalizing genuine and truthful dialogue. The question 'lessons learned?' can be asked regarding a broad set of possible responses to conflict. Peaceful responses and peace strategies might in some cases seek inspiration from existing schemes and traditional forms of arbitration. The focus should be on interactive prevention of violent conflict rather than to plunge into activism producing short-term bandages. In this perspective, it is relevant to look at efforts of capacity building at the middle and local levels. The process of capacity building for the management of conflict in Africa, Eurasia and the Americas is imminent. New regional NGOs are emerging, dealing with problems within specific regions. Approaches range from general ways of resolving conflicts developed in a Western context to culture-specific strategies, which have been used by traditional societies to resolve conflicts.

A number of lacunae are grappling activities in the field of Peaceful Conflict Settlement and add to the various difficulties go-betweens are facing. There is a general lack of comparative studies. Concerning under-researched topics, the main lacunae can be identified:

- a few studies explore the (existing or non-existing) division of labour and interaction between formal diplomacy (track 1) and informal diplomacy (track 2)
- there are no systematic comparative studies of go-between mediation and facilitation, and no such study on go-between activities in the world's most deadly conflict areas
- very few studies have explored what methods of go-between conflict management are suitable (and under what conditions)
- even particularly topical areas of research, such as screening of go-between activities and investigating their working methods against the results obtained were to-date, neglected
- there are no studies focusing on comparing success and failure specific to types of actors in the field of conflict management, more precisely mediation, facilitation and negotiation in cases of severe conflicts; it would be highly relevant to know what actors (civil society actors, state actors and international organizations) can achieve
- nor is there a single comparative study focusing on the work of some of the most significant actors in the field of go-between mediation and facilitation[3]
- current studies rarely relate the go-betweens' views on a particular mediation process with those of the 'users' or beneficiaries of a peace settlement
- studies often focus exclusively on the negotiations as such but not so much on the phase of preparation and, most importantly, on the phase of implementation of the negotiated settlement
- studies do not explore initiatives to build conflict resolution capacities in areas where the real conflicts actually take place; such studies should look at both regional and local level
- conflict dynamics and causes as well as efforts for peaceful conflict settlement and capacity building initiatives should increasingly be reviewed in a regional perspective in order to fully grasp external factors and deal with spill-over effects.

However, there is a body of literature on theories and approaches to conflict resolution on the one side, and a less extended body of empirical studies dedicated to the evaluation and the assessment of the impact of mediation and facilitation in selected cases, on the other side. Regarding the first body of literature (theories and approaches to conflict resolution),[4] reviewing relevant approaches in conflict analysis (for example objectivists versus subjectivists) will not dispense from identifying the lacunae still prevailing. Theoretical frameworks have to be screened in regard to conflict typologies (preferably an actor and objective oriented typology), conflict roots research and structural characteristics of different types of intra-state conflicts. This would be of importance since responding to certain types of conflicts seems to be avoided; some types of conflicts, such as the ethno-nationalist type and certain forms of anti-regime conflicts, seem to be intractable for peace initiatives. A review of current analysis of conflict processes and dynamics in general will identify series of lacunae (as already explored in the introduction to this book). Most conflict resolution approaches do not address the specific causes of today's conflicts in Africa and Eurasia, nor the perceptions of the people involved.

United Nations' involvement in research and conflict resolution efforts in the case of intra-state conflicts in general and ethno-nationalist conflicts in particular, came late, but took an innovative and practically oriented form in matters such as the analysis, management, prevention and transformation of these types of conflict.[5] A newly initiated War-torn Societies Project (WSP)[6] is attempting to create organic links between research and political consultation, with a view to identifying appropriate responses to new global realities and forms of conflict. UNESCO's Culture of Peace programme is aimed at medium- and long-term conflict transformation in postwar situations. These initiatives by bodies within the UN system are also a response to the realization that ethno-national and other violent intra-state conflicts have long since ceased to be secondary threats to the international order.

Some of the problems associated with research into intra-state conflicts and the options for resolving them: the fact that research establishments are concentrated in the North; the shortage of research resources and their one-sided use (too little for topics and researchers from the Third World and eastern Europe); lack of interaction and systematic co-operation between research, NGO mediation-activities and official policy; and a lack of appropriate training facilities for conflict resolution activists. Access to useful resources (such as e-mail and the internet) is still much easier in the North than in the South. The poor co-ordination and lack of interlinks, that has prevailed in peace and conflict research up to the present day, has proven to be obstacles to development in both theory and practice.

3.1 Dispute settlement as an instrument of international politics

The underdeveloped state of political and institutional consultancy in peaceful dispute settlement by 'third parties' – whether through power mediation or go-between NGOs – is particularly lamentable, given that conflict mediation can undoubtedly be successful as an instrument of international politics. According to Bercovitch and Billing, between one fifth and one quarter of mediation initiatives undertaken between 1945 and 1990 were successful.[7] Mediation and peaceful dispute settlement often succeed where third parties have extensive resources at their disposal or are able to threaten sanctions (power mediation); and they are successful, above all, where classical disputes between states are involved (territorial issues, borders). Where there was a substantial input of resources, a positive result was achieved in 40 per cent of cases (Bercovitch 1991: 16). However, there is no indication of how stable or long-lasting these kinds of 'purchased' peace agreements are. Efforts at mediation and conflict resolution are relatively ineffective in the case of ethno-national and ethnic conflicts.[8]

Classic disputes were earlier seen to be an inter-state kind. The potential for such disputes is still great, because most states harbour unresolved territorial or sovereignty claims against one another. Such claims by states 'almost always' collide with one another in practice.[9] Territorial claims are a permanent source of conflicts; in principle they are susceptible to negotiation and settlement, so long as there are no ideological differences as well. There is a high degree of predictability. In five of the seven inter-state conflicts occurring in the period of 1995–2000 territory was/is the main issue.[10] Mediation was in all cases rapidly taken up, although in five cases there were comparably low fatalities, and the manifold go-betweens were fairly effective (except in the bloody war between Eritrea and Ethiopia, lingering from March 1998 to mid 2000).

OAU and UN efforts to mediate in the war between Ethiopia and Eritrea were successful only after two years of fighting, resulting in a direct death toll of 80,000, severe destruction and above one million refugees. In the case of NATO versus Yugoslavia the joint mediation efforts of the Russian Federation (former Prime Minister Chernomyrdin) and the European Union (by EU-Council President Atisari from Finland) brought a halt to 78-days of NATO bombing in June 1999; the responsibility for the administration of Kosovo became a UN matter. In the case of the border conflict between India and Pakistan, internationalization was successful; the diplomatic intervention of several great powers and pressure on Pakistan brought the retreat of the Mujahidin intruders (from the Indian side of the 'line of control' in Kashmir) in mid-July 1999; the potentially explosive situation calmed down.

Mediation is significantly more difficult in the case of intra-state conflicts. Concerted action by local go-betweens (who get the warring parties round a table) and international organizations (UN, OAS, OAU, SADC and so on) and government representatives from neighbouring states (sometimes big powers or regional powers) have nevertheless been successful to strike peace agreements in many instances; the key problem is the implementation of such agreements. In several instances, the last being the efforts to end the world's apparently most deadly war in the Congo, a regional organization (in this case SADC) brokered an accord, which was not implemented for two years by the United Nations and the great powers controlling the UN Security Council decisions.[11] This recalls of 1991–93, when regional leaders successfully mediated negotiations between the Rwandan government and the RPF rebels in Arusha; the implementation of the Arusha Accords of 1993 was to be supervised by a UN mission (UNAMIR), which failed in its task and did nothing to prevent the genocide launched by those who were to lose their grip on the state if power sharing had been implemented.

Where the players include rebel movements that have come into conflict with those in power because of grave social asymmetries and ideological differences, the chances of success are often slim. In the case of armed conflicts involving ideological components, which are often of a protracted nature, it may be that, if internal mediators (such as representatives of the Church and NGOs) pave the way for talks, the solution to a checkmate situation will come from outside – as in the case of El Salvador and the FMLN guerrillas. In the case of Colombia's decade-old insurgency, several rounds of peace negotiations between the government and the FARC rebels have failed to render a settlement. Negotiations between the Colombian government and representatives of guerrilla organizations (FARC, ELN), brokered by 'third parties' from the Church, produced only partial successes, because the government side repeatedly failed to honour its promises. Supervision by an international organization (UN or OAS) or a constructive attitude by great powers (in this case the US) might have prevented failure. Interestingly, in 2001 the government broke the ceasefire declared by the rebels after FARC wanted the official involvement of the European Union in the peace talks.[12]

One type of measure that has proved particularly successful is the regional agreement that restricts the role of big powers and regional powers – Esquipulas II, for example. Building on this kind of regional peace-process, which made possible an easing of the Contra war in Nicaragua from 1989 and helped bring about negotiations between the parties to the civil war in Nicaragua in 1987–89 and in El Salvador in 1990–91 (with the involvement of third parties), the UN initiative in El Salvador was ultimately successful.

In other cases, the role of the United Nations was critical for the success of peace processes. Negotiations between the FRELIMO government and RENAMO in Mozambique, prepared by the International Committee of the Red Cross (ICRC) and representatives of the Catholic Church in and beyond the region – involving the bishops of Mozambique and mediated by the Rome-based Sant'Egido community (CSE) with support from the Italian government – were, again, brought to a successful conclusion by the UN. CSE was less successful in other cases, such as Algeria, where international organizations remained inactive or great powers (in this case France) were not supportive.

3.1.1   Where? Who? What? For whom? To achieve what?

The focal point, both when discussing go-betweens initiatives and capacity building efforts, are questions about the nature of the social – cultural context and how appropriate the chosen approaches are in that context. Some of the pertinent research questions to be asked are the following: what would be the criteria of choosing cases for comparison? What are the basic elements to identify in order to explain the concept of a protracted of conflict? Are there common features compared with other protracted conflicts? Is the understanding of ethnicity in the particular case indispensable to understanding the violent conflict? Is ethnicity a 'cause' for self-propelling conflict dynamics? In the case of 'deep-rooted conflicts' the notion of causality in conflict 'roots' research is bound to run into problems: how to deal with the actors/outsiders view of causality? How to establish a hierarchy of causes and driving factors? How to identify causes, triggers, accelerators to escalation and measures for de-escalation?

More specific questions regarding the actors and parties are: what political and social constituencies do the warring parties and actors to a given conflict represent? What conflicts within the conflict might surface? How are the actors and the go-betweens ('Third Space', INGOs, peace movements, and intermediaries) positioned and what is their legitimacy? Another series of question concerns the go-betweens: what is their status and their role vis-à-vis the parties?, the degree of their intrusiveness, ranging from providing good offices to arbitration? What about the notion of impartiality (impartial outsiders versus partial insiders)? Do certain actors claim a monopoly of knowledge and definition power? Exploring such key questions would contribute to progress in peace work, both with theoretical input and empirical evaluation of specific go-between initiatives and multi-level conflict resolution capacities.[13]

3.1.2   Relationships and management of peace talks

Regarding the relationship between the mediator/facilitator and the warring parties the problem of cultural difference is of course the issue, first and foremost. Questions of the difference or similarity of culture between the mediators and the involved parties are a permanent challenge in the 'quest for understanding'. The motivation behind go-between activities is among the important issues (altruism or hidden agendas?). Why did conflict actors choose the particular mediator–facilitator instead of any other? Who is likely to be successful?[14] Regarding the entry points for go-between initiatives the timing is crucial. As mentioned already, central would be the analysis of the right time for intervention with a view to the issues at stake. The parties and the mediator–facilitator need to agree on the 'terms of reference' for talks and a provisional agenda for the talks.[15] The preparation of talks is another issue of interest.[16]

An inquiry into the approach chosen by the go-between touches on the following issues: (a) selecting the reference persons which allowed entry points into the conflict; (b) overcoming difficulties due to the personal characteristics of those involved; (c) taking into account possible resistance by the respective political constituencies to peace initiatives taken by 'enlightened' leaders. The risk assessment made by the go-betweens is concerning identification of other types of obstacles and for the identification of additional internal and external actors who are not directly involved but might prevent or promote peace talks.

After the difficult starting phase the main tasks of the go-between are coping with the dynamics produced by the talks. They need to gain new insights during the mediation process and to mobilizing the support of the International Community. Roles and functions of the go-between are constantly changing during the process. A long list of possible activities, inspired by Christopher Mitchell, is an attempt to define multiple roles and functions: (1) building confidence and starting-up as trainers, researchers, activists, consultants (explorer/*re-assurer*); (2) empowering the disputants, training them in basic negotiation tactics (*empowerer, enskiller, trainer*); (3) persuading/pressuring external insiders to retreat and let talks go on (decoupler/*disengager*); (4) repairing in-group factionalism and divisions which may impair talks (unifier/aggregator/convenor); (5) bringing up possible of solutions and possible use resources (active convenor/ initiator); (6) bringing-in new ideas, theories, policy options and so on (visionary/fact finder); (7) mediating talks (mediator); (8) guaranteeing a reasonable cost/benefit relationship for the parties (guarantor); (9) chairing meetings and interpreting positions (facilitator, moderator); (10) helping the warring parties to accept the process if it becomes more difficult (legitimizer/endorser); (11) employing more resources for a win-win-solution (developer); and (12) enhancing chances for success (enhancer, strengthener).[17]

Besides the changing roles of the Third Parties there are different categories of negotiators and informers. Among the parties there are soft and hard-liners; mediator–facilitators have to decide on whom to concentrate, the top-level, middle-range and grassroots leadership; most third parties concentrate on the top leaders. Mediator–facilitators can be partial insiders or neutral outsiders; most of the time they 'pretend' to be of the latter type. They have to identify groups at risk, competitors, drop-outs (the best informers), influential users, and so on.

The struggle for trust is at the core of the whole peace process of dialogue, talks, or formal negotiations. The role of the media can be particular disruptive in that respect but it can also help to put pressure on the parties. The media can critically affect the process and outcome of any go-between initiative. Therefore, the question of how to control the relationship with the media during the talks is of considerable importance. There are often no easy solutions (such as strict confidentiality). If no concept is agreed upon several dangers may be critical, such as 'losing face', actors forced to take tough positions, to play hard-line roles and so on. Media coverage can be used as an excuse for breaking down talks, while the leaking of information may be employed as an unfair tactic.

3.1.3 Multi-track conflict mediation in upswing

There is no doubt that preventive measures as well as informal, so-called multi-track conflict mediation will undergo a great upswing in the very near future. The business world (in the case of investment projects in insecure areas), local administrations (in the case of disputed construction projects) and civilian actors (in fights against environmental pollution) have, in the course of numerous negotiation sessions, rallies and round-table talks, long since recognized the value of informal mediation. It is quite conceivable that *ad hoc* methods (and certain aspects of negotiating psychology) be transposed to situations of political and ethnic conflict. Some regime theoreticians who fear competition from non-state actors oppose the use of 'uncoordinated *ad hoc* measures' in the treatment of ethno-national conflicts; that treatment, they say, must 'always' take place within the framework of a comprehensive regional or global security regime (Siedschlag 1995: 6). But this kind of demand is untenable, given that the whole policy-field of mediation, the notion of conflict resolution in general, and the treatment of ethno-national conflicts in particular, has up to now been subject to criminal neglect. The sometimes highly casual pragmatism of practitioners is an indication, precisely, of the lack or non-existence of structured action on the part of the international community. There is no possibility at present of any medium-term solutions to ethno-national conflicts within the framework of security and co-operation regimes.

The way in which the capacities of classical political dispute settlement (arbitration) have been exhausted, and the series of fiascos that have resulted from military interventions by the UN (in Somalia) and NATO (in Bosnia) have stimulated consideration of alternatives in multinational and supranational institutions as well. There have recently been increasing indications of this: the OSCE has latterly been seeking mediation specialists for its long-term missions, though it has a very limited budget for this. In 1998, for the first time, it was the OSCE long-term missions that claimed the greatest share of the budget – 40 per cent (up from 16.6 per cent in 1997 and 15.4 per cent in 1996).

Regarding funds spent on preventive activities, it should be noted that in 1996–98, the share of the overall budget devoted to the high-profile institution of the High Commissioner on National Minorities (HCNM) was a mere 1.5–2.2 per cent, equivalent to an annual average of less than US$1 million the expenses for the Office for Democratic Institutions and Human Rights (ODIHR) amounted to only 5–8 per cent. In the OECD unified budget for 1998 their share was even smaller: less then one per cent (0.65 per cent) of US$190 million for the HCNM and 2.79 per cent for the ODIHR.[18] In 1999 and 2000 OSCE long-time missions continued to consume most of the funds, leaving a tiny share of the overall budget for preventive measures, such as the activities of HCNM or ODIHR. Additionally, the OSCE Court on Concilliation and Arbitration only gets a minor budget.[19]

However, conflict prevention became an issue in most international organizations. The United Nations sends monitors for top-up training in workshops.[20] The European Commission's political directorate has instructed that thought should be given to dispute mediation.

3.1.4 Track-1 mediation: learning the hard way

On the level of institution building with international organizations, the imperative of conflict prevention and peace building was taken seriously, albeit with some remarkable delays. In autumn 1997, at the request of the European Parliament (and on the initiative of Michel Rocard), the EU set up a Conflict Prevention Network. The Commission realized the importance of prevention following the catastrophic events in Rwanda (notably after the submission of the Landgraf policy paper 1995). In the framework of the Organization for Economic Co-operation and Development (OECD), the Rwanda shock had immediate consequences. The OECD's Development Assistance Committee (DAC), focused since 1995, on the growing demands for development co-operation to 'contribute more proactively to conflict prevention and post-conflict rehabilitation and reconstruction'.[21] The DAC established an informal Task Force for this purpose which began to work in October 1995, in collaboration with UN agencies and the Bretton Wood institutions.[22] In 1998–99 OECD–DAC started a series of four comparative case studies on conditionality of development aid. The impact of incentives and disincentives applied by donors in countries experiencing severe conflicts – Rwanda, Bosnia, Sri Lanka and Afghanistan – was studied. The outcome was discussed in May 1999 but remained a 'restricted matter' for the Member States' development bureaucracy.[23]

The first large-scale evaluation of emergency assistance, co-ordinated by DANIDA concerning the case of Rwanda (see: JEEAR-series of studies), was like a 'bombshell' thrown into established institutions and made a deep impact. Given the rapidly evolving challenges and necessity of 'lessons learned' to be applied in the field, the DAC Guidelines on Conflict, Peace and Development Co-operation are a constructive attempt in the right direction. Other international organizations understood the message with some delay and acted accordingly: the World Bank formed a 'Post-Conflict Unit' and the UNDP created a new conflict unit in 1998. Possible synergies are to be expected with the better-established OECD–DAC Task Force. The International Monetary Fund (IMF) and World Bank (IBRD) are required to respond to requests (by G8 and UN) for timely and comprehensive assistance in pre-conflict and post-conflict situations.

The European Union has already acted as a 'third party' in four instances of mediation involving some element of ethnic conflict. It attempted, unsuccessfully, to help normalize relations between the 'independent' Serb republic of Krajina and Croatia: this was followed by Croatia's Krajina campaign of August 1995 and 'ethnic cleansing'. The EU also mediated in the quarrel over the physical assets left over from the Yugoslavian federal republic. It also settled the dispute between one of its own members, Italy, and the new Slovenian state over reparations for the former Italian minority in Istria. An interim agreement in the dispute between Hungary and Slovenia over control of the ecological effects of the Gabcikovo dam on the Danube was also secured under pressure from the EU.[24] Individual efforts at mediation were successful primarily because, as a 'third party', the EU is able, when an agreement is negotiated, to offer perks or material inducements, or to threaten sanctions.

3.2   Third party or go-between?

Most third parties or go-betweens in ethno-national conflicts do not have any kind of material inducements or deterrents at their disposal. The power-based type of mediation, such as was used by the EU in Yugoslavia or by Carter's USA in the Middle East conflict (Camp David agreements), is vehemently rejected by independent mediators.

Because of power mediation, the concept of the 'third party' has fallen into disrepute. The term 'third party' evokes the idea of the football game, with two parties and a referee. Contemporary conflicts rarely have only two parties with a third party to intervene, thus to go-between.[25] Galtung talks of 'outside parties' rather than 'third parties'. He developed a typology of conflict intervention that includes non-intervention and that grades intervention according to criteria of autonomy and good offices or diktat.[26] The typology is set within a framework of dialogue-based conflict transformation. Similarly, Lederach plays down the role of the 'neutral outsider' and talks of the crucial part played by 'middle-range' internal actors.[27] These are well-known figures enjoying cross-sectoral respect – ethnic or religious leaders, scholars, intellectuals, humanitarian activists from NGOs. Belonging as they do to the affected populations, they are, says Lederach, in the best position to build an 'infrastructure for peace', because they can exert influence both on the élites and on the general population.[28] These kinds of internal go-betweens can play major roles in conflict mediation and can effect long-term transformations of conflict in the direction of lasting peace. In regard to the agents of peace strategies, Galtung draws a distinction between élites and non-élites – that is to say, between actors from the state or bureaucracy and those from civil society.[29]

Mediation, dispute settlement and processes of transformation in the case of violent conflicts in deeply divided societies require that civilian actors bring to the peace process the capacity to adopt a dozen or more intermediary roles and functions, approaches and initiatives, in order to be able to respond appropriately to the challenge. In the course of the process, the complex web of roles, functions and activities changes. Mitchell has produced a general typology of roles and functions in this connection.[30]

The process of transformation within a conflictual formation runs from the stage of latent conflict up to confrontation; dispute settlement seeks, via negotiation, to achieve a dynamic but peaceful state of affairs.[31] Ideas about a continuum of conflict, ranging from peaceful to hostile relations, or about progressive development in cycles, have this kind of process of transformation in mind.

Galtung also calls into question the conventional triangle of diagnosis, prognosis and treatment. Instead, he has introduced a six-part flow-chart based on the co-ordinates of time (past, present, future) and treatment (analysis and practical action).[32] The difficulty faced in every conflict settlement – namely, moving from analysis to practical action – is supposed to be overcome by restaging of the conflict situation by those involved.

3.2.1 Non-state mediation and practical politics: Carter in Haiti

Mediation efforts by non-governmental, civil society actors, in the shape of human-rights groups,[33] religious groups, private think-tanks, peace movements, and so on (including some public or partly state-run institutions) will be a major source of stimulus in future. Misunderstandings and disappointments can be avoided if the actors have a precise picture of the aims of mediation and the way it operates. This is particularly difficult because in the world of crisis management, practical politics prevails, and the blazing spotlights of the television cameras fall only on the stars. Success and failure are often not far removed from one another, as the example of Jimmy Carter's mediation in Haiti demonstrates.

Perhaps the best-known examples of civilian dispute settlement are those undertaken by ex-US President Jimmy Carter, founder of the Carter Center at Emory University in Atlanta. The centre developed a Conflict Resolution Program (CRP) for dealing with intra-state conflict and it set up an International Negotiation Network (INN).[34]

The network co-ordinates third party activities and expert studies. The activities range from on-the-spot fact-finding and secret talks with the parties to the conflict to mediation in face-to-face round-table talks. The Carter Center and the INN also offer advocacy and negotiation training for a range of disputants. The INN is a flexible informal network comprising NGOs and government agencies, experts on various trouble-spots, (former) diplomats, and practitioners of conflict management. Different types of individuals work together in the INN, which is directed and advized by a council made up of leading political figures ('eminent persons').[35] The Carter Center organizes regional and international conferences and publishes bulletins and reports.[36]

Carter's 1994 missions to North Korea and Haiti, which he had undertaken as a sort of diplomatic 'secret weapon' at the behest of President Clinton, were successful.[37] In Haiti, a country beset by terrible poverty and a regime that showed nothing but scorn for human rights, something astonishing happened. Via CNN, the world witnessed – as Dieter Senghaas would term it – the first 'humanitarian military intervention' by the United States (carried out with the blessing of United Nations); but it was a humanitarian mission that had some very solid practical and 'internal' political motives.[38] No one now asks whether this success was bought at the price of impunity for mass murderers. Both Carter and the electronic media played their roles in ensuring the ultimate success of the UN operation in Haiti.[39]

The UN plan for Haiti – that is to say, its transformation into a democratic state based on the rule of law – was, politically speaking, the first UN operation of this kind and in this geographic area; the mission was marked by the spirit of the new post-cold war era.[40] UN funds and staff were invested to promote Haiti's transformation and this process came to a close in 1997. The problem remains, even after this, that Haiti is one of the poorest countries in the western hemisphere, having once been its second most important republic (after the USA). Only when genuine democratization (which is making slow progress) is combined with sustainable development will there be any chance for Haiti.

The part played by Jimmy Carter in the first genuine, initially non-voluntary, humanitarian intervention – after the spectacular failure of the UN's Operation Restore Hope in Somalia[41] – should not be underestimated. In ethno-national conflicts, on the other hand, Carter ended up with a number of failures on his score-card.[42]

3.2.2   Peaceful dispute settlement using civil actors: a selection

The most thickly clustered network of mediation and conflict resolution groups is currently to be found in the USA, many of them in the old-established East Coast universities. Associated with Harvard university in Cambridge (Massachusetts) are the Harvard Mediation Service, the Harvard Negotiation Project and the Conflict Management Group (CMG). The CMG does a brisk business (under the direction of Roger Fisher) and organizes training seminars (for example for Americorps, the National Service Program), as well as negotiating workshops and brainstorming sessions (for example with the OSCE high commissioner on national minorities); it also trains trainers, provides mediation services and is involved in missions on the ground (in Cyprus and the former USSR).[43] The US Institute of Peace in Washington, the Center for International Development and Conflict Management (CIDCM) at the University of Maryland, and the nearby George Mason University in Fairfax (Virginia), which runs the Institute for Conflict Analysis and Resolution, headed by Christopher Mitchell, and works with Burton's methods, also offer facilities for conflict analysis and resolution.

In Europe, one of the most important institutions in the area of peace and conflict research, alongside the PRIO and SIPRI, is the Department of

Peace Studies (DPS) at the University of Bradford, which also runs workshops on conflict resolution.[44] The Berghof Research Center for Conflict Resolution has existed in Berlin since 1993 and has some activities in ethnically divided societies.[45]

Informal international networks comprising participants from very different backgrounds take shape around individual conflict regions such as the Horn of Africa.[46] Training programmes for peace activists are run by, among others, the Austrian Studienzentrum für Frieden und Konfliktlösung in Schlaining (partly in collaboration with INCORE) and by the Responding to Conflict group (of the late Judith Large) at Woodbroke College in Birmingham. The ÖSFK now also offers training courses for election observers from human rights organizations, as well as courses for UN conflict observers (who will go on to monitor human rights for the UN High Commissioner for Human Rights), peace-keepers and for development workers.

The work of the Unrepresented Nations and Peoples Organization in The Hague also includes some mediation activities.[47] Among the most active mediators in the NGO domain are: International Alert in London; the Helsinki Citizen Assembly (HCA), based in Prague; the Quaker Peace Service in London; and the human rights organization Memorial, with main centres in Moscow and St Petersburg and active throughout the CIS. Memorial was involved, among other things, in opposition to the Chechen wars. Over the last decade, the activities of International Alert have become widely known. In the earlier years, Kumar Rupesinghe launched an initiative for a Global Coalition against War (in November 1994 via ICON – IPRA's study-group on Internal Conflicts and their Resolution – and IPRA itself),[48] and Jonathan Cohen's mediation in the Caucasus and Moldova,[49] partly in collaboration with the HCA in Euskadi, are remembered favourably. Fortunately, today, the glamour of peacemaking has to be shared with personalities, organizations and institutions based in the south, which are closer to the notorious trouble spots and successfully compete with Western INGOs.

3.2.3 An example of practical conflict research: the ECOR project

The Ethnic Conflicts Research Project (ECOR) was set up in 1987 and started to conduct comparative studies into the causes of lethal conflicts in three world regions in 1988–89.[50] It focuses on multi-layered violent ethno-national conflicts.[51] Nowadays, it also engages in activities that go beyond this – producing a survey of the global phenomenon of ethnonationalism, for example, or analyzing the causes and structural characteristics of ethnic and ethnicizised conflicts, evaluating elements of conflict avoidance (prophylaxis) and conflict resolution, and – one of its principal areas of activity – conducting ongoing field-based research and launching peace initiatives in conflict regions. As regards practical action, within the broad field of the prevention of violent conflict in general and genocide in particular, ECOR is involved in the following specific areas:

- the provision of informal political advice to non-state actors (for example, in negotiations and peace-talks) in the form of *ad hoc* consultancy, process-oriented, of a kind that is instrumental within the framework of confidence-building measures
- research into state policy on nationalities, minority rights, human-rights regimes and forms of self-governance (partly in collaboration with the University of Amsterdam, IWGIA, see Assies and Hoekema 1994)
- provision of advice to the governments of Rwanda and Burundi with regard to the establishment of the traditional *gachacha* jurisdiction (in Rwanda 2001–05), *abashingantahe* (in Burundi since 1998) and truth commissions at different levels; other measures aimed at ensuring conflict prevention, justice and the rule of law, following the genocides of 1993 in Burundi and 1994 in Rwanda (Scherrer 1997*a*), as well as a range of related activities in Central Africa (Scherrer 2002, 2003)
- documenting human rights violations in conflicts
- observation of sessions of the UNWGIP and, since 1989, active participation in 'standard setting'
- consultancy work for indigenous organizations within the framework of UN conferences
- initiatives in the area of inter-ethnic mediation, in close collaboration with organizations representing endangered peoples on the ground and sometimes in association with INGOs.

Training within the conflict avoidance and conflict resolution areas named above is restricted to local ECOR workers – who vary according to the project-area concerned – and to members of indigenous organizations. So far, the project has operated with a modest infrastructure but could be expanded. ECOR also produces a steady flow of publications.

3.3 The process of escalation, timing and type of responses

This sub-chapter will correlate peace strategies such as the possibility of structural prevention of violence conflict management and transformation with six stages of conflict. The role of different actors in preventing violence will be explored, including governments, development agencies, NGOs and the UN system. The question 'what to do in a particular situation?' is linked with the type of conflicts we are dealing with as well as with the stage of escalation of a particular conflict at the particular time of intervention. The focus will be on the importance of the right timing in response to conflict. Types of responses are clearly related to different types of conflicts. Peaceful responses – and peace strategies in general – should learn from existing schemes and aim at long-term structural and interactive prevention of violent conflict rather than plunge into activism that only produces short-term bandages. Proven mechanisms range from minority protection, affirmative action, to autonomy regulations, power sharing, nationality policies and (con)federal schemes. Procedures and instruments include standard setting for international laws and rules, such as those made to protect non-dominant groups, as well as new regimes for controlled partition and secession.

3.3.1 Preventing violence – not conflict as such

Let us think about conflicts in a very general way. In daily social life conflicts make sense. Conflict is an essential form of social interaction.[52] To argue with someone brings problems out. Problems should be expressed (not suppressed), only in this way can solutions be found. To have it out with a person makes arrangements possible affording due respect to different interests and positions. Therefore, the focus is not on 'preventing conflicts' but on 'preventing violence', more particularly 'preventing destructive ways' of dealing with incompatibilities, contradictions, disputes and difference of interests and positions. Interaction becomes destructive through the use of violence.

In processes confronting social groups or larger sections of society the option of using violence should be prevented from the onset. Some may argue that pacifism in inter-ethnic or international relations is a questionable position. For instance they might claim the right to self-defence. Here things already start to get difficult. Others think about revolutionary violence, which should be characterized as *controlled* violence against oppression. The ideal-typical case would be a so-called 'natural right of resistance' against tyranny. But we all know that there are no ideal-typical cases in social life and in the real world. It may only be consequent and genuine *common sense* to say that violence bears violence and that prevention is better than cure.

3.3.2 Collective memory and dormant conflict

Conflicts are a natural thing and mere differences as *such* are not conflictive and therefore do not usually carry or provoke violence. Cultural or ethnic differences can be interesting or attractive and make social life more colourful – as long as such differences are not politicized and exploited for particular interests, especially if states engage in such activity. Immanuel Kant's questions about sustainable peace by banning wars on a global scale 'for all times', thus establishing *eternal peace*, seemed not of this world. Kant wrote his piece about *eternal peace* some 200 years ago – after the French Revolution and at the height of the Enlightenment era. Common sense maintains that wars have always been fought. Therefore, there is always a past full of memories of hostilities and despair. Past violence itself is a source for traumatizing memories.

A constitutive element for each and every society, community, or ethnic group is what has been called the *collective memory*. Other elements would be a common language, being part of a common culture, living in a particular place or territory as a space of communication and social interaction, and feeling some kind of solidarity of belonging to a particular group. It is the collective memory before all other elements that makes up a community of people; this is the most decisive element regarding conflict. The collective memory is a kind of living history book, recording past traumatic experiences. Like official or written history it is full of myths. Common memories about the past reflect all kinds of events, including disputes, past injustices and traumas, violence and victimization, wars and mass violence. In some cases the worst memory is about genocide. Psychologists talk about internalization such as 'sleeping memories' that can suddenly be reactivated. Peace researchers should know very well that memories of past horrors are still virulent after generations of peace and stability.

3.3.3 Use of instruments at the right time

Like memories, conflicts can be held pending in a subconscious or *sleeping* stage and can be suddenly reactivated. That is why this stage is the best time for prevention. Even weak preventive measures have an effect. Targeted measures against renewed violence should take into account the root causes of a **dormant conflict** (stage 1). The adequate choice of procedures and use of instruments is important. Alternative options include either *reliving the tragedy* (Galtung) in order to stop traumatization or to neutralize the trauma through confidence building and *empowerment* – in order to prevent it from emerging again. Galtung asked, 'why should anyone relive a trauma? – to demystify the past'.[53] In a post-conflict situation we deal with reconstruction, reconciliation and resolution (the '3R'), while in the stage of dormant or latent conflict we deal with prevention.[54]

A typology of responses to conflict would have essentially to include all kind of procedures and instruments for prophylactic peace building and peace keeping at the stage of *sleeping conflict*. Thus a typology for crisis prevention and conflict management first identifies institutions, procedures and instruments for peaceful coexistence (see Table 3.1). In a more specific typology for local and global peace building (see Table 3.2), instruments for violence prevention and inter-ethnic balance are listed.

3.3.4 Stages of conflict escalation and constructive responses

Let us now look into conflict stages and possible constructive responses in an abstract way. The Herculean task of peace building is most effectively approached by various ways to structurally prevent violence on different levels. This includes different actors or institutions and can be achieved by using various means. In the general survey of types of crisis prevention and conflict management I tried to specify some aspects of my typology of peace in order to give a structural view of existing institutions, procedures and instruments for peaceful coexistence (compare Table 3.1).

Table 3.1 Peaceful coexistence through violence prevention and inter-ethnic balance: a typology

Coexistence	Scope, realm	Principle	Period	Characteristics/phenomena	Aims/objectives/results
negative peace by **threat of aggression** *pax Americana/ sovietica/etc.*	Global state system – global economy	deterrence (external) and internal control	short and medium-term	Northern states or regional powers against weaker Southern states; exception: mutual deterrence of the super powers (cold war)	imposition of interest/containment/ economic interest; result: hegemony
negative peace by **military intervention** named 'humanitarian'	state system (often against civil society); UN	external; state-centred; powered by legacy of European colonialism	short-term; since colonialism	usually colonial powers, Northern states or regional powers against weaker states at the peripheries; expression of postcolonial dependency (*dependencia*); toppling of unfriendly governments, e.g. US interventions in Latin America since era of President Monroe	often ultimate with no agreement proposed; control/imposition of 'solutions'; result: conflict of interests; partial and non-sustainable effect, perpetuation of dependency
coexistence/peace by **arbitration and settlement of disputes**	state system	external potentially also internal	since 1899 First Hague Peace Conference	establishment of the *Permanent Court of Arbitration* (PCA) 1899 and the Convention for the *Peaceful Settlement of International Disputes* (CPSID) provide for legal base	peaceful settlement of disputes is a good old idea (reaffirmed by the UN-Charter 1945, Article 33c); result: PCA had little impact
coexistence by **agreements**	state system (primary); TNCs	internal/expansive state-centred; *colonialism*	since the early 19th century	settlers versus indigenous nations/weak settler states; conflict reduction by treaties, mostly broken after changes of the balance of power	treaties were made to regulate territorial invasion, for the purpose of control over lands, resources and populations

Table 3.1 Continued

Coexistence	Scope, realm	Principle	Period	Characteristics/phenomena	Aims/objectives/results
coexistence through **welfare state policies and agreements**	state system (primary); economy civil society	internal state-centred; expansive, *internal colonialism*	longer periods since the early 20th century	*mainstream* societies versus indigenous groups/strong settler states; attempted reduction of conflict, postcolonial *trusteeship* ideology; limited agreements with indigenous peoples; reservation-type of system with affirmative action (USA, Australia, NZ)	alien control of most indigenous lands and resources; population control
internal peace and coexistence by means of **modern treaties**	state system economy civil society	internal and state-centred; softened *internal colonialism*	undefined periods since 1948 and again in the 1980s	mainstream societies, indigenous and other minorities; conflict prevention through treaties and agreements with indigenous peoples; partial to full self-governance (Canada, Denmark, Sweden)	control and internal peace as aim; hopeful beginnings in Faeroe Islands 1948, Kalaallit Nunaat, Nunavut, Dené NWT, Saami
coexistence by means of ***autonomy/ conservation*** (in Southern neo-liberal states)	state system (primary); civil society (only corporate)	internal state-centred; internal colonialism by other means	shorter and longer periods	*mestizo* societies versus manifold indigenous communities/weak states (periphery); agreements with selected communities; type: *comarca* (Panama since 1920s); *resguardo*; non-integration often broken by attempts of assimilation; self-rule in Eastern Nicaragua, flawed by neglect/paternalism	traditional institutions (*caciques/congreso*-system); control by concession of self-rule; aim to avoid conflicts by territorial autonomy (passed by law or constitution, often *ad hoc*); real autonomy needs an economy
peaceful coexistence by ***self-rule and***	state system and civil society	associative non-expansive internal/external	medium and longer periods after 1945	enlightened/libertarian societies, indigenous minorities/social welfare states; structural conflict avoidance,	security through respect for others; high degree of oganization development

free association (based on Northern welfare states)				conflict regulation or solution through rights and concessions, self-governance for non-dominant groups (Føroyar or Faroe Islands' home rule 1948)	and prosperity for many; few solid models for indigenous and minority self-governance (traditional institutions etc.)
peaceful coexistence by *neutrality and welfare*	state (primary) civil society	external/internal	Austria, Malta a/o for 50 years	liberal social-democrat societies, protection for minorities/welfare states; structural conflict avoidance, prosperity for many in crisis	conflict regulation through welfare state; proportional representation in parliamentary democracy; non-allied policy in crisis
peaceful coexistence by *neutrality and (con)federation*	state system and civil society	stable self-centred	Swiss model 400 years (?)	decentralization in multi-ethnic pluri-cultural Switzerland: confederation since 1848, big-party concordiality in the central government; respect for other indigenous languages/cultures, but no inclusion of migrants; prosperity for many in crisis	conflict regulation/ solution by self-rule (canton system) and proportional/regional representation; elements of direct democracy overpowered by corporatist interests; abuse of federalism
peace through involvement/ *peaceful intervention*	state system/ UN-System OSCE, OAU, etc.	(re)active civil actors only marginally incl.	since 1945, on the rise since 1990, short term	divided societies/states; UN-operations; OSCE-missions; in between intervention and mediation/facilitation	conflict regulation/ solution through agreements between parties to the conflict; security through inter-ethnic balance and protection of national minorities

Table 3.2 Prevention of violence by peaceful inter-ethnic coexistence: types, instruments and models

Type/instrument	Scope, realm	Principle	Period	Models, processes, deficits	Needs for studies and application
inter-ethnic coexistence by granting of **minority rights**	states multilateral regimes	active preventive internal rule of law	since 1980s; increasingly since 1990	protection of the rights of non-dominant groups (OSCE HCNM); standard setting by UN-CHR towards a *Declaration of the Rights of Indigenous Peoples*	internal peace and external security through inter-ethnic balance and protection of new minorities; application of international law
peaceful inter-ethnic coexistence by **power sharing**	states regimes civil actors	active preventive innovative	for many centuries; more cases still to be established	lessons to be learned from experiences with different existing models of power sharing, representation, ethnically mixed elites and their co-operation (Lebanon, Malaysia, Benin, Nigeria); models of limited attraction	comparison of existing models and their performance; development of new instruments for power sharing and balancing of different ethnic and national groups
inter-ethnic peace and coexistence by granting the **right to self-determination and free association**	co-operation of involved state(s) and peoples; facilitation by UN, regional regimes, NGOs	interactive preventive innovative	increasingly since 1945; still to be established on a larger scale	'lessons learned?' from experiences with autonomy and self-governance in all continents; models: *korenisazia* and autonomization in FSU and China; creation of new states in India, quotas for scheduled castes/tribes; autonomy regulations in Europe	comparison of existing models and their performance; development of new instruments to promote constructive interaction between states and nation(alitie)s; establishment of international regimes in high demand; problem of lack of implementation
inter-ethnic peace and coexistence by establishing **(con-)federal schemes**	co-operation of pluralist people(s); facilitation by relevant actors	interactive preventive	increasingly since 1945; still to be established	lessons to be learned from experiences with federal schemes in all continents; models (also incomplete): FSU/RF, India, Nigeria, Tanzania, Ethiopia, new South Africa, Switzerland, Spain, etc.	comparison and evaluation of existing models and their performance; development of new elements of (con-)federal and regional schemes as well as prevention of its abuse

Table 3.3 Types and methods of/for crisis prevention and peaceful coexistence

Types and ways	Scope, realm	Principle	Period	Models, processes/deficits/needs	Aims/objectives/expectations
preventing violence by **early warning linked to early action**	UN, INGOs, regional regimes, states, civil actors	active preventive	still to be established	increasing capabilities of early warning; full use of conflict prevention networks to be built-up jointly by multilateral regimes, research institutes and INGOs/NGOs	top priority for bridging the gap between early warning and early action
transforming ethnic violence by **preventive diplomacy**	state system primary; civil actors such as INGOs	state-centred regime building	on the rise since 1990; medium term	multi-ethnic societies/states; from actionistic activities to power mediation; conflict regulation as agreements; can be reactive and little impact; often successful enlightened civilized state leaders and civic organizations pushing for change;	*protection*/minimal rights for non-dominant groups; security through respect for others, recognition of multiplicity
peaceful inter-ethnic coexistence **by enforcing accountability and compliance** by states	United Nations; regimes under monitoring and watch by NGOs or INGOs	interventive, rule of (inter-)national law	long-term approach; still at point zero	overall promotion of standard setting in international law in order to force states to obey to the rules and comply with international law	humanitarian minimum and respect of human and minority rights; no double standards; clear-cut sanctions to be introduced against deviation/crimes by repressive and intransigent state governments
peace by peaceful intervention: **mediation/ facilitation**	civil society actors, NGOs /INGOs, some states	reactive–activist interactive preventive	since the 1980s; short to long term	multi-ethnic societies/states; actionistic mediation/facilitation, conflict regulation/ solutions through agreements between inside parties facilitated by outside parties	*empowerment* for non-dominant groups; security through respect for others, recognition of multiplicity/ promotion of minorities' issues
peace building by **constructive dialogue**	states external and local civil actors	active, processual preventive innovative	on the rise; medium term	improvement of overall relationships in multi-ethnic societies/states; recognition and awareness about hidden perceptions/ agendas of involved parties	discovering shared needs; focusing on the future; translating common needs into *'joint actions as stepping stones to agreements'* (Weeks 1994)

Table 3.3 Continued

Types and ways	Scope, realm	Principle	Period	Models, processes/deficits/needs	Aims/objectives/expectations
peaceful coexistence by **structural prevention** of destructive interaction	UN regional regimes, states, societies, NGOs	interactive preventive rule of law	increasingly since 1945; still to be enforced	application of existing instruments/ laws (international pacts, conventions, declarations) as well as development of new instruments in international law; problem: how to break the resistance of states?	new instruments to combat destructive interaction between states and nation(alitie)s; rapid establishment of international criminal justice in high demand; lack of enforcement
coexistence by rules for the realization of **full right to self-determination**	co-operation of involved state(s) and international community	interactive preventive innovative	still to be established	consequences to be drawn from experiences with destructive ethno-nationalist civil wars in all continents; deficit of shared norms/standards for secession; global governance	rules for the creation of new states; regimes for recognition of claims; new instruments to promote constructive transition
peace building by constructive **conflict resolution** approaches	states external and local civil actors	active processual preventive innovative	still to be established	facilitation of conflict resolutions through negotiation about binding agreements as constructive medium and long term approaches	shared needs and joint plans for the future; securing accountability of all parties and building sustainability
peace by peaceful means: education, **culture of peace** by lively cross-cultural communication	civil society civilized states	active interactive preventive innovative	medium periods	enlightened libertarian sectors of societies/civilized states pushing for change; prevention of violence by getting to know each other (multiculturalism versus daily racism; travelling, cultural contacts and exchanges, arts, etc.)	conflict regulation through rights for non-dominant groups (citizenship for second generation migrants); respect for other societies and different cultures/lifestyles

In much the same way the procedures and instruments for violence prevention and inter-ethnic balance are given in a systematic overview (compare Tables 3.2 and 3.3).

3.3.5 Structural prevention at the stage of dormant conflict

Realistically, peaceful coexistence can be approached by means of a minimal level effort. Before creating new instruments the application of existing instruments should be guaranteed. International law is to safeguard international security as well as internal peace. The critical factor in International Law – in general, and in regard to human and minority rights in particular – is the lack or fragmentary nature of mechanisms and procedures for enforcing legal instruments such as declarations, conventions, covenants and treaties.

Enforcing International Law is the real problem. It can be done in three ways:[55]

1. by comprehensive review processes and checks-and-control, as in the case of the European Convention on Human Rights or in the case of the Convention for Indigenous Peoples of the International Labour Organization (ILO convention 169)
2. by institution building, as in the case of OSCE and its institution of a High Commissioner for Minorities, or the latest case, the establishment of an International Criminal Court (ICC), in order to outlaw gross human rights violations such as genocide and crimes against humanity, still meeting strong resistance by large states such as the US
3. by refining an arsenal of sanctions, which shall hurt the non-complying regimes and not the people.

Some states tried to obstruct the process of establishing ICC.[56] The total or almost total absence of sanctions is a phenomenon common to all contractual arrangements in International Law. There is simply no world government that ensures International Law is observed. The United Nations are not a 'World Republic' (Kant) that could engage in global governance in this sense.

Structural prevention has many options regarding the multitude of 'new wars' and conflict characterized by ethnic factors. The best timing for it is to intervene at the stage of *dormant conflict*. This is where/when the obstacles are few but the choices of possible approaches are fairly broad. The scope is large and open. Duplication is not a problem. A range of different actors and institutions can participate to take up their own initiatives.

The most effective forms of structural prevention are those built-in state structures, and combine elements such as autonomy for non-dominant groups, self-governance and (con)federal schemes with power sharing. Peaceful coexistence and inter-ethnic balance can be achieved by a number of models for power sharing. The cases to be mentioned as examples – as you may see at once (Table 3.2) – can not be all that ideal. Other approaches for the realization of free association and internal self-determination of all peoples can be undertaken by way of autonomization – with a range of cases to be studied and compared. More systemic schemes for self-governance were realized by the nationality policies of large multi-ethnic states such as FSU/Russian Federation, China or India. Some cases might be considered as incomplete models. Nevertheless, many lessons can be learned from these long-term experiences. A last type of preventive response is still somewhat utopian. It would consist of regimes for secession and rules for the creation of new states or their international recognition.

Besides domestic forms of structural prevention there are other types of peace building. For instance there is the minority rights approach, which is best undertaken on different levels ranging from international standard setting in the framework of the UN Human Rights Commission and at conferences of the OSCE to the creation of domestic laws. Legislation is best done in an interactive process involving different actors directly or at least by consulting those groups that are to profit from it. An ideal case for the latter could have been the elaboration of the Universal Declaration of the Rights of Indigenous Peoples at UN Geneva.

Annual sessions of the Working Group on Indigenous Peoples included hundreds of delegates from all over the world. The remarkable process of drafting such a declaration was suddenly interrupted – after ten years of hard work.

3.3.6   Emerging conflict: setting the stage for NGOs

Most people in crisis areas never get involved in violent acts and most do not support violence. They are potentially welcoming any initiative for peace keeping and peace building. Peace-loving people who are struggling for mutual understanding are found in every society and sub-group. The more intensively a conflict escalates the more such brave people are forced to be silent. In certain situations they will not be able to expose themselves without running high risks. A second group of people only gets involved if a conflict is already in an **emerging stage** (stage 2).

They may get involved because of persuasive memories of past threats and horrors that were confronting their group, people or party with other parties. Many people get involved only *halfway*. First they do not want 'to have something to do with that savagery'. In many cases they do not even know which party or group they should belong to.

In an emerging stage of conflict there are usually plenty of public threats by the aggressors and plenty of early warnings from the side of targeted groups and local NGOs, but often little or no action is undertaken, at least no comprehensive action as for example in Central Africa. Rwanda of 1994 was the most striking example to show the gap between early warning and early action. In this case there was no early action at all, even in the wake of state-organized mass murder – announced well in advance, incited by extremists by means of radio and reported by several foreign TV stations.[57]

In many cases non-governmental local organizations such as popular associations, churches and politicians try to mediate and facilitate dialogue. International NGOs might get involved. Preventive diplomacy would also include other states and multi-lateral organizations. The aim is to calm the waves and work for a peaceful settlement and constructive resolution approaches. In the non-violent emerging stage of a conflict most options for reactive, active and even interactive responses are still open. The structural prevention approach might already face more obstacles and difficulties to find broad-based political support in order to press for implementation and realization – often controlled by intransigent state bureaucrats. Adequate responses at this stage include early actions by manifold actors and constructive peace building and peace-keeping measures such as dialogue, go-between mediation and facilitation of conflict transformation or sometimes resolution.

3.3.7   Escalation sets increasing limits for constructive responses to conflict

In the **stage of escalation** to violent conflict (stage 3) there is a serious limitation of options as well as a reduction of types of responses and numbers of actors involved. While at an emerging stage many actors are non-governmental, at this stage governments take over and try to control possible responses to conflict. State actors increasingly try to monopolize the public sphere. Especially in ethno-nationalist conflicts this could mean that collaborators of INGOs meet hostility, are harassed, or kicked out of the country. Local NGOs would be banned or restricted. The main conflict actors no longer hear appeals for constructive dialogue. Most parties to the conflict now find it impossible to compromise. The ideological battle is in full swing. In the omnipresent propaganda the *enemy* will be dehumanized, thus preparing the ground for violence.

The **severe phase** (stage 4) is characterized by a now fully violent and militarized conflict. Most doors are closed. Civil actors are out of the picture for the most part. Only combatant parties (governments and rebels), rarely multi-lateral actors, have control. The vested interests of those intervening become clearer. The possibilities for responses other than military interventions are now totally restrained. All parties to the conflict find it impossible to do anything but fight it out.

In the **phase of de-escalation** (stage 5) combatant parties sign ceasefire agreements. All conflict actors now look for *repair* and seek assistance and equipment to be prepared in case of renewed violence. Some NGOs are welcome again, mostly those bringing in humanitarian aid and assistance. Here the classic peace keeping efforts are started. The cases of headline conflicts as depicted by Western mass media (which acquire the status of an involved actor since the media have great influence on local and international conflict actors) have their own externally induced dynamics.

Sometimes peace keeping includes the deployment of troops from major powers or the UN. In this case an eventual military intervention would be named 'humanitarian'.

The decision-making process on the engagement or disengagement of UN peace keeping seems to be dependent on political conjunctures and framework conditions while, the lessons from experiences of utter failure have yet to be learned. A thorough follow up by the UN decision-making bodies to the August 2000 Report of the Panel on United Nations Peace Operations (Brahimi report) is to be expected.[58] As we have witnessed, the number of personnel in UN operations fell from its 1993 peak of 76,000 blue helmets to low of 14,453 peace keepers serving in 17 UN missions, as of mid-1998, but was doubled again by 2001. The drop was the result of the Rwanda shock and several failed Chapter VII operations to impose peace on warring parties. In the mid-1990s the bitter experiences in Somalia, Rwanda and the former Yugoslavia have led to a temporary reluctance by the UN Security Council to authorize new peace keeping and, even less so, peace enforcement operations.[59]

However, in the later 1990s the mood began to change. The number of blue helmets rose to 30,000 serving in 15 UN military operations under way as of 1 January 2001, although there were only three UN operations less than one year before that.[60] Today the number of blue helmets is far from its 1993 peak, and there is a conspicuous selectivity in decisions of where peace keepers are and where they are not. There was no single preventive UN deployment in Africa. The delayed UN operation in Congo and the resulting non-implementation of the Lusaka agreement are just the latest example of this dangerous selectivity and a marked to send UN troops to Africa.[61]

As many examples might show, the danger at this stage is that the cycle of violence turns backward and the conflict relapses to stage 3, only to escalate again. Power mediation, as a state-centred response to conflict, could also again be a possibility. International NGOs would try to push for peace building. They would start confidence building measures (often including 'sugar', which means material assistance for elites and bureaucracies) and try to initiate dialogue between the parties to the conflict.

3.3.8   Peace building and consolidation in postconflict situations

Peace building in the **postconflict phase** of rebuilding and reconciliation (stage 6) has short to medium-term perspectives. War-torn societies need rehabilitation and reconstruction; this is the time for the 'big rush'. The bulk of the NGOs come in at this stage and they are accredited swiftly. They are allowed to bring (often tax-free) any amount of materials they may need for their work (including whatever luxuries they need for their collaborators, for example, expensive 4-wheel-drive cars, mostly for circulation in the capital city). Some of the critical skills of INGOs are in high demand, such as constructive conflict resolution approaches and co-operative planning. Arbitration by neutral outsiders or partial insiders is taken up in order to settle the conflict in a peaceful manner. Building a culture of peace at all levels chiefly includes the grassroots level. Local capacity building is crucial in order to make peace efforts sustainable.

Of course conventional conflict management approaches only deal with the leadership of the former adversaries now searching for a longer-term solution. This would then best be accomplished in way of binding agreements or even spectacular peace treaties – signed under the spotlight of the international media. Donor countries will promise a lot of aid. Rehabilitation and development projects will be set-up in order to consolidate the still-shaky negative peace. However, most donors are still not sensitive enough to conceptionalize the influence of development aid on conflict and to skilfully use incentives and disincentives. Lessons learned from Rwanda?

3.4 Debate about complex political emergencies

The growing number of ethno-national and other violent political conflicts of the last few decades have highlighted ever more clearly the urgent need to redouble research efforts in war zones and postwar societies. Since the 1980s, one of the most disquieting aspects of the international scene has been the emergence of an increased number of complex emergencies, disasters and humanitarian crises of increasingly grave proportions. However, the determining factor in the creation of new research bodies, including large-scale projects, has not just been political decision-makers' awareness of strategic deficiencies; the broad mass of the public – in their capacities as donors, tax-payers and individuals with an interest in politics – have come to realize that interventions to restore peace, and attempts by the international community to provide assistance in emergency and postwar situations, are generally neither efficient nor properly co-ordinated, and this has contributed greatly to the idea that 'mistakes' and defects must be eliminated.[62] There are deficiencies in terms both of peace policy and of humanitarian aid, and they are deficiencies not of a financial but primarily of a political and conceptual kind.[63]

The discussion about the manifest failure of many humanitarian and peace-based interventions in areas of crisis is in full swing. New terminological creations such as 'complex political emergencies', 'multi-mandate relief', 'multi-task approach', and 'multi-track peace building' point to the problem.

The debate initially focused on the problems that were seen as the most important by those intervening – the constant duplication of peace-based and humanitarian efforts, for example, and the general confusion in regard to responsibilities and mandates. What triggered the debate was the piling-up of one failure and one painful setback upon another. Often, despite large financial inputs for peace-keeping interventions by the UN or for humanitarian aid by thousands of NGOs, the results achieved were minimal or, indeed, negative. The assistance given is too expensive, not of sustainable quality, and in many cases politically ambivalent. A second phase of the debate about political emergencies also covered structural defects and 'hidden dangers'. Today, international aid has become an important (sometimes the most important) factor in the political economy of intrastate conflicts and can often be shown to prolong wars.

3.4.1   Reactions to African disasters

The prime example of ambivalent action was certainly Rwanda. The international response to the humanitarian crisis was just as shocking and ill-judged as the bungled efforts of the international community – and the UN in particular – had been in April 1994. The multi-million-dollar aid being pumped into Rwanda lacks any kind of systematic political plan.[64] What is being promoted, involuntarily, is not the reconciliation of a given society following the genocide of 1994, but the perpetuation of the dissension. What has led to this is the ideology of, or obsession with, the neutrality of humanitarian aid.[65] One of the responses to this scandalous situation is the most extensive research-project ever yet conducted into complex emergencies. On the initiative of DANIDA (Danish International Development Agency), a comprehensive, five-volume evaluation-study was produced on Rwanda, and was published in March 1996.[66] A Canadian study on Rwanda had already led to wide-ranging reforms in the crisis response mechanisms of the UN and the international community, with a view to preventing similar cataclysmic events in future.[67] Humanitarian aid – this was the more profound realization – cannot fill a political vacuum.

Because of global political developments and for internal structural reasons, the international peace keeping and humanitarian 'system' has today come up against the limits of its capabilities. Complex emergencies have become a characteristic feature of areas and societies whose 'normal' development has been permanently hindered by a number of interconnected negative factors – namely, the destructive *realpolitik* or power politics of the state, continued economic decline, growing social disintegration and fragility, and progressive cultural breakdown. The emergence of predatory civil war actors has led to traditional structures in many Third World societies being further eroded since colonial times. The collapse of social life and the perversion of values in war-torn societies have led to a blunting of sanctions against social misconduct, as previously imposed by elders and kinship groups, and has produced pathological phenomena such as the existence of child-soldiers, the rape and sexual exploitation of women, the enslavement of members of other ethnic groups, and so on. In many cases, there is the added factor of ecological damage resulting from war, in the form of the deliberate destruction and plundering of natural resources, and also the transfer of property (such as land, cattle, watering-places and so on), all of which undermines the continued existence of the traditional subsistence economy. Lastly, basic preconditions for a resumption and revitalization of traditional set-ups are lacking.

In the case of long-established, persistent and intractable intra-state conflicts, the 'endlessness' leads to a permanent situation of emergency, which in turn leads to new and unconventional survival strategies and extreme forms of political economy (war economies) between winners and losers in war.[68] Criminal modes of fighting and targeted policies of starvation and mass human rights violations acquire a new quality in ethno-national and other intra-state conflicts.[69] Orthodox methods of analysis fail on account of the novelty of the phenomena, as Duffield has shown with the example of the Sudan.[70] War and famine are more and more often the result of deliberate competing strategies on the part of the ruling state-classes and non-dominant social and ethnic groups. The mechanisms involved in the formation of war economies, and the strategy of the targeted destruction of opposition areas has so far not been adequately investigated or taken into account. More and more frequently, dictatorial regimes and movements (headed by 'warlords') are predatory in nature and are regarded as inherently disasterous (Macrae and Zwi 1994: 225). The expulsion and impoverishment of the 'losers' – a defining characteristic of present-day emergencies – is now an inherent part of the survival strategy of dominant groups.

3.4.2 Non-governmental organizations in conflict situations

Non-governmental organizations have become a mass phenomenon only since the mid-1980s. There are three reasons why NGOs have become key players at an international level.

1. The first condition was set when neo-liberalism became state policy in France, under Giscard d'Estaing, as well as in Britain, under the rule of Margaret Thatcher, and in the USA after Ronald Reagan was elected in 1980.
2. Governments created NGOs for intelligence purposes and used them as instruments for activities they could not carry out themselves, especially when intervening in situations of intra-state conflict. To avoid the embarrassment of possible violation of the principle of non-interference, states began to use NGOs more frequently (a phenomenon which actually started during the Biafra crisis).
3. Civil society-building in Western countries, as a result of the 1968 rebellions, increasingly created a more and more complete network and a parallel infrastructure of civil society institutions, which assumed many functions of state institutions.

During the 1980s 'conflict resolution' became an issue and developed into a burgeoning industry, first in the USA. Before the mid-1980s assistance in conflict situations – especially in case of intra-state conflicts – was bound to strict rules. Assistance in war situations was only given after the adversaries agreed to a ceasefire. In the mid-1990s 'conflict prevention' became more and more important. This is a result of large-scale failures of the international system. Effective prevention would make many (international) NGOs jobless. Non-governmental organizations were increasingly operating in conflict areas under ill-defined and self-appointed multi-task mandates that included virtually everything from humanitarian assistance up to conflict resolution.[71]

The Rwanda shock was among the most noticeable events in a period of time which witnessed mounting activities of NGOs worldwide. The genocide in Rwanda resulted in an unprecedented loss of lives: in 1994 more than one million Rwandans were victims of the genocidal state machinery – more than the double the fatalities recorded for all the violent conflicts in the former Eastern bloc, mainly in the former Soviet Union and Yugoslavia, from 1990 to 1999. The genocide in Rwanda sent shock waves throughout the international community. The very role of NGOs in conflict situations came under scrutiny.[72] Some of these organizations were said to have been actively contradicting UN policies.[73] Some NGOs were precipitating the Rwandan government's policy, especially the official policy concerning the internally displaced persons (IDPs). The United Nations created UN–REO, a specialized body to co-ordinate the NGOs in Rwanda.

Since the electronic media became more and more important for generating funding of non-governmental organizations, the role of the media had to be reassessed. During the period of April and May 1994 some NGOs such as Caritas, Oxfam or Care International received donations of up to US$1.2 million per day from deeply concerned citizen, based on the images of refugees beamed into their living rooms by the international news media. The result of these developments is highly ambiguous: in some Third World countries humanitarian aid accounts for up to 50 per cent of the value of the Overseas Development Assistance. The long-term perspective of development as an instrument for conflict prevention is increasingly challenged by short-term NGO activism.

3.4.3 A result of privatization: NGOs implement government policy

For about the last decade – since the triumph of monetarism and neo-liberalism, with its ideology of cut-backs in state provision and of generalized privatization – internationally active organizations, particularly the private so-called 'non-governmental organizations' have become major actors in war-torn societies of the Third World, and recently also of the former Second World.[74] The emancipation of the various sectors of civil society in the rich industrial countries, and the progressive processes of differentiation, interconnection and general increase in influence of the societal world as against the world of states, have played a crucial role in this, as seen from the point of view of the new actors. Almost all INGOs are based in Europe or the USA. Almost all NGOs are dependent on the resources of state or multilateral organizations, powerful partially state-funded foundations, fiscally privileged (state) churches, or multinational Western corporations; only a minority are financed exclusively by individual donations from all sections of the population. Is there a new colonialism in operation – political, economic, cultural and now humanitarian colonialism?

It was the states themselves, or their bilateral and multilateral agencies, that backed the idea of the development of a private, quasi-charitable non-profit-making sector, as a means of implementing and disseminating their policies and predetermined programmes. NGOs as adjuncts to, and agents of, state programmes – this strategy offered states, not only a certain self-generated momentum, but other critical advantages also. Given the limitations of the UN, which were desired and generated by the 'nuclear aristocracy' – that is to say, the permanent members of the Security Council (especially the Western ones) and former colonial powers – for power related interests of their own, bilateral donors are often not in a position to deal directly with civil-war regimes or ethno-national or revolutionary movements. NGOs do not have and do not need an official mandate; their status is negotiable. They operate in a flexible way – on strict condition that they acknowledge the sovereignty of even the most murderous regime. When economic or strategic interests appear under threat, and clientelist regimes seem destabilized, NGOs can be despatched in advance to the 'front line' in areas beset by civil war or emergency. NGOs today are a reliable instrument by which international policy may be implemented, particularly in the domains of humanitarian aid, disaster relief, and political emergencies (which have become the norm in many trouble spots). NGOs have become an important and adaptable conduit of international reaction to crises and wars.[75]

Emergency situations are usually highly politicized (both from above and from below) and are associated with non-conventional warfare, criminal attacks against civilian populations (or inadequate protection of them), anti-regime hostilities, or regional insecurity, sometimes including external attempts at destabilization. The effects of such complex emergencies are generally of a cross-border nature and render the situation of neighbouring states more difficult, often so much so that areas around the border become destabilized. Because of state obstructionism, NGOs (and sometimes UN organizations as well, as in the case of southern Sudan),[76] face the problem of difficult access to the areas of conflict, and this leads to greater (unnecessary) cost, hindrance and delay.

The care and protection of ever greater numbers of victims of structural and armed violence is a new response to conflicts in the Third World and the peripheral areas of the former Soviet Union. Being able to conduct humanitarian operations even in war zones distinguishes the NGO avant-garde from the less adventurous among them. Previously, the rule 'ceasefire

first, then aid' generally applied both to aid and to UN peace keeping operations. Nowadays, some parties to war in Third World states are enabled to
carry on waging war because of the part they play in ensuring supplies to
those expelled and the hungry.

For security reasons, most NGOs operate in government-controlled areas.
Aid can directly or indirectly assist the regime's fight against the rebels.
Government armies seek indiscriminately to clear the areas controlled by
rebels of people, in order to leave the guerrilla forces 'high and dry'. The
NGOs, for their part – working under the eye of the Western media – supply
those who have been driven out with food and medicines, thus 'humaniz-
ing' the expulsion. Some hard-line civil war regimes control aid shipments
and operations by offering fixed, mostly inflated, rates of exchange. This
kind of indirect tax can, in some circumstances, represent an important
economic input and provide the regime with valuable resources with which
to continue the war. Moral dilemmas become even more harrowing where
NGOs have to connive in brutal human rights violations in order not to be
thrown out of the country.

When the Burmese civil war began, the NGO phenomenon was still
completely unknown. Even ten years ago, almost no NGOs were active
in minority areas. Today, there are some areas in which they number several dozen. In other places, the side-effects of this boom are sometimes
extremely contradictory. In 1995, there were over 350 NGOs operating in
the small impoverished, depopulated and devastated Central African state
of Rwanda, most of them in the Rwandan refugee camps. With their dollars, the workers of the NGOs and UN organizations got the service sector
and parallel economy in the city moving, forced rents sky-high, imported
masses of brand new cars (tax free) and created all of Kigali's traffic, including office 'rush-hours'.

3.4.4   Problems of reconstruction in war-torn societies

The new War-torn Societies Project, run jointly by UNRISD and the Geneva-
based Institute for International Relations, is tailored to postwar situations
and emergencies, focusing in particular on reconstruction following violent
ethno-national or political conflicts.[77] The political criticism of privatized
charitable activity together with the failure of UN interventions in some
notorious war zones in the Third World led to a number of positive new initiatives. The launching of this very promising project also constitutes a contribution to the current debate about how the international community
(of states and NGOs) should respond to complex situations of acute crisis –
a debate that has grown even more urgent following the disastrous failure
of humanitarianism in Rwanda.

The aim of the War-torn Societies Project (WSP), launched by UNRISD,
is to identify practical approaches on the basis of sound scientific

investigation,[78] as an alternative, among other things, to the frenzy of unrestricted humanitarianism (as practised in Rwanda in 1994) and its manipulation by cynical rulers. The initial hurdle, as always, is the gap between research and policy. UNRISD is regarded as one of the most efficient, albeit smallest, institutions of the United Nations.[79] In addition to initiating the WSP action-research project, which began its action phase in 1995, UNRISD has, since 1993–94, launched two other research projects on the theme of ethnicity.[80] According to the WSP's findings, strategies of reconstruction in war-torn societies and complex emergencies are hampered by three main problems:

1. the aid given by humanitarian and government organizations is not integrated with the political and military interventions of the UN (or regional organizations) as part, or within the overall thrust, of a coherent political scheme
2. aid from outside is generally not participative in character, and is not adapted to local conditions; there is a dearth of generally accepted models of, and approaches to, the reconstruction of war-torn societies
3. independent local efforts are often choked, ignored, or counteracted by massive and/or indiscriminate aid from outside; the development and promotion of home-grown solutions is thus hampered or precluded.

In view of the dramatic failures of the international community in many crisis areas, what the WSP seeks to do is combine analysis with practical action in a growing number of countries – so far three in total – (as test-cases). The WSP's innovative methodological approach involves integrating different policies, promoting co-operation between different external and internal actors, and advising or influencing policy by pointing up solutions that could produce concrete results. Research and analysis are carried out at country level. Country test-cases are the focal point of the project. The WSP headquarters in Geneva consists of a co-ordinating unit and a high-grade advisory group. It organizes periodic consultations with donors and international actors. The action phase began in April 1995 with missions to selected test-areas.

Local institutional capacity for research and analysis geared to practical solutions is initially to be strengthened or created in three African countries (Eritrea, Mozambique and Somalia). In Eritrea, Africa's fifty-second state, the preconditions seem particularly favourable. In spring 1991, after a long struggle for independence, the Eritrean People's Liberation Front (EPLF) secured victory thanks to its reliance on its own resources. In Mozambique, a large-scale UN peace building operation began following the peace-agreement between FRELIMO and RENAMO. In May 1995 the WSP began investigations in Somalia, where fighting is still taking place in some areas.

In each of the countries, the task is to assemble a country-project group consisting of internal and external experts under the leadership of a director from the country concerned. By preference, the groups are housed (as in Eritrea) in existing local research institutions. Afghanistan may also be chosen as a project area, but not, unfortunately, Rwanda.[81] The project's mode of operation follows UNRISD standards and includes:

- an interdisciplinary and holistic approach to research
- participatory field-research
- development of research capacities in areas of conflict
- co-operation with institutions pursuing the same objectives.

What is innovative about the WSP project is its attempt to get all the affected parties involved in a process of reconstruction and to work out practicable solutions. It also seeks, via experimental comparison, to contribute to overall knowledge about the complex interrelations between peace building measures, reconstruction efforts in postwar situations and sustainable development.

3.4.5 The UNESCO Culture of Peace programme

Within the UN system, the United Nations Educational, Scientific, and Cultural Organization sees itself as a kind of brains trust and 'intellectual space'.[82] UNESCO's long-term Culture of Peace Programme aims to strengthen internal social order, both preventively and in postwar situations, by creating a field of interaction between all those involved. The culture of peace occupied a prominent position in the UNESCO plan for 1996–2001.[83] Projects are developed and implemented in collaboration with NGOs and other UN organizations. A special information system assists the exchange of ideas and experiences. UNESCO's department for human rights and peace is working to 'sensitize world opinion' to the ethnic phenomenon. However, this project is being slowed down by the consensus principle and by the care that is being taken not to offend certain states.[84]

UNESCO sees peace as a dynamic, evolving concept. Peace is far more than just the 'absence' of war or conflict; it embraces social justice and harmony, and the opportunity for each and every person to develop his or her abilities and put them to use in the development of society as a whole – or, in less ambitious terms: the right to a life of dignity and in conditions that make it worth living (UNESCO 1994: 4–5). The culture of peace is a process of confidence-building and co-operation between peoples and states. Its *leitmotiv* is 'dialogue rather than armed violence', fighting against hunger and for more social justice rather than waging war and destruction. The question it addresses is 'how can we escape from the legacy of a culture of war?' (Mohammed Sahnoun).

The unspoken goal is thus the creation of a socio-cultural and peace related environment which makes human rights violations by the state, and other forms of governmental criminality, impossible. Central to this is the development of a socio-political climate which – through the use, for example, of truth commissions such as those operating in South Africa, 1995–98, and for Rwanda – brings political crimes out into the open, arraigns them and (morally if not legally) condemns them.[85] Such a goal requires the creation of a field of interaction that provides security before the law, averts processes of escalation and silences the warmongers. Tribalism and narrow nationalist particularism must not be an option. Possible countermeasures in this regard include the tolerance towards minorities and those who think differently and a practically expressed respect for cultural otherness.

A UNESCO programme for El Salvador, comprising some 25 projects designed, among other things, to benefit the indigenous communities and the victims of war, was mooted in 1992 and became operative in 1994.[86] The country was subjected for decades to despotic regimes and the constant intervention of the military in political life. Five of the projects concerned are therefore aimed at promoting democratic structures and the structures of civil society. A central element is civic studies and the practical everyday application of a culture of peace. The changes in El Salvador, made possible in 1992 by the peace process and the various processes of normalization set in train by the Chapultepec agreement, resulted in the rebel FMLN becoming a political party, enabled the army to be cut back and restructured and led to the holding of free elections.

Reconciliation, a strengthening of the democratic process, the formation of an integrating (not national) identity,[87] the development of binding values that embrace the whole of society, economic and social stability, respect for human rights and security before the law and the promotion of education and training (including non-formal kinds), are the seven pillars on which a culture of peace may be constructed. The results from individual projects – for example, the training of individuals to promote methods and techniques of conflict resolution in El Salvador ('training for trainers') – are to be transferred to other programmes. National programmes in other states and continents have individual but similarly structured programmes that go beyond simple cultural engineering.

In Mozambique, special emphasis is being placed on bolstering the role of women as promoters of peace in rural areas. Training materials prepared by local NGOs with assistance from UNESCO refer to the role of old people and to traditional African methods of peace keeping. Artists and intellectuals are invited to participate. The Mozambican musicians' union organizes peace concerts all over the country. In Burundi, local development helpers are trained in conflict resolution techniques, so that they can work to counteract the eruption of further cataclysmic atrocities (such as those that occurred in Rwanda between April and July 1994) and to prevent destructive behaviour in the inter-ethnic domain.

Further pilot programmes were started by UNESCO in 1995 in the Congo, Cambodia, Guatemala and Nicaragua, and similar schemes were being discussed for Angola and the Horn of Africa (Ethiopia, Eritrea,

Somalia). Comparisons between the experiences in these countries were drawn; these could be particularly instructive for those countries that are in a period of reconstruction following many years of violent conflict. Human development programmes in these places are directed chiefly at refugees, expellees and those injured in war.

The demilitarization of public life and the promotion of actors from civil society ('empowerment of civil society') are prime preconditions for the progress of normalization in former war zones. In almost all the countries where projects are located, the preparation and conduct of multi-party elections, are major aspects of the consolidation of the still-fragile peace process. Great efforts must be made to re-establish authentic spiritual values and ensure the psychological stability of the war-ravaged population, with due account being taken of special local features.

Generally speaking, the elements that have the greatest exponential effects are: improved education and training – beginning with further teacher-training and the formation of trainers for adult education; literacy campaigns for demobilized soldiers; the creation of cultural centres; the organization of activities for young people; and the holding of courses for journalists and other media-producers.[88]

In the initial phase of the culture of peace programme (1994–95), UNESCO launched two or three pilot projects in various countries, working in concert with UN peace building operations and in consultation with other UN agencies and local NGOs. The aim of contact with actors from civil society is to secure a national consensus in favour of a culture of peace. Once problems have been identified, project proposals will be worked out in collaboration with local NGOs. The problem is that funds for the country programmes are to be raised from private and public sources outside the normal UNESCO budget. Most of the trainers will be trained on the ground, with the greatest emphasis on the training of local peace promoters. As far as the management of the programmes is concerned, the guiding notion will be the promotion of creativity and efficiency.[89] Special importance is attached to getting all the parties to the former conflict involved.

The continuation phase, from 1996–2001, attempted to extend the culture of peace programmes world-wide, in concert with various other UNESCO programmes.[90] The framework was a broad one: the ultimate aim of the promotion of a culture of peace is to see non-violent methods of conducting and settling conflicts established. The realization that peace and human rights are indivisible, and that they apply to each and every person, is a leading idea here. At the same time, the creation of a culture of peace is to be seen as a multi-dimensional task, which a broad-based participation by the population will help to expedite. A culture of peace helps to strengthen democratic processes; its realization requires the mobilization of all the resources of education, information and communication. New techniques of peaceful conflict resolution must be learned and implemented.

A culture of peace cannot be imposed from outside; it will only flourish in a process of sustainable, endogenous and just development that is centred on people.

3.5 Low chances for the peaceful settlement of protracted conflicts

In protracted conflicts negotiation or outside party (*third party*) mediation is generally very difficult and rarely successful. In an analysis of the (potential) *success* of on-going mediation efforts (in 22 per cent of 284 wars and crises in the period from 1945 to 1990) Bercovich *et al.* concluded with a negative assessment: the longer the duration of a conflict the lower are the chances of reaching any settlement.[91]

3.5.1 The difficulties of reacting in situations of ethnicization and exclusion

Since the efforts made in Yugoslavia and Nagorno-Karabakh, it has become clear that mediation by the UN and regional organizations in conflicts that have been ethnicized (mostly out of a desire to maintain power) is in danger of collapse. The endeavours of Tanzania, the OAU and the UN in the negotiations between the Habyarimana regime in Rwanda and the RPF guerrillas did, it is true, result in the signature of the Arusha agreements in August 1993. But these agreements were not implemented by the government. Despite the presence of 2500 UN troops on the ground in Rwanda (April 1994) this had very dramatic but unsurprising results. The power struggle between a regime which, throughout the months of negotiations, had also been laying plans for genocide, and an advancing rebel movement (whose victory came too late) was predictable. The genocide in Rwanda had been signalled long in advance and had been systematically prepared.[92]

Attempts at preventing, mitigating and mediating conflict have proved most difficult in the classic case of an ethno-national conflict in which state actors play a major role. This has to do with the causes, the mostly lengthy duration and the high number of victims in these types of conflicts. General and individual case-related knowledge about many untackled, complex, centuries-old conflicts of an ethnic or allegedly tribalist nature ('protracted conflicts') continues to be fragmentary.

3.5.2 No attempt at mediation in many intra-state conflicts

In some sub-forms of ethnic conflict, there has as yet been no mediation. Attempts at mediation by NGOs seem to promise some success in the case of inter-ethnic conflicts where there is no direct participation by state actors. This is a huge but sadly neglected area of activity. The reasons for the neglect of inter-ethnic conflict mediation lie in mediators' fixation on the state, the minimal public impact which such conflicts have in Western countries, and (as the mediators see it) the insufficient prestige to be won.[93]

In the case of most intra-state ethnic conflicts, there is *no* attempt at mediation. During the 46-year-old conflict in Burma, there has, despite a number of favourable opportunities, never been any attempt at mediation, either by the UN, the NAM (Non-Aligned Movement), or ASEAN.[94] In ethno-national conflicts, a military stalemate can go on for a long time without effect – which would seem to contradict the criterion of conflict ripeness (Zartman 1989).

The principle of self-determination is a focal point of the programmes of most insurgencies and ethnic resistance movements. The *multiplication of states* – a substantial growth of the number of independent states (currently nearly 200) – has already started to become a real scenario. Secessionist movements have contributed to many deadly conflicts, but secession has also brought the resolution of a few protracted conflicts, as in the cases of Bangladesh and Eritrea (the latter until warfare was resumed in March 1998). Rules, procedures and regimes for secession, federation and inter-ethnic power sharing need to be developed. These issues may soon be ranking high on the agenda of the United Nations and regional organizations such as OSCE, OAU, OAS and ASEAN. Resolving conflicts in Afghanistan, Somalia, Rwanda, or Bosnia required more comprehensive UN-interventions. Because of the Rwanda genocide and the total failure of the international community to intervene in time, prevention of violent conflict has been put on the agenda of national, supranational and multilateral actors. The talk is mainly about acute prevention and crisis management.

3.5.3   From reactive responses to proactive engagement

However, to prevent or even 'solve' conflicts is an awesome task. The targeted conflicts have, for the most part, already escalated and reached various stages of violence by the time they get the attention of the mass media and (with that) the political class in the West. This reactive approach is likely to overwhelm the capacities of conflict research and conflict management – and necessarily so. The acute prevention approach is bound to become just another failure. More constructive approaches have to be discussed. Most of the latest conceptions are still in a somewhat embryonic stage. The inherent danger is that integral approaches escape the short-term logic of policy makers or do not usually deal with headline conflicts. Their success seems immeasurable (in most cases a questionable perception).

Today there is much talk about crisis control and responding to crises. These are basically reactive responses. On the other hand there is not much talk about structural and proactive prevention. Examples of different forms of national self-administration from all parts of the world should be scrutinized and analysed. There is no mechanic link between conflict intensity and degree of ethnic heterogeneity in a given territory. In many regions of the world distinctly different ethnic groups have for centuries coexisted peacefully. In traditional societies ethnic heterogeneity and cultural diversity were not *per se* sufficient reasons to cause intergroup conflicts. External intervention or asymmetric relationships – and as a reaction to the politicization of ethnicity – brought disorder and violation of rules that often led to conflictive escalation. In the societal realm securing survival requires that the society produce its own mechanisms (of various scales) to effectively calm down, moderate, mitigate, regulate and solve intra-state conflicts. Here, many lessons could be learned.

4
Autonomy, Free Association and Self-governance

The different characteristics exhibited by different types of society have, correspondingly, different types of claims to autonomy or variants in regulatory mechanisms, ranging from cultural autonomy, through regional self-governance, to *de facto* sovereignty. Protection of ethnic and national minorities by means of autonomy arrangements (of all kinds) did not begun until the twentieth century. The challenge of ethno-nationalism and the so-called 'minorities problem', which had been sparked off by revolutions and by the regroupings that have occurred in the wake of the two world wars, began to grow more acute. The progressive nationalities policy, including the right to secession, that had been adopted by the Socialist International in London in 1896 and taken over by Lenin in 1914 ('On the Right of Nations to Self-determination') was applied only in a formalized way in the Soviet Union. At that time, the federal structure of the USSR, with what was initially four republics, contrasted with developments in Western Europe, which had led both to ethnically more unified or homogenized states. Following World War I the imperial multinational states, such as the Ottoman and Austro-Hungarian empires, collapsed and fragmented into a host of smaller states.

From the 1960s, it was the new, recently independent Third World states that became the main locus of conflict and also, increasingly, the main theatre of war in the struggle of nationalities for self-determination. In the 1970s, there were once again violent ethno-nationalist conflicts in Europe – in the Basque country (Euskadi, northwest Spain and southwest France), in Northern Ireland (part of the United Kingdom) and on Corsica (part of France). Towards the end of the 1980s violent ethno-national conflicts became again a sad reality in eastern Europe and Eurasia, first in the Southern Caucasus and later in Tajikistan, as well as in the fragmenting Yugoslavia (Serbian minorities in Slavonia and Krajina versus Croatia; Serbs, Croatians and Muslims fighting each other in multicultural Bosnia; Kosovars defying – until the late 1990s – non-violently the 1988–89 abrogation of their autonomy within Serbia). In the Soviet Union, the 'imperial overstretch' manifested itself ever more clearly from 1985 and dramatically from 1989–90.[1]

Because of the taboo attached to state integrity – that is to say, the inviolability of internationally recognized borders – and because of the acceptance of national sovereignty as a normative principle of international relations, the regulatory mechanisms that would appear to be the most realistic and promising are those that are pitched this side of the aspiration to independent statehood and sovereignty. For some categories of ethnic-cum-national conflicts, the remarks that follow here do not apply, since any realistic solution would entail the creation of a new state or (con-)federation of states. This is true for about 20 per cent of those conflicts that may be interpreted as having an ethnic basis.[2] Federalization, coupled with extensive autonomy rights, is often preferable to secession. To cite a recent example: in Yugoslavia, a confederation would have been much more effective in protecting the rights of the individual nationalities than would secession by part-states, given the rise in group nationalism that would have resulted from this, even under controlled conditions. But the violent follow-up conflicts that resulted from the break-up of Yugoslavia were foreseeable.[3] The same would apply to any further instances of secession in the former Yugoslavia, namely those areas where autonomy was revoked by the Serbian leadership in 1989 (Kosovo/a and Voyvodina) and this is probably why they did not take place. With escalating violence and foreign interference, tensions between the Serbian minority and the Albanian majority in Kosovo/a rose dramatically in 1998.[4] In the name of protecting endangered minorities and safeguarding of human rights, the second NATO war brought large-scale devastation to the region in 1999.[5] The Kosovo/a crisis contained some striking novelties and there seems to be a good measure of 'new anarchy' in the international system. NATO's selective support of ethno-nationalism and the right to self-determination for threatened non-dominant groups raised a number of far-reaching questions. Unintentionally, this might turn out to produce unexpected dilemmas for some of the involved states. The call for regimes for secession suddenly received a boost from an unprecedented case.

The right of peoples to self-determination is laid down in the United Nations Charter and the major texts of international public law (such as the two international pacts, mainly the ICCPR).[6] This basic right to self-determination is considered by some states as not necessarily calling into question the traditional state structure ('internal self-determination'). Emphasis is laid on requiring states (particularly Third World ones) to assume responsibility and jurisdiction ('accountability of states') and on creating procedures enabling national disputes and indigenous claims to self-determination to be brought before the International Court of Justice in The Hague.[7]

The Vienna Declaration, issued by the World Conference on Human Rights in June 1993, contains the first instrument of international law clearly proclaiming a (special) right to secession for peoples 'under colonial or other forms of alien domination or foreign occupation' – that is to say, a right of peoples 'to take any legitimate action ... to realize their inalienable right to self-determination' (article 2). Those states that violate the principle of equal rights and the right to self-determination and thus possess a government that does not '[represent] the whole people belonging to the territory without distinction of any kind' are explicitly excepted from the protection of territorial integrity that is a right of sovereign states.[8]

The right of peoples to self-determination is increasingly being interpreted by some representatives of indigenous peoples in the sense of a free association between indigenous nations and former settler-states.[9] This conflicts somewhat with the legal situation and with the unqualified adherence of most indigenous organizations to the right to self-determination, as repeatedly reaffirmed in such representative documents as the Preamble and 109 articles of the Kari-Oca Declaration of May 1992[10] and the various drafts of the Preamble and 45 articles of the Declaration on the Rights of Indigenous Peoples drawn up between 1987 and 1994 by UNWGIP.[11] Until the creation of a Permanent Forum for Indigenous Issues on 28 July 2000, UNWGIP served both as a forum for bringing complaints against repressive states and as an expert body within the framework of the UN Human Rights Commission. In the final draft of the mentioned declaration, the right to self-determination is clearly interpreted as the right to regulate one's own affairs.[12] However, the form of a covenant or convention would be preferable to that of a declaration; this would afford better safeguards for the activation or enforcement of the rights that are called for.[13]

In the near future, it seems impossible to return to anything below the legal norms and standards stipulated in Convention 169 of the ILO. Despite some worrying and confusing aspects, this convention represents to date the most detailed recognition in international law of the right of indigenous peoples. Any binding codification of the interests of individual indigenous and non-dominant nations would be best achieved via bilateral agreements between states and nations; but there has as yet been no clear precedent for such a course during this century.[14]

The terms 'autonomy' and 'self-determination' are generally used more in relation to voluntary or enforced concessions on the part of states than to the realization of some legitimate legal claim that has been granted binding international recognition. And there are other respects in which the concept of autonomy needs clarification.

4.1 The fundamental right to self-determination in relation to international law

In the case of the Latin American states that emerged after 1840, it was 140 years before any mention was made in their constitutions about distinct, indigenous peoples living within their territory.[15] Efforts have recently been made within the UN system – especially in the ILO and Human Rights Commission – to define the internal right to self-determination more precisely and to secure a revision of international law.

Up to now, the situation of human rights and international law – which, illogically, are often mentioned in the same breath – have been shaped by the following five parameters:

1. As the modern system of states established itself, sovereignty shifted from peoples to states, which meant that indigenous and non-dominant peoples lost their status as independent actors.[16]
2. As a result, the self-declared 'sovereign' state now constitutes the dominant form of political organization on the world scale and the 'highest' in terms of status.
3. Yet only very few new states of the twentieth century (in Africa and Asia) and the nineteenth century (in Latin America) are *nation*-states in the strictest sense (they are, rather, multi-ethnic in structure).
4. This means that the nature of existing communities of states, general international law, the UN Charter, the human rights declarations to be ratified by states, international pacts on civil rights, conventions, other international agreements and International Humanitarian Law (IHL) are an expression of the consensus of the states participating in them, or are dependent on their good will.
5. There are contradictions between human rights and international law; invoking the law of nations, particularly the principles of non-intervention and unrestricted sovereignty, tends to promote dictatorships and these trample on the human rights and minority rights of 'their' own citizens.

The law of nations talks of 'nations' not of states. World-wide there are thousands of nations but only 193 states. The number of nations is declining as a result of genocide and assimilation, whereas that of states is rising, chiefly as a result of the collapse of multinational states. Of the 193 states in existence, only a few are mono-national; most do not have an ethnically/nationally homogeneous population that regards itself as *one* people and *one* nation. In other words, most states are not *nation-states* but multi-ethnic/multinational, pluricultural states.

Yet aggressive claims by so-called nation-states *vis-à-vis* ethnically or nationally distinct groups (so-called 'minorities', which are sometimes actually majorities) and indigenous peoples are a highly dangerous source of conflict. Peoples' right to self-determination is a central item on the agendas of almost all rebel ethnic movements, who claim 'legitimate rights' and see international law and the *law of nations* as backing their case. In general, the demand for rights proves problematic where reference is made to:

(a) the right of divided peoples (nations or nationalities divided up into different states by arbitrary colonial borders) to be reunified
(b) the right of a nation or nationality to secede in order to form its own state
(c) the right of the population of an area that has been incorporated by a state through military annexation (type D, FSO conflict) or contractual cession (colonial agreements, mandated territories) to reject this absorption either by means of a plebiscite or, where necessary, by armed combat.

In international law, it is the sovereign right of states to exist that has dominated in most interpretations of cases (a) and (b) – in other words, there was no recognition of the right to reunification or secession as a form of the right to self-determination. However, the increase in the number of states after 1990 ultimately found expression in the Vienna Declaration of the World Conference on Human Rights (June 1993). The right to secession was recognized as legitimate in cases where the state against which the secession is directed treats minorities, indigenous or historical peoples on its territory unfairly, or discriminates against them in some other way. In case (c), the situation with regard to international law is disputed. In the end, what decides whether legitimate rights are realized is not an abstract claim to a right but the military strength of the respective liberation movements (such as the Eritrea Peoples Liberation Front) that have made it their aim to see that international law is enforced.

International law regulates rights, duties and relations between states. During the 1960s, anti-colonial liberation movements were also recognized by the United Nations as subject to international law. In actual fact, it is states and not peoples that are sovereign and equal. International law affords protection to states, not to their peoples. In other words, it is states that claim power of definition when it comes to determining what is meant by the principle of self-determination in international law. It is they who decide what a 'people' is and which communities may count as such. In political practice, the right to self-determination is not applied, because in most cases it is (allegedly) not connected with territoriality and because as a rule most 'peoples' are recognized not as peoples but as 'minorities'. The appropriate legal basis is then human rights and minority rights, which are generally individual rights.[17] In practical political terms, international law has now become a barrier to the extension of human rights and the rights of non-dominant social groups.[18]

The binding principles of state sovereignty and non-intervention remained resolutely in force *de jure* until a little while ago.[19] *De facto*, there was a series of direct interventions by the major powers.[20] It is true that equality and self-determination of peoples are recognized as rights in the UN Charter (articles 1, 2, 55) and have been embodied in numerous resolutions and pacts (notably the ICCPR, article 1), but they are regarded as general maxims, not as tenets of international law.[21]

Many experts believe that the right to self-determination is the 'opium of the people'; the community of states, they say, will always refuse to grant it in the form of a right to secession, purely out of a survival instinct. 'No one', they claim, is prepared to bear the 'anarchical consequences' of a systematic pursuit of it.[22] Praising the principle of *uti possidetis*,[23] that is the transformation of administrative borders into state borders (as was done from 1840 in Latin America, from 1948 in the colonies and from 1990 in the Eastern bloc, mainly in the USSR), as a 'prudent principle', seems odd. Whether the application of *uti possidetis* prevented endless conflicts, or whether it merely postponed conflicts, or actually caused their eruption (as in Croatia and Bosnia), it is not easy to judge. Postulating a right to secession on a limited scale as 'self-defence against extreme repression' (Fisch) is not sufficient and such resistance involves more than a few isolated cases.[24] Both the right to secession as a form of self-defence and the division into external and internal self-determination are themselves quite advanced ideas in international terms.[25]

International organizations – which consist of government representatives and experts from officially recognized states – often do not deny the right of peoples to self-determination directly, but point to the difficulty of identifying legally binding, tangible criteria for deciding whether a particular nationality can be a subject of the right of self-determination as defined in international law. In order to mitigate these difficulties, the right to self-identification should be defined and embodied in international law. It must be said, however, that this suggestion has little chance of being accepted.

Ethnic nationalities defined as minorities by states are recognized as legal subjects with a partial status in international law. The so-called 'minorities question' ought therefore to be resolved through mechanisms of minority protection, notably autonomy rights. These special rights should entail the replacement of existing state policies of assimilation, segregation and integration of non-dominant ethnic groups by a policy of guaranteed co-existence. The protection of national or ethnic minorities, based on the right of peoples to self-determination as proclaimed by the UN Charter, has not become accepted in international law and international politics. Up to now, the right to self-determination has been applied mainly in colonized areas and in federal substates.

However, the problem of internal colonization and the complex reality of primary ethnic affiliation and identity are being taken increasingly seriously. The explosive power of ethnicity in relation to foreign-dominated (centralized) states, as evinced in the Third World – and, after 1990, in the USSR – clearly demonstrates the need to refine and expand the right to self-determination.

4.2 The concept of autonomy and the minorities question in Europe

Autonomy rights have existed in different forms at different times and in very different societies. In Europe, such rights have been known since the Middle Ages (for the nobility, churches, cities, universities and so on; the two former categories have mostly been done away with, the latter have partly been preserved). The first agreements on minorities – in favour of religious minorities – were concluded within the framework of international law, at the Berlin Congress of 1878. World War I was conducted (from the Western point of view) with the purpose – so the justification goes – of liberating oppressed minorities and ethnic groups in Europe and in the Ottoman Empire. In the Treaty of Versailles, great stress was laid on the ethnic factor.[26] Revisionist claims made by Germany and Hungary from 1933 to the territories of 'their' minorities in other countries (especially Poland and Czechoslovakia) contributed to the outbreak of World War II, which itself signalled the 'final solution' for many minorities – in the form of genocide, flight, enforced resettlement and expulsion.

At the start of this century, the highly explosive minorities question was seen as relating exclusively to Europe and the Ottoman Empire (or Turkey); in the Third World it remained 'undiscovered' within the framework of international relations. The foci of the minorities issue in Europe were: European Jewry, Alsace-Lorraine, Schleswig-Holstein, Friesland (East, West and North Frisians), Upper Silesia and the Sudeten Germans, the Ukrainians in interwar Poland and the situation of numerous minorities in the context of Austro-Yugoslavian and Greco-Turkish relations. The 'solution' to this latter situation came in the 1923 Peace of Lausanne, in the form of a massive enforced exchange of religious and ethnic groups – a tragedy that continues even today to affect relations between the states concerned.[27]

What has been called 'ethnic cleansing' should not be confused with genocide. *Genocide* is a phenomenon known since ancient times; it means actions carried out by a state or ruler with the intent to systematically kill a particular community of people or social collectivity, resulting in destroying the targeted group in whole or in part.[28] After physical eradication (state-directed mass murder, 'democide', 'politicide' and genocide), the type of 'ethnic cleansing' called 'population transfer' is among the most brutal methods states use to eliminate the problem of non-dominant ethnic groups. It is a problem, which, besides being a constant source of ethnic, linguistic and religious discrimination and socio-economic disadvantage, serves as a pretext for external intervention and is responsible for the outbreak of wars.

4.2.1 The issues surrounding non-dominant ethnic groups

The League of Nations system gave priority treatment to the 'problem' of non-dominant ethnic groups, particularly so-called 'borderland minorities'. The Geneva Convention of May 1922 contained 100 or so articles on the protection of minorities.[29] Article 147 provided for a direct right of petition by such minorities to the European Congress of Nationalities in Geneva; and indeed, brisk use was made of this.[30] The congress was officially viewed as an international forum for the collective interests of non-dominant ethnic groups within the framework of the League of Nations – as the Working Group on Indigenous Populations is today, within the UN system. For ethnic groups to be admitted, three criteria applied in 1920: the desire for an independent cultural identity (that is, a distinct ethno-cultural identity); political organization; and the assent or non-opposition of the majority.[31]

The trend toward mono-lingualism or linguistic nationalization that emerged in most European countries after 1880 and to an even more pronounced degree after 1918, necessitated the legal recognition of one or more other languages as official languages.[32] More far-reaching forms of cultural autonomy, such as instruction in the mother tongue and the protection of cultural independence, were often regulated by law. The right to bilingualism (established in 1860) in most cases was far from entailing any kind of political participation or social integration (or non-discrimination).[33] In individual cases, decrees relating to language aggravated inter-ethnic mistrust and fostered negative stereotyping.

4.2.2 Creation of territories with limited autonomy after 1919

The practice of declaring the settlement areas of ethnic minorities official territorial entities with limited (territorial) autonomy began only at the start of this century and was usually prompted by wars. Examples include:

- Lenin's policy of *korenizatsiya* in the Caucasus and the rest of the USSR, adopted as of the 1917 revolution and implemented from 1919[34]
- the Ruthenians in Czechoslovakia in 1919
- the Swedish-occupied Åland islands in Finland in 1921[35]
- the establishment of South Tyrol as one of what is now a total of five autonomous regions in Italy from 1947
- home rule for the Faeroese in the Kingdom of Denmark from 1948
- regionalization and phased granting of autonomy to Basques, Catalonians, Andalusians and Galicians in post-Franco Spain.

In contrast, the safeguards for the Danes in the Federal Republic of Germany (in southern Schleswig, in the *Land* of Schleswig-Holstein) and the Sorbs in the then German Democratic Republic (incorporated into the regional constitutions of Saxony and Brandenburg after reunification) have no clear territorial components.[36] These safeguards contain, among other things, special regulations regarding voting rights, as well as provisions for cultural autonomy.[37] There are no such special conditions in force in the Federal Republic with regard to indigenous East Frisians, Sinti and Roma, Jews, or Poles (in the Ruhr) and especially not in regard to the new minorities.[38] Observers await with interest the outcome of a constitutional appeal lodged by the Sorbs against the destruction of what would be the 129th Sorbian village to suffer this fate. The municipality of Horno/Rogow joined up with ten other municipalities under threat and, with the support of the Sorbian umbrella-organization Domowina,[39] lodged a complaint with the constitutional court of Brandenburg against the coal-mining activities that had been decreed. This action is apparently unprecedented in German legal history.[40]

4.2.3 Non-discrimination, affirmative action and self-governance

In individual cases, the introduction of a number of broad-based classic measures of minority protection have led or contributed to ethno-national conflicts being defused, or in some cases, resolved. The range here extends from minimum non-discrimination against distinct nationalities (defined by states as minorities), through affirmative action (positive discrimination), to a gamut of solutions involving restricted and more extensive forms of self-governance. In principle, they already constitute elements such as might be found within the framework of more far-reaching policies on autonomy and nationalities.

However, major elements of, what should ideally be, pre-emptive, preventive conflict avoidance in Europe (in the function of prophylaxis and anticipative violence prevention) are often actually concessions, made in what is already a fraught situation of crisis in order to avert or contain conflict. Concessions to minorities have been made or demanded at various periods from 1878 to the present, most notably: in the interwar period, in the regulations for borderland minorities; after 1945, in the postwar order; in the 1980s, in autonomy regulations and proto-federal decentralization in Spain; from 1991 in the Russian Federation, in the expanded structures for autonomous territories; and, in a more intensive way, after the end of the cold war, within the framework of the C/OSCE process, with the appointment of a High Commissioner on National Minorities, agreed at Helsinki II in 1992.

The key elements of minority policies in Europe have been:

- recognition of one or more other languages as official languages or languages of communication in radio, television and print media
- instruction in the mother tongue and protection of cultural independence (cultural autonomy)
- political representation, special regulations on voting rights, safeguards such as guaranteed seats (for example, for minorities in scattered settlement areas) and proportional representation without thresholds in per cent of vote

- various forms of power-sharing 'models', consensus-based decision-making, or right of veto[41]
- creation of a special territorial entity or region with full or partial autonomy (territorial autonomy)
- limited, extended, or fully fledged self-governance.

In Europe, the codification of minority rights has usually occurred via constitutional change or legislation. In Anglo-Saxon colonies the rights of ethnically distinct peoples were recognized contractually.

4.3 Transfer of sovereignty rights via bilateral agreements

A major extension of the 'minorities problem' *per se* and the challenge posed by the rising ethno-nationalism has been reflected since the 1980s in demands made by indigenous and endangered peoples for full self-government. They want their own independent judicial administration and the power to decide over economic activities (natural resources, ownership of land). Many indigenous and endangered peoples refuse to be subject to external rule. Such demands are reminiscent of days when the first treaties were concluded between European colonial powers and indigenous peoples, initially respected as sovereign nations.

There are a host of historical examples of relevant treaties dating from the seventeenth to the nineteenth centuries from North America and New Zealand/Aotearoa. The period from 1700 was characterized by a spread of influence of the European powers abroad. This led, among other things, to the development of an extensive system of treaties, notably between the English and French crowns or their successors (mainly the United States) and large numbers of indigenous peoples. Historically, the treaty process was strongest in British settler colonies.[42] For the most part, these treaties were undermined or directly violated – usually after the military situation of the European settlers had improved.

Certain features of contractual law predetermine bilateral treaties as the form in which contemporary issues should be resolved between states and indigenous peoples:

- such a contractual policy would currently fall somewhere between minority law and nationality policy. As in minority law, such treaties generally favour relatively small populations. And as in nationality law, the populations are granted a specific form of self-governance within the framework of a state organization
- the contractual process is extremely bilateral, contains a strong internationalizing element and offers a relatively flexible framework for protected agreements

- but so far there are no contemporary models for protected agreements, only approximations. The 'modern treaties' between Canadian central government/the Quebec government with the Cree and Inuit should be viewed with caution.[43] The debate in Australia about the relationship between (central) government and the Aborigines and the self-governance now in operation in certain areas, were a good beginning.

Treaties of recent times raise a number of legal and political-cum-moral problems.[44] The 'money for land' model of the James Bay Agreement is reminiscent of earlier, nineteenth-century agreements. The package was the product of a bitter struggle waged by the Quebec Cree and Inuit against the building of the huge James Bay hydro-electrical complex on their land, which had been begun without the consent of the landowners. It was only when these owners brought a legal complaint that a negotiating process began between the three parties, placing the government under a certain 'pressure to act'. The Inuit and Cree obtained only about 1.3 per cent of the land they had demanded, but received quite high compensation (Can $225 million for 11,000 native inhabitants). In early 2002 the James Bay Cree signed a new treaty with Quebec.

In the 1992 progress report of his global study on treaties, agreements and other constructive arrangements between states and indigenous peoples, commissioned by the UN Human Rights Commission, Special Rapporteur Miguel Alfonso Martínez announced that he would be looking specifically at the validity of this agreement.[45] His lengthy final report (with some 322 paragraphs) was delayed several times (UNHCR Martínez 1999), and it met with some criticism over its narrow definition of indigenousness and providing insufficient attention to the situation in Asia and Africa.

4.4   Self-government: elements and evaluation criteria

In international law, autonomy is the contractually or legally established limited self-government of a territory that comes under the supreme territorial jurisdiction of a state (territorial autonomy). Autonomy was formerly regarded as being the prerogative of ethnic minorities. The home-rule arrangement created for the Faeroese as far back as 1948 has exemplary status here. Solutions involving fully developed structures of self-governance – such as were implemented early on in the USSR and the Faeroe Islands, or are now employed in Euskadi and Catalonia – exceed the bounds of classical minority protection. The following major instrumental elements are decisive in determining the quality of agreements on self-government for non-dominant nations/nationalities:[46]

- self-governance, with requisite legislative, executive and judicial bodies
- existence of a mixed judicial–political body to act as arbitrator

- control of the territory and natural resources by the nation/nationality bound by the treaty
- stipulation as to who has sovereignty over resources, how these are managed and how profits from them are to be shared between regional and central government[47]
- the autonomous government to have regional sovereignty over taxes: autonomous fiscal law, own revenue, own budget, own financial administration
- central government development in autonomous regions to take place only in consultation with the autonomous regional/local authorities (possibly right of veto)
- protection and promotion of all forms of expression of own culture via own communications channels (especially radio and press)
- fair representation in central government institutions (central parliament, ministries and so on).

Four out of the eight items mentioned relate to the economic basis of self-governance, in line with the motto 'No autonomy without economy'. The areas that affect the life of a nation/nationality most crucially are the land issue and the management of natural resources. Guiding evaluation criteria and principles generally applicable to self-government would be:

- no paternalism in decision-making processes, acknowledgement of a nation's responsibility for itself
- no imposition of foreign (Eurocentric) ways of thinking and concepts of state; respect for differently structured thinking, indigenous institutions and traditional procedures
- clear regulations, verifiability and control mechanisms, in order to preclude non-activity or obstruction by the parties to agreements.

The above-mentioned instrumental elements and evaluation criteria are intended to prevent centralized states from continuing to ensure unilateral power of decision for themselves in certain key areas. States should be persuaded, or forced, to share power of decision on a partnership basis. The number of instruments and elements of self-governance and the extent to which they have been realized, are indicative of the quality of agreements on self-government.[48]

4.5 Examples of self-governance among indigenous peoples in America

Any claim that autonomy arrangements and nationality policies that have been put into practice (or are due to be) in numerous different countries could serve as models must have a question-mark put to it. The degree to which individual models of autonomy are transferable is relatively restricted

and depends, primarily, on the particular region and the specific constellation of circumstances involved. 'Model status' in a broader sense has more
to do with recognition of multiplicity by the states and the use of the
method of open dialogue between states and nations/nationalities. Sharing
sovereignty would go further. The transfer of sovereignty rights in the form
of bilateral agreements – one of the best-protected forms of agreement,
legally speaking and one which is viable internationally – would indeed be a
'model process'.[49]

It remains to be seen whether the following examples can serve as models of self-governance for indigenous peoples elsewhere and whether they
can stand up to detailed scrutiny and comparison. Representatives of
indigenous movements and independent human rights organizations have
at any rate, described them as capable of these things.

One scheme with model status is the system of home rule created, as
early as 1948, for the Faeroes. Almost no one has heard of the Faeroese system of self-governance, and, although it has proved itself over a long
period, it has so far been overlooked in the debate about self-government.
The Faeroese model could be recommended for wider application in the
(post-)colonial territories of France, Britain, the Netherlands and the USA.
The better-known system of home rule in Greenland was first tried out in
the Faeroes.

The Faeroe Islands, which are part of the Kingdom of Denmark, obtained
an autonomy statute that covers everything except the legal system, finance,
defence and foreign policy. The 47,000 Faeroe Islanders are culturally independent and speak Faeroese, which is related to Norwegian. They possess all
the symbols of an independent state, such as their own flag, passport, stamps,
bank notes, a parliament that serves as a forum for the wranglings of seven
political parties and their own separate 'national' soccer team.

All five examples presented below involve special legal provisions for
populations, which are of a relatively small size (ranging from less than
50,000 up to 500,000) but which in some cases inhabit and husband large
stretches of land. Many of these territories are, in addition, of great strategic
importance to the economies of the respective states they belong to. The
reason is that these territories contain huge reserves of raw materials. This
applies to the first three examples – Greenland, northwest Canada and eastern Nicaragua – which have a further characteristic in common, namely
the multi-ethnic composition of their resource-rich, mostly indigenous
populations.

As may be demonstrated by the example of the Nicaraguan region
of Mosquitia, the ethnic composition of a population has a decisive influence on the political model that develops in each case.[50] Along with
eastern Nicaragua, Greenland represents the only model of indigenous self-
governance with a Western-style parliamentary system and a multi-party
set-up (in Greenland there are three parties, in Mosquitia more than a

dozen). One crucial feature in regard to the overall economic and political context of the examples presented here is the irrefutable fact that the indigenous peoples of Greenland and Canada are part of the wealthy First World, whereas the Indians of Latin America occupy some of the poorest and most marginalized rural areas of the Third World.

Issues of (collective) ownership of land by indigenous peoples and the related issue of who has power over natural resources, were the subject of political debate both within Greenland and Nicaragua and also externally, within the framework of the Inuit Circumpolar Conference (ICC) and the international Indian movement. (ICC promotes co-operation between Inuit peoples in four states.) In the case of Mosquitia, the land issue was one of the factors that directly contributed to the outbreak of war. It has been agreed that revenues from natural resources will be distributed equally in Greenland and 'in just proportion' in Nicaragua. In Greenland, a compromise was reached on the subject of underground mineral resources, which elsewhere is generally excluded from provisions – in other words, is subject to the sole power of disposal of the central government (as is the case, for example, with the goldmines in eastern Nicaragua). In Greenland, the independent Inuit government and the Danish authorities decide this issue jointly,[51] whereas in Mosquitia, the law merely provides for the conclusion of relevant agreements between central government and regional governments (without stipulating details). However, the Greenland model has existed for ten years longer and the legal provisions have been implemented in their entirety, whereas unclear or missing provisions in the case of Mosquitia have provided central government with opportunities for inaction and obstruction.

4.5.1 Home rule in Kalaallit Nunaat (Greenland)

Kalaallit Nunaat (as the Inuit call Greenland) is regarded both by North American Indian leaders and by the WCIP as a model for a constitutional-cum-legal solution (in the form of 'home rule') to the problem of autonomy for the indigenous peoples of America.[52] Home rule is interpreted as implying continued national (that is Danish) unity and excludes the option of a federation (of the Kingdom of Denmark).[53] But Greenland can only serve to a limited extent as a model for the two Americas – more so for North America and the Polar Circle, especially the northern territories of Canada, Alaska and northern Russia, which are inhabited almost exclusively by native peoples, Inuit and Indians (and native Siberians). The common features comprise: low population-density (*c.* 55,000 Greenlanders, of whom 45,000 are Inuit and 10,000 Danish; 14 per cent were born outside Greenland), welfare-state provision, mostly modern means of production and a common culture among the native inhabitants.[54] A complicating factor is a variety of restrictions stemming from the cold war (such as being cut-off from relatives in the USSR). The large numbers of military bases (Greenland itself has two US air bases) are proof of the almost unparalleled extent to which the Inuit settlement-areas were militarized during the cold war.

Greenland is part of the Kingdom of Denmark. Denmark has pursued a liberal policy of modernization in its 'provinces'.[55] The fishing industry and the concomitant urban development around the large fish-factories caused profound upheavals in traditional society. But Danes and Inuit never waged war against one another; home rule in Greenland is not a concession made by a state that felt itself under pressure.[56] The Inuit of Greenland were granted extensive home rule between 1979 and 1987. This took place via the successive transfer of areas of administrative competence to the Inuit and the mixed Inuit-Scandinavian population.[57] The transfer of a Scandinavian-style welfare state and of public enterprises in the fishing and fish- and shrimp-processing sectors involved many administrative competencies as well. Constitutional law, together with the legal system,[58] the health service, the finance and currency system and defence (the army), were excepted from the provisions. The educational system, in the authors' opinion, is no more than a copy of the Danish one.[59] Subsidies from the Danish state make up a large part of the government budget.[60] Self-determination also makes itself felt to some extent in foreign policy: following a referendum in 1982 (which took effect in 1985), Greenland withdrew from the EU (then EC), though it remains an associate.[61]

4.5.2   Canada: Indian policy and the Nunavut agreement

The new Canadian constitution brought with it undoubted advances, but the practical realization of these is still awaited. Since 1988–89, a hardening of position has been observable on the part of central government and some provincial administrations (for example, Quebec – see the harassment of Mohawks and their revolt at Oka in 1990). Such unfortunate developments have seriously damaged the reputation which Canada, with its liberal minorities policy, had rightly enjoyed in the 1980s.

Canada did not always pursue a 'liberal minorities policy'. In the 1960s its declared aim was the assimilation of indigenous peoples (as in the USA). At that time, parliament revoked all existing contractual rights. In 1969, the government declared special rights for indigenous peoples to be a form of 'discrimination', but was forced to agree to an investigation into indigenous land claims. In 1973 the Supreme Court (*Calder vs. Canada*) passed what, for that time, was a sensational ruling to the effect that the claim of the Nishga Indians to their forefathers' land was still valid and had not been rendered null and void by their subjection. The Calder case forced the government to adopt a new policy towards Indians and to respect treaties already concluded. Like the Mabo case in Australia in 1992, it triggered a whole series of land claims by indigenous groups.[62]

As of the 1990s, the focus is on control of the rich reserves of natural resources. Despite Canada's progressive policy toward Indians (compared with that of the USA), Indians are still divided into various categories (see 'Indigenous Peoples in Canada' in 4.5.1) and the state still has a say on the important issue of control over resources. Since the 1970s there has been a two-fold division into (1) specific claims, that is special claims that have to do with the revision or interpretation of previous agreements, including those with individual Indian peoples; and (2) comprehensive claims, that is claims relating to the traditional use of land and estates belonging to Indians who have not yet signed any agreements and were not removed from their land. With the exception of the 'modern treaties', the contractual process in Canada took place under the sovereignty of the British Crown. Up to now, the comprehensive claims have proved significantly more important for Indian policy as a whole. The first major case was that of the James Bay and Northern Quebec Agreement in 1975. The present-day agreements, concluded on a 'money for land' basis, do, however, raise a whole series of legal and political problems, to which I have already alluded.[63]

An example of the inconsistencies in the recognition of indigenous territories is the case of the Dene nation. The Dene reputedly became the largest landowner in America (according to the Canadian delegate to the 1989 UNWGIP session), but who, again, have no control over the reserves of raw materials on its territory.[64] One of the recent agreements concerns the 'land claim settlement' of the Gwich'in, who are part of the Dene Assembly of the Northwest Territory. The Gwich'in Dene obtained the title to 20,000 square-kilometers of land and the surface rights to a further 6000 square-kilometers; the amount of land involved is thus much less than in the Nunavut Agreement with the Inuit. The Gwich'in agreement – like the Nunavut Agreement – provides for a share in the royalties resulting from the exploitation of resources and for representation in mixed management bodies that oversee the estates and waters and lay down rules on hunting and nature conservation.[65]

Clearly under the influence of the Greenland scheme of self-governance, the Canadian government concluded, with the Inuit, what is probably the most detailed and extensive exploitation agreement ever made, covering their settlement areas in the Far North.[66] This did not happen in the form of a bilateral treaty, but as an agreement between the Tungavik (the Inuit of Nunavut) and the Ministry for Indian Affairs and Northern Development (MIAND, formerly DIAND). This 'Nunavut Agreement' is due to be fully implemented by 1999; it clearly represents the most detailed variant yet of self-governance for the thinly populated lands of the indigenous peoples of North America.[67] However, given the low legal status of the affected areas in regard to future development, international experts are sceptical, although they see no immediate danger.[68] Territoriality is inextricably bound up with self-determination – and vice versa; according to the late Howard Berman, this is the starting-point from which every agreement must be assessed.[69]

Within a huge area measuring 2.2 million square-kilometers, the agreement transfers a few restricted settlement zones (c.18 per cent of the total area) and any resources located there, as collective property to the 17,500 resident Inuit, on condition they renounce all claim to further rights of exploitation. It also regulates exploitation of most of the remaining areas (excluding any resources located there).[70] Inuit acceptance of the package was secured by means of, among other things, liberal helpings of cash. Over one hundred million dollars are due to be paid out over the next few years, with an additional share of the profits from the exploitation of resources.[71] The main weaknesses of the agreement are the low administrative-cum-legal status of the area and the lack of protection for it against possible mass migration (gold rush, oil finds), settlement and the outvoting of the Inuit on their own territory.[72]

4.5.3   Nicaragua: autonomy for the Caribbean regions

Nicaragua's scheme of regional autonomy for its two Caribbean areas (Región Autónoma Atlántico Norte: RAAN and Región Autónoma Atlántico Sur: RAAS) embraces almost 50 per cent of the national territory but only 9.5 per cent of the population. The two regions are multicultural in composition, comprising four indigenous communities, a somewhat largish African diaspora (mainly in RAAS) and a number of *Mestizos* who have immigrated to both regions. Autonomy in the two Caribbean regions is mentioned in the constitution and has existed on paper since September 1987 (law no. 28: Estatuto de la Autonomía de las Regiones de la Costa Atlántica de Nicaragua) and in concrete shape in a few pilot projects.[73] The provisions for territorial autonomy do mention the indigenous peoples' settlement areas but afford them no further legal protection, as indigenous territories, against *Mestizo* immigrants. In practice, the agricultural border is being constantly shifted eastwards as a result of immigration by impoverished *campesinos*; so far this has mostly occurred to the detriment of the Sumu Indians from Musawas and of the mining areas.[74] Land is the Indians' major resource (along with fishing). Conflicts over it have been going on for decades.[75] The following rights and guarantees set out in law no. 28 may be regarded as positive:

1. Confirmation of the multi-ethnic, pluricultural and multilingual character of the *costeños* (coastal inhabitants) and stipulation of non-discrimination against them (article 11.1). Particularly well developed are the cultural rights, such as bilingualism in education and administration,[76] and financial support, albeit modest, for indigenous and Afro-American cultures (articles 11.2, 11.8).
2. Recognition of the communal property of the indigenous communities (225 Miskitu villages, 32 Sumu and 4 Rama settlements), including the land, waters and forests which they 'traditionally work' (articles 9, 11.3, 11.6 and 36).[77]

3. Establishment of two autonomous regions independently administered by elected regional parliaments and executives appointed by these; the parliaments have jurisdiction over the territory (articles 6, 7 and 8). The division into two regions precludes dominance by one ethnic group (the *Mestizos*).
4. Institutionalization of a plural system of parliamentary democracy, but with elements of a presidential system, since not only a *junta executiva* but also a *coordinador* is elected, who, significantly, is called 'governor' by the population because he has wide-ranging powers; the executive oversees the work of the councils (articles 27 and 28), but without encroaching on the co-ordinator's powers (article 30).
5. The right to self-identification was laid down in law (article 12).
6. The system is based on a balancing and combination of demographic representation and the formal principle of equality *vis-à-vis* the six ethnic communities (termed *comunidades* in the law).

The obvious aim was to reduce inter-ethnic tensions and protect the rights of the small ethnic groups (Sumu, Rama and Garifuna) against the disproportionate influence of the Hispanic *Mestizos* and the Afro-American Creoles (in the RAAS) and the Miskitu Indians (in the RAAN). The division into municipalities is made according to ethnic criteria; there is positive discrimination in favour of smaller ethnic groups in the electoral domain. Every ethnic community must be represented by at least one member in the regional government (*junta executiva*); there are six *comunidades* in the RAAS and four in the RAAN.

Of major importance (though not stipulated in the law) is the fact that radio channels may broadcast in indigenous languages. The radio is either under the direct control of the Indian movement (Radio Miskut in Bilwi) or else is made active use of by it (Radio Caribe). Broadcasters are flexible enough to make spontaneous changes to their fixed weekly schedule to accommodate debates, scandals, or political events – as happened before the annual conference of YATAMA (the Indian organization Yapti Tasbaya Masrika) in 1993.

In the spring of 1990, in 1994 and in 1998 secret, democratic and plural elections to the regional councils (parliaments) took place (in addition to the general elections) in both autonomous regions. Although YATAMA and the pro-autonomy Sandinistas (Frente Sandinista de Liberación Nacional: FSLN) in north-east Nicaragua were approximately equally represented in 1990–94 and represented the great majority of the electors, the implementation of the autonomy law was hampered by political conflicts and conflicts of interests from 1990 onwards. This occurred despite the fact that the pro-autonomy forces still had four members in the central parliament in Managua who were vital to the survival of the centre-left government of Violeta Chamorro. The second light-wing president, Alemán, was elected with the support of the largest Indian faction, led by Steadman Fagoth Muller. The pro-autonomy forces thus no longer held the balance.

The political struggles between Sandinistas and the right parties in Managua are in a way continuing in eastern Nicaragua – and did so to an even more pronounced extent after the elections of 1994. But some conservatives in central government regard the autonomy arrangement as going too far and a small faction of Miskitu Indians saw the same law as not going far enough. In 1990–93, these two camps, curiously, came together, blocked the autonomy government in the northern region and fuelled the political trench-warfare between the left-wing Sandinistas and right-wing former opposition (Unión Nacional Opositora: UNO) in the southern region. One serious setback for the Indian movement was the dissension and infighting before the 1994 regional elections: only a minority of Miskitu canvassed under the banner of YATAMA; others stood on the Sandinista or conservative lists. Despite this, the elections brought no fundamental changes.

The Nicaraguan autonomy law is undoubtedly imperfect, but qualitatively speaking it is the best so far produced in Latin America;[78] how much influence it will have, however, depends on whether and to what extent it is ignored or dismantled by Managua. There are growing signs that this is indeed happening: clear regulations to preclude non-action or obstruction on the part of the government are lacking. The weak point lies in the area of regional council control over territory and resources: neither the respective competencies nor the share of revenues between regional and central government is clearly laid down.[79]

But the process of rectifying the legal weak points and obscurities has been dragged out. The same has been true of the regional fiscal sovereignty of the autonomous governments, which have no independent tax-powers and have only a limited income of their own. One cannot speak of an independent budget or financial administration. In sum: *No autonomía sin economía.*[80]

4.5.4   Panama: the Comarca system

Panama is regarded as progressive when it comes to recognition of certain Indian rights and the granting of cultural autonomy (though not bilingual instruction in schools). Currently, territorial self-governance exists only for the Kuna and Emberá Choco, but not for the more numerous Ngobe (Guaymí) Indians, whose area – due to be designated a *comarca* – has been overrun by large numbers of *Mestizo* settlers and banana companies.[81]

The best-known area is Kuna Yala, the 'land of the Kuna' (official name Comarca San Blas), with its reservation-style system of autonomy and self-governance for 45,000 Kuna Indians. They inhabit a territory extending from El Porvenir up to the Colombian border – where there are also Kuna Indians living – and include some 400 Caribbean coral islands.[82] In Kuna

Yala, too, penetration by *Mestizo* settlers, loggers and drug-dealers (from Colombia) is difficult to halt. The Kuna largely manage their own affairs. However, the school system is currently run monolingually (in Spanish).[83] Thanks to their being relatively sealed off from the outside world, their rigid socio-cultural community has survived and their subsistence system is intact. However, the economy is partly dependent on external factors and unequal bartering goes on.[84]

Native inhabitants have guaranteed representation in the Panamanian parliament; this applies to the Kuna and Ngobe (Guaymí). However, the *caciques/congreso* system of internal Indian organization has its shortcomings. Where necessary, it can be manipulated more easily by the authorities than can an elected representative body (such as those in Mosquitia or in Nicaragua); on the other hand, it keeps traditions alive.

In the case of the Emberá Indians' *comarca*, the official regulatory framework has built into it a provision instructing the state office for renewable resources (Dirección Nacional de Recursos Renovables – RENARE) to ensure the conservation and rational use of such resources 'jointly with' the Emberá community.[85] Such a provision is an invitation for state bodies to intervene. Significantly, there is no mention of such an arrangement in the older statute of the Kuna *comarca*.

In the case of the Ngobe (Guaymí) Indians, the authorities have dragged their feet over autonomy negotiations in a series of protracted conflicts over land and in tussles over the division of political-cum-administrative competencies.[86] Contributing factors have included, on the one hand, the size of the territory claimed, which extends over several provinces and, on the other, the disunity, poor organization and lack of militancy among the Ngobe.[87] The indigenous peoples are now beginning to respond to the government's 'divide and rule' policy and in 1992 the various Indian congresses in Panama came together to form a union.

4.5.5 Colombia: the *resguardo* system

The *resguardo* system in Colombia has its roots in the *encomienda* system of Spanish colonial times (which it began to replace from the sixteenth century). At the outset, it existed only in the Andean uplands (department of Cauca). An early form of self-governance was introduced in the form of the Indian *cabildos* as far back as 1537 and *cabildos* is still the name by which the bodies that run the *resguardos* are known. Some of these early *resguardos* survived the period of liberalism.[88] A *resguardo* is a piece of land that may not be sold and forms part of the permanent property of an Indian community. In addition, there are *territorios tradicionales* (title-less), *reservas indígenas* (state-owned) and *comunidades indígenas civiles*, on land belonging to white landowners. The *reservas indígenas* cannot be regarded as reservations in the North American sense – the history of these is, in any case, much more recent.[89]

Until the 1960s, the upland Indians led a precarious existence. Encouraged by guerrilla activities in Indian areas and by the official land reforms, they began to demand their land back from the large landowners. From 1970, the Indian movement began to organize itself, first as a peasant movement, in the form of the Asociación Nacional de Usarios Campesinos (ANUC) and then as an Indian movement, in the form of the Consejo Regional Indígena del Cauca (CRIC, later renamed the Movimiento de Autoridades Indígenas de Colombia: MAIC). The peasant-based ANUC tried to take over the CRIC but was unsuccessful. Both organizations, together with the Organización Nacional Indígena de Colombia (ONIC), founded in 1982, saw the struggle over land as part of the class war in Colombia.[90] The Paez Indians and later the Guambianos in the Andean Cauca region, proceeded to action as early as the mid-1970s, occupying land claimed by *hacienderos* (large estates of 'Spanish' – that is white – landowners and smaller estates of *Mestizo* landowners). As justification for their action, they cited their historical rights of ownership – in other words, they acted as Indians, not as *campesinos*. In 1980, together with indigenous peoples from all over Colombia, they founded MAIC/AIC[91] as a new organization representing the indigenous Indian movement.

In 1945, the Colombian Institute for Land Reform (Instituto Colombiano de la Reforma Agraria: INCORA) was forced to recognize the claims of the *cabildos*. Since then, 258 new *resguardos* have been created, in addition to the 67 existing colonial ones; 80 per cent of them (covering a total area of 25 million hectares) are located in the Amazonian rainforest region, where there were no *cabildos*. As in Panama, a measure of representation is reserved for the Indians in parliament; but this amounts to only two out of 100 senator's posts, or 2 per cent of the seats – much less than their proportion in the population, which is at least 7 per cent.[92] The rights of the indigenous peoples are mentioned in the constitution in more than 20 articles.[93] Only half a million Indians are identified as such by the state in Colombia. Officially, there are 81 ethnic groups speaking 64 languages from 14 families of languages.[94] MAIC, however, assumes a total of up to 5 million indigenous people.[95] The Colombian Indian movement is one of the oldest in the two Americas; it has become an important political force that can no longer be ignored.

4.6   Constructive structural elements for multi-ethnic states

The political sciences have made an exhaustive study of the question of how stability may be ensured in multi-ethnic states. The danger is that, because of the preoccupation with stability, it will mainly be implications such as solidity, permanence and, ultimately, immobility that will be evoked, with the result that paths to conflict resolution will be distorted. When it comes to resolving issues of nationality policy, what is needed, in total contrast, is great flexibility on the part of all those involved and creativity on the part of the decision-makers. The search is for constitutional solutions, protective mechanisms, and cultural and economic policies that can balance the interests of the individual ethnic groups and thus ensure the proper functioning of the whole. These solutions have to be of a consensual nature and all those affected must be involved in working them out.

The formal, interdependent principles and conditions which must – in ideal-typical terms – be observed when one is trying to create balanced constitutional and socio-political structures in multi-ethnic and multicultural states, can act as guides for innovative policies in the areas of legislation, internal political affairs, culture and the economy. It is assumed that almost all states have a multi-ethnic and multicultural character and that – with one or two rare exceptions – it is not possible to talk of a state as being ethno-politically or culturally neutral.[96] Indeed, one has to presuppose inherent difficulties with such neutrality and sectional interests on the part of the state classes.

4.6.1 Demands for cultural neutrality on the part of the state

For a state to be ethnically and culturally neutral runs counter to the whole European notion of the nation-state, as propagated all over the world in the colonial set-up. The state classes treated ethnicity as a 'political pathology' (Mazrui).[97] Integral to the nation-state model was both a resolve to standardize away ethnic identities and an overt cultural monopolism, often of a hybrid nature.[98] The ideology of the nation-state, the arbitrary colonial drawing of borders and the political constitutions of the new states hampered, or actually ran counter to, any harnessing of ethnic loyalties.

Given this situation, demands for ethnic-cultural neutrality on the part of the state, rather than the culturally monopolistic ideology of the nation-state system and demands for decentralization and federalization rather than political-administrative centralization, require nothing less than an ideological conversion. There has to be a turning-away – if not a turning-around – from certain dubious doctrines of European nationalism and of its successor and imitator, the developmental nationalism in the colonies of the Third World. Only in this way will it be possible to avert the development of destructive forms of top-down ethnicization and the third phase of nationalism – namely, ethno-nationalism.

The degree of 'neutrality' sought and the resolve to eliminate centralism, are crucial determinants of the state's ability to balance interests within society and to resolve ethno-national disputes. The further development of international norms and instruments that provide binding guarantees of equality of opportunity for ethnic groups will help reduce or eliminate the many diverse forms of disadvantage suffered by non-dominant groups. Formal principles of a kind that will avert conflict thus presuppose a civilized state that makes serious efforts to ensure ethno-political or cultural neutrality, that derives part of its legitimacy from this and whose political options are not subject to external constraint.[99] The number and diversity of the following 18 principles for averting conflict reflect the obvious fact that there is no simple cure-all:

1. federalization
2. national self-government based on solid economic foundations
3. internal self-determination
4. protection of minorities, with right of veto
5. equal access to central institutions
6. balanced ethnic representation
7. a state based on the rule of law
8. respect for human rights
9. non-violent resolution of conflicts
10. use of the consensus principle to limit the rights of the majority
11. cultural autonomy and respect for tradition
12. promotion of a democratic culture by means of participation
13. right to equal development
14. fair division of sovereignty over natural resources and land
15. social security and economic equality of opportunity
16. inter-sectoral linkage within civil society; multiple loyalties
17. unity through diversity
18. multiculturalism as a positive feature.

4.6.2 Democracy and human rights as universal values in permutations

The different principles must interact and be brought into relation with one another. Participation, human rights and civil society are parts of a democratic culture. When taken up by a mass movement, the ideals of democracy and human rights can shake authoritarian political structures to their foundations (USSR in 1985–1991, Burma in 1988, China in 1989 and Benin and Mali in 1990, and so on) and bring about their transformation. The demand for democratization, for example, cannot be equated with free elections between two or more parties. Even dictatorships occasionally conduct multi-party elections – only to ignore the results later on (as in Nigeria and Burma) or to resort to armed combat if they find them inconvenient (as in Angola). All the principles listed have to do with democracy and democratic culture. Only in combination with one another and only when linked with what lies ahead and what went before, do they produce the desired result.

Democracy and human rights are truly universal, behaviour-relevant values, which – in their different permutations – have their roots and history in societies and cultures on every continent.[100] The question is: what concept is being assumed? Is there unvarying universalism? Are individual human rights more important than collective ones? Is voting more important than being involved? Is Western representative democracy the ideal form for all societies? Are paid – or indeed bought – parliamentary representatives superior to elders' councils? Is the multi-party system ideal for all societies? Why should a two-party system (such as that in the USA) be better? Why should the majority decide everything?

The sign of a genuine federation is, precisely, that majority decisions are not the measure of all things and that dictatorship of the majority (by the 51 per cent) is prevented. The degree of decentralization and participation says more about the way a true democracy functions than does the number of ballots and parties. Democracy, so the Vienna Declaration of the UN Human Rights Conference (June, 1993), is based 'on the freely expressed will of the people to determine their own political, economic, social and cultural systems and their full participation in all aspects of their lives'.[101]

In their arrogance, writers like Fukuyama wax lyrical about Western liberal democracy as being 'the ultimate form of human government' and even about 'the end of history', rather than about an 'end-product of Western social and intellectual history'.[102] The opposite point of view sees parliamentary democracy as 'capital's extended board of directors' (Ziegler); it highlights what a fragile product of bourgeois society and globally oriented capitalism liberal democracy turns out to be in Third World conditions. At the periphery of the same global economic system, different rules apply. In certain circumstances, military dictatorships make better partners there for global players.[103]

4.6.3 Guiding principles for the creation of balanced constitutional and socio-political structures in multinational states

What is needed is an integrative and holistic viewpoint. In what follows here, the guiding principles, which – by linking forward and backward – can produce the desired result – namely, the creation of balanced constitutional and socio-political structures in multinational states – are described in detail.[104]

1. Federalization and regionalization on the basis of accepted or negotiable ethnic borders (otherwise federalist measures can foster the propensity to ethno-national conflict and encourage the collapse of the state).
2. National self-government for regions and self-governed districts for nationalities/nations with small populations, with a satisfactory, negotiable degree of autonomy for each segment[105] and a secured economic basis for self-regulation ('no autonomy without economy').
3. Abandonment of the option of secession and of (usually bloody) transition to independent statehood, in favour of internal self-determination in all ethnic–national or independent matters; this means an exercise of the right of all peoples to independent development and self-determination within the framework of existing states – assuming free association for individual nations/nationalities or peoples.

4. Constitutional protection for minorities,[106] including affirmative action in favour of nationalities previously neglected or oppressed; right of veto for the affected ethnic groups when changes are made to laws on minorities.

5. Access to central institutions for all ethnic groups; power sharing in mixed bodies and (proportionately) equal opportunities of participation in important decision-making processes.

6. The principle of balanced ethnic representation (for example according to proportion of the population) to be written into the electoral system and to apply to elected representatives in central institutions such as parliament, central government and also, preferably, important ministries (controlled polyarchy);[107] representation in the army and police and also in the secret services; smaller groups to be given guaranteed minimum representation in major institutions, such as the parliament, the administration and the legal system – preferably by the inclusion of relevant articles in the constitution.

7. Rule of law and certainty of the law to be ensured by strengthening democratic institutions; the executive's adherence to the law to be ensured by means of public control and institutional balance; control of state monopoly on force (penalties for arbitrary acts committed by the security forces); reliability and accountability help shape responsibility; formal criteria for democratic rule would not be adequate.[108]

8. Respect for, and institutionalization of, human rights based on practical values and norms corresponding to human needs; regard for the dialectic between rights and needs determines the degree of acceptance and respect accorded to human rights in a particular society; no monopoly on the shaping of binding human rights.[109]

9. Non-violent settlement of conflicts; reinforcement of all methods of peaceful dispute settlement, with involvement and supervision by civil society players; control of emotions; banning of ethnic and racist hate-campaigns.[110]

10. The rights of the majority (where these exist) to be limited by means of the principle of consensus and collective decision-making (negotiation and co-operation of ethnic élites in 'consociational democracies') within the framework of central institutions; or else properly regulated, issue-specific rights of veto for minorities.[111]

11. Cultural autonomy and respect for tradition through the preservation, promotion and development of traditional institutions; cultural autonomy via bilingualism; subsidiarity principle and consensus, based on traditional values.

12. Promotion of a peaceful democratic culture with broad-based participation; democratic behaviour, including peace and democracy education courses for the political élites and officials; civilization of relations through practice of mutual respect and cultural tolerance; development of a constructive conflict culture.

13. Right to equal development and to the satisfaction of basic human needs, with particular attention being paid to the most disadvantaged sectors of the overall population and to all national groups; the right to development is integral to basic human rights and fundamental freedoms.[112]
14. Fair division of sovereignty over natural resources and land; inalienable ownership of land by indigenous peoples and respect for the link between 'Mother Earth' and spirituality.
15. Social security and economic equality of opportunity (fair division of public resources, non-discrimination in the allocation of state posts and on the public employment-market) as social rights and also as guarantees against destructive ethno-populism and as a basis for inter-ethnic and intercultural coexistence; investment in social rather than military security.
16. Promotion of integrating intersectoral linkage within civil society; each individual should have multiple loyalties and frames of reference – as a member of a national community, a religious group, a professional group, clubs and associations, etc.
17. Unity through diversity; ensuring the identity of the whole by promoting individual identity (respect for ethnic identity) while not neglecting joint identity; fostering shared features rather than highlighting differences.
18. Multiculturalism as a positive feature, seen as a rich source of different forms of thought and expression, not as a regrettable lack of homogeneity.

4.6.4   Democracy requires favourable socio-cultural preconditions

Democracy and human rights do not flourish when they are (bilaterally) imposed from outside. Some of the states that formerly propagated colonial oppression, inequality and bondage must now face questions about their right to dictate to other states about democracy and about the legitimacy of their doing so. For democracy to develop, favourable socio-cultural and institutional preconditions are required. Grassroots democracy (as a kind of great palaver) and peaceful dispute settlement are important socio-cultural factors, which may very well be found in many societies of the Third World. What is missing, however, is the institutional preconditions at the state level and/or the political will on the part of the ruling class to share power and privileges. The resistance of regimes that block democratic reforms can often only be broken by a combination of internal and external forces. Democratic movements in repressive states should not be left to cope alone. Use should be made of the international community's existing sanctions options. Regional agreements and the further development of international standards can help to civilize authoritarian states.

Up to now, it is in the Nordic countries (Denmark, Sweden, Norway and Finland) that the above catalogue of ideal-typical proposals for developing balanced structures in multi-ethnic states and societies has been implemented most consistently. These countries have elaborated exemplary anticipatory, conflict-averting schemes for their ethnic-national minorities, indigenous peoples and migrant communities. Progressive minority policies (such as the Faeroese model) are based on solid foundations of political balance and social justice. The high level of political stability in these countries would be inconceivable without a highly developed welfare state.[113] However, as members of the circle of wealthy industrial nations, they have far less pressing problems to cope with than most states in the Third World, especially those in the Afro-Asian space.[114]

4.7 Federation, decentralization and self-governance

Measures for greater decentralization have proved themselves all over the world as an appropriate framework for the coexistence of distinct peoples. In the context of the state system, this means, for example, federal structures based on specific socio-cultural, linguistic, geographic, or ethno-political principles. Decentralization gives the part-states increased responsibility for their own affairs and it delegates administrative tasks to them.

Various large states such as the former USSR, China and India have applied similar methods of decentralization of tasks and of regional or local self-governance, with differing results. The state-based division of the Indian Union shows flexible, regionally adaptable responses to the aspirations of ethnic movements for autonomy and statehood within the framework of the union. The Punjab, Kashmir and the Naga are exceptions here. India can, despite one or two weaknesses, be described as a model that South and Southeast Asia, particularly Burma, would do well to imitate. The underlying principle is to create the greatest possible degree of ethno-linguistic homogeneity in the separate constituent states.[115]

In Africa too, larger multi-ethnic states – such as Nigeria, Tanzania and recently also Ethiopia and South Africa – have experimented with decentralizing, federalist, associative schemes. The new African states (like the Asian ones before them) had the disruptive factor of separatism to reckon with from the time of their creation by the colonial powers. The use of categories such as 'native' versus 'settler' and even the notion of minorities (where there are no majorities), has a very tenuous foundation in large parts of Africa.[116] There is an extraordinary diversity of ethnic components and relations.[117] With the exception of South Africa and the uplands of Zimbabwe and Namibia (and briefly also certain areas of Kenya, Uganda and Tanzania), most areas of Africa were not attractive to prospective settlers from outside. Until recently, racial segregation in South Africa was one of the greatest strains to which the continent was subjected. The perverted form of federalization represented by the now abolished Bantustans was the cause of many violent conflicts in the country.[118] Since 1948, internal colonialism is the major cause of armed conflict, not only in Africa, but in large parts of the world.[119]

In the multinational construct that is Europe, there are also many more peoples than there are states. Some major nationalities – for example, the Basques and the Catalonians in Spain and the Tyroleans in Italy – nowadays enjoy a state-like autonomy. And indigenous and other minorities in the Nordic states and Switzerland enjoy extensive rights. Swiss federalism, with its self-governance by cantons, is an expression of a policy of internal balance between different persuasions, cultures and regions. However, most nationalities in Europe have not yet secured their right to self-governance.

A 'Europe of the Regions', as a counter-model to the authoritarian-cum-centralist Europe of the present-day Union could, at some unspecified time in the future, help resolve acute minority and nationality problems in western and eastern Europe.

4.7.1 African examples: Tanzania, Nigeria and South Africa

In Africa, there has never been nationalism based on linguistic entities (Mazrui 1994). However, as in Asia, the starting problem is the colonial state structure and the phenomenon of internal colonialism. In 1884 the Europeans divided Africa up into 48 colonial possessions. Though the territorial jigsaw puzzle of the new states had been cobbled together in Europe, when decolonization of the first colonial possessions began, the new states and their regional organization (the Organization of African Unity: OAU) declared the borders of these possessions to be 'sacred' and non-negotiable.[120] Colonialism subsequently experienced a continuation, in, as it were, an internal form. Only a handful of states managed to introduce elements and priorities of their own into this process of nation-building and, at least in part, to put their own stamp on it.

One arrangement regarded as exemplary by most African countries is the Tanzanian confederation uniting Tanganyika and the islands of Zanzibar and Pemba (and comprising 70–120 ethnic groups). However, representatives of some minorities and a number of groups in Zanzibar do not consider the state set-up such a good model.[121] Until recently (2001), the existence of tensions and sometimes violent clashes point at unsolved problems. In Tanzania, no ethnic group has a majority or quasi-majority.[122] In March 1964, following the revolution in Zanzibar in the previous December, the islands entered a union with the mainland, under which the individual administrations and political systems were preserved. The Chama Cha Mapinduzi (CCM) party (party of revolution) saw itself as avant-garde during the 1960s and 1970s, striving to create a democratic-socialist system (*ujamaa*).[123] But it was unable to control the bureaucracy and brought about a weakening of existing organs of self-determination. As a result, participation became less attractive to the population (especially the peasants).

Tanzania sought to follow an independent path and was as such sometimes regarded as a model. The wide-spread adoption and promotion of Kiswahili as the national language of Tanzania and as a trans-ethnic, cross-border *lingua franca* is an important binding link in the multi-ethnic state.[124] At the same time, Swahili constitutes one of the politically important shared features of East Africa. However, the *ujamaa* ('community of interests') village co-operative movement was undermined by the bureaucracy and experienced a political and economic crisis during the 1980s. Although external factors (a drop in prices of raw materials, war with Idi Amin, drought) played a part in the economic decline, it was ultimately homegrown errors of judgement (wrong investment policy, badly planned industrialization at the expense of agriculture) that were the determining factor.[125] Lastly, the regions were granted few competencies within the framework of self-reliance. Given that the state structure was never to be brought into accord with the ethnic structure, there also is no basis for segmental autonomy.

A Zanzibari, Ali Hassan Mwinyi, succeeded the charismatic founding president, Mwalimu Julius K. Nyerere, in 1985. There continue to be forces in Zanzibar who are working towards separation; A. M. Babu, who represents Zanzibar in the Unrepresented Nations and Peoples Organization (UNPO), leads one. In 1992 it was decided to introduce a multi-party system. The Tanzanian constitution safeguards traditional and indigenous rights of use and the right to a 'decent' life;[126] every individual has a right to land. However, pastoral peoples such as the Maasai are fighting for the return of their land-use rights and against encroachment by settlers.[127]

Mention must also be made here – though with some reservations – of the Federal Republic of Nigeria, particularly the reconciliation achieved after the Biafra war and the administrative division into 30 constituent states. However, the annulment of the 1993 presidential elections (when Moshood Abiola, a Yoruba, emerged as the 'wrong' winner) once again demonstrated the continued destructive role of the military and the dominance of the Muslim Hausa-Fulani groups of the north (24 per cent of the total population) in the army and state apparatus.[128] As in Tanzania and many other African states, there is no clear ethnic majority – minority situation in Nigeria. The second largest ethnic group after the Hausa-Fulani is that of the Yoruba (21 per cent), followed by the Ibo (12 per cent) in the east, who sought to break away to form Biafra. There are 430 minority language groups concentrated in the oil-rich south-eastern coastal area and Niger delta (15 per cent), in the northeast and southwest (7 per cent each), and in the Benue area (21 per cent).[129]

Originally in order to break the power of the north, a federal structure was introduced. This was expanded to 12 states in 1966, 19 in 1975 and finally 30 states, under the reformist army officers Mohammed and Obasanjo. Under these states are 589 local administrations. In 1983 (after the failure of a corrupt civilian government), the military, who had grown accustomed to enjoying the sinecures of power from 1966 to 1979, carried out another coup and have not relinquished power since (which means there has been at least 25 years of military rule). Although Abiola's struggle against the military had multi-ethnic support, it was depicted in the international media as a purely Yoruba affair and as confined to western Nigeria. The strike staged in 1994 by the oil-workers in the south and by other sectors, in support of the democratization in Nigeria – the first of its kind in postcolonial African history – was scarcely heeded in the West.[130] Writers risk their lives if they speak up for democracy in their homeland: in October 1995, Ken Saro-Wiwa and his fellow campaigners from the Ogoni people were executed. Africa's most famous writer and winner of the Nobel Prize, Wole Soyinka, had to live in exile and was ambassador for the provisional government of the National Democratic Coalition (NADECO), the largest-ever opposition alliance in Nigeria.[131]

In many Third World countries, the holding of elections involving more than one party is no sure sign of democracy – as is demonstrated by developments in Africa following the cold war. Africa's most populous state, Nigeria, probably offered the clearest illustration of this. The local elections held there in March 1996 were merely a ploy by the weakened military regime. Moshood Abiola, the victor of the elections of June 1993, meanwhile, remained imprisoned until his death and opponents were murdered or executed. The sudden death of dictator Sani Abacha brought an unexpected turn in Nigeria's postcolonial history. At the end of 1998, under strong international pressure, a democratic opening-up occurred; but the ultimate test of this is yet to come – after the military had to relinquish power and the winner of the national elections, Olusegun Obasanjo, was sworn in as Nigeria's new president in May 1999.

Since the 1970s, the oil and gas economies and the fluctuation in prices on the world markets largely determined the framework conditions for economic development and the state distribution of resources. If wrangling over distribution grows more acute, the dichotomy between north and south and the opposition between central government and the federal states, may well grow worse. One dangerous scenario would be continued stagnation under military rule. A deepening of the existing antagonisms between the three ethno-political centres of gravity, in the north (Hausa-Fulani), west (Yoruba) and east (Ibo) – within the framework of a badly balanced federal structure – could lead to new prosecession or anti-regime conflicts. The appointment of a sovereign national conference of all the relevant ethnic, social and political groups (as in Benin in 1991–92) would be a first step out of the deadlocked situation. The stepping-down of the military (but their involvement in the national conference as one of the professional groups) and a genuine federalization of Nigeria would seem to be the only way out of the situation of permanent crisis in which Africa's most densely populated country finds itself.[132]

In apartheid South Africa, a number of ethnically/racially based Bantustans were created as an instrument of white power-retention. After centuries of disregard of ethnic languages, the new South Africa has recognized 11 official languages. The enforced schooling of millions of black children in Afrikaans (a Dutch dialect) is over. Up to now, nationalism based on linguistically defined groups has not been very pronounced in Africa (unlike in India). But what South Africa did experience was various forms of so-called tribal nationalism fuelled to the utmost by the apartheid regime. In most regions of Africa, tribalism was a colonial chimera and a useful construct for controlling rebellious colonies. In contrast to the situation in many cattle-breeding communities, tribal structures in most farming societies in Africa had long since disappeared. Violent Zulu nationalism, generated as a means of weakening the multi-ethnic African National Congress (ANC), is one of the burdens of the past, which the new South Africa must bear.[133]

4.7.2   Ethiopia: ethnicization, decentralization and war

The collapse of military socialism in Ethiopia and the overthrow of the Mengistu regime by the allied rebel forces EPLF, EPRDF and OLF led for the first time in Africa to a reorganization along ethnonational lines and to successful secession by the 'province' of Eritrea. In the case of Ethiopia, it remains to be seen how far the newly initiated policy of balance between the 'nations, nationalities and peoples of Ethiopia' (as it says in the Ethiopian Charter of 1991) will succeed. Hopes that the right for 'self-determination' would be implemented were raised by Ethiopia's swift recognition of Eritrea's *de facto* independence but the proclaimed rights were in practice immediately curtailed. Hopes for change among the Oromo majority group were shattered already after one year of relative freedom. Warfare resumed in the south, and, from spring 1998 until mid 2000, also in the north, between Ethiopia and Eritrea. Subsequently, spillover effects threaten to affect the entire Horn of Africa.

The 'New Ethiopia' could have become a model for other multi-ethnically structured states in Africa. Ethiopia (minus Eritrea) was seeking to institute national, regional and local self-governance for its hundred or so 'nations, nationalities and peoples' with elected bodies and fair representation in central government – in other words, a model somewhere between a federal state and a confederation. After the demise of the Mengistu regime in May 1991, the country has been divided into 12 regions, five of which are mononational, the rest pluri-national (designed for larger and smaller ethnic groups). The language of the relevant titular peoples has been made the official language. However, at least since the regional elections of June 1992 the weaknesses of the Ethiopian experiment have begun to show up in practice. The elections were manipulated by the EPRDF coalition, the Ethiopian Peoples Revolutionary Democratic Front, dominated by the small Tigrai or

Tigrawai ethnic group. The opposition – notably the third largest of the victorious guerrilla movements, the Oromo Liberation Front (OLF) – boycotted the exercise after its cadres were harassed and imprisoned. The EPRDF has unilaterally declared its guerrilla force to be the country's regular army.

From summer 1992 a despotic Abyssinian minority regime began once again to take shape. The second-largest minority after the 15 per cent Amhara minority is the Tigrai, whose number, following Eritrea's scission, now stands at only 6 per cent. The Cushitic majority, comprising the Oromo, Somali and Afar, plus over a hundred other ethnic groups (Cushitic, Lacustrine, Omotic and Nilotic), continues to be excluded from power.[134] The general election, postponed until 1995, did little to change this, since all autonomous political movements were banned or remained excluded from any kind of participation. The war restarted in Oromia (OLF) and in the East (OLF, IFLO and ONL). The recourse to old methods of Abyssinian rule ruined the chances of peaceful dispute settlement with the Oromo majority and the peoples in revolt on the margins of the kingdom. The Abyssinians and their new leaders (Issayas Afeworki and Meles Zanawi) even started fighting among themselves again. An all-out war between Ethiopia and Eritrea developed increasing intensity since March 1998. The original issue was a piece of dry territory both sides claimed which spilt-over into southern Somalia during 1999, with Eritrea supporting rebel forces against Ethiopia and Ethiopian forces repeatedly intervening in stateless southern Somalia.

4.7.3   The 'special case' of the Swiss confederation

The 'special case' of multinational Switzerland, at the heart of Europe, officially declared to be a *Wilensnation* ('nation founded on the will of the people'), is an example of almost mulish insistence on self-determination on the part of an ethno-linguistic majority, even at the price of economic disadvantage and political decoupling from the rest of the world.[135] At the end of 1992, association with the rest of what was then the European Community (EC), within the framework of the then European Free Trade Area (EFTA) to be transformed to the European Economic Area (EEA, a prelude to the European Union), was rejected. During the past years, the Swiss electorate has also defeated a proposal to join in international peace-keeping operations (membership in the United Nations was rejected earlier) and scrapped a proposal for free transit for foreign trucks across the Alps. Switzerland's non-EU-compatible transport policy was accentuated even more with the acceptance of the 'Alps initiative'. The consequences of this aloofness are slowly being felt by the Swiss: for the first time since the economic crisis of the 1930s, joblessness in the land of 'social harmony and near-full employment' has risen to alarming levels.

The national minorities in French-speaking Romandie and Italian-speaking Ticino have declared themselves clearly in favour of Europe but were silenced by the majority among the German-speaking Swiss.[136] The continuing economic crisis is having particularly serious effects in the French-speaking area and the *Röstigraben* between Alemanics and Romanics has grown deeper; *Röstigraben* signifies the linguistic or ethnic borderline, jokingly defined in terms of the German liking for and French dislike of, *Rösti* – thinly sliced fried potatoes. Even trivial events saw emotions rocketing.[137] The prophecies of doom have been growing ever more dramatic. A German magazine considered that, as 'a state based on harmony between the different language-groups and therefore also as a model', the Alpine republic had failed; and it went on to ask 'Is there not a danger that the Confederation itself will fall apart?'[138]

The French-speakers have been outvoted half a dozen times since the EEA rejection in 1992 – but this had also happened previously. Anyone analysing the results of elections and ballots in Switzerland will conclude that the split between progressive electors, who are more open to the rest of the world and to new ideas and the conservatives does not run exactly along the dividing-line between the major ethnic groups, but is prolonged into German-speaking Switzerland. Urban Switzerland very often votes in the same way – on both sides of the *Röstigraben*. The large cities of German-speaking Switzerland (Zurich, Basle, Berne and some industrial cities in the central area) are to be found on the losing side in most ballots, alongside the French-speaking area.[139] It is simply the fact that Switzerland is not so much democratic as federalist – in other words, when there are ballots, the notorious no-voters from the rural regions always triumph, despite a majority yes vote.

Ballots fail because of the in-built cantonal majority: tiny cantons such as Appenzell, Uri, Schwyz, Unterwalden, or Zug, which have fewer than 10,000 voters, have as much voting power as large cantons (like Berne or Zurich) with a million or more inhabitants. For instance, a citizen of Appenzell has the voting power of 50 citizens of the state of Zurich. At the level of parliament, with its two-chamber system, the small 'reactionary' *Ständerat* (upper chamber), which is composed of two representatives from each canton, regularly blocks the large *Nationalrat* (lower chamber), which is elected in proportion to the population. To ask whether this form of *Kantönligeist* ('cosy canton spirit') is still suited to the times is to assail the foundations of institutionalized conservatism. Another abuse of federalism occurs in the creation of cantonal tax havens for the super-rich.[140] The case of Marc Rich showed the depths to which this kind of policy can sink.[141] The system continues at the local level where communes have sovereignty over taxes. The result is 'economic apartheid'.[142]

The full might of the Swiss financial marketplace, large-scale global enterprises and the *Kantönligeist* – these all exist side by side, in perverse combination.[143] Tax fraud, economic crime and money laundering have international implications.[144] Every attempt to rectify the system of private wealth and public poverty – for example by doing away with bank confidentiality or introducing a 'wealth tax' – has failed. The Swiss oligarchy, the 'invisible government', has (says Ziegler) 'colonized' the indigenous political class and lulled the population into quietude. Because of excessive influence exerted by the notorious 'thumbs-downers', Switzerland has slowly developed into a model of political immobility.[145]

The political crisis now risks developing into a national crisis for the Alpine realm and it may be less easy to overcome than its economic counterpart. Now that cracks have developed in Switzerland's self-imposed isolation, the power élite at home could further aggravate the problem of acceptance for a policy of opening-up to the outside world. In their unthinking 'stampede' to get things done, the élites became desperate. They seem ready to sacrifice a 'sacred value' and one of the few things that bind the multi-ethnic federation together – apart from William Tell, the *Rütlischwur* (the mythical swearing of the oath at the formation of Switzerland, said to have taken place at Rütli) and the Red Cross: that value is Switzerland's allegedly now meaningless neutrality.

But the overwhelming majority of Swiss people believe that the policy of neutrality continues to be indispensable. In contrast to the imposed neutrality of Austria, that of Switzerland is not a product of the cold war; it is an expression of the Swiss policy of internal balance between Catholics and Protestants, between the *cantons*, and between the ethno-cultural regions of the confederation. Neutrality is nothing less then the essence of the 400-year-old 'special path' of successful self-assertion by the small Helvetian state.[146] All the same, the country does lie wedged between some of the most bellicose nations that history has seen, the process of civilization of which many Swiss people consider is not yet complete. In principle, the question of whether neutrality is compatible with EU membership will not pose itself so long as there is no European system of collective defence, which would necessitate the abandonment of a nowadays allegedly obsolete neutrality.[147]

One possible role for Switzerland within the European framework would be, among other things, to work for the realization of a decentralized, federal structure as a way of satisfying 'the vital interests of smaller communities' (Flavio Cotti).[148] In a changed Europe, neutrality, 'good offices' and direct democracy are political specializations for which the future European Union will have a need.[149] The search for appropriate, democratically legitimated European institutions and mechanisms could, for example, lead to the generalized application of direct democratic referendums (such as Switzerland practices). In September 1995, despite the resistance of the ruling party, Bavarian voters endorsed a bill introducing direct-democratic participation at local-authority level.[150]

4.8   Europe of the regions versus EU super-state?

A Europe of the Regions, which up to now has been regarded as a utopian counter-model to the authoritarian-cum-centralist Europe of the 'Eurocrats', could, at some point in the future, contribute to the solution of acute ethno-national problems in Western Europe (as in the Basque Country, in Northern Ireland, in Corsica and so on). Since the Danish 'No' to Maastricht I and the rejection of membership by the Norwegians, EC and later EU integration has ceased to be a self-propelling process. In Sweden, those opposed to the EU were victorious in the elections of September 1995; they may again call for Sweden to leave the Union. In other Western European countries too, stress is (increasingly) being laid on national self-determination and regional particularities. Like a ritual, Euro-politicians keep repeating in vain the need to create an effective 'Common Foreign and Security Policy' (CFSP) of the Union.

There is a 'fourth level' – in addition to Union leadership (Commission), member-state governments (Council of Ministers) and parliament (European Parliament) – that is not provided for in the treaty of Maastricht I, which came into force in November 1993. No form of democratically legitimated, institutionalized share in decision-making was created for the regions. The only thing envisaged is a consultative committee for regional and other area authorities.[151] Collective rights of minorities and other groups continue to be acknowledged only – if at all – at the individual state level, not at the Union level. Furthermore, regions and minorities continue to have no right to bring actions before the European Court in cases where the 'Eurocrats' – the Council of Ministers and the Commission – violate the principle of subsidiarity.

The second Maastricht summit, in 1996, was prepared by a 'reflection group' representing the 15 EU states. Maastricht I already envisaged the transfer of sovereignty 'upwards', the clearest example being the currency union, due to be fully implemented in the year 2002.[152] Maastricht II was meant to introduce joint policy on issues of internal security, defence and foreign relations. The first of these relates to the reinforcement of 'fortress Europe' against waves of migrants and refugees and to the creation of a European police force – Europol – to fight terrorism and organized crime. Organized militant racism, which became increasingly a serious concern in many EU states, must be added to the list.

4.8.1   The legitimacy deficit of the European Union

As a rule, states consider abandoning a foreign policy of their own more threatening to their national sovereignty than relinquishing economic self-determination, which in any case has long since been called into question by globalization and the world financial markets. A 'Common Foreign and Security Policy' is still a long way off. Individual big-power areas of operation, established by former colonial powers, are seriously disrupting the process of European union and the development towards the formation of a Western European great power.[153] Within the framework of the EU, many aspects of national identities are artificial hybrids and have much more to do with the political arrogance and military or economic striving-after-power of the ruling classes than with the independent cultural and linguistic identity of the peoples.

Although the European Parliament is far from being a rubberstamp parliament, in the eyes of most Europeans it gained status only in 1999, with the dismissal of the entire European Commission (all 20 commissioners, including the president), following an outrageous corruption scandal involving several commissioners. In May the Parliament voted (392 to 72 with 41 abstentions) for Romano Prodi as President of a new Commission. Prodi's first task was to put together a new Commission. However, democracy deficits prevail. The Parliament and the Council have to settle some outstanding differences over the statute.

Maastricht II was supposed to bring about a reform of the EU bodies and of the mechanisms of co-operation between them. The excessive influence of two democratically non-legitimated bodies – the Commission and the Council of Ministers – is to be curtailed. The treaty aimed to bring about increased transparency and foster citizens' acceptance of EU institutions, which are currently somewhat removed from reality. The strengthening of parliamentary aspects has been called for is part of a comprehensive democratization of the justifiably disquieting European super-state. In order to increase democratic control, thought should be given to the creation of a second chamber of the regions alongside a European Parliament with enhanced status.

By way of a feeble compromise, a Committee of the Regions, under the chairmanship of Jacques Blanc, was set up within the European Parliament, as a first step toward an acceptable form of democratically legitimized representation for the European regions. Demands for further institutional rights are to be pressed within the framework of conferences after Nice 2000, where EU enlargement and rules for future decision making had top priority. The most important of these demands are: recognition of a 'Parliament of the Regions' as an independent body, the reinforcement of legislative powers, more parliamentary independence *vis-à-vis* the Economic and Social Committees, the formal reaffirmation of the principle of subsidiarity and clear demarcation of competencies within EU structures.[154]

Regional representatives could become direct 'contacts' for people, if the regions were incorporated into the structure of the state-fixated EU. The call for stronger integration of the regions finds little favour with most of the governments of the 15 EU states. As is natural, it is primarily the states with strong regions, such as Germany, Spain and possibly Italy, who are most supportive of the project; opposition to it comes from extremely centralist France and Greece. There was previously also opposition from Britain, whose conservative government feared increased separatism on the part of Scotland. With the government of 'New Labour', there has been a shift back onto the European track, not only on the question of regional autonomy – which has been partially solved by the devolution process – but overall.

A parliament of the regions, in which not only the geographic regions of Europe, but also its historic nations, nationalities and ethnic minorities are represented on an equal footing, would create a 'directness' that is currently lacking. The demand for representation as peoples could be satisfied in a more regular and more concrete way, which may generate a sense of belonging to Europe. This would also affect minority groups, whose affiliation and representation at national level is often not assured. The number of these kinds of European minorities is considerable and their population figures range from a few thousand to several million.

4.8.2   Recognizing diversity in multicultural Europe

In the multinational construct that is Europe, there are many more peoples than there are states. In some Western European states – notably Spain and Britain – the populations of some minority nationalities or non-dominant nations far exceed those of some small states such as the Vatican State, Liechtenstein and Luxembourg and equal those of medium-sized states such as Denmark, Switzerland, Belgium and Austria. The Tables 4.1 and 4.2 give an overview of official minorities and other ethnic groups in Europe.[155]

In some potential EU member states in eastern and southeastern Europe, the proportions of minority nationalities are even higher. In extreme cases (such as in the Baltic states and Turkey), they rise to one third or one half of the total population.[156] Yet the participatory rights of these national minorities are rudimentary. In some cases, discrimination against them is institutionalized and systematic. Only a few larger nations which do not

Table 4.1   Official minorities and other ethnic groups: a west European overview

State	Historical nations, nationalities, minorities	Population (millions)	% of total
Spain	Catalans (16%), Galicians (8%), Basques (2%), *Gitanos*/Roma (2%)	12–13	29
Britain	Welsh, Scots, Northern Irish, Corney gypsies, Manx. Migrants: Indians and Pakistani (2%), Caribs	10	17
Germany	Turks (2.2%), Kurds, Yugoslavs (1%), Italians (1%), Danes, Sorbs, Roma & Sinti, Friesians, others	8	10
France	Bretons (4%), Arabs (3%), Alsatians & Lorrainers (2%), Basques, Catalans, Corsicans, Flemings, others	4	7
Italy	Sardinians, Friulians, South Tyroleans, Ladins, Catalans, Provençals, Slovenians, Croatians, Albanians, Greeks, Roma	3.5	6

Source: ECOR © 1999

Table 4.2 Minority nationalities in potential EU member states of eastern and southeast Europe

State	Historical nations, nationalities, minorities	Population (millions)	% of total
Latvia	Russians (42%), Belorussians, Ukrainians, Poles and others	1.2–1.4	48
Turkey	Kurds (>15%), Arabs (2%), Roma (1%), Circassians, Armenians, Assyrians, Greeks, Turkomans, Jews, Bulgars, Georgians, Laz and others	13–19.5	25–30
Croatia (1993)	Serbs (15%), Roma (3.7%), Slovaks, Italians, Germans, Chechens, Ukrainians, Ruthenians and others	1–1.2	25
Romania	Roma (8–10%), Hungarians (7.5%), Ukrainians, Serbs, Bulgars, Banat Germans, Croatians, Slovaks, Russians, Chechens, Tatars, Turks, Greeks, Armenians and others	3.5–5.5	15–25

Source: ECOR © 1999

have their own states (such as the Basques, the Catalans and, to my mind, the Scots) currently enjoy a form of autonomy tantamount to statehood, while many among the endangered European nations and nationalities have not yet managed to secure their right to self-governance.

The most marginalized people in Europe are the 10–15 million Roma, who live scattered throughout almost every state on the continent. They were the secondary victims of the Holocaust, the *Porrajmos* (the Nazi genocide against Roma) and continue to this day to be victims of racial prejudice and racist crimes – on an everyday basis.

4.9 Racism, xenophobia and discrimination in Europe

Globalization and the world's current 50 violent conflicts, with its concomitant mass migrations of refugees and people seeking work elsewhere, have been changing the nature of racism.[157] In the globalized market economy, the losers are systematically members of certain national and ethnic groups whose particular vulnerability results from a history of discrimination, oppression and exploitation and the most vulnerable groups being women whose lives are impacted by racism.[158] The 2001 World Conference Against Racism, Racial Discrimination, Xenophobia and Related Intolerance was supposed to deal with this 'new racism', whose manifestations – similar to the 'old' colonial racism – aim at the exclusion of large masses of people in the South from global economic progress as well as the scapegoating and criminalization of migrants and refugees in industrialized North.

The October 2000 European Conference against Racism underlined the importance of combating impunity, to include crimes with a racist or xenophobic motivation, also at international level. Thirty five years after the 1965 international Convention on the Elimination of All Forms of Racial Discrimination (CERD) the international community held the World Conference against Racism, racial discrimination, xenophobia and related intolerance, in September 2001.[159] CERD could serve as a model for dealing with 'new racism' since the convention (which is still not ratified by many states) was the first significant development, particularly in terms of: (i) its definition of 'racial discrimination'; (ii) the establishment of a first treaty-monitoring body, the Committee on the Elimination of Racial Discrimination; and (iii) the provision of affirmative action ('special and concrete measures').[160] Under an often-thin layer of civilization many primitive, atavistic and anachronistic attitudes and mentalities still seem to be part of the European cultural heritage.

Among the concrete and disturbing issues (ranked in order of urgency and threat) partly discussed at the 'European Conference against Racism' in Strasburg, October 2000,[161] and to be discussed at the UN World Conference Against Racism in Durban, August–September 2001, are the following: (i) The existence of forms of racism and prejudice in state institutions, direct and indirect, especially the existence of racist mentality in certain police corps and within the judiciary; (ii) the 'underestimation' or 'banalization' of racism and intolerance by mainstream politicians, in schools and in the media; (iii) the (unpunished) incitement to discrimination against vulnerable groups (immigrants, asylum-seekers, refugees, Roma, travellers and so on) on the part of certain media outlets and politicians, which seem to enjoy impunity for such crimes; (iv) unhindered continuing manifestations of racial or 'ethnicized' violence and restless incitement to racial or ethnic hatred or intolerance by extremist groups, in public spaces, by the press and the use of new technologies of mass communication such as the internet by racist individuals and organizations; (v) the seemingly almost unchecked proliferation and growth of extremist groups in certain European countries, exacerbating such phenomena of hostility against non-dominant groups and inciting to violence;[162] (vi) increase of violent acts against asylum-seekers and refugees in certain European countries; (vii) violent acts against people with darker skin complexion[163] (and the continuing appearance of racism as a theory based on the alleged superiority of a race or ethnic group over others), in some cases including organized racist hate murders; (viii) the existence of violent Fascist extremism in certain European countries, resulting in violent acts against members of Jewish communities, destruction of religious places and dissemination of anti-Semitic material; (ix) persisting systematic discrimination against Roma (Gypsies) in many European countries; (x) the increase in 'Islamaphobia', religious intolerance and the victimization of the large but hidden Muslim communities in

Europe ('Muslims as the Strangers from Within');[164] (xi) the occurrence of contemporary forms of slavery (in the sex industry and beyond), in Europe and in other parts of the world;[165] with continuing large-scale trafficking of women despite efforts undertaken by governments and international organization, due to limited awareness or non-recognition of the intersection of gender and racism.[166] A number of appropriate political and legal steps that need to be taken to mitigate and pre-empt destructive forms of interaction between majorities and minorities in an enlarged Europe are discussed (in the following section).

To talk of racism and xenophobia in Europe one has to be aware that it was in the Europe of the late nineteenth century when the notorious 'theory of the races' was invented (first in the form of the '*Rassenkunde*' in Germany and Austria). This 'theory' (for example, the pathological ideas of Gobineau *et al.*) was derived from the European imaginary superiority complex, which saw other nations and peoples as biologically or culturally inferior. Racism permeated not only the racial teachings of Count Arthur Gobineau (1816–82), the classical European philosophy of the nineteenth century and the science of ethnology – which, armed with the dreadful 'theory of races', exerted a decisive influence on activities of European powers in the colonies. Racism had permeated religious ideologies for centuries, as in the case of the still virulent, age-old anti-Semitism of the Catholic Church and other Christian churches.

Racially based ideologies shaped the thinking of the European colonizers about the peoples they subjugated. For the terrible backlash of such ideologies caused by decades of their 'application' on the colonial subjects, before and after decolonization and the horrendously destructive impact on the thinking of the colonized people has produced countless tragedies in the former colonies until the present day: one of the last but most cruel examples being Rwanda 1994.[167]

The European nations cannot forget the historical role they played for 500 years in the colonization of the South, the magnitude of crimes they committed and the resulting consequences felt to the present day. The memory of genocide and atrocities against minorities committed in Europe in the name of Nazism, Fascism and nationalism is still fresh.

In Europe both societies and state apparatuses are still deeply affected by racism and xenophobia. The relationship between majority and minority populations has never been an easy one in Europe. Contrary to common belief high levels of racism and xenophobia are not necessarily closely related to the appearance of 'new minorities' – indigenous non-dominant nationalities and minorities are equally targeted – nor to their numbers or the proportion of aliens among residents. For instance, in Germany and Switzerland the areas with the highest number of racial hate crimes are the ones with the lowest share of foreigners.[168] The conjunctures for right-wing extremism and racism do not depend on the 'others' or 'foreigners' themselves; it has more to do with long-grown mentalities, the xenophobic bias of police forces and judiciary and with the *laisser-faire* attitude of public institutions.

4.9.1 Recognition and toleration of ethno-cultural difference as essential to anti-chauvinist policies

Efforts to accommodate ethno-cultural difference are an essential part of anti-racist strategies; they have conflict preventive force and contribute to the long-term transformation of ethno-national conflicts. The main topics are collective rights, self-governance and nationality policies. The political-cum-humanitarian concern is to ensure that all possible means of avoiding violent forms of multi-ethnic interaction are exploited, strengthened and made more attractive to the majority populations.

Comprehensive attempts to contribute to anti-racist and anti-chauvinist policies in the Greater Europe start to relate to the subject of formation and construction (in some cases deconstruction) of the ethnic phenomenon with the question of non-dominant identities and the politicization of the ethnic phenomenon (ethnicity) as part of the 'logic' of defensive strategies for 'minorities-at-risk' (Gurr). The victims of racism and xenophobia are usually members from among a multitude of non-dominant groups.

When talking about racism and xenophobia we first think of migrant communities as the object/victims of racism and xenophobia and not so much for other minorities, be it historic nationalities, non-dominant groups, indigenous and other ethnic minorities. The number of indigenous non-dominant groups in the Greater Europe exceeds the number of migrant communities by far. Many of these minorities are either permanently confronted with everyday racism and xenophobia (for example, the sad example of the Roma all over Greater Europe) or they are discriminated against in different forms by respective demographic majorities or otherwise dominant groups. Anti-racist and anti-chauvinist policies ought to address the rejection of non-dominant groups by large national chauvinists groups among the majority populations in many European states.

4.9.2 Victimization by 'racialization' and scapegoating

The victims of racism and xenophobia are usually members of various non-dominant groups. Minority groups or non-dominant groups exist in every EU state,[169] only their composition between indigenous minorities (national minorities including language minorities), religious minorities (Muslims of different communities of belief and origin, Jews, Hindus, Sikhs, Buddhists, and many others), diverse migrant communities, asylum-seekers and refugee populations and so on, and their proportion of the resident population may change from country to country. Especially targeted are undocumented migrant workers, Muslim communities in Islamaphobic environments, the Roma people and women of minority groups. Gender, belief and illegality are factors that profoundly contribute to appalling situations of multiple discrimination.

As a rule, racism is not perceived as the splitting-up of a population but as hostility towards an 'alien' group of 'others' (as opposed to the 'own' breed of 'us-self'); the terms of 'racialization' and 'scapegoating', coined in a decade-old debate by British social scientists, is essential to understand the nature of the 'new' domestic racism that replaced the 'old' colonial racism. With the increase of 'new minorities' in the last two decades racists found it easier to construct scapegoats and to blame aliens and minorities for socio-economic losses.

Violence against non-dominant groups again became a reality in Europe. In the case of migrant communities several of the attributes for ethnic groups defined in the Introduction to this book do apply while others are obviously obsolete due to changed life conditions. As ethnic characteristics are only relevant within the framework of inter-ethnic relations, it is primarily in conflict situations that they become a major focus of perception. In the context of migration previously totally unimportant characteristics suddenly acquire huge significance. For example, phenotypic features are in Western societies the main distinguishing features (unlike the situation in many societies in the South).

What appeared to be a new phenomenon in many parts of Western Europe was racist violence by radicalized members of the mainstream societies against members of non-dominant groups. Large-scale racial clashes in Brixton and racist violence in Rostock-Lichtenhagen, brought to the attention of millions by live televized reports, sent shock waves through the general public. Some urban areas of Western Europe became no-go areas for people with darker skin than that of the resident populations.

For instance in Germany racial hate crimes account for an estimated one hundred people killed and burned by neo-Nazi gangs since 1990. Statistics in Germany show a sharp increase of 58.9 per cent in violent racist attacks (as of 2000).[170] Victims are hunted on the streets of German cities, with hundreds of bystanders witnessing violent acts, and rarely someone intervenes. The police forces and secret services, which have been so efficient in curbing organized left-wing violence in the 1970s, seem powerless or rather inactive in combating organized right-wing criminality. Against this background debates about 'national pride' and the 'guiding culture' (*Leitkultur*) seem out of place. The words of Germany's President Johannes Rau, that one could only be proud of what he/she has accomplished by their own means, seems to be a minority opinion in Germany. Established democratic parties do not hesitate to tap the xenophobic potential for the winning of elections, in violation of more or less established codes of conduct.

4.9.3 Worrying levels of racist attitudes in EU states

Attitude surveys among common folks show high levels of ethnocentrism, xenophobia and racist mentalities, 'a desire to limit immigration and acceptance of refugees and a readiness to exclude foreigners from certain social areas and arenas' (Burns *et al.* 2001: 2). The results of the *Eurobarometer* 1997 survey, which measured the majority populations' attitudes towards minority groups in each member state of the European Union, 'showed a worrying level of negative attitudes in the 15 EU Member States'; a follow up survey in spring 2000 shows an ambivalent, but nevertheless, deeply depressing picture: 'in some ways the attitudes... have changed for the better', for example, in regard to people favouring new policies to improve coexistence between of majorities and minorities (EUMC 2001: 5), but in the year 2000 more people in EU states blame their fear of unemployment and loss of welfare benefits on minorities.[171]

EU-wide only 21 per cent of the population is classified as belonging to the 'actively tolerant' type of people, meaning that they do not feel disturbed by members of minority groups, see diversity as a richness, do not demand assimilation nor repatriation of immigrants, and show strong support for anti-racist policies; this category is higher educated and represents 'multi-cultural optimism'. The relative majority of EU citizens belong to the 'passively tolerant' type, who have positive attitudes but do not support policies in favour of minorities or anti-racist polities. A quarter of the EU population is described as 'ambivalent'; they do not see positive inputs by minority groups, desire their assimilation but do not feel disturbed. However, 14 per cent of the EU-population display strong negative attitudes against minorities, support harsh policies against 'foreigners' and are classified as 'intolerant'; these peoples are usually less educated and less optimistic. Comparing EU member states, the Greeks stand out as the most shocking with only 29 per cent being somewhat tolerant (compared to 60 per cent EU-wide), followed by the Belgians (48 per cent); the Spanish (77 per cent) and the Swedes (76 per cent) see themselves as the most tolerant EU citizens. However, the most telling of the dimensions of 'xenophobic concerns' has been excluded.[172]

As regards the rather positive classification of a majority 60 per cent of European citizens being actively or passively tolerant, serious doubts are cast on such an assessment when looking at the replies on a series of four questions, in which the majority of respondents blame members of minority groups as being responsible for decreasing standards in schools (32–76 per cent, EU average 52 per cent), of abusing social welfare systems (37–66 per cent, EU 52 per cent), increase in unemployment (36–85 per cent; EU 51 per cent) and as being more often involved in criminality (30–81 per cent, EU 58 per cent). Only between 30 per cent and 37 per cent actually disagree with these potentially racist judgements. The EUMC director detects a close relation between rejection of diversity and deteriorating life-standards. 'The data show that rejecting cultural diversity is closely related to this fear for socio-economic changes' (Beate Winkler, in EUMC 2001: 5).

The blaming of minorities for social deterioration such as unemployment, crime, social insecurity, loss of welfare benefits and a drop in educational standards – or the fear of it – felt by large proportions of majority populations, provides right-wing extremists and racists with unlimited recruitment grounds. The persistent threat that – in addition to the notorious, well-known right-wing political parties in most EU states – more radical racist parties and socio-political movements will arise, establish themselves and become more salient.

Today social democrats and a few left-centre parties govern the large majority of the 15 EU states; in only three countries do right-wing extremists and racists have a certain influence on central government policies: in Spain, governed by a shaky right-wing government, Austria, with pro-fascist elements in the central government (Haider's *FPÖ*) since spring 2000 and, unfortunately Italy again, as a result of the May 2001 elections.[173]

Threats that the power-balance between the democratic parties in the three largest EU countries, Germany, France and United Kingdom could be destabilized by a higher turnout of votes for right-wing populists have reduced since the 1990s. Today, the French *Front National*, led by its ardent anti-Semitic and racist leader Jean-Marie Le Pen, once the strongest extremist group in Europe (with some 20 per cent of the vote nation-wide, able to conquer cities like Toulon, Orange, and Marignane in the June 1995 communal elections) is in decay due to factionalism, splits and 'disciplinary' measures taken against Le Pen.[174] In Germany the right-wing parties are split (*NPD, DVA* and *Republikaner*) and remain under the critical 5 per cent line for the most part; much more threatening are the activities of the organized underground of criminal racist, Fascist groupings, who are ready for violence and election campaigns launched around xenophobic themes by the mainstream Christian democrats.[175]

A much more plausible threat is the undermining of established right-wing parties by new racist political agendas, which are 'pressuring established parties to shift their position', and blocking or reversing institutional realignment in favour of pluralism, equality and justice. It is paradoxical that established elites within Europe stand for increased pluralism and opposition to xenophobia and racism, but that they have been largely unable to prevent or limit socio-political movements articulating ethno-nationalism (implying an ardent xenophobia) and authoritarian views on socio-cultural matters (law and order). Nor have they been able to overcome much of the institutional inertia and resistance in order to effectively address the problems of widespread institutionalized discrimination.' (Burns, Kamali and Rydgren 2001: 24). It is the institutionalized discrimination and the institutionalization of racist exclusion practices that are the most worrying aspects of racism and xenophobia in Europe.[176]

Institutionalized discrimination and the institutionalization of racist exclusion practices can only be changed if addressed by specific policies. Regarding the opportunism among the political class it is certainly of particular importance to see support for anti-racist policies by significant sections

of the population in the European Union. In the area of minority protection and equal opportunity for 'aliens' politicians tend to shy away if such
issues do not have majority support.

As part of the *Eurobarometer* opinion polls 1997 and 2000 the respondents
have been asked seven questions about proposed policies that aim at
improving social coexistence between majorities and minorities. While the
replies vary from country to country, the result is shattering: what does not
vary is that all the seven constructive proposals for improving coexistence
have been bluntly rejected by significantly large majorities; EU-wide only
between 22 per cent and 37 per cent of the respondents agreed with the proposals. The percentage for disagreement and 'no opinion' is not indicated.[177]

The most important approach in improving mutual relations between
majorities and minorities is the policy option that discrimination against
non-dominant groups should be outlawed (and some measures for
temporary and targeted affirmative action should be institutionalized).[178]
However, it comes as no small surprise to realize that less then one third
(31 per cent, with variations of 24 per cent to 41 per cent by country) of
the respondents agrees with outlawing discrimination, though 60 per cent
were classified as more or less tolerant!

The equally important basic principle of promoting equal opportunity in
all areas of social life only got a slightly higher rate of approval; though it
met the highest rate of approval among the seven it was only supported by
37 per cent; only in one country, the Netherlands, a majority of 51 per cent
supports this very basic principle. For human rights NGOs and anti-racists
it must be embarrassing to know that only 21 per cent of EU citizens agree
to a greater role for organizations which have already gained experience
in the fight against racism. Only 21 per cent encourage the participation
of members of minority groups in the political life of their country and
only 22 per cent think that trade unions and churches should do more to
combat racism. Again only 29 per cent would encourage the creation of
organizations that bring together people from different races, religions and
cultures. Even the promotion of understanding of different cultures and
lifestyles is a 36 per cent minority position in the European Union, though
the citizens of the three Nordic member states did agree (with rates between
52 per cent and 57 per cent).

4.9.4   'Official racism': the case of Islam in Europe

Even in the case of established national minorities often only a few people
are willing to engage in the discourse on institutional racism, for example
against African-Americans and other 'people of colour'[179] as well as against
Muslim communities in Europe.

Indeed, among the worst example for cultural and structural violence in
Europe would be the enhanced exclusion many of the ten million Muslims
have to face everyday in Christian–Occidental Europe. The Barcelona process

(starting in November 1995) is important for reconciling Europe with the Islamic southern Mediterranean. The question is: will there be Islamic ghettoes or Euro-Islam?[180] So far the EU process has no binding impact on the legal status of the millions of Muslims. The denial of citizenship to Muslims, harassment, the suburb syndrome among France's four million Muslims immigrants, the status of second-class residents for 2.5 million Turks and Kurds in Germany and so on are but a few examples.

As regards Islam two notions seem to be at the top of the European agenda: identity and security.[181] The 'Fortress Europe' has more or less unsuccessfully tried to stem the 'migration flows' from the Islamic southern Mediterranean and south-eastern inner peripheries. These frontiers are hard ones in view of both culture and prosperity. Historically the Islamic civilization was in the midst of Europe (Bichara Khader 1997); its cultural and scientific achievements greatly influenced the Occident, most visibly in Andalusia.[182] Some 300 years of Arab-Moorish presence in Spain, from the south almost up to the Pyrenees and the outcome of centuries of cultural exchange, had a profound impact and are an integral part of the European history and the beginning of the Modern Age.[183]

'Official racism' and animosities against Muslims have deep historic root-causes and are continuously reinforced by biased perceptions of current developments in the Islamic world. As an introduction to the collective imagary of the Occident in the Orient – our 'intimate enemy' and military adversary for 700 years – the works of Khader explain a 'special historic relationship'. Euro-centrism may become dangerous again if not deflected, especially 'in times of cholera'. Algeria with its Rwanda-style atavist slaughters, the terrorist activities of Osmana bin Laden or the Taliban terror regime in Afghanistan continuously reinforced already existing prejudice. The (re-)creation of images of the 'Islamic enemy' by Samuel Huntington, in the form of an alleged *Islamic–Confucian threat* against the West, gained credibility with his bestseller *Clash of Civilizations*;[184] Eurocentric hallucinations about 'Islamic fundamentalism' gained a boost.[185] Another standard argument is that Islamic countries have a human rights deficit; this is well-founded based on many Amnesty International reports. History provides much evidence that this has been very much the problem of Europe when encountering Islam. Khader has exemplified a condensation of hostility against Muslims and Islam in European literature and art. Since Montesquieu and Voltaire the Occident saw the Orient as archaic, despotic and its people compelled to slavish servility. Today's stereotypes can be exemplified in the issue of the veil.[186] Deeply-rooted stereotypes may disrupt the transcultural dialogue between the EU and Arab-Mediterranean space, which was evoked by the Barcelona process.

Many other cases of 'official racism' as exclusion by the state apparatuses are not well documented, especially when 'official racism' goes hand in hand with racism by the majority civilian society, as in the cases of the

Dalit of India, the Buraku people of Japan, the indigenous peoples in most states of the Americas and the Roma people of Greater Europe.

4.9.5 The Roma: the most marginalized people in Europe

The most marginalized people in Europe are the 10–15 million Roma, who live scattered throughout almost every state on the continent. There are 30 countries in which the Roma number over 2000. In Europe, there may be as many as 12 million Roma between Paris and Vladivostok; in some countries, they represent some 10 per cent of the population. Roma life expectancy, educational levels, employment rates, access to acceptable housing and citizenship lag far behind national averages.

The Roma were the victims of the *Porrajmos* (the Nazi genocide against Roma) and continue to this day to be victims of racial prejudice and social exclusion – on an everyday basis. Only lately the crimes of the past have surfaced, even in countries which seemingly have a decent human rights record and which apply minority rights for several domestic minorities or indigenous peoples. For instance, a study commissioned by the Swiss Federal government was published in June 1998; it spoke of more than 600 cases of forced separation of Roma and Cinti children from their migrating parents in Switzerland during the period of 1926–72. Swedes were shocked by revelations, in 1997, that Swedish governments forcibly sterilized 60,000 Roma women to rid society of 'inferior racial types'. The Swedish government set up an inquiry commission. Even more shocking was the fact that the law allowing the sterilizations was not overturned until 1975, 30 years after the Nazis' human engineering policies had collapsed. Such campaigns were practised in Sweden and Norway after World War I resembled racial cleansing. The Swiss – who had come under fire for close business ties with Nazi Germany – reacted mid-1997 with outrage on similar revelations.[187]

In the Central and Eastern European countries Roma especially are often the victims of organized violence.[188] Currently Roma are being ethnically cleansed in Kosovo by the majority Kosovars (as are the Serbs and other nationalities). In NATO-occupied Kosovo the Roma were among the first victims of pogroms and expulsion.[189] Earlier, in 1999, NATO was justifying its war against Yugoslavia with claims of preventing 'genocide' and 'ethnic cleansing'. Despite the KFOR presence the Roma live with death threats but European and NATO politicians do not seem to care.[190]

Only Hungary is renowned for its liberal policies to integrate the Roma. Hungary was commended for its new policy of the active and preventive protection of minorities, based on principles of preservation of their self-identity. The Hungarian state endeavoured to enter into dialogue with the neighbouring countries and concluded a number of bilateral agreements on co-operation and promotion of the rights of minorities. Elections for minority local self-government took place. Sixty-one local governments could be set up by the Roma and some 50 more for seven other nationalities.

Most Roma live in the Balkans, Central Europe and the former Soviet Union; fewer live in Western Europe, Middle East, North Africa and America. The largest communities of Roma live in Eastern Europe.[191] Even though they are one of the largest minority groups, the Roma still have a weak political lobby.[192] Ongoing strengthening of their own organizations at the grassroots, national and international levels could improve their situation. Already in 1997 a respected Roma civil rights activist observed as a positive trend: '[A]lmost unnoticed by the public, more than 300 new Romani groups have appeared across Europe.' (Kawczynski 1997).

At present, Romani organizations are active virtually everywhere in Europe. The best known Romani group is probably the *International Romani Union* (IRU), founded in the early 1970s by a small group of Romani intellectuals led by Ian Hancock. Another international organization is the *Roma National Congress* (RNC); its establishment was connected to the drastic changes which the political transition in Eastern Europe brought upon the Roma. RNC was founded in order to help protect and represent Roma who have become stateless or *de facto* stateless through political developments. Roma in Central and Eastern Europe face increasing discrimination and violence. Many of them have sought refuge in the West, but ago-old anti-Gypsy sentiments have hampered their absorption and protection. Germany, one of the main refuge countries, has become increasingly hostile to Roma.

Other international efforts to represent the Roma include EUROM and the Standing Conference for Co-operation and Co-ordination of Romani Associations in Europe. Strong organizations exist at the national level, for instance the *Roma and Sinti Union* in Germany; the Foundation for Hope and Understanding in the Czech Republic; the Romani CRISS in Romania; *Phralipe* and the Roma Parliament in Hungary. Since the mid-1980s, those organizations have protested against discrimination of the Roma in practically every European country. The legitimate demands of Roma have found their way to the agendas of international bodies. The OSCE established in 1995 a group to record human rights violations against Roma. The UN Committee on the Elimination of Racial Discrimination has held several sessions on the problem. The Roma question will be the litmus test for the democratic new Europe.

4.10 Combating racism – ten steps forward

Ambivalence and conflict are characteristic features of the relationship between immigrants and host societies as well as between indigenous groups and dominant groups. Uncertainties rule the dialectics between 'hosts' and 'guests'.[193] The term xenophobia, the 'fear of others', mirrors these uncertainties, with 'xenos' in Greek meaning both alien and guest. This ambiguity lies at the root of 'otherism'.

The task of exploring policy strategies and measures to address these problems starts with rethinking definitions and core concepts. Instead of looking at racism as a complex of 'prejudices' a good approach would be to say that 'racism is not an opinion, it is a crime' (ENAR 2000). Racism against minority group members can be both individual and structural and it can constitute what Johan Galtung calls 'cultural violence'.

Structural racism is generated by the way economic, political and social institutions operate. Here the works of Michel Foucault about power structures, institutions and the multitude of different techniques they use, might be a source of inspiration.[194] Knowledge and power create what Foucault calls 'rules of formation', an epistemological form he calls a dispositif (or apparatus), which discloses reality while at the same time constructing reality.[195] Structural racism categorizes and marks people, makes minority members visible and denies such people equal access to jobs, education, medical facilities, social welfare, leisure and habitat. Governments, local and state administrations, domestic companies and transnational corporations, the churches, the education system, civil society organizations and (not least) the media, are part of the apparatus which form a dispositif against the different categories of 'others' and 'aliens'; these are the forces producing 'others' and 'aliens' and shaping public attitudes towards 'others', such as national minorities and 'aliens', such as 'new minorities' (migrants, refugees, asylum-seekers and trafficked people).

The challenges of anti-racist/anti-chauvinist policies and the prevention and law-enforcement regarding criminal activities of militant racists/ Fascists are great and the matter is urgent. The EU-wide monitoring of gross human rights violations must be co-ordinated by a special task force.[196] A Racism Alert and Early Warning System is necessary. The imperative to abolish impunity for racist crimes and the consequent prosecution of racist hate crimes must be enforced; the *laisser-faire* policy in many EU states is intolerable. A systematic overview on the tasks, procedures, institutions and voids of anti-racist/anti-chauvinist policies is required.

This overview is focusing on activities, which are essential to combat racism and xenophobia in Europe. Among others a list essential to such anti-racist and anti-chauvinist policies has to combat against militant racism. The conception of new policies to prevent and combat racism and xenophobia follows strategies which are targeting the structural, institutionalized and organized forms of racism which concentrate on the following issues:

1. A number of appropriate political and legal steps to mitigate and pre-empt destructive forms of interaction between majorities and minorities in Europe shall be explored and discussed.
2. Preventive policies are an imperative; there are a number of appropriate political and legal steps to mitigate and pre-empt destructive forms of interaction between majorities and minorities in Europe. Prevention is the

declared policy of the European Union since the mid-1990s. Three problems politicians face in promoting prevention are its long-term character, difficulties to measure their effectiveness and the confusion about diverse institutions, measures and policies that have preventive character but remain unrelated.

3. The contribution of research into preventive strategies ought to be strengthened.

4. Normative, structural and multi-lateral dimensions of prevention of destructive interaction of minorities/majorities have to be valued; unfortunately they are often neglected in favour of more activist approaches and technical aspects.

5. As regards racial discrimination the possibilities for control and legal redress were limited. The year 2000 brought progress: the EU Council Directive of 29 June 2000 incorporated the principle of equal treatment between persons irrespective of racial or ethnic origin and the Council Directive of 27 November established a general framework for equal treatment in employment and occupation (CM-EC 2000a and b). The implementation of these directives, by 2002 in EU countries (and by 2003 in candidate countries), has to be monitored carefully.

6. One of the main tasks is to reinforce practical anti-racist policies aimed at immunizing the European society against racism and xenophobia, the promotion of tolerant attitudes to 'otherness', and the detection and prosecution of organized racism. Of importance to anti-racist policies and, in particular, to combat organized militant racism is the new role a fully established European Union Monitoring Centre on Racism and Xenophobia (EUMC) is going to play in combating organized racism by looking at the perpetrators of hate crimes and their environment. Comparative and investigative research at EUMC ought to be enhanced.

7. The EU-wide monitoring of gross human rights violations has to be co-ordinated by a special task force, as part of an action plan to prevent racist offences and hate crimes.

8. The political will to punish severe human rights violations such as racist hate crimes is increasing. The main problem is the lack of enforcement of existing laws and instruments. In order to anticipate dangers, more attention should be given to the unsung work of civic organizations (such as SOS Racism) at the grassroots. EUMC should assemble a list of organizations and civic movements that combat racism and thus, deserve continuous moral and material support from the EU.

9. The struggle against racism has to establish discontinuities and abolish those institutions that encourage racism and discrimination. To this end, some ideas have been developed and require further development.

10. Finally, rethinking definitions and concepts of racism and anti-racism will add to effective policies to curb racism and to empower its victims.

Multiple discrimination on the basis of race, ethnicity, gender and other factors must be properly addressed. Simply raising awareness or education cannot adequately combat forms of institutionalized racism.

The European Union wants to combat the crime of racism and is searching for appropriate concepts and tools. Social scientists, psychologists and jurists from all EU member states shall be invited to a series of conferences. The main tasks are to develop practical anti-racist policies aimed at immunizing European society against racism and xenophobia and promoting tolerance toward otherness. As a next measure the EU should establish a commission of experts to refine its arsenal of responses to racism and xenophobia. I propose the formation of a Task Force Against Racism, possibly within the already existing EUMC.

4.10.1 Exploring ways of combating organized forms of racism and xenophobia

When looking at political and legal steps to mitigate and pre-empt destructive forms of interaction between majorities and minorities in Europe any attempt to clarify or resolve 'racial', 'ethnic' or other sub-national conflicts must be preceded by the realization that existential questions relating to the survival of an ethnic group and the cultural survival of migrant groups are not factors that are open to negotiation but are essential prerequisites to dialogue. There are a number of destructive forms of interaction between states and ethnic communities which result in the exclusion and persecution of national groups that have not yet been subject to systematic investigation and for which the international community has not yet developed any consistent policy. (This was demonstrated with devastating clarity in the case of the genocide in Rwanda in 1994. The racist hate crimes not only call for prevention but for its elimination.)

The political-cum-humanitarian concern to find ways of avoiding structural and direct, personal forms of racism and xenophobia leads on to questions of:

- how ethnic and cultural difference can be acknowledged and recognized;
- how destructive forms of interaction between states and communities and between majorities and minorities can be prevented;
- how violent, militant forms of racism and xenophobia can be effectively combated; and
- which institutions, legal measures and policies are most appropriate for the purpose.

4.10.2 Preventing conflicts between majorities and minorities

Regarding forms of 'structural prevention' of troubles, I use 'structural' in the sense that new frameworks and institutions are created to avert possible direct violence and reduce structural violence, such as discrimination against non-dominant groups. I am indebted to Johan Galtung, who developed the concept of 'structural violence' in the 1970s, based on his path-breaking distinction between direct personal violence and structural violence; Galtung also reflected on cultural violence, for example, values that promote/justify violence and superiority complexes that result in aggressive attitudes. Structural prevention aims at ending repression, injustice and racism, which is engrained in state policies and which is also an inherent a apart of the cultural attitudes held by many dominant groups.

Today it is common knowledge, and the declared policy of the European Union since the mid-1990s, that it is simpler and cheaper to tackle conflicts preventively and avoid them than to try to put a stop to hostilities that have already broken out. As regards the practical problems politicians face in promoting preventive measures and policies – beyond the rhetoric, when it comes to implementing declared policies, the difficulties are threefold:

- the unimpressive and long-term character of many such measures makes them unattractive if quick results are required;
- the difficulty of measuring their effectiveness adds to confusion about the subject matter; and
- while a number of rather diverse institutions, measures and policies have a preventive character, they often remain unrelated or only partially implemented.

In acting to prevent 'ethnic unrest' among minority groups and in view of the virulent racism and xenophobia present among mainstream national societies there are no 'easy solutions'. The great diversity of cultural and political characteristics exhibited by different types of society produce, correspondingly, different types of claims and regulatory mechanisms. First steps are to mitigate and pre-empt destructive forms of interaction between majorities and minorities in Europe followed by steps to combat racism and xenophobia among the majority societies.

Classic solutions for indigenous minorities range from cultural autonomy, through territorial self-governance, to *de facto* sovereignty. Protection of ethnic and national minorities by means of a variety of autonomy arrangements did not begin until the twentieth century, triggered by a worsening of the so-called 'minorities problem' as a result of revolutions and regroupings that had occurred in the wake of the two world wars.

Too little account has been taken of the policies of certain multinational states when it comes to looking for methods of preventing and dealing with latent or open ethno-national conflicts. Many states have been able to pursue active and successful policies of prevention of troubles by making concessions and negotiation involving elements of reactive minority protection and proactive nationality policy (for example, home rule for the Faeroese and the Inuit in the Kingdom of Denmark from 1948 onwards). Others have – often with limited success – used similar offers to try to resolve armed conflicts that have already escalated (for example, the regionalization and phased granting of autonomy to Basques, Catalonians, Andalusians and Galicians in post-Franco Spain). Nationality policies are generally not conceived of as solutions to conflicts that are smouldering or have already erupted. Some procedures aim more at containment, or pose the nationality question in a purely socio-political context. But such policies are part of the problem. A detailed comparison ought to be made of the different approaches to nationality policy pursued by selected states such as Denmark, Italy, Spain and the USSR/Russian Federation; this may include comparison with lessons learned from China, India, Australia, Colombia, Panama, Nicaragua or Ethiopia.

4.10.3   Enhancing research into preventive strategies

The contribution of research into preventive strategies ought to be strengthened. Practical preventive steps range from initiatives by popular movements to the elaboration of norms and legal instruments within the framework of international organizations. Efforts to change violence-promoting framework conditions through the policing and control of potential perpetrators, bans placed on radical organizations and the promotion of violence and the strengthening of civil society, were often neglected in the debate about how to deal with or prevent violent intra-societal conflicts. Conflict mediation and facilitation in such conflicts can undoubtedly be a successful instrument of domestic politics.

Furthermore, attempts to give a thorough conceptual account of the phenomenon of racialization and ethnicization, to work out elements of a theory of inter-ethnic coexistence, investigate the causes of trouble, to distinguish the many different manifestations of 'ethnic' and 'racial' conflict in industrialized countries, to highlight its potential, to analyse its structural characteristics and the driving forces behind it and to set the phenomenon of 'racial' conflict in a larger context, should all be intensified. The research community ought to intensify international attempts to find methods of preventing and resolving intra-societal conflict. One factor that is of major importance is the extension of international norms and standards of protection for non-dominant minorities and migrant communities, as well as of the rights of these groups with regard to cultural autonomy, bilingual education, freedom of belief, the right to articulate their demands, the right of petition and forms of self-administration of their own communal affairs.

4.10.4   Strengthening the normative and multilateral dimensions of prevention

In the current debate the normative, structural and multilateral dimensions of the prevention of violence are often neglected in favour of more activist approaches and technical aspects. This contradicts the fact that mediation, facilitation, good offices, arbitration and other forms of peaceful conflict settlement by go-betweens are – in regard to their overall effectiveness – of secondary importance compared with long-term preventive policies (for which the European Union has opted).

More lessons should be learned by comparing various regional and local attempts at conflict resolution, ranging from the neighbourhoods to the state level, to link these up with evolving legal provisions at EU and state level. Critical reviews should focus on the activities undertaken by civic organizations, the efforts of the Council of Europe with regard to national minorities, similar efforts by the OSCE, as well as the efforts of the UN Human Rights Commission to work out minimum standards for the rights of minorities and indigenous peoples.

4.10.5 Increasing possibilities of redress for discrimination

As regards racial discrimination the received wisdom is that in legal terms the possibilities for control and redress are limited. All the mentioned institutions and organizations (governments, local and state administrations, domestic companies and transnational corporations, the churches, the education system, civil society organizations, the media and so on) should act responsibly in the interests of human rights and protection of vulnerable groups; for some, codes of conduct could be an appropriate means to regulate their operations. Protection mechanisms provided for by international law often are not translated into legal provisions within the nation states that implement the rules of international conventions; hence they remain inconsequential.

An 'Anti-Discrimination Charter' (ADC), possibly as an amendment to international treaties such as the European Convention on Human Rights, which has a review mechanism and the right for individual petition, could be more effective. Criminal law cases are only in a few instances successful. It is necessary to shift the burden of proof in favour of the victims but the principle of due process of law prohibits such a shift in criminal procedures, hence, the only way for individual redress is the use of civil courts.[197]

The impact of the new Council Directive of 29 June 2000 implementing the principle of equal treatment between persons irrespective of race or ethnic origin and the Council Directive of 27 November establishing a general framework for equal treatment in employment and occupation (CM-EC 2000a and b) have to be explored carefully. In this respect the upcoming incorporation of the EC Racial Equality Directive into the national laws of the EU member states has to be watched closely by anti-racist organizations. In a few countries, however, the protection of minorities is already legally guaranteed in more comprehensive form than the new legislation at EU level.

4.10.6 Reinforcing the fight against organized racism

One of the important tasks to be accomplished by a fully established European Union Monitoring Centre on Racism and Xenophobia (EUMC), based in Vienna, would be the establishment of a Unit for Identifying Common Elements and Patterns of Militant Racism. Analysing and comparing racism and xenophobia in the twenty-first century produces a set of common elements and patterns. Patterns can be found by looking at the perpetrators of hate crimes and their environment. Hence, comparative research at EUMC must be greatly reinforced in order to identify and explore:

- the role of racist, fascist and militant organizations (parties, movements, gangs and so on) and their international network of far-right organizations
- the ideologists, organizers, legitimizers and perpetrators of hate crimes and their relationship to the mass membership, weekend militants, skinheads, petty criminals and so on
- the local and regional conditions they find and create
- the context in which they act, for example, complicity on the part of local officials or state authorities, *laisser-faire* by law enforcement agencies and so on
- the political environment in which they act, for example, complicity of right-leaning politicians, downplaying of their aims by established parties, and so on
- the way extremists gain influence
- the type of victims they choose, for example members of migrant communities, members of ethnic minorities, members of left-wing parties/movements, vulnerable groups such as social weak, disabled, minority women and so on
- the xenophobic, racist or even genocidal ideology they use, and
- the way they plan, prepare and execute hate crimes.

The perpetrators, their ideology, the process of victimization and the way they execute the racist hate crimes are the first focus of attention. A coherent international network of right-wing organizations, guided by an internationally active, vicious elite of militant extremists, is more likely to gain influence among xenophobic elements in the mainstream society and among sympathizers in influential positions. The agenda of such elites is to intimidate, harass, attack, or even eliminate specific domestic groups, which as a rule are in a non-dominant and minority position.

4.10.7 Institutionalizing SOS racism as a European alert system

The EU-wide monitoring of gross human rights violations is a task that has to be co-ordinated by a special task force, as part of an action plan to prevent racist offences and hate crimes. Such a task force would organize efforts to improve early warning and crime prevention by domestic law enforcement agencies with the aim to strengthen the capacity to closely monitor organized political criminality and prevent and prosecute crimes committed by militant racist organizations and individuals. Specific training should be given to staff of national intelligence and police corps to identify warning signs, analyse them and translate warnings into appropriate action. For this purpose a new unit at Europol-Interpol named 'Racism Alert Unit' should be created. This new unit would be closely linked to the commanding structure of national police forces.

A special task would be to filter-out indicators to give early warning about serious risk of racist hate crimes. Similarly, indicators of genocide alert, such as signify 'red alert' for militant racism, shall be deduced, from an indicator box. Translated into practical terms this work could be done in much the same way as the FBI or Interpol assemble and access their criminological database in order to trace organized crime. One of the main tasks for applied research on racism is, therefore, the development of an early warning system. The effective functioning of such a system is only guaranteed if a rapid reaction mechanism can be institutionalized within each EU member state or as part of a regional regime.[198]

The main reason why a future institution for racism alert and early action, in the case of serious threats, should become part of the European Commission is to promote rapid reaction procedures in such cases of alert. The EU member states must agree on new mechanisms and the European Commission will be chiefly responsible for organizing political will to establish a rapid reaction mechanism, which is dependent on purely professional criteria. The concept of 'neutrality' in the case of massive human rights violations has to be dismissed.[199] Capacity building at the European Commission must ensure the necessary resources for law enforcement against militant political extremism.

4.10.8   Strengthening international prosecution of racist crimes

The twentieth century was the age of mass violence and political extremism; in the twenty-first century militant racism (which was the root cause for the death of millions in the twentieth century) has finally to be outlawed. In the spirit of Raphael Lemkin the international criminal law has to be developed comprehensively in order for the international rule of law to be respected by all states and political actors. New developments such as the Pinochet case, the use of universal jurisdiction against Rwandan perpetrators of genocide in Belgium 2001 and the prosecution of crimes against humanity committed in Former Yugoslavia, have in recent years helped to form public awareness. The understanding that the international community is responsible for monitoring the mandatory prosecution of massive human rights violations (racial hate crimes, genocide and crimes against humanity) in any one state is growing.

The political will to punish severe human rights violations is on the increase. It is only now, as a generation has gone by, that all humankind has arrived at the same point. The debate about the International Criminal Court (ICC) and its establishment showed clearly that the time is ripe for systematic international prosecution and deterrence against racism and mass murder. The main problem remains the notorious lack of enforcement of the existing laws and instruments. International instruments rarely provide for law enforcement by comprehensive review processes and checks-and-control, as in the case of the European Convention on Human Rights or the CERD. Law enforcement is a top priority with regard to racial hate crimes and internationally organized networks of far-right and racist criminals.

The international community can learn many lessons from past experiences of militant racism and genocidal ideology. The crime of genocide seems incomparable to the crime of racism and yet, there is no genocide without a racist ideology. Anticipating the dangers posed by organized militant racism is a key area for anti-racist policies. Much more attention should be given to the covert work of organizations such as SOS Racism. EUMC should assemble a list of organizations and civic movements that combat racism, and deserve continuous moral and material support from the EU.

Civil actors should take the lead in fighting powerlessness and passive response to racism and xenophobia taken by many states. The development of concepts of structural prevention of racism and xenophobia is among the noblest of tasks. Charitable funds and scientific funding institutions should prioritize research projects in these fields. Combating racism and outlawing racist hate crimes should become a part of domestic laws and national constitutions as well as a part of relevant international instruments.

4.10.9   Abolishing institutions producing racism and discrimination

At the end of the day, the struggle against racism has to establish discontinuities and abolish those institutions that produce racism and discrimination. Racism today has no scientific platform anymore, since the theory of the races has been found to be pseudo-scientific, inhumane and criminal. All its remaining strongholds must be abolished, one by one:

- starting with racism in schoolbooks being replaced by anti-prejudice educational goals and values of solidarity, conviviality and democratic culture being an explicit part of all curricula;
- racialized or ethnicized citizenship (especially the continuous anachronistic use of the 'blood law', the *jus sanguinis*, by some countries – a curious reminder of a sort of tribal descendence) being replaced by a multicultural and transnational model of European citizenship;[200]
- racist immigration practices and illegal *refoulement* of refugees being rendered useless by open borders and freedom of movement;
- strict political control of police performance towards minority group members and intercultural training courses;
- the production of racial stereotypes in the media is to be replaced by a deconstruction of myths about 'otherness' and the promotion of conviviality;

- conviviality is not a rhetoric term but may start with the most attractive parts of it, such as Brazilian-type multicultural carnivals or the popular annual Afro-Caribbean festivals held in Britain.

To use Foucault's terms, the dispositif of the forces that produce and reproduce racism have to be undermined, weakened and destroyed.[201] Its discourse and practices, for example institutions, arrangements, regulations, laws, administrative measures, scientific statements, philosophical positions, (a)morality and so on, form a specific intensified surveillance and control mechanism, creating policy that aims at policing and establishing discipline among 'out-groups', so as to increase state control over its citizens and non-citizens in a particular area and which in turn leads to resistance among certain groups. In Foucault's broader view of this production of 'truth' via power, contemporary racism would be symbolic knowledge and part of the regulatory procedures and the techniques of domination and thus, part of the dispositif or apparatus of power.[202]

4.10.10 Rethinking definitions and concepts of racism

The structural element for racism and xenophobia is greatly reinforced in situations where certain victim groups face multiple discrimination on the basis of race, ethnicity, gender and other factors. This shows again that issues of gender or class are inseparable from those of racism and other forms of institutionalized intolerance, be it based on ethnicity, descent, social class or caste, age, disability, nationality, citizenship, immigration status, or other factors. Multiple discrimination should become a priority area to be addressed by anti-racist policies;[203] this is of particular importance where particular structural impediments enhance victimization and vulnerability, often aggravated by legal systems and mores.[204]

Such structural, often culturally deeply ingrained, racism is of particular concern; it explains the common tendency (of which evidence was given based on the findings of the *Eurobarometers*) to blame – and even 'criminalize' or violently attack – migrants, foreigners, racial and ethnic minorities or racialized 'others' for all sorts of reasons.

I would distinguish xenophobia, which is a matter of ambivalence, weakness of the Self and problematic individual and collective attitudes towards 'others', 'strangers', 'foreigners' and 'aliens', from racism, which only becomes important and dangerous when it is part of an apparatus displaying a strong structural and processual character.[205]

A workable definition of contemporary racism understands racism as part of the dispositif of societal power relations and the repressive activity of the state apparatus and other institutions, aimed at establishing and maintaining surveillance and control mechanisms, creating policy that aims at policing and imposing discipline and control over citizens and non-citizens. Thus, defining contemporary racism contains the following three core elements:

1. its structural, institutionalised nature, which should be highlighted case by case since common patterns are translated into manifold local forms of rejection, whereby discrimination of individuals is always based on their alleged, asserted or voluntary belonging to a social, cultural, ethnic, religious or national minority
2. the negative dynamics of its production/reproduction are characterized by guided notions and encompass the triple processes, in varying concrete permutations, of
   a. the process of racialization and/or ethnicization as the construction of 'races' and/or 'ethnic' groups in the social imaginary of xenophobic individuals, where by prejudice, stereotype, aspects of cultural or biological 'superiority' or other elements of 'false consciousness' whatsoever may play a role (with the so-called interactive element seen with extreme caution);
   b. the process of victimization along the perpetrator-based definition of the victims, being either 'inferior' or looked at in envy but in both cases 'threatening members' of minority groups; and
   c. the process of selected social exclusion and (often) targeted discrimination of members of minority groups whereby elements of a whole dispositif of the state apparatus, its institutions, the schools, churches, official majority culture, labour markets, etc., play respective roles.
3. racism is always linked to violence (as direct personal, structural or cultural violence). Racism appears in different forms of intensity and degrees of organization; in its genocidal and terminal form racism becomes extremely dangerous; the racists would not be satisfied with discriminating and scapegoating of certain groups of victims but would rather attack, kill and exterminate the constructed victim groups.

Conventional perceptions of racism as prejudice are misleading in several ways. First, the problem of 'new racism' goes beyond a simple question of prejudice, as individual errors or more articulated ideologies. Second, racism is not only a sort of pathological anomy, which could be seen as a social dysfunction, but rather functional and structural in nature. (This can be said despite the difficulty for decent and rational people, and anti-racists in particular, to actually understand the obsessive types of racism and the perception of minority groups as being a threat encountered across Europe and beyond.)

The functionality of racism appears to be obvious when looking at the racially compartmentalized global labour markets, whereby racial exclusion – as 'integration by exclusion' – allows the harsh economic exploitation of often undocumented workers and high profitability for 'informal' business activity.[206] Generally speaking, simply raising awareness or education can barely serve to combat such forms of institutionalized racism.

In this era of globalization, people belonging to minority, migrant and indigenous groups in particular find limited employment, education, training and decision-making opportunities and consequently, hold jobs in grey zones – the informal economy in northern countries, the underground economy of eastern countries, or unregulated or bonded labour sectors in southern countries. Throughout, unionism and labour movements, which could be the foundation for informed advocacy if it stands for social justice and against exclusion, do not exist in grey zones. Most trade unions concentrate on the white 'worker aristocracy'. Rainbow coalitions between labour movements and anti-racism and discrimination movements, able to create a broad, productive alliance, are rather an exception to the rule.

4.11   Enlargement of the European Union: dangers and gains

The challenges of enlargement, from 15 to 27 member states, are great for both the EU and the applicant states. The EU is at risk of losing social cohesion. The East–West divergence between the socio-economic models in operation, the greatly differing levels of economic development, the types of governance, regulatory models and practices are enormous. North–South income disparities between the 15 EU member states are already considerable and even greater disparities will need to be addressed: the large gap between economic standards between West and East. The GDP in eastern Europe is below 50 per cent of the EU average, with great variations from prosperous Slovenia to impoverished Romania.[207]

The enlargement process called 'differentiation' (admission on merit without hard conditionality) advocated by the Swedish presidency wanted the first accession group – probably Poland, Czech Republic, Hungary, Slovenia and possibly Cyprus – to join towards the end of 2003 or early 2004. A decade after the end of the cold war division of Europe there is growing uncertainty about the socio-economic forces soon to be unleashed. While many eastern Europeans fear being relegated to second-class EU citizenship and are anxious to avoid a brain drain, property buy-out and 'economic invasion' by westerners, the expectation of waves of migrating Slavonic workers to the West and the fear of a xenophobic wave among the established West European working classes will put the new EU racial equality and equal opportunity regime to serious test.

Already xenophobia and right-wing agitation is running stronger in eastern Germany, Austria and northern Italy. The risk of a political backlash on enlargement has already played to the advantage of populist demagogues in the May 2001 elections in Italy. Pre-emptive moves against the political exploitation of such anxieties by far-right populists in other countries, by EU leaders, EU members and candidates alike, are in high demand.

Policies of racist exclusion of Roma and other nationalities, denial of rights and citizenship to 'non-national' groups and gross human rights violations are rampant in many of the twelve EU accession states. New members are supposed to introduce EU standards well ahead of accession. Obstacles to regulatory alignment are usually manifold but in the case of anti-racist policies and discrimination things are different. Up to very recently, the European Union's regulatory framework in this area was poor. But, in recasting the Europe, the EU decision-making bodies had to act and 'go over the books'. A European-level response to racism came late and policy formulations were weak.

With the 1997 Amsterdam treaty the problem of 'racial discrimination' was for the first time acknowledged and addressed. Prior to the Amsterdam amendments, the EC treaty contained a clause prohibiting discrimination on the grounds of nationality as citizenship of one of the member states (article 12). In Amsterdam a new title VI (incorporating the Schengen *acquis*) was inserted into the EC Treaty, namely related to 'free movement of persons'. However, freedom of movement has become the sticking point in recasting Europe. Some EU states, in particular Germany, Austria and Italy, fear a wave of workers from eastern and central Europe. Poland and other countries oppose the German proposal of a seven-year delay for the 'free movement of persons' because of the fear of wage dumping; obviously, the Poles do not enjoy the prospects of becoming second-class EU citizens.

The new article 13 empowers the European institutions to take action in order to combat discrimination based on sex, racial or ethnic origin, religion and so on. Despite some weaknesses in the article this was seen as 'a tremendous step forward' (Chopin and Niessen 2001: 9). Article 14 will have the effect of eliminating discrimination between EU citizens and third-country nationals.

Anti-racism appeared formally on the agenda of the European Parliament with the Evrigenis report of 1986, but for the next decade most of its recommendations were ignored although the Parliament continued to press for measures to be taken in Brussels.[208] The 1997 European Year Against Racism passed, several studies were commissioned,[209] and the EU Monitoring Centre on Racism in Vienna was established in 1998[210] but still no major EU level implementation took place; only behind the scenes did 'a lot happen'. The agenda-setting strategies of the anti-racist advocacy coalition operating entered a decisive phase. Carlo Ruzza examined decision-making in the area of anti-racism regulation in EU institutions and described how important policy-making emerged 'from a fragmented coalition of NGOs, politicians and civil servants operating in connected but distinct regulative environments'.[211]

Since the mid 1990s a coalition of activists and EU bureaucrats have attempted to achieve a strong policy response on the challenges of racism, xenophobia and minority discrimination in most EU member states. Among the most active organizations were the Starting Line group, the European Migrants' Forum, the internationally organized anti-racist movement with

SOS *Racisme*,[212] the 1998-formed European Network against Racism (ENAR), the Anti-Poverty Lobby and also the Youth Forum and the Women's Lobby, representing a broad European movement of several hundred organizations.[213] Combating racism – traditionally an activity of the left – 'has in recent years received attention in the media and mainstream politics as a reaction to the substantial advances of the extreme right in several EU countries' (Ruzza 1999: 6).

The year 2000 saw a break-through with regard to equal rights and protection of minorities in the European Union. Two directives and a Community Action Programme to Combat Discrimination were the first measures taken under article 13: the Council Directive of 29 June implemented the principle of equal treatment between persons irrespective of racial or ethnic origin and the Council Directive of 27 November established a general framework for equal treatment in employment and occupation (CM-EC 2000a and b). In this respect the upcoming incorporation of the EC Racial Equality Directive into the national laws of the EU member states and the accession states before July 2003 – as an *acquis communautaire*, in other words a mandatory condition for new members – paves the way for meaningful enlargement.

Not only is a further imposition of restrictive and exclusionary immigration policies by host countries prevented but EU minimum standards are set. Unfortunately, there are a number of weaknesses;[214] for example, while discrimination based on racial or ethnic origin is forbidden, religious beliefs, remain unprotected despite recommendation by the influential NGO-bases Starting Line group (Chopin *et al.* 2001: 25). This is by no means binding for national legislation; NGO pressure will still be effective. The European Parliament and the Economic and Social Committee will closely monitor this transition process and may ask the European Commission for regular reports.

4.12 The search for a new configuration for Europe: obstacles towards a European federation

As we search for a new configuration for Europe – one that goes beyond the old nation-states – the issues of membership, transnational citizenship, democratic representation and demographic representativeness, conflict prevention and peaceful coexistence and social welfare, present themselves in an entirely different light. Remembering the violent past that has seen Europe as the world's major theatre for wars and slaughter, the EU enlargement process, or 'Europeanization', bears a strong promise for a stable, peaceful order in western and central Europe. While threats now lurk outside the defined space for EU extension. Already in 1991, Johan Galtung feared that the end of the cold war might result in ethno-nationalist wars in eastern Europe and formerly Soviet Eurasia and lead to a 'Third-Worldization' of parts of the former Soviet Union, with unforeseen consequences for world peace. Unfortunately this fear is in the process of becoming reality. We recall that even the enlarged European Union is far from representative of a genuine unified of Europe and for the time being the 'stable peace' ought to be questioned. The same applies to the idea of EU enlargement as a sort of 'conflict resolution process', not least for internal or minority 'problems'.[215]

With regard to minority rights and the very notion of 'minority', the conditions for the possibility of a change of paradigm may soon be ready-made: the end to majority rule. The future Europe will not have a 'majority' anymore, hence we are approaching a situation Jean-Francois Lyotard dubbed the 'patchwork of minorities', characterizing the state of art of modernity as its ripeness. Not necessarily a utopia – such a conglomerate of cultures, religions, races, fashions and lifestyles, in amalgamation – but the world of 'minorities' would be able to dump the dominance of the 'majority' and its *Leitkultur* into the rubbish bin of history.

Europe can no longer be a jigsaw-puzzle of nation states and the current debate about a federal new Europe is hugely important for the future orientation of the union. Will there be a sort of 'enlarged Switzerland without Switzerland' as a genuinely federal entity or will there be some sort of 'devolution of powers' model with an upgrading of the regions? So far unitary, decentralized and federal concepts coexist, as a broad spectrum of administrative, legislative and regulatory arrangements, whereby laws and regulations mean different things in each state. Despite marked dissimilarities in their political structures, with a range of characteristic institutional and conceptual variations in each state, similar practices prevail in the federal states such as Germany and Belgium, in the unitary nations Italy and Spain, and in the multinational United Kingdom.

In France many fear that – following Joseph Fischer's advocacy for federalism in 2000 and repeated by the Chancellor at the end of April 2001 – Germany aims at transforming the European Union according to their own model, with the addition of a European constitution.[216] However, even in France, with its long-standing tradition of a centralized model (nurtured as a Jacobinist–Gaullist essential feature of the state apparatus) having already been somewhat revised by the devolution of powers in the case of Corsica (as a measure of appeasement), a genuine change of attitude can be detected in the form of 'a widespread wish for decisions to be taken closer to the grassroots and for further decentralization on the lines of other European countries' (Rémond 2001).[217] So, after more than 200 years of rigid centralization, some notion of decentralization (starting with local governance) became more acceptable only in the 1990s. Paradigmatic changes take time. Currently the French–German 'tandem', which was for decades of decisive importance for the European experience, in concert with the Benelux countries since the times of the European Economic Community, the build-up to the European Community and during its further development in to what has become today's European Union, seems somewhat out of steam.

The European Union will have to sort out what kind of decision-making process is appropriate. Federations and unitary states follow different ways, with power shared in a federal structure because its units wish it to be that way or with powers in a unitary model transferred to the peripheral authorities and the responsibility for the scope and strength of those powers being determined by the centre in Brussels. Opting for a federal administrative arrangement with more grassroots decentralization ('Europe of the Regions') and the subsidiarity principle in operation as at present would certainly reduce some of the in-built weaknesses of the European Union – its decision-making taking place above its citizens, thereby creating a fundamental democracy deficit. A new configuration along these lines would have a profound impact on the emerging European identity.

'EU semantics' have created many incomprehensible terms. The coinage 'external identity', which means a special European identity *vis-à-vis* the outside, is devoid of content to many citizens. For the Eurocrats, 'external identity' is yet to be created. The guiding notion, they say, is not the US melting-pot ideology – whose alleged success they much admire – but the development of a 'European facet' to existing multilayered identities, all the while preserving national, regional, cultural and ethnic identities. The new slogan might be 'Diversity and Coexistence in Prosperity'. The European Union is already the strongest economic block world-wide. Enlargement will make sure that the European economic hegemon will defend its position deep into the twenty-first century before China will retake the place it lost to the Europeans some 250 years ago.

Borders will be continuously changing during the next decades of enlargement and will be shifting eastwards. Nobody knows where the official EU borders will end – at the gates of the Orient and at the borders of the Ukrainian *Rus*? – but certainly, according to the unwritten but not unanimous consensus, at the borders of Russia. And nobody knows when the process will stop (probably around the year 2020). The challenge is how to cater for diversity while trying to avoid exclusion within the future enlarged membership.[218] To give more shape to a 'European facet' of identity the decision makers must think about a process towards European citizenship, as a counterweight and binding framework to the existing cultural pluralism.

The new concept of multicultural citizenship – decoupled from nationality and ethnicity – will greatly contribute to a project, which aspires to more than 'external identity' or a 'European facet' of identity but aims to constitute an emerging European identity. This long-term open-ended project of identity formation will produce social cohesion, identification with democratic culture and a new sense of belonging to a Europe beyond the old nation-states. The new Europe must be, in equal measure, the Europe of the citizens and the Europe of the peoples.

5
Nationality Policy as Violence Prevention: a Brief Comparison of Large States

No more than a cursory glimpse can be given here of the political, military, and economic measures and strategies of control applied by large states – in which about half the world's population lives – to nations and nationalities which they define as minorities.[1] A summary and classification of the mechanisms of conflict resolution provided for by international law, classical minority protection, autonomy arrangements and official pronouncements on nationality policy are still awaited. Deficits prevail regarding attempts at a structural grouping together of the minority and nationality policies of differing forms of societies according to properly defined criteria.

Too little account has been taken of the nationality policies of certain multinational states when it comes to looking for methods of preventing and dealing with protracted and bloody ethno-national conflicts. Such policies are far from merely being part of the historical and political framework that needs to be considered in the search for promising 'solutions'. A whole series of states have been able to pursue active and successful policies of conflict prevention by negotiation involving some element of nationality policy. Others, such as India, have used similar offers to try and resolve armed conflicts that have already escalated; this procedure is a great deal more difficult. Nationality policies that merit the name are generally not conceived of as solutions to conflicts that are already smouldering or have already erupted. Some procedures wrongly labelled 'nationality policy' aim more at containment, or pose the nationality question in a purely socio-political context. But such policies are part of the problem.

A detailed structural comparison ought to be made of the different approaches to nationality policy pursued by selected states such as Denmark, Canada, the USA, the Commonwealth of Independent States (CIS)/Russian Federation, China, India, Australia, Brazil, Colombia, Panama, Nicaragua, Ethiopia and so on. Reference to some of these has already been made. The only – fragmentary – contribution I can make here to this interdisciplinary study is to point out some levels of comparison and some objects that can be practically compared. Official data issued by selected multinational states should be verified by appropriate fieldwork.[2]

5.1 Self-government: cases for comparison

A comparison of the nationality policies of the large multinational and territorial states would be particularly informative. I confine myself here to a rough comparison of the three most populous state structures in the world (China, India and the CIS/USSR). I then go on to draw a few partial and non-systematic comparisons with the large former settler colonies (the USA and Canada). Disparities and inconsistencies will emerge on account of the differing characteristics of the cases being compared. I have already pointed to certain key elements of minority policy in Europe.[3]

Possible areas for comparison would be:

- policies in regard to indigenous peoples in former European settler colonies (the USA, Canada, Australia, New Zealand, South Africa); the situation of the Inuit nation in four different states (Denmark/Greenland, Canada, the USA/Alaska, and the Russian Federation); Indian rights in North and South America (the USA, Canada, Guatemala, Nicaragua, Panama, Brazil)
- minority policies in Europe: in particular the explosive situation of the new minorities in eastern Europe; the new variant of the border minorities problem in states with large minorities outside their territorial areas (Russia, Germany, Hungary) and the possible role here of the OSCE (activities of the High Commissioner on National Minorities, elaboration of minority conventions); policies in regard to nomadic Roma and Sinti in eastern and western Europe (development of political rights, multiculturalism)
- nationality policies in multinational states: in the large states of the (post-)socialist Second World (China, ex-USSR/CIS); also in the large and multinational states of the Third World (India, Indonesia).

The ethnic structure in the three largest multinational entities of the CIS, China and India is extremely varied and complex. The nationality policies that have been realized in the form of decentralization, autonomy and self-governance do actually follow the ethnic borders – at least in the case of small entities. In the case of larger territories, there have been crude attempts to achieve this.

5.2 The USSR model and what remains of it

The Commonwealth of Independent States (CIS) currently comprises, with the exception of the Baltic states, all the successor states of the former USSR.

The fragmentation of the Soviet Union was pre-programmed by its ethno-national subdivision, and it was because of this that the collapse initially proceeded without violence. It was only a second phase of disintegration, together with unilateral declarations of autonomy (or abrogation of minority autonomy by the majority populations in the new states) that led to a number of violent conflicts on CIS territory. Most of these conflicts have been halted. After 70 years of *pax sovietica* (broken only by the German invasion), there has been a total of nine wars on CIS territory, seven of which have been brought to a close. Violence in Chechnya and Tajikstan continues, while wars begun in Kyrgyzstan and Kazakhstan incurred cross-border spill over effects.[4]

- From 1922 to 1989, the USSR had a composite structure comprising: 18 autonomous republics, 8 autonomous regions and 10 autonomous districts. Of the autonomous territories, 16 republics (now 21), 5 regions and all the districts were located in the Russian Federation and non-Russians made-up 17 per cent of the Federation's total population.[5]
- Twenty-three nations of the former USSR have a population of more than one million; these are followed by 26 nationalities with 0.1 to 1 million, 13 with 0.01 to 0.1 million and 68 with up to 10,000. Until 1990, there were 130 languages in official use, representing seven linguistic families (a unique phenomenon in world terms).
- In the USSR, about 50 per cent of the population belonged to a variety of non-Russian nations and nationalities. In some successor states, such as Georgia and Moldova, the autonomy rights of minority nationalities were revoked; war resulted in four cases.[6]

5.2.1   Abrogation of autonomy as a trigger to war in the CIS

The abolition of autonomous territories – occurring in several of the new states after gaining independence – was an attempt by nationalist-cum-chauvinist state classes to 'turn back history'. This aggressive policy, combined with the abolition of the constitutionally guaranteed rights of minority nations, led in several cases to an escalation in ethno-national tensions.[7] This abrogation of autonomy led to the emergence of a form of conflict previously unknown in the former USSR[8] – namely, violent ethno-national opposition *from below*, a type of conflict which up to now has predominated chiefly in the Third World.

In all of the four cases in which abrogation of autonomy has triggered war,[9] the 'rules of play' were changed unilaterally by the respective state peoples or titular nations, to the detriment of the minority or minorities concerned. A number of other ethnic conflicts had been generated or aggravated in the Soviet period, chiefly by the Stalinist deportations, by unfair demarcation of borders, or by discrimination against certain nationalities. Payne has identified four types of ethno-ideological conflict in the CIS.[10] The objects of contention in each case are: (1) historically disputed territories (3 conflicts);[11] (2) the administrative status of an ethnic territory (Abkhazia, Gagauzia, Pridbestrovye, Chechnya and so on); (3) the threat of peoples in indigenous territories being outnumbered by settlers, as in the Baltic, Moldova, certain Russian republics, and elsewhere (for example Abkhazia); and (4) the consequences of Stalinist deportations.[12] In addition, there are several ethnic conflicts in the CIS that are not new; they were only superficially brought to peace by the *pax sovietica*, without the underlying causes of the conflict being removed.

5.2.2 No 'Third-Worldization' of the former USSR

From 1989, a dramatic and belated revival of nationalism was shaking the peripheral areas of the former Second World. After the collapse of the *pax sovietica*, a wave of violent ethno-nationalism overtook eastern Europe – the former nominally socialist states and the Balkan states, notably the once-proud non-aligned Yugoslavia. The breaking-away of many 'nations oppressed by tsarism and forcibly incorporated into the state', and of nations later 'forcibly confined within the state borders' by the Soviet Union – contrary to Lenin's assertions – is still under way.[13] The present-day ethno-national trouble spots are the small south-western and central Asian states of the CIS and some Russian mini-republics in the Caucasus.[14]

After clashes between Chechen and Ingush (as well as Osetians) between December 1991 and March 1992, the first bloody war on Russian territory began in December 1994 in Chechnya. This war assumed the character of a secessionist conflict with the destructive potential for escalation. There was a danger that Dudayev's (and later Yandarbijev's) 'holy warriors' might internationalize the conflict by further hostage-taking and acts of terror. The war ended in August 1996 with a 'gentlemen's agreement' between former generals (Lebed, as Yeltsin's envoy, and Mashkhadov) – without the core issues being 'resolved'. The seemingly moderate leadership under Mashkhadov managed to calm the situation only for a short period.[15] Some three years later, in October 1999 the war reignited, with Chechen rebels attacking Dagestan. The 'victory' of the Russian army in Chechnya gave Vladimir Putin a decisive advantage in becoming elected president of Russia – again, without Russia being able to put an end to the secessionist's guerrilla war and without searching for a lasting resolution to this conflict dating from the nineteenth century.

In contrast, the Armenians and Azeris have so far held to the agreed ceasefire, though the Armenians have continued to occupy one area of Azerbaijan. In Tajikistan, in Central Asia, the bloodiest civil war so far launched (in 1992) by the Islamists against most of the clans around President Rakhmanov, seems for the moment to have been quelled by CIS troops; but exchanges of fire on the Afghan border will continue. Violent ethnic conflicts continue to rage in neighbouring Afghanistan (between the Pashtun-based Taliban against Uzbeks, Tajiks, Hazari and others).

Compared with a wide range of conflicts in the Third World,[16] the violent conflicts in the ex-USSR display a number of significant differences:

1. only in a third of the cases (three out of nine) are the conflicts protracted. They are located in areas running along the borders with the Middle East and Central Asia – that is, in the Southern Caucasus (Armenians versus Azeris, Chechnya) and in Tajikistan as part of an arc of cross-border conflicts in the Afghanistan–Tajikistan–Uzbekistan–Kirgistan region (see Table 1.4)[17]
2. the recruiting bases for these conflicts are members of what, in Soviet times, were largely non-dominant nations or nationalities, who now find themselves in the position of being titular nations (often in the role of aggressor) or national minorities
3. the majority of these conflicts do not have the characteristics of guerrilla wars (Chechnya and Tajikistan are exceptions), rather they are either disputes between aggressive armed factions (army or police units) or intrastate civil-war-like power struggles (Georgia, Tajikistan) or occasionally disputes not involving the state (pogroms). Generally there is noticeable support from outside (Russians/Russia, CIS troops, intervention by Turkey and Iran in the Southern Caucasus). Occasionally an insurgency is conducted in concert with other rebel movements (for example, Abkhazia with help from the Caucasian 'federation') or supported by Islamist mercenaries (in Chechnya, Uzbekistan and Tajikistan), partly al-Qaeda.
4. the deeper causes of the violent conflicts in the ex-USSR do not lie invariably in the fact of colonization by a previously ethnically mixed but ideologically unitary power élite. Local élites exercised repressive rule, implemented centralized policies (deportations, settler colonialism, division of territories) and acted with the support or in the name of a dominant nation. Other causes lie, rather, in the administrative or political status of particular areas, or in some long history of conflict.

The explosive nature of these conflicts is due to two structurally different patterns: (1) the subsequent abrogation of the autonomy of non-dominant nations (or smaller nationalities) by a chauvinist titular nation or nations, whose threat to the identity and well-being of the minority nations/nationalities provokes resistance in the form of ethno-nationalism from below and/or civil disobedience; (2) the resumption of historical conflicts between hostile nations/nationalities which had been quelled but not resolved by the *pax sovietica*.

5.2.3   Russia continues to define itself as a plurinational state

The Russian Federation is currently the only successor state to the Soviet Union that defines itself constitutionally as a multinational state. The *de facto* highest-ranking geographic entities in terms of prestige and status (alongside or above the *oblasts*) are the 21 minority-nationality republics, most of which (16 out of 21) are former Autonomous Soviet Socialist Republics (ASSRs). The following minority republics exist within the Russian Federation:

- eight republics in the North Caucasus: Adygea, Karachay-Cherkessia, Kabardino-Balkaria, Ingushetia, North Ossetia, Chechnya, Dagestan, Kalmyck;
- two republics in the European north: Karelia and Komi; *two krais*: Nenetsk and Komi
- six republics in the central European part of the Volga–Kama–Urals triangle: Mordvinia, Chuvashia, Mari El, Tatarstan, Bashkortostan, Udmurtia
- four republics in Central Asia, along the Mongolian border: Altai, Khakassia, Tuva, Buryatia; and two Buryat*okrugs*: Ustyurt-Buryat and Aga-Buryat
- a republic in the far north of Siberia: Sakha-Yakutia; four *okrugs*: Khanty-Mansi, Yamalo-Nenetsk, Taimyr and Evenk[18]
- an autonomous *oblast* in the far east: Jewish autonomous area
- two *okrugs* in the far north-east: Chukot and Korjaken.

The 21 republics and ten autonomous districts belonging to non-Russian minorities are concentrated in the most southerly and most northerly parts of the Russian Federation. With their population of 7–8 million, the nine territorial units in the Far East, along the coast and in the Amur area, are very sparsely populated compared with the neighbouring growth areas of Japan, China and Korea. It is from here that the great wave of migrants (especially Chinese farmers and traders) will come in future. The far-eastern region of Russia will thus be sharing directly in the East Asian economic miracle, the Confucian work-ethic and Japanese technology. (Giant China was virtually untouched by the crisis that hit Korea and most South-East Asian countries from autumn 1997 and has enjoyed steady growth since the 1980s.) But the Russians and indigenous peoples living in the Far East could soon be demographically outnumbered, and this would elicit a defensive response, particularly on the part of the resident Russian population. The indigenous minorities are threatened with the same fate as the neighbouring Ainu in Japan.

5.2.4   Enhanced status means more resources

For territorial units (such as republics) which have exportable natural resources, declaring sovereignty is a great temptation. Enhanced status generally means a greater share in export income. As the example of Sakha-Yakutia (which is the size of Western Europe and has one million inhabitants) shows, this can produce the oddest of effects. With a total population of almost 400,000, the Yakuts are the largest nation in the north. Together with Russian migrants and five other minority indigenous peoples, they

inhabit a territory covering one fifth of Russia which is equivalent in size to
Western Europe or the Indian Union.[19] Twenty per cent of the world's diamond production is conducted in the republic of Sakha-Yakutia. Life there
is better than elsewhere, since the republic receives 27 per cent of its export
income in hard currency. The down-side being the unbridled plunder that
goes on in these fragile permafrost areas.[20] The Russian settlers living in
Yakutia have given full support to its otherwise implausible claim to independent statehood and declaration of sovereignty because they hope a dol-
lar economy will bring them a better standard of living.[21] The Volga Tatars,
like the Yakut, live alongside Russians in their territories; as titular nations
they are seeking to lay claim to the massive reserves of natural resources
(Sakha-Yakutia) and developed oil-industries (Tatarstan).

The present republics are territories, which, in contrast to the now-
independent Soviet republics, did not have a right of secession. They would
find it difficult to secure political recognition from the international community (as the case of Chechnya again made clear). None the less, some former autonomous republics and autonomous regions (*oblasts*) of the USSR,
and even nationalities without their own territory (for example the Crimean
Tatars) now pursue an active foreign policy. Twelve autonomous territories
or republics became members of UNPO.[22]

5.2.5 The difficulty of consolidation and self-identification in the CIS

At the global level of bloc-formation, the process of fragmentation in the east
was in direct and startling contrast to the process of ever-closer enmeshment
going on in Western Europe.[23] In the regions on the southern periphery of
the former Soviet Union, patterns similar to those in the Third World have
begun to take shape, though up to now – excepting in the Caucasus and
Tajikistan – this has been a largely civilian and constitutional process.[24] Soviet
federalization and nationality policy did make a decisive contribution to the
break-up of the USSR, but thanks to the high standard of ethno-national
interaction, it also prevented large-scale wars. A number of positive elements
of the model continue to demonstrate their validity even today. Given the
adverse circumstances, characterized by continued economic decline, growing poverty and new-found chauvinism, the problems of consolidation and
self-identification in the successor states of the Soviet Union will not be
solved in a matter of a year or two, and not without conflict.

5.3 China: a large multinational-style state

China defines itself as a multinational-style state. The 1982 constitution stipulates equal rights and duties for all nationalities, and this may be interpreted
as marking a break with thousands of years of Sino-centrism.[25] Since the
1940s, in addition to the 24 provinces patterned, with modifications, on the

USSR, a large number of territorial entities have been created, including five large autonomous regions, a host of smaller autonomous departments and districts, and hundreds of cantons in which there are different gradations of minority self-government. The Middle Empire has a 4000-year-old history to look back on when it comes to relations with non-Han peoples.[26]

Scattered over more than half the surface area of the People's Republic of China are 55 officially recognized, state-defined nationalities (*shaoshuminzu*):

- the Western half of China is home to populous nations such as the Turkish-speaking Uighur, Tibetans, Muslim Hui and, on the borders with the CIS, the Tajiks, Tatars and Russians;
- in the north-east there are Mongolians, Manchu and Koreans;
- in the mountainous regions of the centre there are She and Tu;
- in the south-west there are Lhoba, Yi, Naxi, Maonan, Miao, Achang, Hani, Jingpo (Kachin), Lahu, Lisu (Kachin), Drung, Nu, Pumi, Wa, Dai (speaking Lao-Tai), Bai, Yao and Hui;
- in central and south(-east) China there is the populous Sinicized Zhuang people, more Yao, and Jing, Li, Tujia and Gaoshan.[27]

5.3.1 China's minorities: a critical mass

According to official statistics, China's officially recognized minorities make up 7 per cent of the total population (the other 93 per cent are Han) – in other words, they number 89–90 million (out of a total of 1200 million). This is equivalent to the population of the Federal Republic of Germany after reunification.[28] For various reasons, China's minorities, despite their comparatively small share of the overall population, constitute a critical mass – in qualitative as opposed to purely quantitative terms.[29]

- nineteen nationalities have populations of over one million (over 0.08 per cent). These are: the Han (93.3 per cent), Zhuang (1.33 per cent), Hui (0.72 per cent), Uighur (0.59 per cent), Yi (0.54 per cent), Miao (0.5 per cent), Manchu (0.43 per cent), Tibetans (0.39 per cent), Mongolians (0.34 per cent), Tujia (0.28 per cent), Bouyei (0.21 per cent), Korean (0.18 per cent), Dong (0.14 per cent), Yao (0.14 per cent), Bai (0.11 per cent), Hani (0.11 per cent), Kazakh (0.09 per cent), Dai (0.08 per cent), Li (0.08 per cent). The next, the Lisu, have 600,000 or 0.05 per cent (Census of China cited in Yin 1989: 431)
- the Zhuang (15 million), the Hui (8 million), the Uighur (7 million), the Yi and Miao (5.5–6 million each), and the Manchu, Tibetans and Mongolians (each with 4–5 million) also constitute a critical mass in demographic terms
- about one million people still belong to 'unidentified nationalities'[30]
- fifty-six official languages belonging to five language groups are in use in China

- the territories occupied by the minority nations/nationalities cover half the surface area of China and are of major economic (raw materials) and strategic importance
- every official minority has a seat in the People's Congress (parliament) and enjoys autonomy rights (*zizhifa*) in autonomous areas (*zizhiqu*).

5.3.2 China's well-developed structure of autonomous areas

Demands for self-government for the various nationalities of China were accepted in petition form as early as 1922 by the Chinese Communist Party and were formally proposed in 1928.[31] The party and its central government began to implement this resolution from the 1940s, using a modified version of Lenin's nationalities policy.[32]

Immediately after the emergence of the People's Republic of China, Inner Mongolia became the first component in what was to be a sophisticated hierarchical structure of autonomous territories. By 1985 China had five autonomous regions, 31 autonomous prefectures, 96 autonomous counties, and 800 autonomous 'banners'; most of the larger entities were demarcated as early as the 1950s. The first entities to be created, between 1947 and 1958, were the autonomous units in the north (Mongolia), west (Tibet) and east; from the 1950s a similar process took place in the south and west (especially Yunnan).

The system was steadily extended in the 1980s and 1990s with the addition of over twenty more territories. The obvious positive results are cultural pluralism and ethnic revival. Observers talk of a new tolerance towards religious practices and of a new prosperity based on economic reforms.[33] There are a number of internal and external threats to autonomization:

- the Uighur in the first place[34] and the Tibetans, might be described as dissident nations;[35] in my opinion, so can the Muslim Hui, the Mongolians and the Yi.[36] Some border areas (especially Yunnan, Tibet, Xinjiang/East Turkestan and Nei Mongol) are not under the firm control of the government
- the rise in living standards of the *yuanzu minzu*[37] as part of the unique Chinese 'economic miracle' by no means guarantees the success of the state's strategies of integration – as the events in Tibet in 1987 and 1988–89 and also the unrest in 1990–91 in East Turkestan (Urumqi) and Inner Mongolia show
- the state borders are not ethnic borders. Some peoples have never given up their marriage relations across international borders
- the Burmese civil war and, in recent years, the opium trade from the Golden Triangle are contributory factors in the fragility of security and order in the border areas of south-west China.

5.3.3   Conflict aversion and nationality policies in Yunnan

Comparison of the situation in the strategic province of Yunnan with that in the neighbouring states of Burma, Laos and Vietnam would be of great value in assessing the conflict-averting effects of Chinese nationality policy.[38] Members of 20 nationalities (out of the total of 56 official minorities in China) live in Yunnan, which lies in an exposed position next to the infamous Golden Triangle. Non-Han peoples account for more than a third of the population there. Over 40 autonomous territories have been created in Yunnan since 1953 (the first was Xishuangbanna, the Dai area along the Mekong).[39] The Dai form part of the Lao-Tai linguistic group. The name 'Thai' was also used as a vehicle for a particular political standpoint and is therefore rejected by many non-Siamese.[40]

Some autonomously administered territories of minority nations/nationalities in China lie immediately next to liberated areas belonging to the same or another non-dominant nationality that extend, on the Burmese side, along the troubled border from Arunachal Pradesh (north-east India) and Tibet to Laos. The differences on either side of the international border are huge.

Large rebel areas on the other side of the international border are *de facto* autonomous (or were so until 1989–90). The Burmese army was never able to quell or control them completely; this applies to the territories of the Kachin Independence Organization (KIO) and of the Wa, who previously served as soldiers for the Communist Party of Burma and in 1989 formed the United Wa State Army (UWSA).[41] On this side of the border, the Chinese Lisu (one of six Kachin groups in Burma), who, with a membership of 500,000, are the largest nationality, administer the autonomous prefecture of Nujiang, which runs along the upper reaches of the Salween (Nu in Chinese), Mekong (Lancang) and Yangtze (Jinsha). These lifelines for Burma, Indochina and China, which rise in Tibet and flow out through impressive gorges across northwest Yunnan and into Burma and Laos or the Chinese plains, cut across the land of the Lisu.[42]

The contrast between the situation of some mountain peoples in China and those in Burma – notably the Lisu, Jingpo and other peoples (such as the Drung and Nu) who belong to the group of nationalities known as Kachin in Burma and are fragmented by present international borders – could not be greater.[43] On this side of the border, the Lisu and Jingpo live tranquil, peaceful lives in their bamboo houses, mandarin-groves and pastures. On market-days, the taverns and the market-places, overflowing with gaily coloured Chinese and local goods, are full of farmers and people from the surrounding area. Health-care and all schooling are free in the autonomous prefecture of Nujiang; on Sundays, the churches are well-attended.[44] On the other side of the border, the standard of living is much lower: most children do not go to school, there are no clinics and life is perilous. Until the present ceasefire, which the KIO was forced to conclude with the SLORC dictatorship under pressure from China, many Burmese Lisu, fighting in the ranks of the KIO had been engaged, since the 1960s, in a brutal jungle-war against the much better-equipped Burmese army.

The plateau-country of Yunnan has always been a marginal region, which only attracted Chinese settlers from the time of the Han dynasty. It was originally a quasi-independent region, with the Nanzhao kingdom as the regional power.[45] Nanzhao was later forced to pay tribute to the Chinese empire, as was the Bai kingdom of Dali.[46]

The creeping Sinicization of the upper classes of almost all nationalities can now be detected, even by outsiders, all the way into Burma (in the form of the spread of Confucianism, of the Chinese language and Chinese dress, cuisine and nomenclature).[47] Yunnan is not only an ethnic 'multi-verse', it also lies at the point of intersection between no less than seven religions, including four world religions.[48] Because it was not fully under Chinese control, it remained closed to foreigners until a few years ago, but the tourist invasion has now begun.[49]

5.4   India's nationality policy as a model for conflict resolution?

The postcolonial policy of the Indian Union can, with some reservations, be cited as an example of a reasonably successful constitutional form of conflict resolution. The problems that *can* be observed, and whose causes I shall try to identify in what follows here, do not lie in the instruments and mechanisms of conflict aversion, nor in the structure of the state, the laws, the affirmative provisions for protection or the regulations stipulating positive discrimination for the socially weak. Problems and flaws occur, rather, by way of poor implementation, bureaucratic sabotage and half-hearted enforcement of existing provisions.

The normative and instrumental bases of the Indian system of conflict aversion are similar to those used in China and the former USSR: secularism (with 83 per cent of the population being Hindus), socialism (non-aligned) *de facto* one-party rule and self-reliance. These elements are bound together by a specifically Indian form of syncretism in respect of state ideology and its symbols. The emblems of the state, such as the eternal wheel, are not of Hindu origin but are Buddhist symbols. For almost half-a-century one-half of the population embraced by the coalition of minorities united under the umbrella of the Congress Party has on occasion translated into 60 or 70 per cent of the seats in the central parliament.[50]

The component parts of the Indian system of conflict prevention are:

- a federal state structure allowing flexibility in the creation of constituent states according to cultural/linguistic/ethnic criteria (mostly on the basis of official language-areas);

- bilingualism at central-state level (English and Hindi);
- transfer payments for disadvantaged constituent states; and
- well-developed protective regulations for indigenous groups (aboriginal Adivasi), Dalits (also indigenous casteless peoples) and people from low castes.

The parallels with previously mentioned examples are clear: the Indian Union is the largest multi-ethnic state with no homogeneous majority population acting as its mainstay, as do the Han in China, for example, or the Russians in the Russian Federation. As in China and the former USSR, a long-established ruling *de facto* unity party – the Congress Party – views an integrating nationality policy as a form of conflict prevention, enforces it and has, over decades, adapted it to developments.

5.4.1 Cultural diversity and state structure

The cultural and ethnic diversity of India is extraordinary:

- the total population of India is estimated to have passed one billion in 2001; of this number, 90–100 million (almost 10 per cent) belong to the indigenous minority-nationalities, with little overlap between these and the 180–200 million indigenous casteless Dalits (17–20 per cent)[51]
- fourteen major languages (out of a total of over 100) from six language families are in official use; like the Dalit, Mongolian – especially Tibeto Burmese – Austro-Asiatic and Negritic nationalities, the Dravidian-speaking south also does not belong to the mainstream Hindi-speaking population.

The Indian Union today consists of 24 union states and a number of union territories.[52] Some of the new states, notably Nagaland and Mizoram in the north-east (formerly Assam),[53] came into being as a result of the pressure of armed uprisings by the Naga and Mizo against the union of India. In the case of the Naga (National Socialist Council of Nagaland: NSCN) and Boro, insurgency has continued at various levels up to the present day.[54] Autonomous districts for nationalities that have been recognized as minorities exist in various constituent states. The Andaman, Nicobar and Laccadive islands have a special status.

A number of elements of the Indian state system were taken over from the British Empire, but in an Indianized form. India did not, like other Third World countries (especially non-British colonies) inherit an over-centralized colonial state structure: its federal division did, however, resemble that of Burma, which created problems from the very outset. The initial division of India reflected more the peculiarities of British indirect rule than the ethno-cultural realities. Demographic concentration in large constituent states, a series of small feudal-cum-colonial principalities, and a number of separately administered mountain regions, were the distinguishing features of British India.

5.4.2   Protection of the Aboriginal peoples, Dalits and people of low caste

The legally stipulated protection of the Aboriginal Adivasi population, the casteless Dalits and people of low caste (scheduled tribes and castes) had already been introduced under British colonial rule. These protective regulations are particularly important because, despite its formally democratic institutions, India may be regarded as one of the most socially repressive countries in the world. Sixty million Adivasis and up to 200 million Dalits are treated as second- or third-class individuals.[55]

The Aboriginal population is almost exactly congruent with the 60 million Adivasis. Subsumed in this category are nationalities from four overall groups:

- populous Dravidian groups of the Gond people of central India (in Madhya Pradesh and five neighbouring constituent states), the Bhil in western Deccan and the Oraon in eastern Deccan
- Austro-Asiatic peoples such as: the Santals[56] (who are related to the Mon-Khmer group) in West Bengal, Bihar and Orissa; the Munda and Ho in eastern Deccan; smaller tribally structured peoples such as the Maria and Muria in southern Madhya Pradesh; the Chenchu and Yanadi in Andra Pradesh; the Kadar, Allar and Kurumba in the forests and mountains of Kerala and Tamil Nadu
- Mongolian peoples of the Himalaya range and north-east India, but who do not at all identify themselves as Adivasis
- a huge and varied number of small and very small groups living in reserves on the subcontinent; they include the group of Negrites (now to be found chiefly on the Andaman islands), who, again, do not identify themselves as Adivasis.[57]

Most of the Adivasi groups live in the dense forests which, though still covering one-fifth of India's surface area, is being converted into cultivable land at an alarming rate – with the familiar side-effects of erosion, flooding and disruption of the water economy.[58] Whereas for the last Andaman islanders living on an island-reserve, and for the already decultured Onge Negritos, ethnocide is moving ever closer, the cultures of the large Dravidian and Austro-Asiatic peoples have stubbornly preserved themselves, despite expulsion and discrimination.

Only exploitation as urban coolies or rural debt-slaves sets the Adivasis on the same footing as the large social class of the Dalit. Adivasis are now active in a number of political movements, especially the campaign for autonomy in Jharkhand and the new ethno-ecological mass movements (Chipko, Appiko, Narmada).[59] The Chattisgarh Mukti Morcha (CMM) trade union has been set up in the Chattisgarh region of Madhya Pradesh, in central India. It is the first to employ the notion of cross-sectoral activity, bringing together the struggle of the Adivasis and that of people in insecure employment.[60]

The Dalit ('oppressed' in Hindi) are regarded as the most oppressed section of the population – the 'lowest of the low'. They live either as bonded labourers without rights or as much-despised coolies; their children do heavy labour and many of them are forced into prostitution.[61] This huge Dalit section of the population lives cheek by jowl with the Hindus of caste, scattered throughout most of India's 200,000 villages and in hundreds of cities.[62]

The Dalits themselves consider that they belong to the Aboriginal peoples of India, subjected to Aryan oppression from 1500AD.[63] The self-appellation 'Dalit' as used by the more politically aware sections of the untouchables embraces certain lower castes and Adivasi peoples. Some low castes (such as the Sadan) became ethnicized as a result of the peculiarities of Indian society (or else are, or were, true ethnic groups). Discrimination against the Dalits, although prohibited since the 1950s, is almost universally tolerated and is perpetuated through the violent structures of exploitation and through the agency of most of the Dalits themselves: feelings of inferiority have been internalized over three centuries by the millions and millions of members of this humiliated underclass.

5.4.3 The use of quotas in the allocation of state jobs

The Indian constitution contains provisions for protection of weak sections of the population against social injustice and 'all forms of exploitation' (article 46).[64] Additional protective regulations provide for quotas in the allocation of some 18 million state jobs and in the award of student places. The quota of 22.5 per cent for disadvantaged indigenous populations and members of casteless and low castes is divided between the Adivasis, Dalits and the 'Scheduled Castes':

- 7.5 per cent to the 600 official groups of the 70-million-strong sched-uled tribes, including the six mini-states of the mountain peoples of the north-east
- 15 per cent to the 150–200-million-strong Dalits (given the name 'Harijans' or 'children of god' by Gandhi and generally known as 'untouchables' or casteless peoples) and to the incredible figure of 3743 'backward castes'.[65]

These provisions, important and positive as they may be for enhancing equality of opportunity in India's socially repressive, hierarchical, caste-based society, are, in fact, poorly enforced and in practice the quotas are not fulfilled. The permanent power-holders, the Brahmin, account for 5.5 per cent of the population and occupy most top jobs; the next five high-ranking forward castes claim most of the rest.[66] The caste system and the strong sense of hierarchy are peculiar to Hindu society. In social prac-tice it may also 'pervade the non-Hindu communities in India in various degrees'.[67]

According to the Mandal Report of the 'Backward Classes Commission' in 1980, for example, Adivasi representation in the highest echelon of the hierarchy, the Indian Civil Service, is in reality only 2.2 per cent and that of the Dalits only 8.5 per cent.[68] Following the recommendations of the commission, Prime Minister V. P. Singh's intention to reserve additional quotas of state jobs for other disadvantaged groups – some 27 per cent for Other Backward Castes and Classes (OBCs), besides the 22.5 per cent for the Scheduled Castes and Tribes – led to unrest in 1990 and brought about his government's downfall.[69]

Religious freedom, as laid down in the constitution, also forms part of the protective regulations for minorities in the wider sense. It guarantees free exercise of religious beliefs to the large Muslim minority (110 million or 11.2 per cent of total population of 985 million in 1998), the Christians (2.2 per cent), the Sikhs (1.7 per cent), the Buddhists (0.7 per cent), the Jains (0.5 per cent) and the Animists (no figures available), despite an overwhelming Hindu majority.[70]

5.4.4   Agitation for Jharkhand: a state for the Adivasi

The Indian system of conflict avoidance suffers from another, not insignificant, drawback. If a conflict remains below the threshold of armed hostility for a lengthy period, nothing much happens – in other words, the governments of the Union and constituent states show no inclination to make any concessions. For example, as regards the agitation in favour of Jharkhand, a potential Adivasi state comprising the four constituent states of West Bengal, Bihar, Orissa and Madhya Pradesh, the politicians turn a deaf ear.[71]

A multi-ethnic Jharkhand would offer improved conditions of survival to a population of over 30 million Aboriginal inhabitants living in an area the size of France. A special status is planned for the 10 million non-tribals in the area under claim. However, Chota Nagpur, which is part of Jharkhand, contains half of all India's natural resources, and this is another reason why the goal of a separate constituent state still lies a long way off.[72]

The Adivasis in the Jharkhand Mukti Morcha (JMM) and the umbrella-organization, the Jharkhand Co-ordination Committee (JCC), were not taken seriously until they took-up arms, and this, according to Wallensteen and Axell, began in 1992.[73] Since the uprisings of 1967–68, the Naxalites have also become active again in the region.[74] Since the crushing, by the British colonizers and their mercenary forces, of the great rebellions by the Santals in 1855, the Munda in 1797–1800, 1807 and 1819, the Kolh in 1832, and the Sardar movement of Birsa Munda in 1875–99, the Adivasi movement for autonomy in central and eastern India has been largely non-violent.[75]

It is as much as 150 years since the first white missionaries came to the Gond and Kolh. They taught the Adivasis that 'violence and alcoholism were sins'.[76] The most successful were certain Protestant churches (including

German Lutherans). The churches undertook various administrative and social tasks in the Adivasi villages. Not surprisingly, they soon came into conflict with landowners and the colonial authorities. Teaching the Adivasis to read and write made them more independent of the rich estate-owners and also more self-confident. After the expulsion of the white missionaries from the region, the churches began anew and today play an important role.

Religious awareness (of a caste-free minority religion), the chance of education, and the struggle for human rights, land rights and trade-union rights, were combined – as in the north-east, among the Naga and Mizo, but in a less radical form – with a growing awareness of national identity among the Adivasis. A series of politically motivated murders of leaders of the autonomy movement, attempts to cause schism within it, efforts by the ruling Congress Party to entice supporters away from it and the attempted corruption of prominent figures, all so far have been unable to break the Adivasi movement.[77]

As in the north-east, one solution might be to begin by creating a union territory, and at some later stage upgrade this into a constituent state for the Adivasis. This form of autonomy and federalization, combined with a fair distribution of the profits from resources, would be quite sufficient in the case of Jharkhand.

5.4.5 The special status of the hill tribes

The tribal Adivasis ('primitives' in Hindi) are despised, oppressed and marginalized by the Hindus of caste. This is also true of the hill tribes, though to a much lesser extent because of their isolation. Such hill tribes include: the Naga, Mizo, Kuki, Jamatia, Khasi and Boro in the north-east, and the Monpa, Nishi, Apa Tani in the Himalaya region (from Ladakh, Himachal Pradesh and Uttarkhand to Sikkim and Arunachal Pradesh). Few have remained Buddhist (in Ladakh, for example) or even Animist; larger nations such as the Naga and Mizo have been successfully Christianized since the end of the last century.

Some peoples, especially the Tibeto-Burmese hill tribes of the north-east, cannot be regarded as disadvantaged for a number of reasons: they now have the highest rates of literacy (60–70 per cent); in the case of the Dalits, it is 10 per cent. The central governments sought – with little success – to break their resistance by means of repression and massive transfer payments. Their economic situation, political mobilization and cultural independence therefore cannot be compared to the entirely different situation of most Adivasis in central and southern India.

Comparing north-east India (formerly the state of Assam) and civil-war-torn Burma from an ethnic standpoint (as well from the point of view of their comparable area and population) is a reasonable undertaking, given their similar compositions. A leader of the Chin National Front (from Burma) has stated that the Chin should join the Indian Union; they would, he said, have more rights there than in Burma. He said this with an eye on the culturally and geographically disadvantaged Mizo. In February 1987, Mizoram (the land of the Mizo), which had been a Union territory since 1972, was proclaimed the 24th union state of India. Separate statehood for the Mizo people was accepted as a solution to, or method of settling, the armed conflict between the central state and the Mizo guerrilla fighters. The 20-year-long fight for self-determination waged by the Mizo National Front ended with the latter's incorporation into the political process.

This development, which should be regarded as positive, had begun with the Nago rebellion of 1953–54; Nehru and Indira Gandhi had previously tried to resolve the 'minority problem' without making any substantial concessions. Six rounds of talks ended in failure; the breakthrough came in 1972, when the Revolutionary Government of Nagaland (RGN) got its 1500 fighters to disarm and entered into negotiations. In November 1975 the Shillong Agreement was concluded with two other Naga organizations (the FGN and NNC). This extended the autonomy status established in 1963. The National Socialist Council of Nagaland, on the other hand, rejected the Shillong Agreement as 'treason' and continues to fight for independence, partly from bases in Burma. Between 1963 and 1987, seven new (union) states were created out of the former state of Assam, and this served to pacify this, along with Kashmir and the Punjab, extremely sensitive region of India. Because of the ethnic diversity of the region, any solution based on autonomy eventually reaches limits.[78] In Assam, the UTLNF and ULFA are fighting against the constituent state's AGP-led government.[79] In Nagaland and Manipur, the NSCN is fighting for independence from India; as are the PLA and UNLF in Manipur. These latter armed movements have their hinterland in the Somra mountains of Burma and previously maintained good links with the ethno-national organization of the Kachin. Since 1987 the NSCN held highest-level negotiations with India in four countries. A Bhutan-type status for Nagaland may be the solution.

5.4.6 Creating new states does not solve all the problems

The Indian speciality of 'muddling through', combined with the creation of new states and autonomous districts and protection for the Adivasis, has not produced complete peace. Fighting by separatists such as the diverse groups of Sikhs trying to secure Khalistan, or the Jamait-e-Islami movement and 180 other groups seeking an independent Muslim state incorporating the whole of Kashmir (including Hindu Jammu and Buddhist Ladakh),[80] or the NSCN, PLA and ULFA in the north-east, marks the limits of the conflict resolution system even in India. However, compared with the situation in neighbouring Burma and in the Chittagong Hill Tracts (in Bangladesh), the intensity of the armed conflict is significantly lower and more discrete. More serious eruptions of violence (besides those in the north-east) took place in Kashmir (and earlier in the Punjab).

The Kashmir issue seemed to become less conflict-prone after a series of peace initiatives by the former centre-left Indian governments of Deve Gowda and Inder Gujral in 1996–97; the latter had already signed several agreements with Pakistan when he was foreign minister under Gowda. It was obvious that the second attempt by Vajpayee's Bharatiya Janata Party (BJP) to form a government (in March 1998) would threaten these historic advances towards a de-escalation of the Indo-Pakistani conflict. In less than two years (May 1996–March 1998), the national front government accomplished what the Congress Party had failed to achieve in almost 50 years of monopoly power. With the nuclear tests, only a few months after they took the power – forcing Pakistan to do the same – the BJP was aiming at reducing these historic advances to rubble.

Notwithstanding the mentioned areas of difficulty, certain elements of the Indian system of conflict avoidance have much to recommend them.

5.4.7 Secular India – under threat from Hindu nationalists

India's constitutionally guaranteed religious freedom and its character as a secular state are today being increasingly cast into doubt by fanatics and Hindu nationalists and fundamentalists. Operating at the trans-regional level is the Bharatiya Janata Party (BJP), which cultivates good relations with extremist local parties (such as Shiv Sena in Maharashtra, which triggered pogroms against Muslims in Bombay) and even more radical splinter groups. The most dangerous force is the Rashtriya Swayamsevak Sangh (RSS), a fundamentalist Hindu cadre-party which has dozens of smaller militant organizations (some armed) under its control. For a while, the BJP formed the government in three northern constituent sates in the Hindi belt. In 1993, its agitation against Muslims (via the Ayodhya mosque) had devastating effects and ended in a bombing campaign and bloody pogroms. The bloody rioting in Bombay, India's multicultural 'secret capital',[81] acted as a signal. Since the beginning of 1995, the state of Maharashtra has been ruled by a coalition including the xenophobic anti-Muslim Shiv Sena party.

The Congress Party, which along with the regionally strong left is the guarantor of secular India, has been weakened by internal power struggles and, since the assassinations of Indira and Rajiv Gandhi, has been without a charismatic leading figure. The first-ever use of an (IMF-style) neo-liberal economic recipe and the opening-up of the country to externally directed 'modernization' which occurred under the Rao government led to increased social polarization. By abandoning its policy of self-reliance for India, the historic Congress Party (founded over a century ago) violated its own principles. Five years ago I wrote that: 'the BJP may team up with chauvinist regional parties in a bid for power'.[82] The results of the elections of April–May 1996 brought the BJP near to this kind of scenario.[83] Although the National Front, a centre-left alliance of communists, low castes and some regional parties (such as Janata Dal in Karnataka) won 180 seats (33.5 per cent) and became the strongest force, it was the BJP who was charged with forming a government. This is a signal: it was the first time that a chauvinist Hindu government had gained power at central-state level in India. Without a parliamentary majority, however, the BJP's fate was uncertain. The demoralized Congress Party must choose between left and right, between pluralism and Hindu chauvinism.

All the parties were a long way from holding a parliamentary majority. But the BJP became more than a 30-per-cent party: with its fundamentalist partners, it already commanded a blocking minority (195 seats out of 537). The government of Atal Behari Vajpayee, the 'acceptable face of an unacceptable organization',[84] attempted to win the support of the large regional parties of south India and in order to prevent a Congress-tolerated centre-left alliance or minority left-wing government (under Jyoti Basu or Deve Gowda), but it failed. The left-wing alliance was the true victor in the elections and can only be kept from power by a 'conspiracy' between the BJP and the Congress Party. Both ideologically very different parties are led by Brahmans and represent the interests of India's ruling castes.

Vajpayee had already in May 1996 threatened Pakistan with war and advocated the incorporation of Kashmir without a referendum; he was openly pursuing the 'nuclear-weapons option' and was resolved to maintain *swadeshi* (self-reliance).[85] The 1996 BJP election platform bluntly stated what the effects of the fundamentalist variant of *swadeshi* would be – namely, a shift away from pluralism and towards 'one nation, one culture'. In May 1996 I wrote that 'This would be tantamount to the end of the progressive Indian nationality policy – which, despite all its weaknesses, has proved its worth, or at least prevented anything worse from happening. An end to Indian nationality policy would mean the enforced integration of Muslims, of the non-Hindi-speaking south, of the Dalits, the Adivasis, and the rebel mountain-peoples. The Indian subcontinent could once again be threatened with war and destruction.' (Scherrer 1996: 170). This turned out to be rather prophetic.

After less than two years, India found itself at the same crossroads. Vajpayee was again sworn in as prime minister. His declaration that 'India [has] all rights to produce nuclear weaponry' (19 March 1998, *Lok Sabha*) was bound to set the subcontinent aflame once again. And yet there has been no immediate reaction to this grave threat; the response of the UN and the big powers was conspicuous by its absence. The geopolitical players have remained silent and seem to be hoping for the impossible: that a much stronger BJP will stay in power for an even shorter time than in 1996. This turned out to be a very mistaken assessment. The world powers reacted almost hysterically when the announced nuclear blasts really took place, only months after the BJP took the power. Pakistan reacted promptly by doing the same. Both regimes seemed to ride on a wave of popular nationalist sentiment of the 'we also go nuclear' kind. The arms race on the Indian subcontinent was preprogrammed, and so were new tensions and war in Kashmir, as soon unfolded. The BJP-led government collapsed again in April 1999 (after 13 months); the right-wing coalition lost its parliamentary majority by one vote. A party representing lower caste interests had switched sides. Commentators rediscovered 'India's divisive ethnic and regional politics' that had produced continued political uncertainty.[86] India had five governments in eight years and instability continued.

After four decades of almost one-party system, only twice interrupted by short-lived non-Congress governments, the last decade saw the multiplication of smaller parties, thus the political scenery became 'unpredictable, scattered, immature – and far more democratic'.[87] Small 'ethnic', caste-linked or local parties vie for influence. Sonia Gandhi, the Congress Party leader, had difficulties in forming a temporary coalition government. Those who had trumpeted 'the rascals are gone' when the BJP left power soon felt disappointed. Since no stable anti-BJP coalition could be put together new elections were the only solution. The Hindu chauvinists returned, even stronger.

Although BJP and sectorial parties have caused repeated political upheaval at a time when the 'Asian economic crisis' destabilized a number of countries in the region, India has remained a giant with a steadily growing economy and its peculiar political system – even under rather hostile conditions – proved fairly robust, flexible and accommodating.

5.5 The settler states of North America and the Indians: self-governance instead of tutelage?

In former settler colonies, there was a common pattern of interaction with indigenous peoples, oscillating between cultural encounter, trade relations and campaigns of eradication. The Indians of North America, the Aborigines in Australia, the !Khoi and San/Zhu Twasi in South Africa were all subjected to these. The genocide perpetrated on the Aboriginal population in the (later) USA reduced the number of Indians from about 12 million in around 1500 to less than 250,000 survivors at the start of this century! Even after the drafting of the United Nations anti-genocide convention of 1948, the USA continued to engage in anti-Indian activities that are banned by article 2 of the convention: removal of children, forced sterilization and medical interventions detrimental to health – as emerged in the 1975 scandal over the Indian Health Service.[88]

In contrast to the multinational states of Asia and the former USSR, the political structure of the former settler states of North America allows few inferences as to numbers of indigenous peoples. Parcels of reservation territory, both large and small, are scattered as isolated entities over the whole surface area of both states, with a concentration in the north.

5.5.1 Indigenous peoples in Canada

In Canada, the immigrant population of about 30 million (2001) inhabits a narrow strip averaging 100 to 300 km in width, along the border with the United States. Canada's indigenous population of about one million (3.6 per cent of the total) is a heterogeneous entity, made up of four groups: status Indians – that is to say, indigenous peoples who, by virtue of the fact that their ancestors and line of descent are recorded in the central register of Indians, are officially recognized as such and are 'cared for' from Ottawa, by a special department of the federal government;[89] the Inuit of the north; the *métis* (*mestizos*); and Indians without status.

- of the 500,000 officially recognized status Indians, about 55 per cent live on a total of 2250 small reservations scattered over approximately two-thirds of Canada's surface area. The status Indians are officially made up of 604 groups ('bands'). The nations (a term the Indians use for themselves) or 'tribes' (not an Indian term) belong to 10 linguistic groups comprising 53 languages. Differences of interest between the various treaty groups persist even today[90]
- 66 Inuit communities with a total population of 40,000 are scattered over the remaining third of the Canadian territorial area; almost half are located in Nunavut,[91] which is officially designated as a 'settlement area' and which was in 1994 the subject of an agreement[92]
- 50 per cent of the 200,000 *métis* (people of mixed French and Indian birth) live on the land, particularly the prairie region
- in addition, there are about 300,000 Indians without status, of whom two-thirds are reported to be living in the large cities.[93.]

The Canadian status Indians are organized into an Assembly of First Nations, with a centralist institution of an elected Grand Chief. The differently focused, less privileged interests of the 600,000 or so Indians living outside the reservations are represented by the Congress of Aboriginal Peoples. Both groups are susceptible to being played off against each other where the need arises.

The government of Jean Chrétien talked of an 'inherent right to self-governance' by the indigenous peoples and promised negotiations about 'models of autonomy', and also a stage-by-stage dismantling of the Indian ministry through the delegation of administrative tasks to new, autonomous structures. The Canadian government's policy *vis-à-vis* the Indians is regarded as progressive.[94] Despite this, the 'trusteeship' scheme is to be retained by Ottawa, and is to continue to be dealt with as a federal matter. Meanwhile, tensions between the Indians and the nationalist Francophones (the 'Bloc Québécois') and reactionary groups in western British Colombia are becoming more acute.

5.5.2 Indigenous peoples in the United States

The number of indigenous peoples living in the United States is only slightly more than in Canada:

- about 1.5 million (0.6 per cent) of the approximate total of 250 million US Americans belong to the indigenous population. This number is made up of 266 official 'tribes' and 55,000 Inuit living in 216 Inuit and Indian communities in Alaska.[95] The most populous Indian nation is the Dine (Navajo) nation in the south-west,[96] with 300,000 members. It occupies the largest reservation in the USA, comprising 17 million acres (out of a total of 50 million acres for all reservations – that is 2 per cent of the total surface area of the US)
- the 229 reservations for Indians in the USA together occupy only 223,000 square km. A large proportion of the Indians are forced to live there, mainly for economic and socio-cultural reasons, in conditions of great depravation.

Much of the land is of poor quality; the western reservations have insufficient water. It is precisely on this land that most of the uranium reserves and one third of the coal reserves in the USA are to be found (mainly on the territory of the Dine, Hopi and Oglala-Sioux/Lakota). These resources are being exploited against the will of the Indians, bringing pollution to their reservations.[97]

The US Indians are on a par with the populations of poor developing countries in terms of income (theirs is the lowest of all the ethnic groups in the USA), literacy, life expectancy (45–48 years), child mortality and health status. Thanks to tax exemptions and to some social welfare provided by the Bureau for Indian Affairs (BIA) about half of all North America Indians manage to hold out in these kinds of poverty stricken reservations. Demanding self-governance on the basis of the present distribution of reservations and under the present trusteeship regime (and its mediation through the BIA) seems a precarious undertaking.[98] Some reservations have turned out (ironically) to be rich in natural resources – resources over which the Indian landowners and inhabitants, however, have no control.

5.5.3 The doctrine of trusteeship and state appropriation of resources

Under the influence of the doctrine of federal trusteeship over the Indians of North America, the latter were assigned to reservations – a process periodically interrupted by attempts at forced integration into mainstream society. In the USA, this 'melting-pot' ideology found expression in the Dawes Act of 1887;[99] and in Canada in Law No. 857 on Gradual Civilization. The banning of the north-west-coast Kwakiutls' practice of the potlatch in 1884 (via the Indian Act) and a large number of other laws and provisions which effectively outlawed indigenous cultures were aimed at 'deculturing' the Indians and integration into mainstream society.[100] The Indians in the USA did not obtain civil rights until 1924 (in Canada this was never in question!). Since the 1930s, the idea that the indigenous nations must be granted cultural autonomy has gradually gained acceptance. It was only in the 1980s that there began to be a call for self-government to be granted (in the reservations) – a development which the Indian movement has been working towards since the 1960s.[101]

North American Indians are increasingly setting themselves against the exploitation of natural resources in their territories. In 1988, for example, the Stl'atl'imx (Salish) and Lil'Wat Indians opposed the clear-felling of the forests in British Colombia, as did the Lubicon Cree, whose forests in northern Alberta were suffering the same fate – harvested ruthlessly and without compensation. The discovery of oil and gas, or the construction of huge dams, are other factors that led to the Indians being driven out of their hereditary reserves.[102] They are now insisting on their attested (land) rights. In the USA this is being done by the Western Shoshone (in California and Nevada), the Lakota (Sioux) in the Black Hills (South Dakota) – on whose reservation gold has been found and mined despite the fact that the Fort Laramie agreement of 1868 assigned them the area around the Black Hills 'in perpetuity' — and the Apache, engaged in a struggle over the Big Mountain area (in Arizona).[103] Nowadays, there is a network of Indian organizations and a (partly foreign) support committee that is able to respond rapidly to acts of aggression by the state – as it did when Quebec brought in police troops against the Mohawk Indians in July 1990 (the 'Oka incident').

5.6 Significant differences between multinational and settler states

If one compares the world's three most populous multinational states (China, India, the CIS) with the former settler colonies (the USA, Canada, Australia, New Zealand and, I believe, South Africa), clear structural and demographic differences, and differences in the quality of nationality policies, emerge, as well as a few similarities. The fundamental differences between multinational states and settler colonies are significant and this is clearly reflected in the core ideologies governing nationality policy.

5.6.1 Three axes of nationality policy in former socialist countries

Cultural pluralism (cultural autonomy), administrative autonomy and economic integration are the three axes of nationality policy in nominally socialist countries (the former USSR and China). In India, the economic integration element is weaker, but the administrative autonomy of the national territories more pronounced. Whereas in the former USSR and, to an even more marked extent, in China, there is a clear majority/minorities relationship, this is not the case for India.

Despite efforts to revitalize the various national and minority cultures in the former USSR and China, deep and irreversible processes of transformation has been triggered within the minority societies by state measures such as:

- 'cultural enhancement' of minority nationalities (elementary education, literacy/development of a written language);
- economic development programmes;
- introduction of social-welfare institutions;
- infrastructure projects by central state, with the aim of 'overcoming isolation'/gaining better control over outlying areas.

Internationally, all measures relating to nationality policy served the declared aim of integrating the minorities into nominally socialist society. In this process, unintended dynamics of ethnic revival were triggered. In China, ideas about the 'liberation of nations under the yoke' (for example, the Tibetans) or the 'raising-up of the culture of the indigenous societies' (for example, the traditional societies of Yunnan) continued to play a key role until recently.[104] Indigenous communities were to 'skip the feudal and capitalist stages' and be catapulted straight into the socialist phase. A unilinear mechanistic-cum-evolutionist theory of stage-by-stage development was enlisted to justify the transformation of autonomous, autochthonous societies.

The principle of self-determination, which was proclaimed to be a right of colonized peoples by the United Nations in 1945, had already been applied in the USSR as early as the 1920s, in the form of territorial self-governance, and subsequently also by China and India at the end of the 1940s. As a rule, the extent of the territorial entities and their administrative status is geared to the demographic size of the various nations, nationalities, or minority peoples. A genuine right of secession was only recognized in the former USSR, but long remained a formality – until its dramatic materialization in 1989–90.[105] The ethnicized structure of the Soviet empire became the basis for what is probably a historically unique process — namely, the initially largely civilized and peaceful collapse of that empire, followed by a second, bloody phase.[106]

5.6.2 Indigenous peoples of North America: from contractual partner to 'ward of court'

In the nineteenth century, against the background of colonial rivalry, indigenous peoples were acknowledged as contractual partners and allies in the settler colonies (except Australia and South Africa). Between 1785 and 1885, numerous treaties were concluded between the (expanding) United States and various Indian nations. Negotiations with Indian tribes are even mentioned in the American constitution of 1787/91.[107] Between 1871 and 1885, the process of treaty negotiation was broken off. Since then, the achievements of the treaty-era have been largely rendered null and void. The US government (like its Canadian counterpart) claims direct authority over the Indians. The status of the Indians as contractual partners remained in force from the end of the eighteenth century (when the youthful United States excluded the possibility of a confederation with the Indian nations, as demonstrated by the treaties with the Delaware and the Six Civilized Tribes) until the middle of the nineteenth century.[108] This initial status as contractual partners is in sharp contrast with the later status of 'wards of court' under the protective trusteeship of the Bureau of Indian Affairs.[109]

It was not until 1919 that the Indians began once again to assume a higher political profile (with the call issued by the Snowhomish leader Frank Bishop). Up to now, what has been at issue was not so much the political status of the Indians, but various legal questions. Only since the 1970s have the indigenous peoples managed to secure (limited) rights of self-governance.[110] This was due, among other things, to the way in which the Indian movement was radicalized by the AIM (American Indian Movement). Between 1972 and 1978, the AIM undertook a series of militant actions.[111]

The largest minority in the USA is that of the Afro-Americans, who account for 15 per cent of the total population. The white establishment has never viewed them as a national minority that could claim any kind of right to self-determination.

5.6.3   Differences in nationality policy and human rights policy

An initial comparison of the multinational states of Asia and the former white settler colonies points up significant differences in nationality policy and human rights policy.

After a brief phase of contractual negotiating, the United States endowed itself with dictatorial plenary powers *vis-à-vis* the Indians.[112] Neither the chauvinistic theory of the Great Han, nor Chiang Kaishek's expository statements, or indeed, the anti-minority assimilation policy of the Kuomintang in Taiwan, claimed these kinds of wide-ranging powers. On the mainland, the policy of autonomization proclaimed as early as the 1920s was extended in a systematic and controlled way, in accordance with a modified version of Lenin's policy of *korenizatsiya*.[113] This nationality policy proved a success even beyond the regional framework.

US human rights policy will also have to be measured by the minimum standards that are fulfilled within the framework of minority policy. The caustic criticisms which Western government departments and mass media periodically level at, for example, China's human rights policy lack credibility given that China's nationalities enjoy a number of rights and a type of political status which North-American Indians may want to achieve.

6
The Imperative of Genocide Prevention and Elimination

Humanitarian law [...] has reached new heights today with the Rome Statute of the International Criminal Court. We are talking about a Court that will take on genocide, crimes against humanity and all the kind of barbarities that we witness every day [in the media], coming from diverse parts of the world – enforced disappearances, sexual crimes and torture – that affect the most elementary rights of every human being. It is difficult to believe that countries that take pride in being champions of the fundamental rights [may make any] attempt to question this instrument.

Judge Baltasar Garzón, 2000[1]

The challenges of genocide prevention are great and the matter is urgent. A systematic overview on the tasks, procedures, institutions and voids of genocide prevention is required.[2] My above toolbox covers the most important areas to reduce, prevent and eliminate genocide. Today effective instruments, practical procedures and respected institutions necessary to achieve these noble goals are only partly in place: most instruments and institutions for averting, preventing and outlawing genocide have yet to be created.

The questions to be asked are:

1. What deficits of scientific research on the origin and nature of genocide and its practical applications can be identified?
2. What policies, procedures and institutions shall be developed that can effectively prevent genocide in the local and global space?
3. What can be done to enforce the existing international law on the punishment of the crime of genocide (that is UN 1948 convention) and to counteract genocide and other massive human rights violations in the future? What sanctions or interventions are necessary to force the parties to the anti-genocide convention to act? And what incentives and initiatives can be developed to have still some 50 states yet to ratify the UN anti-genocide convention?

4. What instruments, practical procedures and institutions can be strengthened or created that are effectively reducing genocide and finally eradicating genocide once and for all? By whom and where? And what would facilitate the process of genocide eradication domestically and internationally?
5. How can the media be influenced to provide current and comprehensive information on the crime of genocide? How can journalists be enabled to identify relevant information on the topic, determine what information is not yet available and to avoid questionable or discredited information? How can the awareness and attention of the public be raised with regard to the crime of genocide and mass violence?
6. What can the emerging global civil society do against the crime of genocide? How can an effective genocide alert and rapid response network be created? How can the public be mobilized to prevent or halt an outbreak of genocide?[3]
7. How can government, international organizations and the United Nations be invited, urged and pressured to act against the genocide and work for averting and eradicating it?

The overview on genocide prevention hereafter is focusing on activities which are essential to combat and eliminate genocide. I believe that different actors should collaborate to that end. The synergies between the organizations of states in general and the United Nations in particular, the world's 193 states, international non-governmental organizations and locally active NGOs could be used. However, genocide prevention is among the most important tasks for global governance: the global monitoring of gross human rights violations is a task that has to be co-ordinated by a special United Nations task force. The world organization is called to implement the recommendations made by the remarkably candid and forward looking Carlsson inquiry report of 1999. In Table 6.1 six areas of activities to combat the crime of genocide are explored.

Deadly threats and the vulnerability of civilian populations in intra-state conflicts and particularly in genocides both grew at a fast rate in the past twentieth century. Civilians are seen by many actors as soft targets and easy to assault. They are murdered, tortured, terrorized, starved, pillaged, put their health at high risk, chased, expelled and displaced, rather than protected. Violence is more often used without any purpose than destruction of lives and livelihood. International law and international humanitarian law are not enforced. There are generally no sanctions linked to gross violations of international law. Perpetrators of large crimes still have a chance to get away with it. This is an invitation for others to act in the same way.[4] I now explore the mentioned six areas of activities with the objective of searching for ways and means to combat the crime of genocide.

Table 6.1 Systematic overview on genocide prevention: tasks, procedures, institutions and voids. A tool box

1 Genocide Alert/Early Warning System	2 Early Action/Rapid Reaction Mechanism
• Global monitoring of gross human rights violations shall be co-ordinated • Clear-cut indicators for early warning about serious risk of genocide • Development of an integrated early warning and early response system • Special UN task force for processing data on minorities-at-risk and development of behaviour of dangerous regimes • Permanent information of UN Security Council and other key decision makers about high-risk situations	• High level diplomacy in cases of alert • Development of new mechanisms of rapid reaction in cases of 'red alert' • Organizing political will for averting genocide • Organizing political will for mandatory military intervention of UN and protection of the victims in case of genocide
3 Prosecution and Deterrence	**4 Enforcing International Law**
• Mandatory prosecution of perpetrators of genocide in anyone state • Establishment of special prosecution institutions to end impunity for mass murder • An international tribunal for the crime of genocide to be institutionalized as integral part of the UN system • The International Criminal Court (ICC) shall be established in due time • International criminal law has to be developed comprehensively in order for the rule of law to be respected by all states and political actors	• by comprehensive review processes and checks-and-control, as in the case of the European Convention on Human Rights or in the case of the ILO convention 169 • by institution building, e.g. the OSCE High Commissioner for Minorities • by establishing an International Criminal Court (ICC), in order to outlaw gross human rights violations such as genocide and crimes against humanity (ICC met strong resistance by large powers, esp. by USA) • by refining an arsenal of sanctions, which shall hurt regimes not the people
5 Pressure, Vigilance and Protection	**6 Lessons Learned**
• UN, regional organizations and donors to impose conditionality on aid in cases of abuse, violations, threats, state criminality • Incentives shall promote democratization, respect for basic human rights and minority rights, rule of law, good governance • Monitoring risk areas and minorities at risk (by INGOs, local NGOs, IGOs) • Averting genocide/breaking escalation through presence and media coverage • Rapid and broad system of protection of possible victims	• Learning from experience of genocide-free world regions (such as East Asia) • Fighting powerlessness and passive response on genocide • Development of concepts of structural prevention of genocide • Writing genocide prevention into statutes, domestic laws, constitutions, international conventions, pacts, etc. • Standardizing prevention of genocide and mass violence internationally

6.1 Genocide alert and early warning system

As part of an 'Action Plan to Prevent Genocide' a UN commission of inquiry headed by Ingvar Carlsson recommended in December 1999 that 'efforts at improving early warning and preventive capacity should include the prevention of genocide as a particular component'.[5] The inquiry panel recommended that 'specific training should be given to staff both at Headquarters, in agencies and programmes and not least, personnel in field missions, to identify warning signs, analyse them and translate warnings into appropriate action'.[6]

For this purpose I launched the idea to establish a new unit at UN Headquarters named 'Genocide Alert Unit' (for discussion at the UN millennium forum, May 2000). This new unit could be closely linked to the commanding structure of a future UN 'Rapid Reaction Force'; the unit could share some offices with the existing 'Lessons Learned Unit' of the United Nations Department of Peace keeping Operations (DPKO). It would also be appropriate to increase the capacities of the present 'Lessons Learned Unit'. The proposal might be combined with the one made by the humanitarian organization *Médecins du Monde* 'to create, within the heart of the United Nations, a special body to evaluate humanitarian situations in times of crisis'.[7] The organizations propose to give the new body a 'high degree of authority and legitimacy', and that it should be attached directly to the UN Security Council.[8]

Genocide scholars from all over the world shall be invited to a series of conferences. The main task is to filter-out indicators for early warning about serious risk of genocide on a global scale that allow us to predict the threat of genocide in a particular area, more precisely, to detect ongoing preparation of a genocide. On this basis 'red alert' can be given to stop genocide by rapid reaction. Indicators of genocide alert and signifiers for 'red alert' shall be deducted from an indicator box. Translated into practical work this could be done in much the same way as the FBI or Interpol does when assembling and accessing their criminological database in order to trace organized crime. One of the main tasks for applied comparative genocide research is the development of an integrated early warning and early response system.

There are already a number of early warning systems, the most globally active are PIOOM in Leiden, the Carter Center in Atlanta (with bi-annual conflict up-dates) and the London-based early warning network FEWER.[9] However, the sharing of early warning information among IGOs and (I)NGOs is still not formalized and synergies are underused, although now improved thanks to informal channels and networking among organizations and agencies working in humanitarian assistance and development.[10] The problem is not the existence of early warnings in the case of genocide (as in Rwanda from 1992 onwards) or a system to receive such warning, the problem is the non-existent linkage between early warning and early action. This gap is wide and its effects are deadly when it comes to genocide. In situations of low intensity conflict, early action can be undertaken by the international civil society, as long as they are non-military means. The effective functioning of such an integrated system in a severe crisis is only guaranteed if a genocide alert and rapid reaction mechanism can be institutionalized within the United Nations system and as part of regional regimes or regional prevention mechanisms. The recommendations of the Millenium Forum point to similar deficits that ought to be addressed by UN.[11]

Learning the lessons from the Rwanda genocide shows that there were a great number of early warnings between 1990 and April 1994 – some of them not only credible but also detailed – but no early action followed. The main key reason for the non-implementation of Arusha accords and the unhindered preparations for genocide was the failure of the international community in general and the UN in particular to monitor the Arusha process and the situation in Rwanda. The international community failed to act tough against non-implementation of the accords and to take credible measures against gross violations of human rights and the upsurge of Hutu extremism. Feeble attempts to make development aid conditional on respect for human rights were resisted by both the United States and the Europeans (Jentleson 1998, 10). In their inquiry on the role of the United Nations in Rwanda, the inquiry panel headed by Ingvar Carlsson clearly recommended that a 'dialogue' between the top UN institutions should focus on 'the need for enforcement measures to counteract genocide and other massive human rights violations in the future' (Carlsson *et al.* 1999, IV, §1).[12]

Comparative genocide research aims at contributing to the short-term development of a global early warning system, chiefly by working on reliable indicators. The long-term objective is to establish effective structural prevention of genocide. The first task is to search for signs of imminent danger. Based on this work the second task is to identify indicators for red alert. Thus, the main task for applied genocide researchers is to develop indicators for a system of effective early warning. Indicators warning of serious risk of genocide or mass violence against vulnerable groups can be deduced from patterns of escalation.

On an abstract level I explored such patterns within a scheme built around 12 broad comparative categories, which shall be applicable in different conflict areas. In order to deduce indicators of alert for the purpose of on-the-spot monitoring of human rights violations and early warning it is necessary to assemble the identified steps and elements of genocidal processes according to stages of urgency and significance. Table 6.2 contains steps to successive escalation within 12 areas and broad categories.

The following 12 indicators for alert should be tested for reliability.

Indicators of Genocide Alert

- Indicator 1: reinforcement and manipulation of old stereotypes
- Indicator 2: construction of dichotic collectivities: us/them; nationals/ vermin
- Indicator 3: ensuring and reinforcing victims are defenceless
- Indicator 4: dehumanizing of the victims
- Indicator 5: impunity for crimes against the victims
- Indicator 6: appeals to complicity and supply of more privileges.

Indicators of Red Alert

- Indicator 7: recruiting, indoctrination and training of a 'willing executioner' force separate from army/police
- Indicator 8: surge of hate propaganda in the state controlled media (e.g., gossip, lies and fabrication about victim group)
- Indicator 9: liquidation of the political opposition
- Indicator 10: breaking resistance among the 'national' population
- Indicator 11: skilful use of framework/smoke-screen of 'crisis'
- Indicator 12: pre-emptive launch of well-prepared cover-up operations.

Quantitative indicators to measure economic and political discrimination of ethnic groups by state governments are also in demand; Gurr and Harff have developed indicators to measure the use of violence by governments.[13] The idea is to develop qualitative indicators for minorities at risk of genocide – without excluding possible quantitative aspects. Global data collections showing low and high scales of state discrimination of minorities are of special interest since discrimination is an essential aspect of the victimization process that characterizes every genocide.[14]

Danger is imminent when the category of highest state discrimination is present, indeed, the 'Minorities-at-risk Project' (MAR) defined genocide and politicide as the most severe indicator.[15] Other drastic measures applied by states, such as formal and 'deliberate exclusion' and/or recurring repression, are steps in which genocidal intent becomes apparent. A genocide alert must be issued and followed up before all-out escalation; for the final phase of a genocidal process only red alert would be appropriate. The findings of the MAR project show that nearly a fifth of all minorities at risk suffer deliberate exclusion and repression by state actors, with a disproportionate concentration of minorities at high risk in Middle East and Africa. The severity of discrimination is greatest in the Middle East and among ethno-classes; the latter category is particularly prominent in the African Great Lakes region. Genocide prevention includes the eradication of impunity for gross human rights violation and gives a clear signal to potential perpetrators. Reconciliation needs justice.[16]

Table 6.2 Early warning – escalator box with indicators for alert

Genocidal society (1)

- 'National characteristics' vs. 'non-national minority' seen as 'foreigners'/'outsiders': manipulation of the perpetrator society
- Mobilization of past negative experiences (general)
- Construction of the 'problem'

Indicator 1: Reinforcement and manipulation of old stereotypes

- Reinforcement of prejudice, intolerance and antipathies
- Encouraging disposition and readiness use of violence against the victims
- Construction of threats
- Building a *solid base* of 'confusion' and insecurity

Development of an exterminatory ideology by the perpetrators (2)

- Replacing unitary emancipatory categories of nationhood by narrow ones
- Categories of order in 'nation building'
- Purified exclusive 'national idea'
- Futility, 'falseness' and 'danger' of *aliens* being assimilated into the nation
- Primitivization of alleged 'utopian concepts', borrowed from ethno-centric philosophy and nationalist ideology
- 'Purposeful rationality' vs. psycho-pathological aspects
- Anti-individualistic bias in state ideology

Indicator 2: Construction of dichotic collectivities:us/them; nationals/vermin

Construction of the victim group by the perpetrator (3)

- Identifying victims
- Defining the grey zone of 'mixed' elements
- Signifying victims
- Deluding vigilance among the victims
- Destroying unity, solidarity and resistance among the victims by all means

Indicator 3: Ensuring and reinforcing the defenselessness of the victims

The process of victimization (4)

- Excluding victims from the scope of 'normal procedures'
- Systematic spreading of gossip
- Heinous rumours about the victims
- Public humiliation and harassment of victims by extremists in daily life
- Associating victims with all evils
- Unsanctioned hate propaganda

Indicator 4: Dehumanizing of the victims

- Demonizing victims

Making of a genocidal state (5)

- Infiltration of the state machinery/silencing moderate leaders
- Deepening the general situation of politics crisis, disorientation
- Creation of more confusion/fear
- Collusion between authors–ideologists and state apparatus
- Free hand for planers of 'total terror' and genocide
- Free hand for propagandists
- Extremists take over state-controlled (or private) media
- 'Spontaneous' acts of violence

Development of a conductive social-political environment (6)

- Propagandist onslaught to win over the 'national' population
- Supply of ambiguous identification possibilities
- 'Normalcy' and 'necessity' of escalation
- Undermining social solidarity with victims among the perpetrator society
- Diffusion of 'normalcy'
- 'Normality' of 'special procedures'

Indicator 6: Appeals to complicity and supply of more privileges

Table 6.2   Continued

Indicator 5: Impunity for crimes
against the victims
- Coercion of the state bureaucracy
  for 'purification' (campaign of fear)
- Exclusivist ideologies in schools
  and public places

Dynamics of totalitarism (7)

- Establishing lines of command for
  the 'final solution'
- Mobilization of the state bureaucracy
  for organizing genocide
- Coercive mobilization of civil
  servants on all levels
- Secret systematic preparation of the
  'final solution'
- Organization of special troops,
  militias and/or gangs

Indicator 7: Recruiting and training
of a 'willing executioner' force separate
from army/police
- Spreading of mass hatred
- Creating of the 'ripe moment'
- Planned systematic and ruthless
  execution of the crime by all means

Development of a genocidal environment (8)

- 'Brainwashing' in schools/public
  places

Indicator 8: Surge of hate propaganda in
the state controlled media (e.g. gossip,
lies and fabrications about victim group)
- Compulsory use of derogatory
  expressions for victims
- Humiliating expressions for alleged
  accomplices of the victims
- Attempt for breaking down the
  (traditional) moral order
- Public chasing and beating of victims

*Establishment of a totalitarian state and
total control (9)*

- Decapitation of opposition
- Humiliation of 'neutral' personalities
- Showing resolute leadership
- Open criminal agitation
- Intentions of the genocidal
  elements become known to all
- Appeal to the 'most primitive
  instincts'
- Arbitrary arrest of 'doubtful
  nationals'
- Exhibiting 'final' determination of
  the top leader(s) and ring leaders
- Open 'public acts' of violence
  against last rest of former opposition

Indicator 9: Liquidation of the political
opposition
- Liquidation of all dissent
- Increasing violence against victim
  group

*Preference for the option of outright violence
and extermination (10)*

- Construction of the 'problem'
- Reinforcing its plausibility

Indicator 10: Breaking resistance among
the 'national' population
- Supplying a 'problem-solving' model
- Invitations for fatalist acceptance of
  state terror
- Creating the atmosphere for
  genocide and extermination
- Spreading and generalizing fear
- Executing the 'problem-solving' model

Table 6.2 Continued

Conductive context for genocide: War situation and crisis as smoke screen (11)	Misinformation and denial (12)
• Pretention of 'contradictions' in top leaders' policy' ***Indicator 11***: Skilful use of smoke-screen 'crisis' • Delusion of the international community • Use of emergency situation to cut access to information • Play of diplomatic dementia • Tricking international media • Use of the 'ripe moment' • Presentation of systematic extermination as singular acts for foreign consumption	• Misinformation campaign claiming 'punitive acts' and 'preventive action' ***Indicator 12***: Pre-emptive launch of well prepared cover-up operations • Banalizing the crime of genocide claiming 'isolated events', 'unfortuate incidents', 'individual cases of wrongdoers', etc. • Threatening or silencing witnesses • Destruction of evidence (esp. official documents) • Outright denial of genocide

The challenge for genocide alert is threefold: (1) the search for quantitative indicators measuring structural discrimination of victim groups and targeted repression (indicators for alert), (2) the identification of aspects of significant aggressiveness against victim groups and the deduction of qualitative indicators, which allow timely reading of signs of growing determination on the side of the discriminators/oppressors and their intent to commit crimes against humanity (indicators for genocide alert) and (3) the identification of triggers and dynamics of rapid escalation, translated into indicators for red alert. Indicators will be deducted and will become, depending from the stage of escalation, signifiers for 'genocide alert' and 'red alert'. Such indicators have to prove their usefulness in comparative studies, which would screen an array of cases. A few years ago this work had not started yet in any systematic way; today, deliberations in this direction are in progress but with only a few scholars involved.

All these important pioneering works would be rendered useless without strengthening the political efforts to narrow the existing gap between early warning and early action and red alert and rapid enforcement respectively. The role of the United Nations will be critical for enhancement of the capabilities of early action and rapid response in situations of severe crisis, chiefly by building public awareness and political will as well as by securing effective political decision-making, namely the timely issuing of mandates for intervention and the deployment of a permanent rapid reaction force in case of genocide alert.

6.2   Early action: the creation of a rapid reaction mechanism

The main reason why a future institution for genocide alert and early action should become part of the UN General Secretariat is to have rapid procedures and solid facilitation of high-level diplomacy in cases of alert. Annan has put it clearly: 'without early action, early warning is of little use'.[17] The UN member states must agree on new mechanisms of rapid reaction; in cases of 'red genocide alert' traditional diplomacy is not the appropriate means.[18] Traditional methods of conflict management such as negotiation, mediation, good offices, fact-finding missions and judicial resolution might all be involved at a much earlier stage.[19] In case of 'red genocide alert' only the plausible threat of a UN military intervention will be appropriate. Averting genocide is in principle the duty of all signatory states of the UN Anti-Genocide Convention.

The UN Secretariat will be chiefly responsible for organizing political will to establish a rapid reaction mechanism which shall not depend on political criteria but will be a purely professional venture. To create the political will to stop genocide within the system of the United Nations is also to prevent unilateral interventions, which usually have their own agendas. Reforming the UN anti-genocide convention should include organizing the political will for the mandatory military intervention of the UN in case of genocide alert. The effective protection of potential victims in case of genocide is definitely a duty the United Nations must accept.

The most important recommendations of the Carlsson Report of December 1999 deal with establishing a UN enforcement capacity. For the first time in a UN-sponsored document, the concept of 'neutrality' in the case of massive human rights violations has been dismissed.[20] In addition, the inquiry recommends that 'action be taken to improve the capacity of the United Nations to conduct peace keeping operations and in particular to ensure the sufficiently rapid deployment of missions into the field'.[21] Within the United Nations system an Executive Committee on Peace and Security was created in 1999; the intention is to enhance co-operation (between the different parts of the UN system), policy coherence and the sharing of information.[22] The establishment of physical links between the OAU and the UN to ease transmission of information and facilitate practical steps started with a new United Nations liaison office at the OAU headquarters in Addis Ababa; it aims at improving co-operation between the UN and this regional organization. Since Africa currently has the lion's share of armed conflicts and mass violence – including areas at high risk of genocidal atrocities – new links may improve a co-ordinated deployment of political efforts to prevent, contain or resolve violent conflict.

Capacity building at the UN must ensure the necessary resources – not only for peace-keeping (UN Charter, Chapter VI) but for peace-enforcing

(UN Charter, Chapter VII). In case of red alert, the permanent members of the Security Council ought to decide on the airlifting of crack troops at short notice.[23] Concerning blue helmet missions the Carlsson inquiry panel made a number of detailed recommendations, which draws on the lessons of the disastrous inaction of the United Nations during the Rwandan genocide.[24] Looking to African conflict spots, some operative recommendations were made, such as to make logistical resources rapidly available to contingents lacking in material (for example OAU peace keepers) and to enhance the use of the logistic base at Brindisi. Other preparations since 1998 have begun to take shape (see UNDPKO 1999). The UNDPO is developing a strategy for improving African peace keeping, among others – from a longer-term perspective – the development of regional training institutions and operational mission management capacities until 2002. Carlsson *et al.* 1999 also recommended increasing preparedness in different fields.[25] The world organization – in particular the UN Security Council and the troop contributing countries – must be 'prepared to act to prevent acts of genocide' (Carlsson *et al.* 1999, IV. 3) without applying double standards.

6.3 Prosecution and deterrence

The twentieth century was the age of genocide, in the twenty-first century genocide has finally to be outlawed. In the spirit of Raphael Lemkin the international criminal law must be developed comprehensively in order for the international rule of law to be respected by all states and political actors.

New developments such as the Pinochet case, the indictment of Rwandan perpetrators of genocide and the prosecution of crimes against humanity committed in Former Yugoslavia have in recent years helped to inform public awareness. The understanding that the international community is responsible for monitoring the mandatory prosecution of perpetrators of genocide and crimes against humanity in any one state is growing. The attempt by the Spanish prosecutor, Baltasar Garzòn in Madrid, who issued an international arrest order against the Chilean dictator Augusto Pinochet – arrested in England in October 1998 but freed on health grounds in 2000 – failed for the time being but it will greatly influence the contemporary prosecution of humanitarian crimes.[26] Garzòn may have got the idea from the father of the anti-genocide convention. Lemkin's idea was to outlaw Nazism, Fascism and other such ideologies by punishing its leaders and agitators in any one state.[27] The effect of deterrence would have been enhanced if Lemkin's ideas had been applied by the member states of the League of Nations; Nazism could have been stopped.

The political will to punish severe human rights violations is on the increase. The Pinochet case has already developed its own African version: early in 2000 a judge in Dakar interrogated Hissène Habré, former

French-supported tyrant of Chad who lost power in 1990 and currently lives in Senegal, on charges of torture and 'barbarity' committed against the Chadian opposition in the 1980s. The establishment of special prosecution institutions in several states (such as Nicaragua, Ethiopia, Rwanda and Uganda) is another important element in the international effort to end impunity for organized mass murder.

Ad hoc tribunals such as those at the UN International Criminal Tribunals (the ICTR and the ICTY) are not enough. The International Criminal Court (ICC) will be a permanent court that will investigate and bring to justice individuals who have committed the most serious violations of international humanitarian law, namely genocide, crimes against humanity, war crimes, torture and large-scale aggression acts. Unlike the International Court of Justice (ICJ) in The Hague, whose jurisdiction is restricted to state parties, the ICC will have the capacity to indict individuals. The ICC will be created on the basis of the Rome Statute, a treaty adopted on 17 July 1998 at the United Nations diplomatic conference in Rome.[28]

The debate about the International Criminal Court, the signing of the Rome treaty to create the court by half of the world's states in 1999 and its expected establishment in due time shows clearly that the time is ripe for systematic international prosecution of most severe crimes and deterrence against mass murder. This important development also marks one of the most crashing defeats the USA (and other great powers) suffered in the international arena; the obstruction by the Pentagon and superpower arrogance serve to isolate the USA in the international community and reinforce new isolationism at home. Besides the USA two other great powers (China and India) remain hostile against establishing the International Criminal Court. In July 1998 at the ICC conference in Rome some 120 of the 148 countries present voted in favour of the Rome Statute; only seven countries voted against it and 21 abstained. Among those seven states voting against ICC were, besides the great powers United States, China and India, the pariah states of Iraq and Libya.

However, in many parts of the world the Rome Statute of the International Criminal Court gets support. The European Union countries, many Latin American countries, as well as many countries in Africa are marching ahead; the EU countries are expected to provide the bulk of ICC's expenses. Most notably, in June 2000 the first permanent member of the UN Security Council, France, ratified the ICC statute; Britain followed in October 2001.[29] Tajikistan became the first country of the former Soviet Union to ratify. So far ratification is missing in Asia and the Middle East; Nauru became the first state in Asia-Pacific to ratify the ICC statute in 2001. Some 90 governments signed the Rome treaty to establish the ICC in 1999. As of end 2001, 139 states have signed the Rome Statute and 48 state parties have ratified this historic treaty which is 80 per cent of the number required for it to come into force.[30] On the last day of the twentieth century even the United States, Israel and Iran signed the treaty, though, there is little chance that they will ratify it in due time, while, by end 2001, some half dozen states were close to ratification.[31] Many states have already begun revising domestic legislation to permit ratification of the treaty and some 30 more states have taken initiatives toward ratification.[32]

Establishing the International Criminal Court will be one of the most important projects of the international community in the first decade of the twenty-first century. Hopefully, the ICC treaty will enter into force in due time, in a couple of years or in the best scenario already in 2002 – after having secured the 60 ratifications that are needed to establish the court. The international system needs a permanent international criminal tribunal to deal with the crime of genocide and other crimes against humanity; it should be institutionalized as an integral part of the UN system. The repression of genocide should be internationalized in every form and should become effective in any one place. There should be no safe havens for *génocidaires*.

The culprit should be liable not only in the state where the crime was committed but should be detained in any country on earth. Here the Pinochet case already had its follow-up in Africa (Habré arrested in Dakar, Senegal). Such important developments may constitute a trend toward decentralized responses to make the world's worst human rights offenders accountable. Another trend can be seen in the tendency that the principle of national sovereignty can no longer be invoked to neutralize accusations of severe human rights violations. Today even powerful states (such as China or Indonesia) can no longer deny the validity of international human rights norms, although such norms have their local expressions.[33]

The more than 50 states that have not yet signed and ratified the UN anti-genocide convention should persuade their world citizens to join with the 130 countries now party to the convention, the last state being Switzerland. The background of it is that the crime of genocide has not been incorporated into the Swiss penal code by international treaty; when dealing with several Rwandan *génocidaires* arrested in Switzerland at the request of Rwanda, Swiss courts had no sufficient legal basis upon which they could act.[34] Among those 50 states are many weak, dangerous or war-torn countries, such as Angola, Central African Republic, Chad, Congo, Equatorial Guinea, Eritrea, Guinea, Indonesia, Japan, Kenya, Mauritania, Niger, Nigeria, Paraguay, Sierra Leone, Somalia, Sudan, Tajikistan, Uzbekistan and others. In many or by many of the above-mentioned states, genocide or crimes against humanity have been committed in the past one hundred years. In some cases governments are committing such crimes, as recently in Congo, Equatorial Guinea, Indonesia and Sudan. In other countries non-state actors are the culprits, as in Somalia, Sierra Leone and Tajikistan.

6.4   Enforcing international law – new institutions, sanctions or interventions?

> In the most extreme cases, the innocent become the principal targets of ethnic cleansers and *génocidaires*. International conventions have traditionally looked to states to protect civilians, but today this expectation is threatened (...). States are sometimes the principal perpetrators of violence against the very citizens that humanitarian law requires them to protect.
>
> Kofi A. Annan/UNDPI 2000[35]

The main problem in protecting the vulnerable is the lack of enforcement of the existing international law instruments. Either no institution has the formal mandate to do so or the existing institutions are too weak. International instruments rarely provide for law enforcement by comprehensive review processes and checks-and-control, as in the case of the European Convention on Human Rights or in the case of the ILO convention 169. Law enforcement needs more institution building. The establishment of the International Criminal Court in the first years of the twenty-first century, in order to outlaw gross human rights violations such as genocide and crimes against humanity, is one of the noblest tasks for global governance. The heart of global governance must be prevention of destructive violence. The ICC is an important step in that direction. Unfortunately the ICC has already met strong resistance from the great powers; among those exhibiting the most resistance are countries known for their official human rights discourse such as the USA and France!

As coercive measures the United Nations should establish a commission of experts to refine the UN arsenal of sanctions. UN sanctions should hurt regimes not people. Unfortunately, the enforcement of international law became a justification for military intervention – in outright breach of international law – as in Kosovo.[36] A human rights organization found that the most dramatic developments in 1999 were that twice, in Kosovo and in East Timor, 'members of the international community deployed troops to halt crimes against humanity' – although these crimes very much continue.[37] Although an important question was not asked: why was there no military intervention in Rwanda 1994 pursued in Kosovo 1999?

The two cases of military interventions in 1999 – carried out in the name of stopping human rights violations – have not only raised questions of utter selectivity but also of legitimacy and abuse of human rights discourse in pursuit of war aims. The case of Yugoslavia is particularly controversial: those who wanted to stop severe human rights violations themselves violated international law, the Geneva Conventions and its Protocols in particular. Targeting of civilians was utterly disproportionate.[38] The damage and death toll caused by NATO was kept secret.[39] In the case of East Timor the intervention fulfils the provisions of international law and was generally felt to be justified. But the intervention came too late to save thousands of lives. In fact, it came 25 years too late. A partial genocide unleashed by the Indonesian army has killed 200,000 Timorese since 1974.[40] The UN failed to intervene in Rwanda, and today the UN hesitates to intervene militarily in Congo, as called for by the Lusaka ceasefire agreement 1999, in order to prevent further mass violence. Double standards in enforcing international law are intolerable.

6.5   Pressure, vigilance and protection

Development aid should be suspended in cases of gross violations of human rights. Threats against groups of citizens must be dealt with immediately. UN agencies such as UNDP, regional organizations and donor states should impose conditionality on development aid in cases of organized forms of state criminality in weak states. Incentives shall promote democratization, respect for basic human rights and minority rights, rule of law, good governance and the promotion of a free media. Projects in these sectors should attract priority funding.

Genocide alert and the monitoring of risk areas, in particular the evolving situation of minorities at risk, is still largely underdeveloped. One of the key lessons to be learned from the Rwanda shock is the failure of early warning and the failure of the donor states, UN agencies and the established international human rights organizations to react promptly and to monitor the situation. Generally, international and local NGOs as well as IGOs should be more active in monitoring risk areas and minorities at risk. Averting genocide must become a main area of activity for all NGOs working in conflict areas.

Where were the international watchdogs in Rwanda 1993–94? NGOs have for some time been the 'good guys', allegedly without hidden agendas and with much humanitarian commitment. In the Rwandan case this image has been dashed. It is hard to believe that the largest, well funded and globally active human rights NGOs, Amnesty International, Human Rights Watch and Fédération Internationale des Ligues des Droits de l'Homme/International Federation of Human Rights Leagues, failed to understand the danger and failed to monitor the situation closely – despite series of warnings from local informers and despite the postcolonial history of Rwanda and Burundi providing all the necessary evidence for vigilance and to keep watch on the evolving situation with determination and care.

Those NGOs, who claim to be the 'conscience of the world', failed to urge the donors and the UN, ahead of time, to put pressure on the government and to take action. They did not listen to their local counterparts; they failed to echo local warnings and give them more weight; and finally they failed to alert the media and draw world attention to an extremely dangerous situation, which was going out of control. When the most barbaric crimes happened on the African continent in the twentieth century the human rights watchdogs were just about to wake up.[41] After the disaster there was little attempt made to understand what happened and the human rights NGOs, offered no apology for their own failure. Amnesty International never published a special report on the Rwandan genocide. Human Rights Watch, together with Fédération Internationale des Ligues des Droits de l'Homme, waited for more than five years to publish their report, which is full of gaps. The most pervasive gaps are the most fundamental questions 'why?', 'what went wrong?', and 'what can be done?'. Is it possible that a catastrophe of the magnitude of that in Rwanda was no reason for the three most established human rights organizations to be alerted – at least *post eventum*! The three seemed to do precisely the contrary: there was no self-criticism of their own failures and no exploration of the genocide (in time), but a continuation of their limited understanding of the general situation. While the same three largest human rights organizations seemingly saw it as their duty to nail the new government of Rwanda, composed of survivors of the genocide. In my view, based on my experience in Rwanda, the credibility of these three human rights organizations is at stake.

In the case of Rwanda some INGOs were talking about reconciliation before any justice was done. Massive contradictions and shortcomings characterized the approach of Amnesty International. Their global campaign against the death penalty is only at first sight a noble cause; in some countries, in some cultures and in the aftermath of genocide, it is totally out of place. The protest against the public shooting of mass murderers at massacre sites in April 1998 was hypocritical. The campaign does not distinguish between the type of crimes committed: genocide and crimes against humanity are the 'crimes of all crimes' and punishment must be appropriate. In Rwanda nobody believes in a life sentence as punishment for the top *génocidaires*. Amnesty International would be better advised to stick to what they advertise on their home page, where – concerning the Pinochet case and crimes against humanity – a quote is displayed prominently, that justice needs to be done and people need to see that justice is done.

Working within the historical context of any troubled region is the key to understanding complex situations. In cases of genocidal violence it is mandatory to explore the root causes, its ideology and the sequence of past traumatic experiences. The INGOs did not engage in addressing questions of what to do after genocide. Recommendations of how to break the cycle of violence were missing. The government of Rwanda, which was in dire need of support, was left alone.

In some cases, for instance in situations of rapid escalation, averting genocide can only be done by military intervention as *ultima ratio*. In latent conflict situations the one could envision of TRANSCEND as an 'international nonviolent peace force' (similar to the 'Shanti Sena', a nonviolent army, proposed by Mahatma Gandhi more than 50 years ago), possibly as a joint venture between the UN and INGOs. This force should be well trained and prepared to work in conflict areas – at the invitation of local groups committed to a peaceful resolution of conflict. A nonviolent peace force could become a regular mechanism for most lower and medium risk conflict situations.[42] Such a force may also reduce the financial burden of armed UN peace keeping operations.[43] However, future UN peace-enforcement missions in high risk situations, especially in cases of genocide alert, should be better prepared and co-ordinated. Besides improving the early warning capacity of the UN, 'in particular its capacity to analyse and react to information' (Carlsson *et al.* 1999, IV.4), the UN should enhance co-ordination with organizations outside the UN system, improve the flow of information and seek the protection of civilians, local staff and personnel in risk situations.[44]

Escalation processes can often be broken through permanent presence, monitoring and appropriate media coverage of the plight of minorities. A rapid and broad system of protection of possible victims should be organized by a NGO coalition in every conflict area. Civil actors shall intervene in addition to and as correction of parallel efforts by the UN, IGOs and regional organizations.

6.6 Anticipating dangers – learning lessons from past experiences

The international community can learn many lessons from past traumatic experiences of genocide as well as from relevant experiences of genocide-free world regions. Genocides are not a natural disaster; genocide can be prevented. If the response comes too late, it can be and it must be stopped by force!

Two generations ago, the German Fascists and their willing executioners in many occupied countries committed the worst genocide of this century. Many knew about the mass murder of Jews, Roma, Russian prisoners of war and others Slavonic groups in extermination camps.[45] The Allies had known it since 1941 but they kept complete silence.[46] This 'conspiracy of silence' enabled the Nazis to exterminate their victims without restrain.

In January 2000, fifty-five years after the liberation of Auschwitz (by the Red Army), world leaders convened in Stockholm to commemorate the death and despair and to remember the breakdown of civilization in Europe two generations ago. The aim was to draw lessons for the future but the talk was only about the past. In December 1998 the Task Force for International Cooperation on Holocaust Education, Remembrance and Research (composed of the governments of Sweden, UK, US, Germany, Israel, Poland, the Netherlands, France and Italy) had issued a declaration stating that 'Holocaust education, remembrance and research strengthen humanity's ability to absorb and learn from the dark lessons of the past, so that we can ensure that similar horrors are never again repeated'.

The hypocrisy cannot be overlooked. Although we all sympathize with the initiative as such, it must nevertheless be remembered that at least two Task Force countries were in a good position to 'ensure that similar horrors are never again repeated'. However, they failed to ensure that Rwandan lives are as important as lives in multi-ethnic Bosnia or the lives of Albanian Kosovars. And, unfortunately, the genocide in Rwanda may not have been the last genocide to occur. In October 2000 the Committee on Conscience of the Council of the United States Holocaust Memorial Museum issued a (late) genocide alert: 'We cannot remain bystanders as this remorseless fire consumes the people of Sudan.' The Committee accused the Sudanese military regime of perpetrating genocidal crimes against the Dinka and Nuer peoples in the south and the Nuba in central Sudan.[47] For the three million people (in a cumulative count), who have died in the Sudan since 1955, this alert came too late!

The UN could have prevented the Rwandan genocide, chiefly by careful monitoring of the Arusha process and by taking the necessary precautions. The UN could have stopped the implementation of the state organized mass murder, once the alert was received, in this case having received full insight via Dallaire's cable on 11 January 1994. The slaughter could have been stopped in the four months to come, and it could even have been stopped during the first weeks, when France and Belgium flew in thousands of additional troops – only to save their own citizens! The main recommendations of the official UN inquiry into the organization's own failure in Rwanda 1993–94 include ensuring that 'Lessons Learned from previous missions are integrated into the planning of new peace keeping operations' (Carlsson *et al.* 1999, IV.1).

The United Nations has since taken a number of steps to follow-up this very important recommendation. The 'Report of the Panel on UN Peace Operations', known as the Brahimi report (named for Lakhdar Brahimi, the chairman of the high-level 10-person panel) represents the first systematic effort to critically assess UN peacekeeping operations and address a number of mainly technical problems such missions face. The report was mindful of past UN failures, stating that 'genocide in Rwanda went as far as it did in part because the international community failed to use or to reinforce the operation then on the ground in that country to oppose obvious evil' (Brahimi *et al.* 2000: §50). Though the report particularly mentioned that the UN must be prepared to deal more effectively with 'spoiler' groups, that is, genocidal elements and warmongers with vast economic means at their disposal, and to focus on the causes of conflicts it wants to appease (ibid., 20–4), it did not elaborate much on these key issues.

I have accused the UN Security Council decisionmakers of double standards and apparent lack of will (Scherrer 2002*b*: 303–26). In order to disarm genocidal 'spoilers' from Rwanda roaming the Congo – called 'negative elements' by the Lusaka Accords – the United Nations would need to deploy a well-armed, professional military force, at least 50,000-strong peace-enforcement mission. In Bosnia some 20,000 troops were not enough and in Somalia 28,000 could not do the job. But the UN sent a small force (as proposed by the US) to a country the size of Western Europe. This was another indication that there was no consensus in the Security Council about the size and deployment strategy of a UN peacekeeping force. The UN has not learned the lessons of the Rwanda disaster: in the Congo the worst tragedy of humanity since Rwanda 1994 continues to unfold. The United Nations must intervene and stop this unspeakable mass violence.

The first step in such a learning process is to acknowledge that something went seriously wrong. The United Nations, meaning its most powerful components such as the Security Council, the Secretariat and the General Assembly, should 'acknowledge its part of the responsibility for not having done enough to prevent or stop the genocide in Rwanda' (ibid., IV.14). In my view, the UN inquiry report could have explored the question of responsibility more precisely.[48] This would include the exploration of the responsibility of its member states, the US and France, in causing the deadly UN inaction.[49] This work has still to be accomplished, in order for future occasions and a new generation of politicians to learn valuable lessons from the utter failure of their own governments – be it as an actor, as an accomplice or as a bystander. More attention should be given to the silent work of violence prevention and confidence-building measures; they should be compared and studied carefully. Civil actors should take the lead in fighting powerlessness and the passive response on genocide taken by states and state organizations. New alliances and coalitions are currently being developed to respond to the global threat of genocide, in order to identify and prevent crimes against humanity wherever they may occur.

The development of concepts for structural prevention of genocide and mass violence are among the noblest tasks of peace research. Charitable funds and scientific funding institutions should prioritize research projects in these fields. Research results must equip a growing civil movement with critical and effective tools in the struggle against genocide. The prevention and elimination of genocide should be written into the statutes of many more associations. Standardizing the prevention of genocide and mass violence internationally should become a key task for the United Nations in the twenty-first century. Genocide prevention must come to form part of domestic laws and national constitutions as well as become part of all relevant international conventions and pacts.

Summary and Conclusions

Today, internal conflicts occur much more frequently than those between states. Wars and mass violence of a predominantly ethnic character account for more than half of all violent conflicts. The global trend to 'ethnic', ethnicized and ethno-nationalist conflicts has increased over the last decades. But ethnicity cannot serve either as a rationale or as a fig-leaf to be used when other interpretations fail. Ethnic violence is a response to difficult, protracted crises. The question of what drives it leads on to the question of the nature of ethnicity itself and of what constitutes the ethnic basis of nations. Responses to conflict can only be effective if informed by a comprehensive understanding of contemporary mass violence.

Starting from this base, the study addresses the themes of prevention, management and transformation of 'ethnic' intra-state conflicts. The main topics are responses to conflict such as constructive approaches to dealing with violent conflicts, peaceful conflict settlement and the question of the timing of responses, autonomy arrangements, collective rights, self-governance, nationality policies and federal arrangements. The political-cum-humanitarian concern is to ensure that all possible means of avoiding violent forms of interaction in a multi-ethnic setting are strengthened and made more attractive. This leads on to the question of how ethnic or cultural difference is to be understood and acknowledged.

The introduction of this book deals with concepts and their progress. Given the almost routine mingling of ethnic groups, nations, states and nation-states that is already taking place in both the conceptual and the real world, there is a need for some basic definition here. The concept of a minority, so often used in the context of ethno-national conflicts, seems to be in need of elucidation on a number of counts. To list characteristics that enable an ethnic group or a people to describe itself as a nationality – which is a nation without its own state but in search of statehood – is not just an academic exercise. These kinds of definitions acquire more and more political relevance the more clearly the relationship between nationalities, nations and states is viewed as part of international relations. Nationalities are distinguished from nations by the degree of political organization, readiness to fight and particular external circumstances. Most politicized ethnic groups see themselves as nations entitled to govern their own affairs.

The book (in Chapter 1) deals with contemporary mass violence. Conflicts in the poor and impoverished countries of the southern hemisphere have many different causes and are a manifestation of a variety of partly autonomous influences. The difficulties of identifying the various factors in violent conflicts are manifold, stemming from confusing terminology, tendentious accounts by those involved, and a general lack of research into, and elucidation of, intra-state conflicts, which are much more frequent than those between states. Typologies should not just be drawn up for war; they should also be drawn up for peace (see Chapters 2 and 3). With the aid of a typology of intra-state conflicts based on the major driving forces combined with an actor-orientation, some of the problems inherent in attempting to distinguish between various types are discussed. Their actual merging in concrete conflicts has repercussions for both theory and practice. The complex formation of conflicts is analysed by a combined process of primary, secondary and (in some cases) tertiary classification. The ECOR index for the ten years 1985–94 lists 102 violent conflicts and 107 cases during the six years 1995–2000 alone; a global count is presented, the results are specified and compared, and trends in contemporary mass violence are identified.

Since the late 1980s, political conflicts have been militarized to a degree unknown since World War II. The hope for a more peaceful world, cherished since the end of the cold war, has come to nought. The claims which false nation-states or ethnocracies, ruled by dominant ethnic groups who have secured 'possession' of the state, make with regard to ethnically distinct nationalities (so-called 'minorities', who are sometimes the demographic majority) have shown themselves to be the major source of violent conflict. Evidence of an urgent need for research is discernible for every subspecies of ethnically interpreted conflict. Depending from the period of observation, conflicts of a predominantly 'ethnic' character (the four type of ethno-nationalism, decolonization wars, inter-ethnic conflict and genocide) account for between more than half and two-thirds of the world's violent conflicts. In some indexes of contemporary wars, these major types of conflict are still listed under the shameful rubric 'miscellaneous intra-state conflicts' or are not registered at all. The main trends show that in the period since the mid 1980s there has been a decline in the proportion of inter-state conflicts, and now stands at less than one-twentieth of all conflicts; decolonization conflicts remain at a constant one-twentieth of all conflicts. Disquieting facts are that the proportion of gang-style wars and inter-ethnic wars have almost doubled in the space of ten years. In these types a peaceful conflict settlement is particularly difficult to achieve. Though endemic chaos and 'warlordism' continue to be a feature in only a small proportion of all conflicts, although where it has almost became a 'way of life', there is a realistic danger that their number will increase. In summary, the most dangerous trend points towards further fragmentation within existing states and signifies an increasing loss of hegemony on the part of state actors.

Approaches to dealing with intra-state conflicts in general and 'ethnic' types of conflicts in particular are explored (in Chapters 2–5). Appropriate political and legal steps need to be taken to pre-empt destructive forms of interaction between states and peoples. This has not yet been subject to systematic investigation. The new research priorities should involve, first and foremost, greater attention to causes. My critique of some of the approaches is intended to broaden the debate about prevention and conflict resolution. The self-determination of peoples is one of the main planks of ethnonationalist revolt. But structurally, international law protects states rather than peoples. From the 1920s, and again since World War II, autonomy arrangements of all kinds have helped resolve ethno-national conflicts in Europe. Classic measures include recognition of lesser-used languages, protection of cultural independence, political representation and special electoral regulations. The creation of territorial units has produced various forms of self-government by minorities. I explore various elements of, and evaluation criteria for, self-government.

Outside Europe, the demand of many nationalities for self-governance led to a broadening and deepening of the classic form of minority protection. The search for regional ideal–typical examples of autonomy and self-governance produces a number of more or less successful 'models' that could become paradigms for the particular regions concerned. Prevention through appropriate autonomy arrangements and generous nationality policies is not only cheaper than intervention it is in fact the only really ideal method when it comes to dealing constructively with the problem of ethno-national difference.

Conflict averting structural elements for multi-ethnic states entail a turning-away from the culturally monopolism of nation-states and the political centralism that goes with it. The move towards ethno-political neutrality and the principle of decentralization constitutes a change of paradigm. There is no simple cure all here. Constructive structural elements can be explored in the global context. To sum up, federalization, decentralization and territorial self-governance have proved themselves all over the world to be means of averting conflict.

Comparison of the nationality policies of the most populous countries of the world (the multinational Asiatic states of China and India and the CIS/USSR) with the minority policies of the former settler colonies of North America (the USA and Canada) is of major importance when it comes to positing international legal standards in regard to indigenous and endangered peoples. The nationality policies of China and India in particular are little known or appreciated. More attention should be given to the silent work of violence prevention, confidence building and dialogue. Successful experiences should be compared and studied carefully.

Civil actors should take the lead in fighting powerlessness and the passive response on genocide taken by states and international organizations. The development of concepts of structural prevention of genocide and mass violence is among the noblest task of peace research. Charitable funds and scientific funding institutions should prioritize research projects in these fields. Standardizing the prevention of genocide and mass violence internationally must become a key task for the United Nations in the twenty-first century.

Notes

Introduction: ethnos, nations, ethno-nationalism and conflict

1. Let us take a topical example: in non-aligned Yugoslavia, there was no fighting or dying for the nation – a concept that appears to have been surmounted. The media coined terms such as 'ethnic cleansing'. Religious communities were ethnicized on the basis of, and in memory of, the last chapter in a barbaric, externally imposed history of genocide scarcely two generations old. According to my definition of an ethnos (see below), the parties to the conflict in Bosnia are lacking certain major objective attributes that would justify speaking of a nation of Croats as distinct from that of the Serbs or Muslims. The differences between the Slav peoples of Yugoslavia lie at the level of confession/religion and (concomitant) colonial history, and of affiliation to two empires – the Habsburg and the Ottoman. The crucial objective attribute of language, and many cultural features of the parties to the conflict, are largely identical (Serbo-Croat). The talk of 'ethnic cleansing' makes little sense in this context.
2. The example of Yugoslavia involves a hybrid ethnicization of religious groups (Muslims, Roman Catholics and other Christians and so on), that accelerated or was revitalized as the conflict escalated. The existing group cohesion (however weak) was 'confirmed' by the traumatic events of World War II, or was reinforced by ongoing atrocities. This form of ethnicization of political and social conflicts became a vehicle through which the ex-Communist élite maintained power.
3. The concept of the majority is a political-cum-territorial one: this is also true of its 'counterpart', the minority. As a rule, minorities are the majority in the areas which they inhabit or to which they lay claim. The state often tries to ensure such so-called minorities are outnumbered in their own areas, through settlement by members of the state peoples. Almost all states have one or more minorities. In Africa in particular, there are rarely state peoples capable of forming a majority demographically.
4. The saying that there are as many definitions of an ethnos as there are ethnologists is exaggerated, given that many ethnologists show no interest in having an easy-to-handle definition; too narrow a definition, meanwhile, would entail a risk of abuse in the political domain.
5. For a detailed definition, see Zimmermann 1992: 75–118. Isajiw investigated 27 definitions of an ethnos, involving up to 12 characteristics: see Wsevolod W. Isajiw, 'Definitions of Ethnicity', in Bienvenue and Goldstein 1980, also Wsevolod W. Isajiw 1999.
6. A figure of 10,000 or more ethnic groups has been mentioned. The variation in figures is due to the differences in the criteria or attributes used to define an ethnos.
7. There are two opposing points of view on this: (1) religion is tantamount to a marker of ethnic identity, because it gives the individual a collective identity and security (Durkheim's 'religion as social cement'); in this scheme, functional and structural implications remain obscured; (2) religion is an instrument of social control that works in a subtle way through internalized value- and belief-systems, cosmologies, and so on, or that secures subjection and obedience and/or provides

the powerful with a justification for their power, through direct command and instruction from authoritative institutions. This second point of view does not deny the power of religion to form identities and to confer authoritarian structure on sectarian factions in politics.

8. The attributes of an ethnic community cannot be regarded as uncontroversial. P. Smith (1991: 21) lists six: distinct name; myths about origin; historical memory; shared culture; 'homeland'; and a feeling of solidarity among significant sectors of the population. Barth (1969: 10 ff.) names four groups of attributes: biological reproduction; shared cultural values; shared area of interaction; self-identification; and distinctiveness.

9. Ethnic communities may be imagined (Anderson) but as imagined entities they are significantly more concrete and more tangible than that of the nation.

10. Despite this, many ethnologists seem to regard peoples defined thus as a kind of 'island' in themselves (Barth), which can be arbitrarily wrenched from its social context and removed from the area of inter-ethnic communication for the purposes of description.

11. Barth 1969: 11. Thus, a shared culture would not be a primary, defining characteristic of an ethnic group (in Barth's opinion). If we would put the cultural aspect first this would interfere with the chronological continuity of an ethnic group (which we presuppose as one of the most enduring forms of social organization) and with those factors that determine its form. One-sided concentration on the social aspects, for its part, would result in too great an emphasis on the identification of Self and Other.

12. For a discussion of primordialism versus constructivism/situationism in anthropological theory see Scherrer 1997, 20–32. For a thorough critique of primordialism, the claim that ethnicity is entirely socially constructed (an exaggerated thesis in my eyes) and the consequences colonial primordialism had in some cases, see Eller 1999.

13. The authoritative six-point definition of an indigenous people given by Burger (1987: 9) allows for the conquest and dominance aspect but imposes unnecessary restrictions (nomadism, acephalousness, 'different world-view').

14. The term 'homeland' (used by among others Smith 1991) seems unfortunate to me, because it is vague and because it names a mythical area to which an ethnic group can lay claim without living or working there. In our definition, territory as an objective criterion is closely related to the mode of production and life of an ethnic group. Obviously, different yardsticks apply for nomads than for those who work on the land.

1   Contemporary mass violence

1. See 'Neue Weltordnung: "Dialektik zwischen Orient und Okzident". Ein Gespräch mit Johan Galtung. Groningen. July 1990' in IRECOR Working Paper 3. Moers: IFEK-IRECOR 1997.

2. A two-volume handbook on ethno-nationalism attempts to avoid the systematic distortion of facts by most belligerent parties through participatory observation. See: Scherrer 'Ethno-Nationalismus. Münster' *agenda* 1996 and 1997. Case studies are based on first hand information and field experience and are published in the IRECOR reports series, no. 3–6.

3. Ted Robert Gurr developed a sophisticated typology of nations and minorities at risk; he distinguishes two different types and seven subtypes of 'politicized

communal groups' (Gurr 1993, 18): 'National peoples' (what I call – according to ranking in size and status – nations, nationalities and peoples) subdivided as ethno-nationalists and indigenous peoples and 'minority peoples', subdivided into ethno-classes, militant sects and 'communal contenders', again subdivided as disadvantaged (losers) and advantaged (winners).

4. Gurr's definition of ethno-nationalism differs from mine in a few aspects. It carries an essentialist element by the implicit identity of social base and political actor. In defining the actors and the political realm Gurr combines ethnonationalists as 'a people' ('large, regionally concentrated peoples with a history of organised political autonomy') with a particular political agenda as 'a people' (having 'pursued separatist objectives at some time during the last half-century'). Separating indigenous peoples from other ethno-nationalist peoples makes sense with regard to international law provisions.

5. Different potentials for resistance to stateless (*acephalous*) and centrally organized societies are outlined and illustrated with three series of examples in Scherrer 1997 (Handbook 2, chapter 6).

6. The two Koreas are the best cases for homogeneity. Japan is also relatively homogenous, with indigenous Ainu, former Korean slave workers, so-called Asian 'comfort women' and migrant communities as relatively small non-Japanese communities. The 'sex slaves' issue had been kept secret as a result of 'the warrior-macho logic of governments that the suffering of women was outside the responsibility discourse' (Galtung 1997, 28), ignored by the Tokyo Tribunal, the 1952 Peace Treaty with South Korea.

7. Northern states direct intervention in the South was carried out mostly as a (former) colonial power or as an intervention power. The states with most war involvement were Britain, France and USA, see SEF 1997, 369. These findings are contested by Herbert K. Tillema who compiled interventions for the period 1945–1991, see '690 foreign overt military interventions, 1945–1991'; in Duyvesteyn 1995. Also compare note 12.

8. Some 38,000 transnational corporations made a turnover of more than US$5500 billion. World trade grew from 10 per cent of the world-wide production of goods in 1970 to 25 per cent in 1995 (SEF 1995, 2).

9. The term *internal conflict* became invalid concerning conflicts about asymmetric resource distribution, economic underdevelopment and ecologically induced conflicts. The latter may well escalate because of global and regional disruption of the natural environment (*greenhouse effect*) or sudden large changes of climate caused by hydro dams. Dams can be an issue in wars for water in the Middle East (Turkey versus Syria and Iraq; Israel versus Lebanon, Syria and Jordan) and in Western Africa (Senegal versus Mauritania) where there is a considerable mixing of ecological issues with ethnic issues.

10. Some 6267 ethnic groups in 159 countries (1979), see Boulding 'Ethnic Separatism', in Kriesberg 1979, 276. The 'Ethnologue' of SIL/Grimes *et al.*, 1996 listed 6700 language groups.

11. ECOR Register in Scherrer 1997 (Handbook 2), 105–43; Summary see: Scherrer in Kurtz *et al.* 1999, vol. 3, 381–430.

12. Due to a difference in criteria the number of cases range from 88 to 390: states of the North were 88 times (of 363 cases) directly involved in wars according to SEF 1993: 181; others say that states of the North were, since 1945, directly involved in over 390 wars fought by state actors in the South. For the period of 1945 to 1991 compilations go as high as 690 foreign overt military interventions.

Northern states direct intervention in the South was mostly carried out by former colonial powers or by super powers. The countries with the highest level of war involvement are Great Britain (19), France and USA (14 each), USSR/Russia (7) and Turkey (5). See SEF 1997, 369; Tillema, *op. cit.*, in Duyvesteyn 1995.

13. See: African Rights 1995, Scherrer 1997a, Human Rights Watch 1999. In this century the number of war-related victims was fewer than the victims of slaughter. It is not a viable solution to register (for the sake of a narrow definition of war) non-war violence such as 'massacres' only if they constitute 'mass murder or exterminatory actions occurring during a war or in close relation to a war' (Gantzel 1997, 259), as exemplified in the cases of Bosnia 1992 and Rwanda 1994.

14. AKUF translates as *Workgroup for Research on Conflict Causes* (Arbeitsgemeinschaft Konfliktursachen-Forschung, Hamburg). AKUF data is quite accurate, though the criteria for their compilation are somewhat outdated and impractical. Earlier the AKUF-register excluded whole sections of contemporary violent conflicts (analysed by Nietschmann more than a decade ago; see: Nietschmann 1987), more recently some criteria have been modified; see AKUF: 'Kriege und bewaffnete Konflikte 1999' on http://www.sozialwiss.uni-hamburg.de/Ipw/Akuf/ home.html.

15. As UN Special Investigator I experienced the consequences of the world's fastest genocide very personally and directly (see: Scherrer 1997a). Statements such as 'the Rwanda genocide...was part of the war' or 'part of the war aim' (*Journal of Peace Review*, March 1998) are outrageous. This is based on a deeply erroneous definition of genocide as being part of warfare, and trivializes the Rwandan genocide. One can only imagine the outcry if the same were claimed to be applicable to the *Shoah* (the Nazi Holocaust against the European Jews).

16. Lately a research deficit on *ethnic* conflicts was acknowledged. After critics AKUF revised its typology (Gantzel 1997, 321; Rabehl and Trines 1997). The definition of war is still state-centred and expects legitimate state monopolies of violence in force almost everywhere. In times of state collapse such approaches suffer a loss of credibility. The AKUF-typology needs further revision to indicate other dominant actors or decisive factors. Ethnicity is seen as 'secondary construct' (Gantzel); the risk is that such a 'definition of ethnic conflicts becomes so restrictive that their absence becomes nearly tautological' (Wiberg 1997, 311).

17. Private armies and *post-modern warfare* see: Shearer 1998. The journal *Civil War* dedicated a good part of its first issue to that type of warfare. Shearer's conclusion that the UN should hire 'professional' mercenaries for 'peace keeping' duties is highly questionable, to say the least.

18. Mediation and outside intervention are much more successful in C type cases than in any of the other conflict types. In the case of Ethiopia versus Eritrea there was a conspicuous lack of success. From May 1998, Colonel Ghaddafi, Hassan Gouled of Djibouti, Italy, Rwanda, the USA, Zimbabwe and others rushed to intervene and mediate in this absurd war. Amid a famine both countries spent scarce resources on war, continued the spiral of escalation and even exported proxy conflict to neighbouring states. Only with the Cessation of Hostilities Agreement (18 June 2000) the war abated, followed by the Peace Agreement (12 December 2000), disengagement and the rapid deployment of UN troops. The war took a high toll (80,000), if compared with other type C cases in the 1990s.

19. Some of the frequent clashes between settlers and indigenous peoples do not have to include criminal elements (at least with no higher participation of criminal actors as for other types of conflicts). However, such conflicts become gang

wars and not 'normal' inter-ethnic conflicts because the settlers would often not be grouped together and armed without the support of the state they belong to. Individual settlers conceive indigenous territories as *terra nullius*, as settler states have done during the centuries.

20. Compare the authoritative work of Kiernan 1996.

21. On the Rwandan genocide compare: African Rights 1995; ECOR 1995a; Prunier 1995; Scherrer 1995/1997a; JEEAR 1996; Human Rights Watch 1999.

22. The perpetrators of genocide in South and Central Sudan are the Sudanese Army and tribal Arab militias. Irregular forces were armed and recruited by central governments since the reign of Sadiq al-Mahdi. In October 2000 the United States Holocaust Memorial Museum issued a genocide alert regarding Sudan.

23. Among those 50 nonsignatory states are many weak, dangerous or war-torn countries, such as Angola, Central African Republic, Chad, Congo, Equatorial Guinea, Eritrea, Guinea, Indonesia, Japan, Kenya, Mauritania, Niger, Nigeria, Paraguay, Sierra Leone, Somalia, Sudan, Tajikistan, Uzbekistan and others. In many or by many of the above-mentioned states, genocide or crimes against humanity have been committed in the past. In some cases governments are committing such crimes, as in Congo, Equatorial Guinea, Indonesia and Sudan.

24. *Homicide:* mass murder and crimes on a scale characterized by the intention of the perpetrators/a group of perpetrators to kill individuals belonging to a particular social group; homicide, as configured as organized criminal violence of some degree of duration and intensity, thus having structural aspects and a particular unique configuration. Type H had been under discussion for some time; the type was neither included in the ECOR typology nor finally rejected.

25. Mixed types such as AB, BA, BC, CB, AC, CA, AE, EA, ABC, BAC and so on. The first mentioned letter indicates the type which in a given period is the dominant type in combination with a less influential secondary type and an even less influential tertiary type.

26. Scherrer 1988, 1997, 1999; ECOR studies; AKUF; HIIK *Conflict Barometer*; SIPRI *Yearbooks*; Gantzel *et al.*, 1994, 1997; Nietschmann 1987; SEF, *Global Trends*; Seybolt 2000; Uppsala Conflict Data Project, 'Major Armed Conflicts', in SIPRI *Yearbooks*; Wallensteen *et al.*; UNDP, *HD Reports*; FEWER, *Situation Reports*.

27. Gurr identified for 1990 some 233 minorities at risk in 93 countries, representing nearly one billion people or 17.3 per cent of the world's population (Gurr 1993, 11). In 1945–49 26 *ethno-political* groups were in conflict, 1950–59 there were 36 groups, in 1960s the same number, in the 1970s the number rose to 55, in the 1980s it reached 62, and in the mid 1990s 70 ethnic groups were at armed struggle (Gurr 1994).

28. The most recent cases of dominant inter-state conflicts: the war between Pakistan and India in Kashmir 1998–99; the war between Ethiopia and Eritrea being fought with increasing intensity since March 1998, with spillover effects on Southern Somalia during 1999, ceasefire and the deployment of UN peace keepers late in 2000; and, the 78-days air war of the NATO alliance against Yugoslavia 1999, resulting in ongoing violence and reversed 'ethnic cleansing' in Kosovo in 2000. The most costly of the three wars is the one in the Horn of Africa; the original issue allegedly was territorial but underlying was a power struggle between competing leaders and former liberation movements.

29. The new trend is evident in Africa. In 1996 and 1997 there were several cases: Angolan military involvement in October 1997 gave decisive support for Sassou Nguesso's 'cobra' militia who had tried since June 1997 to seize control over

Congo-Brazzaville from the Lissouba government. The intervention of Rwanda and Uganda in November 1996 had helped AFDL-rebels to topple the Mobutu regime in May 1997. Rwandan troops had crossed again into Congo DR in August 1998 to support the anti-Kabila revolt. The result was a rapid internationalization of the new war in Congo, which is currently the world's most deadly and most complex war. Sudanese state army battalions are fighting an 'endless' civil war in South Sudan and occasionally crossing the borders into Congo and Northern Uganda 'in hot pursuit' since 1996. A similar scenario exists whereby the Ethiopian EPRDF-army, when fighting Ethiopian Somali rebels (Ogadeni), across the border of stateless Southern Somalia since 1996/97.

30. There is talk about 'Africa-War-I' relating to Congo-DR, Angola, Zimbabwe, Sudan (unofficially), Namibia and Chad (until May 1999) propped-up the faltering government army (dominated by Kabila's Lubakat officers and the main faction of the Katanga tigers/gendarmes along with FAR-Interahamwe and FDD as troops) while Uganda, Rwanda, Burundi and the SPLA supported the RCD rebels (dominated by the Banyamulenge). Some of the states are only involved in order to clear the hinterland of their respective insurgencies, for example Angola versus UNITA, Uganda versus LRA, ADF, and WNB, Rwanda versus FAR-Interahamwe and Burundi versus FDD. Some dozens of militias and gangs in Congo-DR struggle in changing alliances with state actors and rebel armies while undergoing frequent splits.

31. From 1995 to 1996 there were 23 cases of foreign state interventions, of which six cases of intervention started before the mentioned period. The number of interventions has further increased since.

32. In all rules, no so-called 'Third Parties' take immediate part in combat in the case of ethnic conflicts. Exceptions to the rule are ethno-national conflicts that have earlier been named 'regional conflicts' or proxy wars during the cold war period (escalated by the intervention of super powers).

33. All successful rebel organizations have or had their hinterland in one or more neighbouring states. This fact will be officially denied by the respective states out of diplomatic necessity. Dependent on political conjunctures and the current state of interests, a number of states provided a hinterland for resistance movements of neighbouring countries. Such support has a long tradition and even includes criminal organizations (organized crime, for example drug cartels and terrorist groups).

34. Quantitative criteria (such as 1000 victims per annum) remain tentative. *Contrary to the Correlates of War Project* and others, AKUF/Gantzel refuse to apply (mechanic) quantitative criteria and followed Istvan Kende's definition of warfare (Gantzel 1997, 259). The way Small and Singer apply their criteria showed inconsistencies of a marked quantitative approach. Wallensteen *et al.* (see chapter on 'Major armed conflicts' in various SIPRI yearbooks 1994–99) used the 1000 victims criteria to distinguish *intermediate armed conflicts* (1000 'battle-related deaths' for the entire course of conflict) and *wars* (1000 during a particular year). The cardinal problem: genocide-related deaths can not be classified as battle related and are by definition excluded. Thus, the data remain flawed.

35. In 1996 seven African countries were among the 15 countries affected by major armed conflicts: Algeria, Burundi, Congo-Zaire, Ethiopia, Somalia, Sudan and Uganda; outside Africa eight major conflicts were being fought in Afghanistan, Burma, Chechnya/RF, Colombia, India, Philippines, Sri Lanka and Turkey/Kurdistan. In 1997 the number of African countries with major conflicts claiming

more than 1000 violence-related deaths rose to ten (Angola again, Rwanda again, Sierra Leone again and Congo-Brazzaville) compared to seven other cases in the rest of the world (the above mentioned without Chechnya). In 1998 already 13 major armed conflicts had occurred in Africa: Algeria, Angola, Burundi, Congo-DR, Congo, Ethiopia versus Eritrea, Guinea-Bissau, Rwanda, Senegal, Sierra Leone, Somalia, Sudan and Uganda; seven major conflicts were fought in the rest of the world: Afghanistan–Tajikistan, Burma, Colombia, Sri Lanka, Turkey–Kurds, US–UK versus Iraq. In 1999 again 13 major armed conflicts occurred in Africa: the above mentioned with Nigeria new, Senegal less; eleven major conflicts were being fought in the rest of the world: the above mentioned, less US–UK versus Iraq, and five new or newly igniting conflicts: NATO versus FRY-Kosovo, Kargil–Kashmir (Pakistan versus India), Lebanon–Israel, Indonesia–East Timor and Russia versus Chechnya.

36. The regional war in Congo broke out in mid-1998; eight states and two dozen armed non-state actors are fighting each other. Only African actors are directly involved. Observers talk about an 'Africa War I'; its outcome will be decisive for the new order in Africa. Two alliances with some in-between parties are fighting it out. 'The Kabila regime survived since August 1998 due to marginal or non-existent links between the internal political opposition and the armed groups, because of their influence areas and ethnic base being apart or their differences too great. The power struggle in Central Africa became truly regional. The old Francophone networks were revived by Kabila, reinforced by several SADC countries, against the axis Uganda–Rwanda–Burundi, backed by most East African states.' (see ECOR 1999: 122–40, 130). The Lusaka peace agreement of July 1999 was seen as a turning-point in the war and called for a UN peace enforcement operation. For the implementation of the agreement, however, there was no political will by the UN Security Council; a proposed African peace force did not materialize either.

37. Rudolph Rummel's estimates conclude that four times as many people were murdered by their states than were killed in war, see Rummel 1994*a*. 2–3; also 1994 and 1997. For a good presentation of the issue compare Grimshaw 1999.

2   Approaches to identifying and dealing with violent conflicts

1. 'Palaver democracy' is a central element in this, one example being the *gada* system of the Oromo in Ethiopia, see A. Legesse, *Gada: Three Approaches to the Study of African Society*. London: Macmillan, 1973. Traditional *gachacha* arbitration was spontaneously revived in Rwanda after the genocide: see Kagabo, and Thahirwa, *Droit coutumier au Rwanda: Cas Gacaca* (Kigali: UNAR, 1995); Karega, (c-ord.): *Gacaca: Le Droit coutumier au Rwanda. Rapport final de l'enquête sur le terrain* (Kigali: UCT-HRFOR, 1996). Ntahombaye and Manirakiza UNESCO–Culture de la Paix: *La contribution des institutions et des techniques traditionnelles de résolution pacifique des conflits à la résolution pacifique de la crise burundaise* (Bujumbura: Presses Lavigerie, 1998).

2. Roman law reputedly contains concepts for the forensic treatment of 'ethnic' conflicts.

3. The plan of justice minister Jean de Dieu Mucyo is nothing less than to launch an unprecedented response to genocide, on an unprecedented scale, in order to

start prosecution and trials where the crimes were actually committed and where the witnesses are to be found: on the thousand hills of Rwanda, 220,000 or more grassroot judges will be trained and sworn in to serve in countrywide 11,000 gachacha courts. Their task will be the largest ever operation in justice after genocide the world has seen. This huge scheme will be launched in 2001. See 'Participative Justice on Scale 2000–2010' in Scherrer, *Responses to Genocide: African Solutions and the Role of the International Community*, 2003 (forthcoming).

4. What is needed is an 'integrated early warning analytic system' with direct access to executive levels of international organizations: 'Early warning was less critical in the Rwanda crisis than the willingness and ability to respond. Nevertheless, the failure to respond adequately was in part influenced by the failure to collect and analyse the data that was available and to translate this information into strategic plans', in JEEAR 1996, *Early Warning and Conflict Management*: ii. The path-breaking UN inquiry report on the role of the UN in the Rwandan disaster, delivered in December 1999, made a number of detailed recommendations to that end, including 'initiate an action plan to prevent genocide involving the whole UN system' (Carlsson *et al.* 1999, IV, §1–14, §1).

5. Barbara Harff and other scholars developed an early warning system of genocide and mass violence for the US government; the project was 'adopted' and supported by the then vice-president Al Gore, see: Harff B. 'Strategic approaches to genocide prevention', presentation at AGS Conference 'The future of genocide', Madison: University of Wisconsin 1999. The US State Department is learning from its failure in 1994 and is going to instal an early warning system. At the Stockholm International Forum on the Holocaust in January 2000 the German minister Michael Naumann called on the EU to develop such a system.

6. Where were the international watchdogs in Rwanda 1993–94? NGOs had for some time been the 'good guys', allegedly without hidden agendas and with much humanitarian commitment. In the Rwandan case this image has been dashed. It is hard to believe that the largest, best funded and globally active human rights NGOs, Amnesty International, Human Rights Watch and Fédération Internationale des Ligues des Droits de l'Homme/International Federation of Human Rights Leagues, failed to understand the danger and failed to monitor the situation closely – despite a series of warnings from local informers and despite the postcolonial history of Rwanda and Burundi providing all the necessary evidence to be highly vigilant and to keep a watch on the evolving situation with determination and care.

7. East Timor is a former Portuguese colony, which was occupied by Indonesia in 1975, after the Portuguese revolution liberated the country. More than a quarter of the population had died in the late 1970s; the death toll was a result of a merciless Indonesian counterinsurgency campaign against rebel FRETILIN. In 1998 Indonesia was bogged down by economic and political crisis. After the fall of the dictator and political change in Indonesia, a referendum was allowed on 30 August 1999: 80 per cent East Timorese braved Indonesian threats to vote for independence. In the aftermath of the referendum, military-backed militias unleashed an orgy of destruction, driving three quarters of the population from their homes. The late UN intervention secured their return. The chief responsible for the massacre, General Wiranto, lost his positions in 2000 and might be brought to trial.

8. The main recommendations of Carlsson *et al.* 1999 to co-ordinate between the Secretariat, other affected agencies and INGOs, and to co-operate with regional and subregional organizations, to improve efforts to protect civilians in conflict

and potential conflict situations (IV 5), to secure the UN personnel as well as the local staff, to improve the flow of information within the United Nations system (IV 8), particularly between UNHCR, UNHCHR, Special Representatives, and UN funds or programmes with the Security Council (IV 9), to improve information on human rights issues (as a base for decision-making in conflict areas), to co-ordinate national evacuation operations with UN missions on the ground (in order to avoid the retreat of an important contingent, as in the case of the Belgium contingent in UNAMIR I) and to exclude criminal states from being members of the Security Council (as in Rwanda in 1994).

9. See Scherrer 1998a. For the latest developments in the establishment of the ICC see the home page of the Coalition for an International Criminal Court on www.iccnow.org.

10. See the overview of minority/majority dictatorships by N. Pietersee in *der überblick*: AGKED 1993: 14 ff.

11. These would appear to be unfortunate appellations for movements that sprang from asymmetrical postcolonial 'starting-conditions'. The conflict in Sri Lanka (Singhalese army versus LTTE), for example, may be regarded as a classic case of ethno-nationalism by provocation, which has nothing to do with 'demands' but much to do with 'defence' and survival in a situation of threat (see Scherrer 1997, 95–6, esp. fn. 121). While 1915 saw the first of seven pogroms by the Singhalese against the Tamils, the start of the armed struggle by various Tamil organizations began in 1983, following a series of repressive measures taken by the state in the period since 1948.

12. Ropers and Schlotter 1993, 866 ff.

13. See Hofmann 1992: 2. For comments on the resolution of the EU Council of Ministers, *ibid*. n. 2.

14. The Fascist Ustacha (operating under SS direction) murdered 655,000 Serbs, Jews and Roma in the four years between 1941 and 1945.

15. Together with Pol Pot's Cambodia (1975–79: 2 million victims) and Young Turk Turkey (1909–23: mass murder of 1.4 million Armenians 1915–18 plus a million further victims), Croatia under the Ustacha was one of the three most murderous regimes of this century measured in terms of deaths per year (see Rummel 1994a, 4, Table II).

16. The agreement consists of one page of general text plus 35 pages of appendices (ten in total) on the major questions relating to: security, borders ('interentity boundaries'), elections, constitutions, dispute settlement, human rights, refugees and expellees, national monuments, public services, civilian implications and international police. The crucial appendix on the peaceful settlement of disputes (12 lines long!) leaves everything open and refers to the 'basic principles' of Geneva of September 1995. 'General Framework Agreement for Peace in Bosnia and Herzegovina. Dayton, 21 November–Paris, December 1995', *Review of International Affairs*, 67 (1996).

17. What has actually happened is counter to the agreements of Dayton (December 1995) and Rome (February 1996), according to which Sarajevo is to remain united 'Sarajevo Will be a United City', *Review of International Affairs*, 67 (1996).

18. The Serb settlement-areas in Croatia (Krajina, Slavonia) were described as 'Serb-occupied'. Croatia claims ownership of the Gulf of Piran in Slovenia. The Slovenian parliament declared the Slovenian settlement-areas in Croatia to be a separate republic in October 1994, in order to force Croatia into formal agreement about the inviolability of joint borders. Tudjman led Croatia to lay claim to Croatian areas in south-west Bosnia.

19. Including, at that time, US Secretary of State Warren Christopher.
20. The way the intervention was prepared by NATO states (Rambouillet diktat), the way it was implemented (indiscriminate bombing of civilian targets during 78 days), and the results that came out of it (perpetrator and victim of the ethnic cleansing and massacres were reversed) seem in no way to justify the NATO intervention.
21. Human Rights Watch 2000, 6–8. Now the 'liberated' Albanians kill Serbs and Roma under the eyes of NATO soldiers; common law criminality in Kosovo has also massively increased. For the Serbs it is history repeated: after the Axis powers invaded and dismembered Yugoslavia in 1941, Kosovo Albanians formed military units to fight for the Nazis, killed more than 10,000 Kosovo Serbs, drove more than 100,000 out of Kosovo and brought immigrants in from Albania. Fifty-eight years later the price was paid by the ordinary Serbs of Kosovo, who were killed in 'revenge acts' and driven out, and by ordinary citizens of Serbia proper, whose country was bombed almost into 'pre-industrial times', while their leader remains in power; parallels with the case of Iraq are striking. Why was there no military intervention in Rwanda 1994 but in Kosovo and in East Timor?
22. On his visit in Yugoslavia 1999, Cornelio Somaruga, head of ICRC, claimed the destruction of water supply systems, electrical power stations and grid, all kinds of industry facilities, oil refineries, heating plants, broadcast facilities, numerous bridges (including large bridges over the Danube), public building (including schools and hospitals); this disrupted civilian life in a way that was clearly disproportional thus 'excessive in relation to the concrete and direct military advantage anticipated' as codified in article 57 of Protocol I to the Geneva Conventions.
23. According to GoYU estimates NATO's air war against Yugoslavia inflicted US$20–30 billion worth of damage. The HRW and AI 1999 reports do not detail the devastation caused by NATO, and the number of NATO victims was given as 300 (official numbers are around 2500). 'NATO is bound by these basic rules whenever it goes to war. Particularly when it fights in the name of human rights, it should abide by these standards scrupulously.' (Ibid., 5) HRW rightly criticized disturbing violations of international law by NATO and especially mentioned the Geneva Conventions of 1949 and their Additional Protocols of 1977 with contingent prohibition to target non-combatants.
24. Legal provisions for the protection of the Sorbs are included not in the national constitution of Germany but in the regional constitutions, laws, and decrees of the *Länder* of Saxony and Brandenburg. See Bund Lausitzer Sorben 1994; also Elina Hilza, *The Sorbs in Germany* (Bautzen, n.d.).
25. The NCGUB is led by Prime Minister Sein Win, currently living in exile in Washington. (Dr Sein Win is a cousin of Nobel Peace prizewinner Aung San Suu Kyi.) See Josef Silverstein, 'Burma's Woman of Destiny?', in Aung San Suu Kyi *et al.*, *Freedom from Fear* (New Delhi: Penguin, 1991), 277; and *pogrom*, 188 (1995) (spec. issue on Burma).
26. Wars in the former Soviet Union: Moldova/Trans-Dniester, Georgia/South Ossetia, Georgia/Abkhazia, and Chechnya/Ingushetia. Yugoslavia: wars in Croatia/Krajina and Slavonia (Serb minority) and tripartite Bosnia. In Bosnia, the abolition of power sharing and of the principle of rotation of high office meant that the complex rules of play (in a system involving three actors, each without a majority) were invalidated. In all cases (except that of Bosnia) the 'rules of play' were changed unilaterally by the state or titular nation in a way that is detrimental to the minority or minorities.

27. See Scherrer 1998*a*: 298–9. In the Russian Federation, there are currently 21 autonomous republics (five more than during the Soviet era), independently governed by large minorities as titular nations.
28. The same ethnic élite has already provoked one war (against Ingushetia) and has been involved in two others (Abkhazia and the rebellion led by Zviad Gamsakhurdia).
29. Forerunners of present-day peace research emerged in the USA and Britain as a form of pacifist doctrine of international law originating mainly with the Society of Friends (Quakers). The two main reference points of present-day peace studies – namely, concern with (potential or actual) conflicts of a violent kind in both the world of states and the societal world, and the gearing of both theory and practice to a positive guiding concept of peace – were ones which the Quakers also respected.
30. In West Germany, these influences were taken up above all by Dieter Senghaas, Hartmut Elsenhans and Klaus Jürgen Gantzel. See Senghaas 1972, 1974.
31. Being fetishistic about state borders and ignoring the reality of multinational heterogeneity, particularly in the Third World Galtung said is 'ethnocentric and short-sighted': Galtung 1964: 2.
32. Scherrer 1994: 68–74, 1997: 134–42 and 1999: 392–5. In order to illustrate the dynamics and composition of present day mass violence, the ECOR index includes, in addition to details of the dominant type in each case, a second/ third mention detailing the phase of the violence. This allows for the hetero-geneous-cum-dynamic character of most cases of mass violence.
33. According to the ECOR index the most frequent dominant type of mass violence is the ethno-national type, which accounts for >40 per cent; running at some distance behind these are: anti-regime wars (dominant in ca 20 per cent of cases), inter-ethnic/tribal wars (>15 per cent), inter-state wars (>10 per cent), decolo-nization wars (<5 per cent), gang wars (<5 per cent) and genocide (2–3 per cent).
34. P. Weishaupt, 'Kalt erwischte Männerbastion: Friedensforschung in der Krise', *WoZ* 1992/32.
35. Johannes Schwertfegen, Egon Bahr, Gert Krell (eds), *Friedens-gutachten 1991* (Hamburg/Münster: LIT Verlag, 1991).
36. Exceptions to the rule were the North–South research projects conducted by the Deutsche Gesellschaft fur Friedens- und Konfliktforschung (DGFK: German Research Foundation) and some studies by regional researchers in the 1970s. The heading of this section is not meant to imply that the whole of peace and conflict research had to do with military science: in the Federal Republic of Germany – unlike in Switzerland – the pacifist tendency has predominated since the emergence of critical peace research; there are also many non-pacifists who are not, or were not, military scientists in the broad sense of the word.
37. According to my information, 102 wars occurred world-wide over the ten year period 1985–94. Regionally they occured as follows: 42.2 per cent in Asia (including 15 in Southeast Asia), 29.4 per cent in Africa, 14.7 per cent in Europe and 13.7 per cent in Latin America.
38. The Peace Research Institute in Oslo (PRIO) started a research programme on ethnic conflicts (formerly labelled as 'internal conflicts'). Harvard University's Center for International Affairs has conducted risk analyses on ethnic and other intra-state conflicts, as has the University of Uppsala's Department of Peace and Conflict Research (DPCR).
39. The Institute for Ethnography of the USSR Academy of Sciences, the Moscow-based IMEMO Institute and the Centre for Ethno-political Studies, set up by

Edvard Shevernadze in Moscow (with Emil Payne as its first director) all realized which way the wind was blowing. See Emil Payne: 469–80.

40. The acronym INCORE resembles that of ECOR, without having a connection; ECOR was started five years earlier, in 1987. In 1992, the first international conference of the Ethnic Studies Network (ESN), which has some 300 members, took place in Northern Ireland. In 1993, an initiative launched by John Darby led to collaboration between the UN University and the University of Ulster in Coleraine, and to the launch of The Joint International Programme on Conflict Resolution and Ethnicity (INCORE), which 'will set out to provide a systematic approach to the study of ethnic conflict' (INCORE 1993, 2). The ambitious goal INCORE sets itself was 'to encourage links between research, training, policy, practice and theory'. UN funds of $US770,000 were provided for an initial phase of activity. INCORE publishes a regular bulletin and a series of books.

41. INCORE 1993, 3. See also *AFB-INFO* 1993/2: 8–10.

42. UN Doc. S/24111, §11. He talks of states being threatened by 'brutal ethnic… strife'. Often the opposite is the case. Furthermore, the term 'strife' is derogatory, generally used by professional military men to describe non-professional players; in other words, ethnic players are not acknowledged as equal or fully-fledged adversaries.

43. This is true of one of the UNRISD research programmes on ethnicity.

44. ASEN (the Association for the Study of Ethnicity and Nationalism) was set up at the London School of Economics and Political Science. It aims to promote research on this theme by organizing seminars. ASEN published lists of literature on the subject as well as a regular bulletin.

45. The problem is often reduced to that of the ethnically based mobilization engaged in by ethno-élites, especially members of the urban middles classes, for the purpose of satisfying particular interests in the redistribution of collective goods. Such ethno-élites present the splendid image of a (rather unappetizing) permutation of the Western liberal welfare-state, incapable of effectively managing 'wage-disputes' between ethnic groups and social classes.

46. The identification of serviceable distinguishing criteria and the execution of a detailed regime analysis are tasks that cannot be covered here.

47. At the IPRA conference, 1994, in La Valletta, Malta, there were sessions devoted to preventive diplomacy in intra-state conflicts and conflict transformation. Rupesinghe (then ICON) pursued its work with a view to forming a global coalition for war prevention.

48. This fear also derives from the widespread ignorance about the internal conflicts and ethnic structure of the former USSR.

49. Research into the countries of origin and motives of refugees could demonstrate that intra-state armed conflicts, not economic factors, are the main trigger for refugee flows.

50. See expert report: Merkel 1995: vii.

51. Examples for conflict preventive institutions: within OSCE, for example, the high commissioner on national minorities and the new long-term missions of the OSCE in member states facing severe internal problems; the high commissioner for human rights at the UN; the OAU conflict prevention mechanism; and confidence-building measures instituted by the Council of Europe.

52. INCORE/ESN, 'Report on the INCORE Research Workshop', in *ESN Bulletin*, (1994) 6. The research agenda outlined was an ambitious one. INCORE was to become a primary source and resource for researchers – 'the world's leading information centre on ethnic conflict'. This, however, has not been achieved.

53. Important publications that seek to plug these gaps are coming out of the 'Minorities at Risk' project at University of Maryland (see Gurr *et al.*).

54. On this, see the research project 'Ethnic Atlas of the World' which has been run by the ethnology department at the University of Zurich for several years. The outcome, however, seems to be at odds with the resources spent.

55. Whereas the West gave human rights political priority, the East backed the notions of peace, disarmament and security. Collective economic, social and cultural rights are more important to the East than individual civil and political rights, see Balkrishna Kurvey, 'Human Rights: Prerequisite for Peace, Democracy, Freedom, Justice and Security', paper given at Loccum, 1995, 3.

56. Declarations of human rights followed on from wars of independence or 'national' revolutions. This was the case with the 1689 Bill of Rights in England, the 1776 American Declaration of Independence and shortly after this, the Declaration of the Rights of Man under the French Revolution's banner of liberty, equality and fraternity. This quasi historical-cum-organic melding of international rights and human rights in the European-dominated modern age represented from the very outset an unhappy concatenation of nationalism and civil rights.

57. The fact that the existence of second-class citizens – whether as colonized subjects of the British Empire, as *sans-culottes* (literally 'without breeches'=members of the underclass) peasants without rights in revolutionary France, as black slaves in the United States, not to mention as women of the time – did not cast doubt on the idea of human rights from the very hour of their inception but points to the ambivalent notion of human beings and society, or of humanity.

58. In their 'Core Questions for Peace Research in the 1990s', divided into five domains, Senghaas and Zürn called, in 1992, for a 'rethinking of normative goals'. The question was whether, after the collapse of nominal socialism, the Western notion of human rights should be established as the basis for all politics, or whether, when considering value related questions, tolerance should be the 'prime precondition' and a global ethic should be developed via dialogue between the cultures. Although the latter was soon challenged by Huntington with his 'clash of cultures' thesis. It would be interesting to have some indication as to what this 'global ethic' might contain.

59. Though Senghaas and Zürn (1992) confined consideration of this question to the OECD world (the First World) the formulation of the issues relating to the long overdue adjustment to categories and analytical instruments was weak. (Ibid, extracts also in *AFB-Info* (1992) 1: 5.)

60. The authors (*ibid*) disaffirm the postulated notion of multi-polarity by asking whether 'new world-powers (China, India, Russia, Brazil) are in the making' – suggesting that there is only one world power. The question as to whether 'there is any chance at all that...the relatively successful development-path (of the OECD world) will be repeated elsewhere' is incomprehensible, given that China has spent two decades doing just that. Many still refuse to believe the ongoing Chinese economic miracle (since 1980).

61. Whether the predatory privatization propagated by the West really does promise development (something which is being called into question in an obvious way in CIS and eastern Europe), or whether a combination of state and market, exists such as in most countries in Southeast Asia, would be more likely to help bring about the desired development has yet to be decided. Set against the successes achieved in the Far East combining the market with centrally-planned or state-directed economies, the obvious limitations of the doctrines of privatization and the lean state begin to show.

62. International institutions organizations and regimes should all equally promote the principles of cultural tolerance, the inviolability of basic and human rights, and the primacy of ecological conservation. Regarding the latter, the OECD countries, which have 20 per cent of the world's population and cause 80 per cent of its pollution, face the toughest adjustments.

63. Karlheinz Koppe talks with Kant of positive peace (and of justice, security and health) as an unattainable condition. Scholars, he says, should highlight successful approximations to peace; they should expose the function of the military as an intra-societal instrument for preserving power structures and blocking reforms; identify the factors that make peaceful coexistence possible and utilize those factors; point up types of social action that are of significance in peace terms; and they should outline policies for peace (Koppe 1995: 13).

64. Ideas about ethno-nationalism being 'the expression of a global unintelligibility' or 'an act of desperation by backward economies' or 'petty nationalism [without] any real development basis' (Senghaas and Zurn 1992: 4, 5) obscure the real problems and are ultimately only restatements of the question of the size or 'viability' of potential states.

65. The term 'aetiological' contains the idea of a situation of social disease, i.e. a concern with pathological phenomena (analogous to the pathogenesis of visible phenomena in medicine). However, in most cases, rather the absence of violent conflicts would be pathological.

66. Wallerstein talks of 'historical social sciences' (1995).

67. Most peace researchers lack on-site observation; they find the topic 'fascinating'. The modern discourse about war and violence is concerned 'not with truth but with suitability' and does this in a 'purified language'. Empirical material is derived from a small handful of people with first-hand knowledge of the violent conditions on the ground. Even this material appears 'in a very curious way, not to extend, theoretically and conceptually, beyond particular lines' (Richard Rottenburg, 'Reden über Gewalttätigkeiten und Kriege, die andernorts stattfinden', Berlin, 1996).

68. Anyone who sees the modern age as 'non-violent', and associates violence with 'primitiveness, the archaic and nature' is turning a blind eye to everyday racism in modern industrial states. Was the industrial-style annihilation in Auschwitz not 'modern'?

69. I learned of Mengistu's flight via the BBC in the liberated region of the Oromo rebels. My heavily armed escorts remained sceptical and at first believed this to be deliberate disinformation – 'just another trick of the government'. The largest army in black Africa collapsed within weeks.

70 The Greek term *polemos* was translated as 'war/warfare'; originally the old Greek meant 'struggle', mainly the 'exchange of ideas' (not the exchange of fire), as the current usage polemic reveals.

3 Peaceful conflict settlement, go-between facilitation and the timing of responses to conflict

1. The term 'mediation' is used for types of activities requiring active influence by the go-between, while the term 'facilitation' is used for activities such as inviting the warring parties to talk to each other and providing framework conditions for talks as well as (what could be called) 'quiet diplomacy' and 'good offices'.

2. Galtung proposed the term 'go-between' to mean 'n + first parties' (rather than civilian third parties), since it can be very useful to involve fourth and fifth parties.

He says, the term 'third party', has Aristotelian and thus, Western connotations. The idea of neutrality is one he totally rejects which, he says, has never existed in matters of peace and war – only 'in death'.

3. Possible go-betweens or facilitators for example in Africa are the African Dialogue Center (Arusha-based), the OAU Conflict Prevention Mechanism, the Mwalimu Nyerere Foundation, Comunità di Sant'Egidio, Nairobi Peace Initiative and so on; for FSU: Popkov/Weeks/Cohen, Memorial, Brown University (Dennis Samut), the International Circassian Association, UNPO, Islamic INGOs, HCAs; generally: the South Center, Quakers' Society of Friends, Quakers Peace Teams, Carter Center, Conflict Management Group, Institute for Conflict Analysis and Resolution, International Alert, International Crisis Group and others.

4. A selection from the body of literature on conflict resolution: Azar and Burton 1986, Bercovitch *et al.* 1991, Bercovitch and Rubin 1992, Bercovitch 2000, Burton 1990 and 1996, McDonald and Bendahmane 1987, Mitchell and Banks 1996, Ropers and Debiel 1995, Ropers 1995 and 1998, Zartman 1989, 1992 and 1997, Zartman and Deng 1991.

5. Research within the framework of the United Nations University (UNU) only began in 1993. The United Nations Research Institute for Social Development (UNRISD) in Geneva has run two projects on ethnicity since 1994: the Ethnic Diversity and Public Policy project, which also raises the question of ethnic violence (UNRISD 1995) and the Ethnic Conflict and Development project, as part of which seven country reports will be or have been published. See esp. UNRISD Haynes 1995*a*; Bangura 1994; Tishkov 1994*a*; Young 1994*b*; Premdas 1993; Rashid and Shaheed 1993*a*.

6. The WSP is run jointly by UNRISD and the Geneva Institute for International Relations.

7. The two authors take different numbers of conflicts as a basis and operate within different categories and theories. None the less their end results are not very far apart. Billing (1992) investigated 288 cases, Bercovitch *et al.* 1991: 79 within the same period. See also Debiel 1994: 9.

8. Jimmy Carter's mediation attempts in disputes involving states (Haiti, North Korea) were much more successful than those involving intra-state conflicts (Ethiopia, Sudan and Burma).

9. There are only 20 continental and a dozen island states that do not lay claim to territories already claimed by other states. See Kidron and Segal 1992: 11.

10. In 1995 and 1996 there were three cases of dominant inter-state conflicts and four more with inter-state interference as a secondary or tertiary component (see ECOR index 2):

11. Ecuador	Peru	C	Jan. 1995–Feb. 1995
38. Ethiopia	Somalia: ONLF, WSLM, others	CE	August 1996–
54. Lebanon	Israel, Syria, SLA, Hisb-Allah, AL, Amal, PFLP	EC/CE	1982–93/1993–

During 1997–2000 there were four more dominant C cases: Eritrea versus Yemen (Hanish Archipelagos) 1997, Eritrea versus Ethiopia 1998–2000 (Badme district, spillover and escalation in 1999, peace treaty in December 2000), in 1999 for two months between India and Pakistan (about the 'line of control' in Kashmir) and for 78 days NATO versus Federal Republic of Yugoslavia (Kosovo/a). Non-dominant C cases: the UN intervention in East Timor was a decolonization conflict (with limited fighting between UN troops and others but a heavy death toll due to the slaughter of civilians by pro-Indonesian militias). The NATO intervention against Serbs in Bosnia 1995 (NATO; Chetniki, Muslims, HOS and others) was, in my view, not a dominant inter-state conflict (but ECB=) since the war was older, most of the fighting was between local parties on the ground according to their own agendas.

11. In the highly internationalized war in Congo-DR mediation efforts by Zambia's president Chiluba on behalf of SADC brought a ceasefire agreement in mid-July 1999. The agreement, after 11 months of war and dozens of failed attempts, was signed by six (of an initial eight) involved states and (separately) by the three rebel forces of RCD, RCD-ML and MLC. Because of the intransigence of the regime of Laurent Kabila the outcome of the Lusaka talks was threatened from the very beginning, giving the UN arguments against implementing the accord and deploying the agreed peace keeping force. Several other parties to the conflict (local gangs and genocidal elements from Rwanda) were not subject (not parties) to the deal. Only the assassination of Kabila by his generals, in mid-January 2001, brought about change and removed a stumbling block to peace.

12. FARC controlled the pace and direction of the two-year-old peace talks until January 2001, when the government deployed some one thousand soldiers on the border of the FARC-held 'liberated zone' in southern Colombia against the FARC which had declared a unilateral ceasefire. The reason being that FARC wanted the official involvement of the European Union in peace talks, a disengagement agreement and a partial prisoner exchange (involving 550 soldiers captured by FARC). This will not be the last round in the continent's oldest insurgency; the army has little chance of winning a war against FARC's 17,000 well-armed fighters and the broad-based support for the 'revolution' among the poor. For a US perspective see Stratfor: 'Colombia: Adopting a Tougher Stance Against The FARC', 25 January 2001 (www.stratfor.com/home/giu/archive/ 012501).

13. This was ECOR's intention with its project 'Peaceful Conflict Settlement: Mediation, Go-between Facilitation, and Preventive Diplomacy'. The project has an innovative aspect: go-between activities are *post-festum* 'reconstructed' and screened to allow an overview and insights beyond the moment. The intermediaries' working methods are investigated. The project aims to assess initiatives to build conflict resolution capacities at regional and national levels (in a few cases examples might be taken at local level) in two regions: the Central African Great Lakes region and the Caucasus region. The research methods used are also innovative; they include in-depth interviews with members of top/middle level go-between organizations and archival investigation; on the spot documentation, in-depth interviews with users and beneficiaries (middle-level leaders, civil society leaders) and observation of the peace process by Participative Observation according to PAR standards.

14. Some research questions are: who is likely to be acceptable to the parties and under what conditions? What are the role expectations? What is more important, to stick to a role or to change it with the consent of the parties? Who is likely to offer their services? What is the intermediary's status, reputation, influence, role, function and legitimacy?

15. Specifications concern the questions where, when, in what form, with whom (parties, go-betweens, 'observers', others), and under what conditions (for example media in attendance or complete secrecy?) talks will be held.

16. An inquiry on the preparation of go-betweens will look at their training, case knowledge, if fact-finding missions and best case analysis is carried out beforehand and so on.

17. See Mitchell, 'External Peace-Making Initiatives and International Conflict', in Midlarsky 1992.
18. All the OSCE's institutions, negotiating activities, *ad hoc* meetings and missions are financed by contributions from the participating states. In 1996 the secretariat employed approximately 90 staff, excluding interpreters and other language-staff, who bring the total up to 125 or so. In addition, there are 25 staff working in the Office for Democratic Institutions and Human Rights (ODIHR) in Warsaw, and ten in the office of the High Commissioner on National Minorities (HCNM) in The Hague. As a rule, OSCE staff are paid out of the OSCE budget. The total budget for 1996 was US$52.9 million, including US$24.5 million (that is 46 per cent) for the OSCE action in Bosnia and Herzegovina. The 1997 budget was stable at US$50 million, with the activities in Bosnia taking up 44.17 per cent. The unified budget for 1998 went up to US$79 million. The cost of the OSCE action in Bosnia fell to a third of the total budget (38.8 per cent). See http://www.osceprag.cz. In the 1998 budget of US$190 million, the share of preventive institutions such as HCHR and ODIHR was 3.5 per cent.
19. The Convention entered into force on 5 December 1994. The number of signatures is 33; the number of ratifications/accessions is 27. Conditions for entry into force were formulated by 12 participating states. The budget was preliminarily fixed at 250,000 Swiss francs (see: www.osce.org/indexe-inb.htm). The signatory states of the Convention on Conciliation and Arbitration within the OSCE will cover these expenses.
20. Such workshops are run by the Österreichische Studienzentrum für Frieden und Konfliktlösung (ÖSFK: Austrian Study Center for Peace and Conflict Research) in Stadtschlaining.
21. The OECD Development Assistance Committee (DAC) is seeking ways to improve the efficiency, effectiveness and coherence of efforts in the areas of shaping development co-operation as an instrument of conflict prevention and post-conflict rehabilitation and reconstruction. DAC is providing policy guidance with their *Guidelines on Conflict, Peace and Development Co-operation*, OECD-DAC 1997: 7.
22. The DAC Informal Task Force work has drawn on the operational experience of development co-operation agencies and the knowledge of outside experts and practitioners. Participating were most West European countries, the European Commission, the International Monetary Fund (IMF), Japan, the United States, United Nations Development Programme (UNDP) and the World Bank. Other UN agencies such as UNHCR and DHA joined later. Academic research in the field of development co-operation and conflict may give more input in the future.
23. The final four reports delivered by the consultant groups have so far remained confidential; the same applies to the synthesis report compiled by Jon Ebersole (DAC special co-ordinator), see OECD-DAC Task Force on Conflict, Peace and Development: workshop on the limits and scope for the use of development co-operation incentives and disincentives for influencing conflict situations. Documents 1–5. Paris: DAC 1999.
24. In the case of the Krajinas the EU 'shuttle diplomacy' between Belgrade, Zagreb and Knin did not succeed in bringing about genuine negotiations on an agreement regarding the situation of the Krajina Serbs; the issue remains virulent up to the present. See: Richard Lewis, 'Mediation Disputes: A View from the European Commission', in Callieβ and Merkel 1995: 556–9, 557 (former Yugoslavia). Lewis is a member of the staff of EU Directorate-General IA (External Political Relations) and works with Unit A2 on Human Rights and Democratization.

25. Reviewing James Rosenau's operational definition of the term 'intervention' ('The Concept of Intervention', *Journal of International Affairs*, vol. 22, 1968: 165–76) avoids the narrow military conception of intervention, Strazzari rejects Rosenau's criteria of the convention-breaking character and authority-oriented nature of intervention with regard to new types of non-coercive 'third party' intervention. Forms of 'constructive intervention' would be 'essentially legitimised and pre-authorised' (Strazzari 1998: 14).
26. See Callieβ and Merkel (eds) 1994. Galtung rejects the notion of the third party and talks of 'inside' and 'outside'. Communication takes place without/with an outside party as an asymmetrical process or as a symmetrical/dialogue-based process with outside facilitators (in line with Burton) or as an imposed asymmetrical process with a conflict-manager or conflict-dictator.
27. He perceives a division between 'top-level', 'middle-range' and 'grassroot' leadership. On middle-range leadership, see Lederach 1994: 18 (on actors) and 21–5 (on activities).
28. Lederach worked as a mediator in (eastern) Nicaragua and the Horn of Africa (Somalia and Ethiopia) – regions in which I too have carried out empirical research. His analysis of the peace process in eastern Nicaragua stresses rather different aspects from my own (Scherrer 1993) and this, in my opinion, leads to an inflated assessment of the role of the third parties from the Church (partial insiders versus neutral outsiders)(Wehr and Lederach 1991).
29. Civilian peace-workers will become more and more important in future. Responding to the question 'Who Are the Carriers of Peace Strategies?' (in Galtung 1996: 7–8), the reply was 'In principle, the answer is everyone. But in practice there are problems in having the state system as carrier.'
30. Christopher Mitchell, director of the Institute for Conflict Analysis and Resolution at George Mason University, is also a practitioner and runs Burton-style conflict resolution workshops. In outlining the various roles, he envisaged rather outside mediators.
31. Lederach 1994: 36–9, 62.
32. Galtung 1994: 13 'Why should anyone relive a trauma? To demystify the past…' (*ibid.*). The fictional reliving has to be envisaged as a brainstorming dialogue ('counterfactual approach calls for imagination'). This concept and its eight-fold path to peace and Galtung's manual on conflict transformation should be put into practice. The mini-version (Galtung 1997) has now been tried out over 40 times on training courses see: Dietrich Fischer: TRANSCEND Circular Letter 98–11, 22 September 1998, on website www.transcend.org.
33. In most cases human rights groups confine their activities to observing elections.
34. The CRP has been or is active in Ethiopia (in Mengistu's time and again in 1993), Sudan (reconciliation of the SPLA factions), Liberia, Burma (KNU-SLORC pre-negotiations), and over a dozen other conflict regions. Since secrecy is recommended for many negotiating efforts, and since CRP mediation is generally discreet, the exact number of regions in which CRP has been involved will probably never be known; the public often only gets to hear when there are successes to celebrate, and that is rarely the case. The Carter Center needs this coverage, because its multi-million budget is financed not from government coffers but by private fundraising.
35. The council has 12 members, including Jimmy Carter (chair), Oscar Arias (ex-president of Costa Rica), Pérez de Cuéllar (ex-UN secretary-general), General Obasanjo (ex-president of Nigeria) and Archbishop Desmond Tutu (head of TRC, South Africa).

36. CRP publications: *INN Newsletter*, reports on about 20 ongoing conflicts (with weekly updates); a global report (*The State of World Conflict*).
37. In North Korea, shortly before Kim Il Sung's death (June 1994), Carter secured an agreement on the non-production of nuclear weapons; and in Haiti, just hours before the planned invasion by USA and other troops in September 1994, he secured an agreement with the rebels led by Raoul Cédras whereby they were forced to hand-over power.
38. Carter's immediate goal was to secure the peaceful 'deployment' of UN troops on Haiti and the hand-over of power to the elected president, Jean-Bertrand Aristide in October 1994. In practical political terms, the aim was (1) to keep losses among USA troops to a minimum, in exchange for a guaranteed Panamanian haven and freedom from prosecution for the rebel leaders, the Duvalierists, the financiers and the chiefs of the Tonton Macoute death-squads; (2) to stem the flood of Haitian refugees to the 'promised land' (USA) at source and be able to send back the refugees held in US camps; and (3) to be free of the bothersome Aristide.
39. Day after day, the US peace enforcement troops and the American television watching public looked on as demonstrators were beaten to death in Port-au-Prince (the Haitian capital). Haiti was already a hot 'internal' topic in the USA at this time (autumn 1994). The pressure applied by the black lobby and the shocked television watching public on the dilatory Clinton administration increased and in response, the US troops confiscated the Haitian army's heavy weaponry (something not provided for in the agreement) and opened fire on baton-wielding police officers.
40. The peace keeping operation in Haiti had a human rights component built in. The elections of June 1995 were admittedly not blemish-free, but they were the best that had ever taken place on Haiti. However, Aristide was soon accused of autocratic leadership; he remained the strong man behind the scenes even after his constitutional term was over.
41. The intervention in Somalia had begun with the launch of US marines' Operation Restore Hope on the beach at Mogadishu on the morning of 9 December 1992, in the full glare of the American media. By June 1993, if not before, the operation began to change complexion (with the killing of 24 Pakistani UN peace keeping troops in an ambush) and it subsequently developed into an out-and-out disaster. The 'humanitarian intervention' became a war operation, in which thousands (mainly civilians) lost their lives.
42. The INN was also called upon to mediate in long-standing ethno-national conflicts (protracted conflicts), for example in Ethiopia, Sudan, Burma and so on, without any visible success.
43. See *CMG Update* (quarterly). Harvard is working on, amongst other things, the Middle East (Herbert Kelman and Jay Rothman, *From Conflict to Cooperation*, Harvard University Press, 1992); the transition in South Africa (Robert Ricigliana, *Assisting the Process of Transition in South Africa*, Cambridge, Mass.: CMG, 1994); on the OSCE (Diana Chigas, *Early Warning and Preventive Action in the CSCE: the Role of HCNM*, Cambridge, Mass.: CMG, 1992); and the former USSR (Valery Tishkov, *Nationalities and Conflicting Ethnicity in Post-communist Russia*, Cambridge, Mass. CMG). (All but the first have appeared in the CMG Working Paper series.)
44. The department employs up to 40 staff. Practical activities currently focus on former Yugoslavia, Bosnia, Croatia and Macedonia. See University of Bradford, Dept of Peace Studies, *Newsletter*, 6 (September 1994).
45. Directed by Norbert Ropers, it is already engaged through problem-solving workshops (run in line with the ideas of John Burton) in work in ethnically divided

societies, sometimes in co-operation with organizations on the ground, for example, a Romania programme run jointly with the Romanian Youth League with financial support from the Protestant church, see Petra Haumersen, 'Romanian-Hungarian-German Workshops on Conflict Management', in Callieβ and Merkel (eds) 1993: 457–62. In 2000 the centre also became active outside Europe and CIS, in Sri Lanka on concepts of ethno-national conflict settlement, see Ropers 1995.

46. On the Horn of Africa, there is an International Resource Group on Disarmament and Security, comprising a dozen experts and organizations from various countries, including the former UN special representative for Somalia, the Algerian ambassador Mohammed Sahnoun, Wolfgang Heinrich (who grew up in Ethiopia) and Manfred Drewes of the Arbeitsgemeinschaft Kirchlicher Entwicklungsdienste (AGKED: Association of Church Development Services), Herbert Wulf, then of INEF; John Paul Lederach of the Mennonite Central Committee, USA, and Lt. Gen. Emmanuel A. Erskine. The Life & Peace Institute (LPI, Bernt Jonsson) in Uppsala and the Institute of Peace and Conflict Studies at the University of Waterloo, Ontario, also conduct studies and mediation projects in north-east Africa. The LPI has published the *Life & Peace Review* since 1986, it employs 14 staff, financed by SIDA.

47. UNPO engaged in attempts at mediation during the conflict in Abkhazia. See the interview with Michael van Walt van Praag, former General Secretary of UNPO, in ECOR 1995c: 175–83. See also UNPO, Ennals *et al.* 1992c.

48. IPRA/ICON (Elise Boulding) 'Global Coalition for War Prevention. Round Table Report' (Valetta, 1994). Rupesinghe headed ICON, the major study group run by the peace research umbrella body, the International Peace Research Association (IPRA); he also co-ordinated the United Nations University's programme on Governance and Conflict Resolution. In 1992 he moved from the PRIO in Oslo to become secretary-general of International Alert (until 1998).

49. Cohen is a historian and Slavist; he knows his way around the baffling complexities of the conflicts in the Caucasus and has first-hand knowledge of the area. See interview with him. See also, J. Cohen and Gus Meijer, 'Conflict Resolution Training in North Caucasus and Georgia', in Callieβ and Merkel (eds) 1994: 436–40, also: International Alert, *Conflict Resolution. Report of the Nalchik Seminar* (London: International Alert, 1993).

50. Until 1992 the project was financed by the Canton of Zurich, working in co-operation with, amongst others, the Development and Peace Institute in Duisburg and the department of the sociology of law at the University of Amsterdam. An extensive body of literature has been gathered (notably in the form of interview transcripts) and the project is developing its own research frameworks. It is also working to perfect its empirical/practical methods, as set out in the ECOR Outlines: 'We understand our work as a form of action anthropology. Field studies in the areas mentioned are only possible on the base of mutual confidence and long-standing personal contacts with the respective nationalist movements. For more on ECOR, see the peace-work report in Merkel 1995: 46–9; also online www.oneworld.org/euconflict/guides/orgs/eu_h-s366.htm; www.sidos.ch; www.inesglobal.org/eudb/; http://regulus.cis.pitt.edu/cgibin/giant1-9.pl?orgid=3983.

51. The areas covered by the field work are extensive and very different in nature as regards their colonial pre-history and ethnic composition. The main foci of interest are Central America (esp. Nicaragua, Panama), the Horn of Africa (Ethiopia/Eritrea, the Sudan), South-east Asia (esp. Burma and comparisons between north-east India and Yunnan/China).

52. Conflict is a natural thing. The term conflict might be a representation of energies and an expression of an emotional or rational way to address a problem.
53. Galtung questioned the triangle of diagnosis, prognosis and therapy. He correlated the time dimension with peace work (analysis and practice). For a typology for conflict intervention compare: Galtung 1994: 13.
54. Galtung made concrete proposals for conflict prevention, transformation, or resolution in 35 conflict cases 1997*a*.
55. The status of some instruments is essentially that of a declaration of human rights principles. In International Law, a declaration of principles has political-cum-moral force and implies legal obligations. See 'Fundamental Human Rights must be Protected' IRECOR Working Paper.
56. It became clear that *ad hoc* International Tribunals as those for Former Yugoslavia (in The Hague) and for Rwanda (in Arusha) represent important steps toward a permanent Criminal Court. However, it became also clear that some states want the ICC to be closely connected to the UN Security Council. The old 'nuclear aristocracy' among the permanent members of the UN Security Council have little possibility to use their veto or try to seize the definition of power on what would be considered as crimes to be persecuted by the ICC. Such action would be unacceptable and contrary to the very idea of an independent court. It should also be guaranteed that individuals and citizen groups (as in the case of the European Convention on Human Rights), as well as the Court's prosecutors and governments, are allowed to bring cases to the Court.
57. After the testimony given by General Romeo Dallaire (force commander of UNAMIR I) in Arusha 1998 we established that the details of the planned extermination of the Tutsi minority were known in the headquarters of UN and Western governments well in advance.
58. The cash-strapped UN has been forced to pay out large sums. The expensive and not very successful operation in Cambodia was forgotten after the failure in Somalia 1993 (under US guidance) and the total disaster of UN troop engagement in Rwanda 1994. In former Yugoslavia, the UN actually withdrew in favour of NATO. More recently, in East Timor 1999, UN peace enforcement was judged as relatively successful (after a series of diplomatic failures to secure the transition process, the failure to make the Indonesian army accountable, and the UN's late reactions to-scale massacres on the island) and, thus, was the UNs reparation for its one failure to prevent the genocide committed by Indonesian troops in East Timor in the mid 1970s.
59. Largely successful operations, such as those in Mozambique and Namibia, could not alter the general picture. The development of a 'UN rapid troop deployment capacity' never materialized. There is a lack of political will; some UN member states wanted to go it alone.
60. Among the 15 UN peace-keeping operations in 2001 five operations from the 1970s or older remain: two 'endless missions' are as old as the United Nations itselves, dating from 1948, the ones in Palestine (UNTSO) and Kashmir (UNMOGIP); next was Cyprus 1964 (UNFICYP) and two others in the Middle East: the UNDOF on the Golan Heights (Israel/Syria) since 1974 and UNIFIL in Lebanon since 1978. The other ten UN operations are those from the early 1990s (Iraq, West Sahara, Georgia, Bosnia and Croatia-Pevlaka), four from 1999 (Sierra Leone, Kosovo, East Timor and Congo DR), and one from end 2000 (Ethiopia/Eritrea). The dates given do not necessarily mean that there was a deployment of troops in that year, as the example of Congo DR illustrates, where troops were only deployed in spring 2001. The three UN missions terminated in

the year 2000 were those in Tajikistan, Haiti and Central Africa Republic; in the latter, two of these countries (Tajikistan and Central African Republic) the United Nations did not achieve anything that comes near to peace.

61. Annan wrote that 'providing support for regional and sub-regional initiatives in Africa is both necessary and desirable' (Annan 1998, §41); some 15 months later a regional initiative brought about the Lusaka agreement but no UN support has been seen since. Annan also admitted that 'This reluctance appears to go well beyond the lessons that Somalia offers, and it has had a particularly harsh impact upon Africa.' (UN Secretary-General 1998: §29).

62. See Matthias Stiefel, editorial, in UNRISD 1995*b*: 3.

63. African Rights 1994. Also see Conclusion by Duffield, Macrae and Zwi in Macrae and Zwi (eds) 1994: 222–32; UNRISD 1995*c*.

64. On development aid and its impact in the pre-genocide and post-genocide phase, see Scherrer, 1996*c*: 61–86, 2001: 167–216.

65. Rakiya Omar, 'Rwanda: The Limits of Neutralism', in African Rights 1994: 28–39.

66. JEEAR 1996; also DANIDA 1995, 1995*a*.

67. Paul LaRose Edwards, *The Rwandan Crisis 1994: The Lessons Learned* (Ottawa: IHRDCR, 1994).

68. In the literature such conflicts are given labels such as 'protracted', 'intractable' and 'intransigent'.

69. Katerina Tomasevski, 'Human Rights and Wars of Starvation', in Macrae and Zwi (eds) 1994: 70–91.

70. Mark Duffield, 'The Political Economy of Internal War: Asset Transfer, Complex Emergencies and International Aid', in: Macrae and Zwi (eds) 1994: 50–69.

71. NGO fields of work are manifold (according to Ropers 1997): monitoring; fact-finding; advocacy; and so on. The empowerment of disadvantaged groups (that is, most discriminated groups) may result in a cut in the perceived excessive privileges by privileged groups. What is necessary are measures to mitigate conflict and accommodate just demands: peace education, for example school text-books about what happens/happened in conflicts is of great importance in divided societies; crisis management activities in general combine humanitarian assistance with conflict transformation, although there is a serious danger of prolonging conflict by providing humanitarian assistance (as seen in the case of Rwanda after the genocide); strengthening information exchange between actors, mobilization of the media and public opinion for the peaceful resolution of conflicts. Working directly on the conflict: negotiation and mediation should be introduced (without social engineering). However, track 2 does (often) not reach the top leadership level. Post-conflict tasks include reconciliation (as a long-term process) and cohabitation, integration of combatants, physical reconstruction, training and capacity building. The development of institutions linked to conflict resolution and working for conflict prevention should be linked to early action (compare: Ropers, 'The role of NGOs in conflict situations' Paper, Moscow: IFPR, 1997).

72. Under the title of 'Humanitarism Unbound' the London-based human rights organization African Rights has criticized the behaviour of NGOs in the case of the Rwanda crisis. For instance when I arrived in Rwanda there were about 120 NGOs and when I left, four months later, there were about 500 NGOs operating in Rwanda.

73. On the Rwanda disaster and the response of the international community see African Rights 1994 and 1995, Scherrer 1995, 1997 and 1999*e*, JEEAR 1996 and Human Rights Watch 1999.

74. Anja Weiß and Aleksej Nazarenko gave an analytical overview of the activity of local and international NGOs in conflict areas in the former Eastern bloc, based on 56 interviews. The authors highlighted the problem of the shortage of resources and the dangers associated with outside funding and intervention by Western NGOs ('academic tourism'): in *Strategies and Needs of NGOs in the New Eastern Democracies* (Berlin: Berghof Stiftung, 1996).

75. See Macrae and Zwi (eds) 1994: 126–228 ('The International Community: Putting NGOs on the Front Line').

76. ECOR 1992; David Keen, 'The Functions of Famine in S. W. Sudan: Implications for Relief' in: Macrae and Zwi (eds) 1994: 111–25.

77. Dharam Ghai, 'WSP: A New Dimension in UNRISD Work', in UNRISD 1995b: 7.

78. The participative methodology comprises the three steps of integration, participation and impact. WSP seeks to influence emergency aid and emergency policy and to help identify political solutions in particularly difficult situations. UNRISD 1995c: ii.

79. Despite having a small staff of fewer than ten professionals and a mini-budget of US$2–3 million per year, UNRISD produces a dozen books and as many discussion papers each year, organizes half a dozen regional and international conferences, thus achieving a profile and effectiveness which is remarkable within the UN system. From the point of view of it (cost) effectiveness, UNRISD provides a good model. (See Dharam Ghai, 'WSP: A New Dimension in UNRISD Work' in UNRISD 1995b: 7.)

80. These are: the 'Ethnic Conflicts and Development' project, in connection with which several country studies have been published, and the 'Ethnic Diversity and Public Policy' project, which also considers the question of ethnic violence; see various publications on this theme.

81. Interview with Matthias Stiefel, WSP director, Geneva, July 1995. The reason cited was the ongoing DANIDA study; but other possible reasons are the obstructionism and sensitivities of certain UN member states.

82. UNESCO sees its function as being to provide an international arena for the 'exchange and free exploration of ideas' by scholars, researchers, NGO practitioners and conflict resolution trainers (UNESCO 1994: 12).

83. The year 2000 'is not the end of history, but it should be the end of this story, the story of war' (Frederico Mayor, former director-general of UNESCO *op. cit*).

84. UNESCO was set up in 1946 as a special UN body and has since developed a life of its own, regarding itself as a kind of 'think tank' and concerning itself, amongst other things, with urgent issues of the day (such as Western media domination and development aid). It employs a staff of about 4000 and has a budget of more than half a billion US dollars. The 'ideal' preconditions therefore exist, in terms of infrastructure, for UNESCO also to become a 'brains trust' on issues of peace and conflict research. However, it took time to establish the themes of conflict prevention and resolution as major programmes or central areas of activity.

85. This is to be done via dialogue and reconciliation, not so much by blaming and stigmatizing individual people. See Galtung in Calließ and Merkel (eds) 1994: 395–417. On South Africa, see Alex Boraine, *Justice in Transition* (Rondebosch, 1994); Alex Boraine, Janet Levy and Ronel Scheffer, *Dealing with the Past* (Claremont, 1994); Alex Boraine *et al.*, *The Healing of a Nation* (Cape Town: JiT, 1995). On Rwanda, see Scherrer 1995 and 1997.

86. 'The Case of El Salvador', in UNESCO 1994b: 8–10. 'Methodology of the El Salvador Programme and Activities', in UNESCO 1993: 8–12; on support for the

revival and development of manifestations of indigenous culture (for example in art and language), and on the promotion of indigenous crafts and small industries, education, access to science and technology, the protection of natural resources, see *ibid.* §40.

87. In multi-ethnic and multinational or pluri-cultural state constructs the idea of so-called national identity cannot apply, since this generally entails some strategy of domination of a conflictual, hierarchical, assimilative and anti-minority nature.

88. For a practical proposal see: Scherrer and Oberg 1999.

89. Periodical evaluation of the programmes will generally take the form of internal assessment by the participants themselves, under the guidance of their own experts.

90. Talks with David Adams in Durban, July 1998.

91. Bercovitch, *et al.* 1991. 'Some Conceptual Issues and Empirical Trends in the Study of Successful Mediation in International Relations' *Journal of Peace Research*, 28/1: 7–17; Debiel 'Kriege' in SEF: Globale Trends 1993/94, Frankfurt/M.: Fischer 1993: 177–97.

92. The massacres of the Tutsi minority by the army, the presidential guard and armed elements of the unity party in Rwanda claimed more than a million victims between April and July 1994. The genocide erupted after the plane that was bringing back the presidents of Rwanda and Burundi (from peace negotiations in Arusha mediated by Tanzania's President Hassan) was shot down. The outcome of the negotiations would have meant that the Hutu guard would have been disbanded and the Tutsi monopoly of the army in Burundi done away with. In Burundi, there had been repeated massacres and genocidal attacks by Tutsis on Hutus, the last being in 1993, following the murder of the newly elected president, Ndadaye (a moderate Hutu). Africa is once again being described as a continent without hope (*Der Spiegel*, 94/16: 138–40), which is even in need of 'gentle neo-colonialism' [*sic*!]. Area specialists and peace researchers have in vain spoken out against the false ethnicization of many conflicts and urged that socio-economic facts be taken into account.

93. The sufferings of the victims evidently count for less than their suffering in front of the cameras of international television monopolies such as CNN, CBS, or the BBC.

94. As a result of increasing pressure from Burma's two dissimilar neighbours, China and Thailand, which both have economic interests in Burma (primarily teak, minerals and markets for Chinese consumer-goods, and gas, water and fish in the secondary case), but not because of any real efforts at mediation (probably rather because of the political vacuum that emerged in the north following the break-up of the CPB rebel movement into seven sections in 1989). There have been a number of ceasefires between certain rebel groups and the military regime, but no peace accord or reform of Burma's political system.

4 Autonomy, free association and self-governance

1. Johan Galtung feared that ethno-national wars in the FSU–CIS might lead to a 'third-worldization' of parts of the former Soviet Union, with unforeseen consequences for world peace. See Scherrer 1991.

2. This applies in particular to the following situations: (1) post-colonial occupation – (FSO: 'foreign-state occupation'); (2) to the position of large-scale ethnically unified peoples in various states – a situation of SSvN: 'several states versus one nation' (as is the case in, for example, Europe's neighbourhood with the Kurds in Western

Asia, the Oromo in the Horn of Africa, or the Turks in Central Asia); and (3) to certain conflicts of the 'state versus nation' (SvN) type. On the typology, see Introduction.

3. The right to self-determination was granted to the Slovenians, Croatians and Bosnian Muslims in 1990–91, but not to the 600,000 Serbs in Croatia or to the Bosnian Serbs (40 per cent of total population) and Croatians (20 per cent). The anti-Serbian propaganda in many Western European media and Europe's amnesia concerning Yugoslavia obscured the fact that it was the Serbs who must have felt under the greatest threat. See Carl G. Jacobsen, 'War Crimes in the Balkans', *Coexistence*, 30 (1993), 313 ff. Most of the Serbs in Krajina were driven out by the Croatian army in August 1995. Until a comprehensive solution is found for the entire FYU there seems little likelihood that they will return to their native territory.

4. Following the refusal in 1989 by Serbia's national communist leadership, under Slobodan Milósevic, to further grant a degree of autonomy to Kosovo/a, there was until 1998 contrary to all expectations no genuine ethnic armed conflict between Serbs and the Albanian majority in the former autonomous area of Kosovo. The new element was the upsurge of armed struggle by the irredentist ethno-nationalist 'Kosova Liberation Army' (KLA/UCK), launching attacks on Serbian forces partly from their Albanian hinterland. With violence escalating in March 1998 (and more so from July 1998), the Kosovo/a conflict could have very probably escalated into an inter-state conflict with spillover effects into Albania and Macedonia (and possibly also Greece). Albania was shaken by another internal crisis in September 1998, while NATO prepared for aerial bombing of what they call Serbian installations in Kosovo/a. Since the USA was engaged in bombings with cruise missiles against three countries far outside of NATO's area, the warning had to be taken seriously. See Jan Oberg's urgent 'Questions before bombing Serbia' (TFF press information 47, 2 October 1998, on: http:// www.transnational.org).

5. Surprisingly, the NATO bombing of the Federal Republic of Yugoslavia did take place and went on for 78 days from March to June 1999. The aerial warfare resulted in masses of refugees, atrocities committed mainly by Serbian paramilitaries against Kosovars (from June 1999 by UCK against Serbs), civilian fatalities in FRY, large-scale destruction in all of FRY and an uncertain future for the whole region. The KFOR troops occupying Kosovo and the Yugoslav troops pulling back to Serbia proper failed to prevent another wave of 'ethnic cleansing' carried out against local Serbs and Roma. The costs of repairing the damage will be exorbitant; a good part of it will be financed by European taxpayers' money.

6. 'All peoples have the right of self-determination. By virtue of that right they freely determine their political status and freely pursue their economic, social and cultural development' (International Covenant on Civil and Political Rights and Economic, Social and Cultural Rights, article 1) article 27 concerns minority rights.

7. See 'Dutch Government Policy' in NCIV 1993. The recommendations of the 'Voices of the Earth' congress call on the EU and the Netherlands government to create procedures to enable the International Court of Justice to be invoked.

8. World Conference on Human Rights: The Vienna Declaration and Programme of Action June 1993 (United Nations: New York, 1995), 29.

9. See Fourth World Center 1993 and Assies 1993. The claim to full national sovereignty for indigenous peoples is in contradiction to their supposedly freely chosen association with the settler-colonies.

10. World Conference of Indigenous Peoples on Territory, Environment and Development, 'Kari-Oca Declaration and Indigenous Peoples Earth Charter',

Kari-Oca (Brazil), 25–30 May 1992, esp. III: 'Human Rights and International Law', articles 1–30.

11. In 1995, after almost ten years of intensive work to produce a draft universal declaration on the rights of indigenous peoples, this project suffered a severe setback in the Commission; a new working group was established with the sole purpose to water it down. This shows states' high degree of sensitivity to, or fear of, demands from 'their' nationalities. At the 51st session of the Human Rights Commission, in February–March 1995, a resolution (1995/32) was passed instructing a new working group 'to elaborate the draft provisions further'. On the WGIP's original text, see UNCHR 1994, also 1993, 50–60. However, the conference draft of 22 July 1993 (E/CN.4/Sub.2/AC.4/1993/CRP.4) contained only 42 articles.

12. UNCHR 1993, §3: 'Indigenous peoples have the right to self-determination ... they have the right, *inter alia*, to negotiate and agree upon their role in the conduct of public affairs, their distinct responsibilities and the means by which they manage their own interests' (cf. UNCHR 1993: Add. 1, p. 3).

13. See the contribution by the Indian Law Resource Center (ILRC) to E/CN.4/Sub.2/AC.4/1990/3/Add.2, p. 5. The ILRC proposes introducing, among other things, the right 'to be left in peace'.

14. See details in Section 2.4. The three 'modern agreements' in Canada are not the kinds of accords that could be properly established as agreements. The international aspect is lacking and the internal socio-political aspect predominates.

15. The new constitutions of Nicaragua (1987), Brazil (1988, ch. VII), Mexico (1991, rev. art. 4), and Bolivia (1994, art. 1) are the first to make any mention of indigenous peoples or (as in the reformed Bolivian constitution) of a multi-ethnic state.

16. Stavenhagen 1994: 27.

17. The rights of ethno-national communities are located in the grey area between collective international law and individual human rights.

18. Following the acquisition of statehood, dominant-group regimes have upheld international law as the yardstick for the territory to which they lay claim. They have demanded that others (including the UN) do not intervene in their internal affairs, and have stressed their 'sovereignty', in order to be free to trample the human rights and minority rights of their citizens, as they wished.

19. The principle of 'non-intervention' in 'internal affairs' is coming under pressure internationally. The enforcement of minority rights by other states or by multilateral organizations (for example within the framework of the OSCE) will no longer constitute intervention in internal affairs. The OSCE and the Council of Europe are drawing up binding minimum measures for the protection of minorities. Some third-world countries fear that revised regulations may encourage future attempts at intervention of a general kind. Western power politics *vis-à-vis* third world countries has been furnished with new tools for legitimating intervention. This emerged in the unprecedented restrictions on sovereignty imposed by the UN on Iraq and in the intervention of Western troops in the former Zaire (in September 1991). Contrary to this colonial pattern (repeatedly applied in Congo–Zaire), the overthrow of Mobutu became an internal African matter, with troops from Rwanda, Uganda and Angola supporting the AFDL rebels until their ultimate victory. The second rebellion in Congo DR was seemingly a consequence of 'Mobutism without Mobutu' and of the outright failure of the Kabila regime to deal with the burning questions of citizenship, power-sharing and broadening of the alliance.

20. Military interventions have often served directly as a means of preserving and securing vital economic interests (such as oil in the Middle East and strategic

raw materials in Zaire). The overthrow of 'unfriendly' regimes (for example in Chile in 1973) or the protection of tame local potentates have been the aim of many US military interventions in Latin America.

21. See Hector Gros Espinell, *The Right to Self-determination: Implementation of United Nations Resolutions* (New York, 1980). On the minority question, see ICCPR, art. 27.

22. Out of a fear of bringing 'anarchy' to the world system, jurists and politicians have removed all the 'teeth' from the right to self-determination. See Jörg Fisch, 'Selbstbestimmungsrecht: Opium für die Völker?', *NZZ* 209, 10 September 1995, 17.

23. A principle (re)adopted after 1945, according to which colonial administrative borders were to become the borders of independent states, see Fisch, *ibid.*

24. I know of too many such 'isolated cases' to concur with Fisch on this. However, Fisch gave a brilliant exposition of the complex situation and the intersections within it. His proposed emergency right to secession is designed to deal with similar problems that I am attempting to address with my call for secession and recognition regimes.

25. Article 1 of the ICCPR is interpreted in a variety of ways with regard to internal self-determination. Thus, the government of the Netherlands recognizes such self-determination 'in the sense that it must be possible to hold national governments accountable', and at the same time views art. 27 of the ICCPR as implying 'a certain amount of scope for distinctive identity within a state' (NCIV 1993: I; Political Rights, 1).

26. 'The ethnic argument was given much strength' (Paul Smith 1991: 154).

27. The 500 years of peaceful coexistence between members of the Greek Orthodox church and Turkish Muslims in Asia Minor and Eastern Thrace was permanently poisoned within a short space of time by nationalist ideologies such as Panhellenism and Kemalism (or the Young Turk movement). Greece took in over one million refugees (about 20 per cent of its total population at that time) and almost half a million Muslims were deported to Turkey. See K. Koufa and C. Svolopoulos, 'The Compulsory Exchange of Populations between Greece and Turkey: The Settlement of Minority Questions at the Conference of Lausanne and its Impact on Greek-Turkish Relations' in Paul Smith 1991: 275–308.

28. 'Genocide means ... acts committed with the intent to destroy, in whole or in part, a national, ethnic, racial or religious group as such' (article 2) United Nations: Convention on the Prevention and Punishment of the Crime of Genocide 1948. U.N.T.S. no. 1021, vol. 78 (1951), p. 277. The convention was adopted by UN General Assembly (resolution 260 (III) A) on 9 December 1948. *Modern genocide* is state organized mass murder and crimes against humanity characterized by the intention of the rulers to exterminate individuals belonging to a particular national, ethnic, religious or 'racial' group, to a particular cultural group (*ethnocide*), to a particular political group (*politicide*) or to a particular social group (*democide*). Genocide is a premeditated mass crime that has been systematically planned, prepared and executed. See Scherrer 1999*a*.

29. Stanislaw Sierpowski, 'Minorities in the System of the League of Nations' in Paul Smith 1991: 20.

30. Forty-one petitions were addressed to Josip Wilfan, president of the congress (Paul Smith 1991: 135).

31. The third condition proved problematic and was dropped in March 1928.

32. In many multi-ethnic societies in Europe, social and professional groups had a much higher level of bilingual or trilingual competence than is the case today.

33. See Arnold Suppan in Paul Smith 1991: 340.
34. Certainly the USSR under Stalin has to be distinguished from the USSR as 'invented' by Lenin and from the USSR since the 1960s. Stalin's expansionism as concerned Central Europe in 1939–40, including the Molotov–Ribbentrop Pact, should be noted. In the Stalinist period the centralized state left the sub-units without any choice or the possibility of 'freedom of action', with strongly developed repression mechanisms to punish even the slightest notion of deviation, sometimes with very sophisticated, Machiavellist solutions applied to different ethnic groups to ensure a state of alert with their neighbours, thus strengthening their dependence from the centre.
35. The Åland Islands Autonomy Act of 1921, concluded between Finland and Sweden (and the inhabitants of Åland) under the aegis of the League of Nations, is regarded as exemplary for its time, because it contained a far-reaching autonomy statute and because it brought about reconciliation between the parties involved. See Tore Modeen, 'The Åland Islands Question' in Paul Smith 1991: 153–68, also *ibid*. 335. The incorporation of Finland into Tsarist Russia in 1809 resulted in a major Russian military presence on the Åland Islands, and between 1836 and 1853 these troops built the fortress of Bomarsund (which was destroyed during the Crimean War). At that time, Sweden had a far greater interest in seeing the islands demilitarized than in securing guarantees for the Swedish minority. Given that Finland enjoyed extensive home rule under the Russian imperial regime, the subsequent application of the principle was preordained.
36. The constitution of the *Land* of Brandenburg (art. 25) stipulates the 'right of the Sorbian people to the protection, maintenance, and cultivation of its national identity and indigenous settlement-area'; the constitution of the Free State of Saxony talks only of the preservation of the 'German–Sorbian character of the settlement-area of the Sorbian ethnic group' (art. 6.2).
37. On the situation of the Lusatian Sorbs, see Leo Satava, 'The Lusatian Sorbs in Eastern Germany', in Minority Rights Group (MRG) (ed.), *Minorities in Central and Eastern Europe* (London: MRG, 1993).
38. That is to say, the seven million migrants and their offspring living in Germany. Turkish is the most commonly spoken first language in the Federal Republic after German.
39. Domowina was founded in 1912 in Hoyerswerda and represented what was then a total of 200,000 Sorbs belonging to the two 'tribes' of the Lusatians (resident in the Spreewald area) and the Milcenians (in the region around present-day Baudizin/Bauzen). Nowadays, only 100,000 or so people still identify themselves as Sorbs.
40. A citizens' initiative has been fighting since 1989 to stop the destruction and resettlement of the village, scheduled for the year 2000. A court decision ruled that Horno would disappear but destruction was postponed.
41. Dieter Senghaas mentions the right of veto and 'procedural guarantees and guarantees of legal protection outside the political system as well'. In considering the use of self-governance and territorial autonomy as conflict averting measures he looks only at the European context. See Senghaas, 'Das konstruktive Programm', in idem, *Friedensprojekt Europa* (Frankfurt/Main: edition suhrkamp, 1992), 130–4.
42. Most of the indigenous parties to the treaties were Indian peoples from North America: the Iroquois Confederation (for example Mohawks), the Micmac, Delaware, Creek, Shoshone, Sioux and Cree. But the Inuit from the North and

the Maori in New Zealand (Treaty of Waitangi, 1840) also entered into agreements. See UNCHR 1992*a*: 31–52.

43. The agreement/conventions with the peoples of the North have treaty status – see esp. the James Bay and Northern Quebec Agreement (Convention de la Baie James) of 11 November 1975, see Hoekema 1998. According to M. A. Martínez (UNCHR 1992*a*: 52), they involve two types of treaty demands: Aboriginal rights and specific claims.

44. The Canadian government's offer in the James Bay affair consisted of a 'forced purchase' of strategic land; it could not be refused, because the complaints brought by the Cree had no power to delay matters or halt construction, see Peter Cumming, *Canada: Native Land Rights and Northern Development* (IWGIA Document 26; Copenhagen, 1977), 17. See also George Brown and Ron Maguire, *Indian Treaties in Historical Perspective* (Ottawa, 1979), and Bennett McCardle, *Canadian Indian Treaties* (Ottawa, 1980).

45. UNCHR 1992*a*: §324.

46. Cf. less far-reaching provisions under section 2.2.3. See also Assies 1993: 19, and idem, 'Self-determination and the "New Partnership"' in Assies and Hoekema 1994, 31–71 (49).

47. Ideally via the right of a nation/nationality independently to enter into agreements with regard to the exploitation of its natural resources. This is provided for, for example, in the draft law drawn up by independent experts for regulating relations between the Russian Federation and the indigenous peoples of the North and for establishing their legal status (Hoekema 1994: 11). Berman (in Scherrer 1993*b*: 6) regards the contractual process as 'a very good model' for the conclusion and operation of major agreements.

48. André Hoekema, 'Do Joint Decision-Making Boards Enhance Chances for a New Partnership between the State and Indigenous Peoples?', in Assies and Hoekema 1994: 177–202, esp. 179 and 188–9 (Greenland).

49. See Scherrer 1993*b*.

50. Described in detail in Scherrer 1998*a*.

51. Hence each party has a right of veto. There is a mixed commission made up of equal numbers of representatives of Denmark and Greenland. However, up to now there have only been exploratory operations, no actual production of minerals. The crunch has, therefore, not yet come. See Hoekema 1994: 9.

52. The Greenland Home Rule Act (No. 577 of 29 November 1978). Kalaallit Nunnat has been described as a model for the indigenous peoples of both Americas. The island remains part of the territory of the Kingdom of Denmark but enjoys extensive self-government (see Hoekema 1994: 9).

53. Emil Abelson, 'Home Rule in Greenland', in UNCHR 1992: 109–16 (109).

54. Two centuries of contact with Europeans have left their mark on the Inuit of Greenland; external influences are least strong, relatively speaking, in northeast Greenland. The situation in Canada is more serious (loss of language, abandonment of traditions, criminality, alcoholism and high suicide rates among young people). Only in northeast Russia does the Inuit culture seem to have survived intact.

55. This modernization policy has its down sides: see NCIV 1993: Introduction B, 'The Inuit', 3–4.

56. Finn Lynge, 'Economic Rights', paper given at 'Voices of the Earth' congress, organized by NCIV, Amsterdam, November 1993.

57. The mixed population is the result of intermarriage since the time of the Vikings (who reached America in about 1000).

58. Native lay judges are empowered to deal with minor offences.
59. Assies 1993: 21.
60. So-called 'block grants' currently make up 56 per cent of the government budget of US$650 million. See Assies 1993: 23.
61. The Inuit rejected EC membership as early as 1972.
62. See Plant 1994: 16.
63. See Sections 2.3 and 2.2.5; notes 40 and 41.
64. Interview with the Grand Chief of the Dene, Geneva 1997.
65. Plant 1994: 16.
66. The Inuit make up 75 per cent of the population in this area. See 'The Road to Nunavut', in Ian Creery, *The Inuit of Canada*, (London: MRG, 1993), 16.
67. Tungavik/Canadian Ministry of Indian Affairs and Northern Development 1993. The agreement is 281 pages long and has 42 articles, divided into subsections. 'Nunavut' means 'our land' in the Inuit language. André Hoekema of the Department of Sociology and Anthropology of Law at the University of Amsterdam, together with a team of researchers, has carried out an analysis of agreements and settlements between states and nations and is of the opinion that this is the most comprehensive accord of this kind so far (Hoekema 1994).
68. On the expert debate, see 'Agreement between Canada and the Inuit of Nunavut May Develop New Regimes', interview with Kevin Knight (of Unaaq), in ECOR 1995: 16–19; also 'Comarcas Have Potential to Provide for a Higher Level of Indigenous Control', Howard R. Berman, *ibid.* 19–25.
69. On the question of territoriality and on the treaty process as a whole, see 'Indigenous Peoples and Self-governance: A Model Process for Arriving at Self-determined Political Situations', interview with Howard R. Berman, professor of International Law at the California Western School of Law, in ECOR 1995: 11–16.
70. The Nunavut Agreement is the most detailed so far: Tungavik/Canadian Ministry of Indian Affairs and Northern Development 1993: 129–33 (municipal lands); 135 (marine area); 137 (outer land fast ice zone); 139–67 (purpose of and title to Inuit owned lands); 189 (taxation of real property); 203 (resources royalty sharing); 211 (petroleum); and 277 (Inuit harvesting rights in Manitoba).
71. *NZZ* 103, 4 May 1994, 9.
72. See Berman in Scherrer 1993*b*. One could counter by saying that the climatic conditions in this area (and the necessary adjustments in social life to the harsh natural conditions) is almost too much for Europeans to tolerate.
73. República de Nicaragua 1987, also República de Nicaragua, Constitución Política, *La Gaceta, Diario Oficial,* Año XCI, No. 5, Managua, 9 January 1987. The declamatory nature of Latin American constitutions, and the continued existence of differing conceptions of law among the *Indios* and the *Ladinos,* is pointed out (in relation to Brazil) by Wolf Paul ('Die Rechte der "Indio" in Südamerika', in S. Armborst *et al., Sieger und Besiegte im Fünfhundertjährigen Reich: Emanzipation und lateinamerikanische Realität.* Bonn, 1991).
74. In some areas, the so-called 'agricultural border' (an ethnic border between *mestizos* and Indians) has already reached the limits of the land that is suitable for long-term cultivation (see Gabbert 1991: 262). Since the 1950s, however, land-related conflicts in the mining area have increased and in some places are now threatening the cohesion of the Miskitu subsistence-system (esp. in southern Tasba Pri – 'good land' in Miskito – and in Llano Sur).
75. There is a concentration of conflicts along the highway (built by the former Sandinista government) that runs from Managua to Siuna, Rosita, and then on

to Puerto Cabezas, and also in those areas in which the former Chamorro government settled *mestizo* former Contras and their families.

76. Bilingual school-system (11.5) and official use of indigenous languages (and Creole English, art. 5).

77. These are: 'To direct the executive activities, name functionaries, "discuss" [*questionnaire*] competence matters with the central authorities and administrate funds [special funds for development]' – art. 30.6 (see Scherrer 1994*c*).

78. ECOR 1989. Update in ECOR 1993, 1995.

79. Law No. 28 (the autonomy statute) talks of 'just proportion' (see República de Nicaragua 1987: art. 8). The implementation provisions were negotiated in 1993–94.

80. 'No autonomy without economy.' See Scherrer 1994*c*: 109–48.

81. Congreso Guaymí, 'El Ante-Proyecto de la Carta Orgánica de la Comarca Guaymí', Hato Corotú (Chiriqui), 1986; Miguel de León, 'The Indian Political System of the *Congresos Generales*', in ECOR 1994: 53.

82. Arysteides Turpana, 'The Dule Nation of the San Blas Comarca: Between the Government and Self-government', in Assies and Hoekema 1994: 149–56. On the question of the reunification of the Kuna, León remarks, in somewhat syblline fashion, 'we can one day be unified with our brothers in Colombia': ECOR 1994: 59.

83. Interview with Leonidas Valdez, Cacique principal, Kuna Yala 1989, also interviews with Miguel de León in ECOR 1994: pt. 3. According to the representative of the Congreso de Organizaciones de Indios de Centro America, Panama y Mexico, the indigenous peoples of Panama account for 10 per cent of the total population: *ibid.* 21.

84. León in ECOR 1994: 58. León talks of an 'exchange of lobsters for beer' with Colombian sailors and also of unfair trade.

85. The words used are 'conjuntamente con': art 19, law no. 22 of the Republic of Panama, November 1983. See André Hoekema's comments on Panama in Assies and Hoekema 1994: 189.

86. 'Guaymies, the largest indigenous group, do not have a Comarca, only the Kuna after the Tule uprising in 1935', Miguel de León, ECOR 1994: 57; 'Big landowners possess the lands', idem, *ibid.* 60.

87. Both the autonomy arrangement for the Kuna in Panama (1927) and that for the Miskitu, Sumu, Rama, Garifuna, and Creoles in eastern Nicaragua, were secured by armed force.

88. See Assies 1993: 24 ff.

89. See J. Kloosterman, 'Indigenous Self-government in Colombia: The Case of the Muellamués Resguardo', in Assies and Hoekema 1994: 157–76 (158 ff).

90. *Ibid.* 163.

91. 'Movimiento de Autoridades Indígenas de Colombia' or 'Autoridades Indígenas de Colombia'.

92. *Weltatlas* (London: George Philip Limited, 1992/93).

93. Autoridades Indígenas de Colombia, *Los derechos de los pueblos indígenas en la constitución* (Bogota: AIC, 1992).

94. Indians live in 27 of the 32 departments in Colombia. According to the AIC (*op. cit.*), the four largest ethnic groups are: the Paez or Nasa in the southwest (Andean Cauca region), with 110,000 members (1991) or 21 per cent of the total Indian population; the Wayuú in the northeast, with 95,000 or 18 per cent; the Emberá in the northwest (Pacific coast, also Panama), with 50,000 or

9 per cent; the Quillasinga or Pasto on the border with Ecuador, with 40,000 or 8 per cent. These four groups represent just over half of the indigenous population.

95. The government figures are notoriously inaccurate. Other sources cite figures of 7 per cent indigenous, 68 per cent *mestizo*, 20 per cent white and 5 per cent black (see George Philip, 1993). Assuming a total population of 35 million Colombians, this would make 2.5 million Indians.

96. This idea was inspired in part by the reports of the United Nations Research Institute for Social Development (UNRISD) and the Deutsches Institut für Föderalismusforschung in Hanover (see Hans-Peter Schneider, 'The Multi-ethnic State: Can it Be Kept Stable?', lecture, Bonn 1994), and also papers delivered by Prof. A. G. Zdravomyslov (Center for Sociological Analysis of National Conflicts, Moscow), Vincent Maphai (University of Western Cape, Belville South Africa), and Jakob Rösel (Arnold Bergstraesser Institut, Freiburg i. Br.), at the expert hearing 'Keeping Inter-ethnic Conflicts Non-violent: Interests, Strategies, Institutions', held by the Ebert-Stiftung, Bonn, September 1994.

97. Ali Mazrui, 'Ethnicity in Bondage: Is Its Liberation Premature?', in UNRISD 1995: 31–40 (31).

98. Details in Scherrer 1997: ch. 2, 47–98.

99. Restriction of political options may result from many different causes: (perverse) historical developments (cultural chauvinism, notions of superiority on the part of dominant groups); other political priorities; lack of democracy (for example threats of intervention by the military); primacy not accorded to matters political; dominance of sectional interests; and so on.

100. 'Demokratie und Menschenrechte', SEF 1991: 55–60.

101. World Conference on Human Rights: 'The Vienna Declaration and Programme of Action June 1993' New York: UN, 1995: 30–1.

102. Tetzlaff 1993: 84.

103. Democratically elected governments are less suited to 'dirty deals' (for example that of the multinational oil-company Shell with the Nigerian military leadership) that promise extra profits. Free elections can be ignored with impunity by local potentates – under the benevolent eye of international capital.

104. 'Democracy, development and respect for human rights and fundamental freedoms are interdependent and mutually reinforcing' World Conference on Human Rights: 'The Vienna Declaration and Programme of Action June 1993' New York: United Nations, 1995: 30.

105. See Lijphart in J. J. A. Thomassen (ed.), *Demokratie* (Samson: Alphen, 1981), 128–45. Following investigation of 21 plural societies, Arend Lijphart concluded that 'consociational democracy' had four defining characteristics: co-ordination and co-operation between the élites of various ethnic groups ('segments'), high levels of autonomy, a right of veto for every 'segment', and use of the principle of proportionality. The internal differences or splits within a plural society should not be obvious ('no clear cleavages'), in other words they should not constitute unbridgeable differences, which can only be the result of oppressive practices. Cf. Lijphart 1984, 1977; also PIOOM 1994: 26–7.

106. There is an urgent need for international norms here – for example based on the minimum standards of the OCSE – and for the protection of indigenous peoples in line with the standards set out in the Declaration on the Rights of Indigenous Peoples drafted by the UN Human Rights Commission's Working Group on Indigenous Populations but so far not adopted.

107. According to Rothschild (1991), a characteristic feature of a polyarchy would be an inclusive and accountable system. Representatives should be elected – not co-opted – in order to ensure genuine representation. Good electoral systems foster inter-ethnic co-operation, because the votes of particular groups are needed; examples are cumulative voting systems and mixed bodies in ruling committees (UNRISD February 1995: 11–12).

108. Formal criteria for democracy are regular elections and a minimum of two parties. Such criteria is inadequate, as demonstrated by a whole series of states, for example Turkey, Peru, Guatemala, the Philippines, South Korea, and so on. These states undoubtedly fulfil formal criteria but violations of human rights is an everyday occurrence and the political opposition is completely at the mercy of the police and army (see Nuscheler in Tetzlaff 1993*a*: 87; SEF 1993: 94).

109. Johan Galtung has pointed out that there are rights that have no corresponding needs, and vice versa. He identified 28 needs and 49 rights: Galtung 1994*a*: 91–164, 235. For one billion people forced to live in utter poverty and under conditions of 'structural violence', social rights have a higher status than political rights.

110. On the civilization of society, see Senghaas's hexagon of conditions, comprising the state monopoly on force, the rule of law, interdependences, democratic participation, social justice and constructive dispute culture (tolerance, dialogue, empathy and so on), which produces reliability of expectation within and without (Senghaas 1995*a*).

111. Lijphart 1984; UNRISD 1993; consociational democracies as multi-ethnic coalitions of élites (for example Switzerland, Belgium, the Lebanon, Malaysia).

112. UN Declaration on the Right to Development, GA Resolution 4/128, 4 December 1986.

113. The well-developed welfare infrastructures in these countries also benefit an extra-European people – the Inuit of Greenland (part of the Kingdom of Denmark). See Section 3.5.1 on home rule in Kalaallit Nunaat.

114. The development co-operation policies of the Nordic states are regarded as highly efficient and innovative in the Third World. International solidarity and committed foreign policy are products of domestic policies built on a foundation of solidarity.

115. See the section on 'India's Nationalities Policy' in Chapter 5.

116. As well as the Khoisan and Pygmy minorities, the Negroids are also indigenous in the wider sense. Most of the 55 states of Africa, particularly the larger ones, have no clear ethnic majorities or minorities. In many cases, there is only a quasi-majority in demographic terms.

117. Of the 2500 to 6500 ethnic groups and subgroups that exist world-wide, almost half are to be found in Africa. (The figure given clearly depends on the way in which the calculation is made – that is on the definition of an ethnos or ethnic group.)

118. The framework conditions for a consociational democracy outlined by Lijphart are too strict and narrow, and also questionable in their requirement for geographic separation of the ethnic segments. This was the principle on which apartheid was founded; 'separation as segregation' has failed, and that is precisely what has made the South African experiment in plural democracy possible today.

119. Current examples in Africa are: the conflict between north and south in Sudan; the oppression of the Oromo peoples by the Abyssinians; the marginalization

of the Tuareg in Mali, Niger and Algeria; the enslavement and deculturization of the !Khoikhoi and San in southern Africa; the dominance of the Hausa-Fulani in Nigeria and the dangerous crisis in the federation.

120. See Moringo Parkipuny, 'In 1884 Europeans Partitioned Africa into 48 Possessions', in ECOR 1994: pt. 4: Africa, 69–72. Parkipuny states that the starting problem was the fact that 'New states received territory puzzles drawn in Europe – and held on to [them]' (69) and 'Internal colonialism launched intensified assaults in the name of national unity' (70).

121. Tanzania's 'indigenous peoples' include the Maasai, the Hadsa, the Sandawe, the Rodbo, the Basrow and the Datrow. They continue to trust in their own culture, 'despite relentless onslaughts by state and mainstream society' (Parkipuny in ECOR 1994: 71). Dissension is greatest among the two branches of the Maasai: see idem, 'The Maasai Pastoralists in East Africa', *ibid.* 72 ff.

122. Over 90 per cent are Bantu, the rest Nilot (Maasai) and Cushitic. No one people plays a dominant role. The largest people (the Sukuma in the northwest) accounts for 13 per cent of the population, followed by the Makonde in the south, with 4 per cent, and a number of 3 per cent-groups (Chagga, Haya, Nyamwezi and so on). See Rolf Hofmeier, 'Tanzania', in Nohlen and Nuscheler 1992–93: v. 178–200 (179).

123. The CCM was formed in 1977 out of the Tanganyika African National Union (TANU, founded in 1954 by Nyerere) and the Afro-Shirazi Party (ASP). TANU was the leading force and represented a broad multi-ethnic, anti-colonial (nationalist) alliance that led Tanganyika into independence in December 1961.

124. Kiswahili is a kind of proto-Bantu reconstruction comprising elements of Arabic and Indian. Some classes of words are given prefixes (and singular/plural indicators): *bantu* is an example (*ba* is the plural for the class of humans). *Ki* is the prefix for the class of 'instruments' (thus *kitabu* = book, *kikomputeri* = computer). Swahili, meanwhile, derives from the Arabic *swahil* = coastal region. It is there (for example in Zanzibar) that the best standard of Swahili is still spoken.

125. Scherrer 1988: 37–63 ('Tanzanias versuch selbstbestimmter Entwicklung').

126. NCIV 1993: Introduction C (Maasai), 6.

127. The interests of the Maasai in Tanzania are represented by Inyuat e Maa (the organization of the Maa-speaking communities in Tanzania) and by KIPOC. The Maasai's situation in Kenya is comparable, but the organizations that represent the Kenyan Maasai are dominated by corrupt, so-called traditional leaders (co-opted as deputies and administrators by the KANU (Kenya African National Union) government).

128. The Hausa and Fulani have entered into a kind of symbiosis. As a result of historical developments, these two ethnic groups came together to form a pre-colonial state. The Hausa states, with their urban culture and wide trading network, first emerged during the eleventh century; they were Islamized during the fourteenth century, and, at the start of the nineteenth century they were taken over and reorganized by the Fulani movement, led by Usman Dan Fodio. Meanwhile the Fulani of northern Nigeria (Hausa-Fulani make up about 25 per cent of the total population) and southern Niger (Hausa-Fulani = 50 per cent of Niger's population) adopted certain aspects of Hausa culture (notably the language). The Fulani (Peul, Fulbe) are a people of traders and cattle-breeders who are spread all over the west of Africa.

129. See Heinrich Bergstresser, 'Nigeria', in Nohlen and Nuscheler 1992–93: iv. 344–63 (344 ff).

130. Mazrui (in UNRISD 1995: 32–3) laments both the double standards of Western governments who merely gave lip-service to Abiola (but ultimately preferred the repressive stability guaranteed by the military in oil-rich Nigeria) and the Western media's ignorance about the heroic struggle waged by Abiola and the oil-workers. By way of contrast, Mazrui cites the massive support for the Solidarity trade-union and Lech Walesa in 1980s Poland ('African villains got more coverage than African heroes' (p. 34)).
131. 'Nacht über Nigeria': interview with Wole Soyinka in *Tages-Anzeiger* suppl., 45 (1995), 46–8.
132. See Scherrer 1996*b*: 46–8.
133. See 'Kollaborateure unter der Zulu-Aristokratie', in Scherrer 1997: 274-5.
134. See Scherrer 1994*a*: 133–205.
135. Although some UN organizations have their permanent headquarters in Geneva, Switzerland itself is not a member of the UN. The option of membership was rejected by the electorate in 1986.
136. As against the Alemanic majority of 4.3 million (about 65 per cent of the total population), there are 1.3 million French-speaking inhabitants. In addition, there are 350,000 Italian-speakers in Ticino, 50,000 Rhaeto-Romanic Swiss in Graubünden and two smaller indigenous minorities. Not much is known about the attitude of the Rhaeto-Romanics to the issue of EU membership. At one million, the proportion of 'foreigners' without civil rights is proportionally much higher than in all four neighbouring countries (Germany, France, Italy and Austria).
137. The cause of the latest escalation was downright ridiculous – but highly symbolic: Swissair did away with a number of intercontinental flights that started from Geneva.
138. 'Beben am Röstigraben', *Der Spiegel* 96/19: 144–7.
139. The ruling middle-class bloc comprises the Protestant liberals (FDP, Freiheitlich Demokratische Partei – the party of the upper middle classes), the Catholic party (CVP, Christliche Volkspartei), and the smaller populist right-wing party (SVP, Schweizerische Volkspartei). This centre-right coalition dominates politics as compared with the social democrats (SPS, Sozialdemokratische Partei der Schweiz) who also form part of government and the left-wingers and Greens who are almost completely excluded – on all sides of the linguistic borders. Switzerland has only coalition governments, both at federal and at canton level. Since the Second World War, the seven posts in the *Bundesrat* (national executive) have been filled, according to an unwritten 'magic formula', by the above-named parties in a ratio of 2:2:2:1 (1 for the right wing SVP), irrespective of their exact share of the vote. Some years ago, it seemed as if the three middle-class *Bundesrat* parties would sink below 50 per cent of the vote – a development that would have caused the social democrats (who, with 20–25 per cent of the vote, were the strongest party) a major headache, given the broad spectrum of a dozen or so national parties plus a host of local and regional parties.
140. The cantons of Zug and Obwalden have such low rates of tax (virtually non-existent for assets) that large numbers of foreigners are also attracted there. Many tax evaders have a nominal home there, for example in Zug, but work in nearby Zurich. Some of the many tax-exiles – for example German heirs to large fortunes, such as Sachs, Flick and others – have been the cause of considerable upsets.
141. In order to avoid pursuit by the US authorities for tax fraud involving several hundred million dollars, the world's largest speculator in raw materials,

Marc Rich, took refuge in Zug and availed himself of the services of a former member of the *Bundesrat* as a legal adviser. A shameful tug-of-war began, which went on for several years, eventually developing into a trade war between the USA and Switzerland – a war that was kept secret from the Swiss public. When tariff barriers against Swiss cheese exports failed to produce any effect, the USA suspended delivery of enriched uranium for the Swiss nuclear reactors. The end result being that the multi-millionaire March Rich was eventually forced to pay up.

142. Tax concessions for the wealthy lead to some bizarre situations in Switzerland: while the city of Zurich is bleeding to death financially, the local authorities on the right bank of Lake Zurich (known popularly as the 'Gold Coast') are building their second public indoor swimming pool. Property prices (and therefore also rents) on the 'Gold Coast' are so high that people earning normal salaries cannot afford to live there. The market is producing a form of social segregation. Wealthy local authority areas and cantons are resisting a redistribution of the tax burden.

143. Swiss mega-corporations number among the global players. They include the world's largest chemical company, Novartis (born of the merger between Ciba-Geigy and Sandoz), the food giant Nestlé (which derives less than 5 per cent of its staff and turnover in Switzerland), ABB (formerly BBC), Hoffmann-La Roche, the Schmidheini group and so on. The turnover of each far exceeds the Confederation's budget.

144. Since the sociologist Jean Ziegler, an establishment critic and member of the *Nationalrat* published his book with the title 'Switzerland: Beyond All Suspicion' (*Die Schweiz – über jeden Verdacht erhaben*. Darmstadt/Neuwied: Luchterhand, 1976), there has been an animated debate about the Swiss banks' role as an international 'fence', about bank confidentiality, flight capital and money-laundering ('Switzerland washes whiter'). The merger of the two major banks, the Schweizerische Bankgesellschaft and the Kreditanstalt, attempted in March 1996, would have produced the largest bank in the world.

145. The findings of a study by the political scientist Hans-Peter Kriese on decision-making processes in Swiss politics were unequivocal: indecision predominates.

146. Swiss neutrality dates back neither to the cold war (as in the case of Austria) nor to the Vienna Congress of 1815 (as claimed by Frazer Cameron, adviser to the General Secretary of the European Commission for External Relations). In fact, Swiss neutrality dates back to the time of the *Tagsatzung*, which was the Confederation parliament in Solothurn, about 400 years ago, see F. Cameron, 'Neutralität – im heutigen Europa noch relevant?' in Bächler 1994: 63–71 (63); and my contribution in the same book.

147. On compatibility of neutrality and EC/EU membership, see Scherrer 1994*b* and Gärtner 1992: 74–5.

148. 'Without any lecturing', as Cotti, then minister of state and president of the OSCE, emphasized in 1991.

149. Frazer Cameron has adopted the position that neutrality (as a deviant form of independent foreign policy?) is not compatible with the Maastricht Treaty. The great majority of the Swiss (82 per cent in November 1993) has declared themselves in favour of continued neutrality.

150. The signatures of 10 per cent of the voters are sufficient to demand a ballot on a particular issue or to reverse a decision by the executive.

151. What is more, the members of the committee are appointed by the states. See Tomas Benedikter, 'Die "EU"', *pogrom*, 174 (1994) 3.

152. The majority of EU states have long since ceased to pursue individual monetary and interest rate policies. The currency union is thus a recouping of sovereignty by the EU super-state. The intention is that currency speculation by powerful financial markets be curbed.

153. Nuclear have-nots such as the economically powerful FRG want to strengthen the Western European Union and integrate it into the EU. The nuclear powers France and Britain, on the other hand, want to continue to play their roles as major military powers – a fact which (for example in the framework of the UN) also pays off politically. The significance of the French nuclear tests in the South Seas (Mururoa) was purely political. Protests against them were loudest in the FRG – and not just out of pacifism or love of peace.

154. Klaus Walraf, 'Ausschuβ der Regionen will mehr Mitsprache in EU', *Das Parlament*, 23 February 1996, 1.

155. Sources: United Nations Population Division, *World Population Prospects: The 1998 Revision*, 1999 (http://www.popin.org/pop1998/) *Internationaler Weltatlas* (Hamburg: Xenos, 1999, 112–45); *pogrom*, 174, Dec. 1993–Jan. 1994: 11; Minority Rights Groups, var. reports.

156. Outside the EU the proportions of minority nationalities in some OSCE states are even higher.

157. As an acknowledgement, the following sections are the outcome of two workshops organized by Tom R. Burns (University of Uppsala) in Brussels (April 2001) and Uppsala (June 2001) as a contribution to the Swedish EU presidency in the framework of European Community Research of 'Improving the Socioeconomic Knowledge Base', with the participation of members from several Directorate Generals of the European Commission and the EU Presidency among international experts and NGO representatives. Key themes of the workshops were: (1) core mechanisms and institutional strategies to deal with racism and xenophobia; (2) preventing institutionalized and everyday racism – strategies to combat it, especially its organized forms; (3) local mechanisms of racism and xenophobia – and local counterstrategies; (4) the politics of racism and xenophobia: comparative perspectives; (5) EU enlargement as a source of increased xenophobia and racism in Europe; (6) racism and xenophobia as 'cultural and structural violence' and as part of the legacies of Eurocentrism.

158. According to the Asian NGO report (2001: 6) the globally most vulnerable groups are women in situations of armed conflict; Dalit women; women in migration; women in trafficking; refugee women and displaced women; women of ethnic/national minorities; women of religious groups; and indigenous women.

159. The UN world conference 'United to Combat Racism: Equality, Justice, Dignity' took place in Durban, South Africa, 31 August–7 September 2001.

160. For general views on affirmative action see Martiniello 2001.

161. The landmark European Conference against Racism brought together governments and civil organizations from across Europe. On the government side, the Council of Europe (CoE) with its 41 member states, as well as states with observer status to the CoE, participate in the conference. Council of Europe bodies, including the European Commission against Racism and Intolerance (ECRI), institutions of the European Union, for example its European Monitoring Centre on Racism and Xenophobia (EUMC), the Organisation for Security and Co-operation in Europe (OSCE), and the United Nations, most importantly its High Commissioner for Human Rights, together with its human rights

treaty monitoring bodies and mechanisms, were taking part. A large forum for 600 or so non-governmental organizations immediately preceded the European Conference.

162. 'Discrimination, hostility and violence against migrants, refugees and other non-nationals are vividly apparent in all world regions today; manifestations of xenophobia have been reported in virtually every country, in some cases widespread and brutal.' NGO Working Group on Migration and Xenophobia 2001 (www.migrantwatch.org).

163. 'The intersection of racism and xenophobia is manifest in the presumption that anyone whose physical characteristics are distinct from the idealised national norm is assumed to be foreign.' (Ibid.)

164. See the extensive research project on 'Muslim Voices' in the EU and the major report compiled by Glavanis *et al.* 2001. Additional collections of documents can be accessed at http//les.man.ac.uk.cgem (username eumuslim, password mus99lim). Also see Kamali 2001: 6–9; Samad 2001.

165. The situation of migrant women directly concerns Europe and beyond: 'Migrant women are treated as second-class citizens in their countries of destination. Racist state policies of host countries, particularly on labour and immigration, account for the exploitation of migrant women. Migrants are discriminated against in terms of wages, job security, working conditions, job related training, and the right to unionize. They are also subjected to physical and sexual abuse.' See Asian NGO Forum 2001; also see European's Women Lobby EWL 2001 and the 1995 Beijing Conference on Women's Rights: Conclusions and Recommendations.

166. Violence against women is the most abhorrent manifestation of racism. The root causes for ethnic, religious, gender and caste-based discrimination, in the case of discrimination against women, thus the intersection of gender and racism, may include globalization, migration and trafficking of women and girls, poverty, political and social oppression, and situations of violence and armed conflict (mass rape of women from ethnic minorities or indigenous communities).

167. In my book *Ethnicization and Genocide in Central Africa* (Campus 1997) one of the main entries was that the same German-manufactured ideology (the *Rassenkunde*) provided the impetus and 'justification' for two sets of monstrous crimes against humanity: it was the same theory of race and racist *übermensch–Untermensch* ideology that provided the basis both for the genocidal anti-Semitism of the Nazis and as for the extremism of the Rwandan Hutu power regime. The unease in the face of historical parallels is referred to under the title 'From Auschwitz to Africa'.

168. In the five new East German states where the share of 'foreigners' is the lowest, between 1.4 and 1.8 per cent, the number of crimes is the highest, between 2 and 3 crimes per 100,000 residents; contrary to that, in the six central and southern states where the percentage of 'foreigners' is between 7.4 and 13.9 per cent the number of crimes is the lowest, between 0.2 and 0.5 crimes per 100,000 residents. The three city-states and the two northern states range in-between, with 0.9 to 1.4 crimes and 5.2 to 18.7 per cent foreigners. See Globus 6514: 'Rechte Gewalt', based on Verfassungsschutzbericht 1999, Statistisches Bundesamt. In the year 2000 there was another dramatic 50 per cent increase of racist hate crimes in Germany. In Switzerland racist crimes against refugees in the 1990s were highest in rural areas of the centre where the share of foreigners was lowest. In towns like Geneva and Basel permanent residents without Swiss citizenship constitute almost half of the population (among the

highest degrees of non-nationals in Europe); they only have communal voting rights, if any.

169. When talking about racism and xenophobia we first think of migrant communities as the object/victims of racism and xenophobia and not so much about other minorities, be it historic nationalities, non-dominant groups, indigenous and other ethnic minorities. The number of indigenous non-dominant groups in the Greater Europe is exceeding the number of migrant communities by far. Many of these minorities are either permanently confronted with everyday racism and xenophobia (for example the sad example of the Roma all over Greater Europe) or they are discriminated against in different forms by respective demographic majorities or otherwise dominant groups. Anti-racist and anti-chauvinist policies ought to address the rejection of all non-dominant groups by large national-chauvinists groups among the majority populations in many European states. See my presentation in Brussels (Scherrer 2001).

170. According to statistics from the *Bundesamt für Verfassungsschutz*; see 'Mehr rechtsextreme Straftaten', in FAZ, 12 April 2001: 4.

171. *Eurobarometers* are a EU polling tool. The aim is to monitor change of values and attitudes twice a year; the sample size is usually 1000 (which is rather low). The 'Public Opinion Analysis Unit' of the DG Education and Culture of the European Commission is responsible for the *Eurobarometer*. For earlier surveys see Commission of the European Communities: *Eurobarometers* 30, 1988; 39, 1993; and 47.1, 1997 (*Racism and Xenophobia*), Hargreaves and J. Leaman *Racism, Ethnicity and Politics in Contemporary Europe*, Aldershot: Edward Elgar 1995 (see 'Racism in Contemporary Western Europe: An Overview').

172. See EUMC 2001: 24–5. The typology is based on six of seven dimensions for measuring attitudes towards minorities, the most telling of the dimensions (of xenophobic concerns about the alleged negative social impact of minorities), labelled as 'blaming minorities', which is 'the most important set of questions asked in the survey ...[that] seems to constitute the core attitude within the set of negative and positive attitudes' (*ibid.*, 9). The reason given is 'poor comparability'; my concern is that the result could be very different. Apart from critics about the way questions were asked the evaluations also seem to be problematic.

173. The 'great communicator', TV-tycoon Silvio Berlusconi, promised almost everything – and won. His *Forza Italia* party conglomerate contains fascist MSI remnants as well as xenophobic *Lega Norte* elements (with Umberto Bossi's Northern League weakened at the ballot box).

174. Le Pen lost his deputy mandate and was facing several trials and prosecution due to multiple charges. Of the three cities only the right-wing mayor of Orange remained in power after the March 2001 elections.

175. Unsuccessfully so by CDU in Northern Rhine-Westphalia (Germany's largest state), with a racist 'Kinder statt Inder' campaign, and, successfully so in Hessen (Germany's richest state).

176. Lately there is a legal workable definition of institutional racism: '...the collective failure of an organisation to provide an appropriate and professional service to people because of their colour, culture or ethnic origin. It can be seen or detected in the processes, attitudes and behaviour which amount to discrimination through unwitting prejudice, ignorance, thoughtlessness, and racial stereotyping which disadvantage minority ethnic people.' (McPherson Report on the Metropolitan police investigation into the death of Stephen Lawrence, London, in April 2000: §6.34.)

177. See EUMC 2001: 26–31 and 50–1.
178. See general principles about affirmative action in Martiniello 2001: 5.
179. US statistics speak of stark disparities: 'African-Americans have an unemployment rate of 7.3 per cent and are incarcerated at seven times the rate of whites. Thirteen percent of black males in the U.S. cannot vote due to felony convictions. Twenty-three percent of African-Americans live in poverty and live shorter lives than their white counterparts. The African-American infant mortality rate is on par with developing countries with 14.2 per 1000 live births which is more than double of that of 6 per 1000 births for white Americans.' See Clarence Lusane (author of *Contemporary Racism and African Americans*) in *Report on the IMADR Symposium Forms of Discrimination, Racism and Anti-Semitism*. New York City, 28 November 2000.
180. Small countries sometimes catch the winds from outside their space. Luxembourg was the ideal place for the Euro-Mediterranean dialogue (Luxembourg, 25–7 September 1997), since it is far from it. The debate with participants from Maghreb, Mashrek, Turkey and west European countries gave sense to the 'Dialectics between Orient and Occident' see Lehners 1997.
181. Contrary to the view that the Arab Muslim world poses a threat to European security there is no evidence for that with regard to military hardware. Disruption of security is more likely in the eastern Mediterranean, as a fall-out from ongoing violence in Israel–Palestine, its influence on the entire region and the plight of the Middle East peace process after the election of Ariel Sharon.
182. The Crusades started in 1291 as an aggressive attempt at religious–cultural hegemony, as did the later *Reconquista* in Spain. Islam was narrowly intertwined with power, state, politics and culture, since the demise of Francoist Spain is slowly rediscovering its history.
183. Gotfried Liedl was looking at the Spanish–Arab frontera, between confrontation and exchange, and exemplified how Europe and the 'Islamic civilization' coexisted. As Liedl 1997 ('Die spanisch-arabische Frontera im Spätmittelalter: Konfrontation und Austausch'), Bichara Khader (CERMAC) and Peter Feldbauer argued against mainstream orientalism, the 'Arabs' were themselves beaten by the arms and tools they gave the Europeans. The long exchange between northern Africa, Spain and Europe (also via Sicily) brought military technology (firearms), nautical and navigation skills and many elements of cultural, scientific and ideological nature of the seafaring Arabs into the possession of Europeans which not only jump-started modernity in Europe but greatly contributed to its 'ability' to start the first globalization which led to the colonization process.
184. For a critique see Scherrer 1997: 79–98.
185. The case of the short-lived Refah government in Turkey can exemplify how hollow the fundamentalism argument can be. For a debate on political Islam also see Carlos Echeverria: 'L'activism islamique autour de la Méditerranée et sa perception en Europe', in Lehners 1997.
186. Haleh Afshar reviewed the clash of European versus Islamic feminists and the influence of European liberation ideologies on the (re-)construction of Islamic feminism. She showed that the position of women in Islam has pros (never seen) and cons (mainly seen), exemplified in the issue of the veil. See Afshar's contribtion in Lehners 1997.
187. The historian Hans Ulrich Jost (University of Lausanne) reported that doctors had sterilized so-called 'mentally handicapped patients' against their will. Sterilizations were done under a law passed in the state of Vaud in 1928; it was

requested by Adolf Hitler in 1934 as a basis for Nazi Germany's own racist legislation. In Vaud the practice was only stopped some 20 years ago.

188. Claude Cahn described how a nationalist mob descended on the Romani quarter
in the village of Velyka Dobron, Transcarpathian Ukraine. 'An Ordinary Pogrom';
www.geocities.com/Paris/5121/pogrom.htm. Against the background of rising
Ukrainian nationalism and a collapsing economy many Roma fled to Hungary.

189. A 38,000-strong KFOR (NATO) peace keeping force in a population of two million Kosovars was unable to prevent the violence against non-Albanians. Only a
few years back, in 1999, Western leaders tried to legitimate war against
Yugoslavia by talking about 'deliberate and systematic acts of genocide' (Clinton
in *The New Statesmen*, 15 November 1998) in Kosovo; Blair was talking about
'racial genocide' committed by Milosevic (*Guardian*, 28 October 1998).) Was
there 'genocide' in Kosovo? Realities on the ground turned out to be radically
different than reported: the International Criminal Tribunal for Former
Yugoslavia (ICTY) found no genocide. Inquiries by the ICTY other international
bodies and a number of journalists, 'show a radically different train of events'
than the one presented in the media. The ICTY has announced the discovery of
some 2018 dead bodies, many of them might be Serbs and Roma.

190. The NATO bombing of Yugoslavia was started in March 1999 with the
expressed aim to 'stop a genocide' in Kosovo and received unprecedented
media attention; the result appears to be outright failure which will prove to be
expensive for the UN. For the expressed purpose of 'stopping genocide' in
Kosovo the NATO alliance unleashed (on the night of 24–25 March 1999) air
attacks followed by 78 days of bombing on Yugoslavia. While the suffering of
the Kosovar Albanians ended mid-1999, and the refugees returned, the Serbs
and Roma (Gypsies) living in Kosovo have in turn been forced to leave, while
the remaining non-Albanians live under threats of death – even under the eyes
of NATO troops – ever since the 1999 war. See Noam Chomski: 'Lessons of War:
Another way for Kosovo?'; in *Le Monde Diplomatique*, March 2000.

191. Roma live in large numbers in Romania (2–2.5 million: 8–10 per cent of total
population), the former Yugoslav republics (1–1.5 million: 4–10 per cent),
Bulgaria (<800,000); Hungary (670,000: 6.2 per cent); Turkey (650,000: 1 per
cent), the former USSR (640,000); Slovakia (500,000); but also in the EU, for
example in Spain (900,000) and Greece (est. 500,000), figures cited for the
Roma population according to Puxon 1978: 13. Estimates are generally lower
than in reality: many Roma are unwilling to give details about their identity for
fear of discrimination. Collaborators of the European Roma Rights Centre monitor Romani communities and estimate the Romani populations in Central and
Eastern Europe: Romania 4,900,000; Hungary 2,500,000; Bulgaria 1,500,000;
Greece 1,000,000; Russia 1,000,000; Slovakia 900,000; Czech Republic 350,000.
In Romania there are 40 different Roma groups; about 60 per cent speak the
Romanes language; in Hungary there are four different groups and only 25
per cent speak Romanes.

192. Useful links are www.gypsies.net/; www.romnews.com/; literature see Puxon
1997. UN Committee on the Elimination of Racial Discrimination: RD/858
(Report of Hungary) Geneva, 7 March 1996; RD/860 (on Spain), 8 March 1996.

193. Identity formation and reformation take place as a result of societal developments as well as interactions between host and immigrant populations.
Ambivalence on the part of host populations relates to, for instance, the
value of immigrants as workers, entrepreneurs or human capital versus alleged

socio-cultural and economic threats as foreigners and/or potential deviants. The ambivalence of immigrant populations to the host society relates to the dilemmas and difficulties of 'integrating' or 'remaining distinct, thus separate' – in either case, not without feelings of 'hostility and resentment'. See Burns 'Racism and Xenophobia: Key Issues, Mechanisms, and Policy Opportunities,' European Community Research Programme 'Improving the socio-economic knowledge base', Brussels, 5–6 April 2001.

194. Michel Foucault, 1926–84, was a French historian and philosopher beyond structuralism and Marxism, psychologist and social scientist. A student at ENS he became at many professor universities and at the age of 43 a member of the Collège de France, a political chameleon and human rights activist always a non-conformist and controversial character.

195. The dispositif is almost synonymous with Louis Althusser's 'apparatus', which rather camouflages reality while at the same time constructing it. For a good Foucaldian discussion of racism and the 'racial knowledge' see Terkessidis 2001: 38–41.

196. EUMC in Vienna does not do any monitoring itself but is supposed to co-ordinate it.

197. ADC as proposed by Rainer Nickel (2000) 'Criminal law … when it comes to racist or anti-Semitic hate speech or racist defamation. But many forms of discrimination cannot be fought effectively by criminal law as it is almost impossible to prove certain facts before the courts. It takes a higher degree of proof for a criminal sentencing than it takes for a civil claim to succeed … It would be much more effective if violations are made expensive for the violators. In case of discriminations civil courts should be enabled to award reasonably high compensations and additional punitive damages to the victims and/or to victim support groups.'

198. This could work in much the same way as the UN Action Plan to Prevent Genocide, as recommended by Carlsson *et al.* 1999 to 'establish networks of cooperation with humanitarian organisations, academic institutions and other non-governmental organisations with the aim of enhancing early warning and early response capacity.' Carlsson *et al.* recommended 'intensified dialogue' that would not only involve the UN Secretariat and the UN Security Council, but also INGOs, IGOs and regional organizations such as OSCE, OAU, OAS, ASEAN and others.

199. Such a system could learn from the findings and recommendations of Carlsson Report of December 1999 on the role of the UN in Rwanda 1993–94; consequences have yet to be drawn. Its most important recommendations deal with establishing a UN enforcement capacity. In cases of 'risk of massive killings or genocide it must be made clear in the mandate and Rules of Engagement of that operation that traditional neutrality cannot be applied in such situations' (*ibid.*, IV, 1.). In its second recommendation the inquiry recommends that 'action be taken to improve the capacity of the United Nations to conduct peace keeping operations, and in particular to ensure the sufficiently rapid deployment of missions into the field'.

200. See good ideas developed by Delanty; the author believes that 'The Canadian model has much to offer European transnationalism, namely the need to separate three domains of group rights: national determination, rights for national minorities and special representations rights. Only by devising a multi-tiered citizenship that is capable of responding to these three realities, will a genuinely democratic multiculturalism be possible. But beyond this the US and Canadian experience is limited.' Delanty 2001: 10.

201. According to Foucault the concept of a paradigm (*episteme* as governing discourse) is insufficient and the concept of dispositif fills the gap. The term *dispositif* links theory with practice, thus discursive knowledge with social practices and techniques of power. A paradigm is researched through the analysis of discourse (thought, speech, text), but there are practices in addition to discourse, which we may use to provide a genealogical analysis. Genealogies again are not solely based on established knowledge but on other bodies of knowledge such as dissenting opinions and theories that did not become the established and widely recognized local beliefs and understandings of some particular situation. For Foucault knowledge has very different forms, practical, instrumental, paradigmatic–scientific (say theoretical) and symbolic. Foucault was interested in themes such as sexuality; power, power structures and its multitude of different techniques; different kinds of knowledge; death, madness, disease in general; asylums, the hospitals, the prisons system; the ways to produce disciplined and docile people and so on.

202. For Althusser the reproduction of the relations of production is carried out through ideological state apparatus. Althusser reached this conclusion through a critique of Karl Marx's theory of the state. Marx believed that the state was a 'machinery' of repression; the repressive elements of the state are what Althusser calls the 'state apparatus'; it basically consists of the government, the administration, the army, the police, the courts, the prisons and so on. In addition to this, according to Althusser, the state also consists of ideological state apparatuses, which translate into a number of distinct and specialized institutions for normalization and control of the potentially deviant individuals, such as religion, education, the family, the media, official culture and so on.

203. Women, more than men, are subjected to double or multiple manifestations of human rights violations. Hence, sex and gender should not be left out of the discussions on anti-racist strategies. Gender discrimination is a human rights violation intersecting almost all other forms of discriminations.

204. Women often are further hindered by a lack of access to remedies and complaint mechanisms for racial discrimination due to structural gender-related impediments, for example gender bias in some legal systems and the general discrimination against women in all spheres of life.

205. Compare the critical approach to, definition of and expertise about racism by Mark Terkessidis (2001: 40), inspired by Robert Miles and Michel Foucault. Terkessidis is presently the best reading in Germany; he comprehensively presents and criticizes the specific German approach to the problem of racism. Some of his lines of thought should be developed further, especially with regard to the processual and structural character of contemporary racism (with some inspiration from Galtung).

206. The series of Targeted Socio-Economic Research (TSER) project reports on inclusion/exclusion are a good resource, for example a large TSER report (though with a problematic title) was dealing with informal economies and so-called 'deviant behaviour' among migrants, so large groups of undocumented poorly paid workers such as Albanians in Greece, Portuguese-speaking Africans in Portugal, Moroccans in southern Spain and North Africans in France, representing the lowest categories of (illegal) migrants in the EU (Reyneri *et al.* 1999). Also see Chamberlayne *et al.* 1999, Cars *et al.* 1999, Siim *et al.* 2000, Berkel *et al.* 2001 and Glavanis *et al.* 2001.

207. The EU has already spent some €10 billion (besides €16 billion in EBRD loans) to prepare candidate countries for the 'EU shock' and will spend €3 billion

annually during first accessions. This seems 'peanuts' compared to the €40 billion annual cost of the Common Agricultural Policy, which still is the largest share of all items. See James 'Recasting Europe', *IHT*, 23 April 2001: 16.

208. Of the 40 recommendations only a few have been fully implemented so far and – until the year 2000 – none has led to significant changes in anti-racism legislation.

209. The European Commission's Targeted Socio-Economic Research (TSER) Programme commissioned several studies on social exclusion and inclusion.

210. The EUMC has a staff of 20 but only one single researcher. The centre does not monitor racism but co-ordinates what is being done by others (including the NGO community). For this purpose some seven (of 15) national focal points remain to be established.

211. Ruzza (1999: 1) did 'field research' in Brussels; his data was drawn from observation, personal interviews and analysis of archive materials. The paper analyses the role of different concepts of anti-racism and their implications in the policy process. Diverging definitions of the nature, causes and ideal solutions of racism coexisted but '[a]ll together these conceptions give identity and professionalism to the relevant policy network, but in a fragmented and contested fashion.' (*Ibid.*) Some of Ruzza's conclusions are now obsolete since the report was written before the breakthrough while his inquiry into the anti-racism lobby is not at all obsolete.

212. Anti-racist movements became prominent first in France, where the problems were monumental (along with the rise of FN and other extremist parties) already in the 1980s; broad-based anti-racist groups such as *SOS Racisme* have been supported by left-wing parties, mostly by the socialists. Today *SOS Racisme* exists in several countries and *SOS Racisme International* has an office in Brussels.

213. The anti-racist movement overlaps with a variety of other movements concerned with social exclusion; the largest networks are the Social Platform (which co-ordinates two dozen umbrella organizations, some with several hundred member groups), *Solidar*, the Youth Forum, the European Federation for Intercultural Learning, the European Human Rights Foundation and a number of religious organizations.

214. The EC Racial Equality Directive (in article 13) is disappointing in that it establishes no independent bodies or ombudsman for receiving complains about racial discrimination (as exists in the UK Race Relations Act 1976 and amendments, the Dutch and Swedish laws) and places the burden and the financial risk on the plaintiff, see Chopin *et al.* 2001: 47–8.

215. 'In assessing *Europeanization* as a method for conflict resolution, at this level of generality, the answer remains ambiguous. The uncertainty about the eventual shape of European integration undermines the credibility of the EU in playing this role.' (Trimikliniotis 2001: 58–9).

216. In Germany the *Länder* (similar to the *Cantons* in Switzerland) are responsible for drafting and applying local legislation, with each *Land* being free to draft its own constitution within the ideological and institutional framework and principles of the 1949 Basic Law (*Grundgesetz*), and the *Länder* even participate in the federal legislative process through the *Bundesrat* (Federal Council). The *Bundesrat* has a right of veto, which can only be overturned by a majority vote of the federal parliament (the *Bundestag*). Compared with the German Schröder's ideas of a federal Europe the French press reacted by rejecting it: 'L'Europe qu'envisage Gerhard Schröder serait une réplique exacte du modèle fédéral allemand, couronnée par une Constitution européenne.' (*Le Figaro*, 30 April 2001: 4).

In fact, what Schröder presented (see *Der Spiegel* 22, 27 April 2001) was not exactly a copy of the German model described above. The reaction of French Prime Minister Leonel Jospin of end May 2001 was, as expected, rather defensive and certainly cautious about federalism.

217. According to Rémond, judging from the point of view of French state traditions, it was 'noticeable that territorial autonomy [as administrative autonomy introduced on the unruly island of Corsica, my addition] does not always imply self-determination, nor does it necessarily entail independence.'

218. See Ulrich Sedelmeier: 'Enlarging Europe', in European Commission/Liberatore 1999: 77–9, this ref. 78.

5 Nationality policy as violence prevention: a brief comparison of large states

1. On the Soviet model of nationality policy, see Scherrer 1997: 276–316.

2. Possible areas of exploration may be: the nature of inter-ethnic relations; majority/minority numbers; distribution of resources; resolution of the land problem (land reform); data on/analysis of the political or state set-up (confederation, federal state, centralized state) and presence/absence of autonomous regions or areas; relevant provisions in the constitution, laws, edicts and so on. Official statistics should be compared with those provided by the groups affected/endowed with autonomy and so on, and with the results of empirical studies on the ground.

3. Such as basic components of, and evaluation criteria for, arrangements for self-government (Section 2.4) and constructive structural elements for multi-ethnic states (Section 2.6).

4. Wars in the USSR/CIS 1988–95: Azeris versus Armenians; Georgians versus Gamsakhurdia's ARK; Georgia versus South Ossetia; Georgia versus Abkhazia; Ingushetia versus North Ossetia; Romanian Moldova versus Dniestr coalition (with Cossacks); Tajikistan versus clans (including Russian soldiers and Afghan Tajiks); Chechnya versus Russian Federation. There were armed hostilities between Chechens and Ingushetians (formerly a joint autonomous republic) at the beginning of the 1990s. Three of the 18 districts of Chechnya wanted to return to the Russia federation. On this, see the detailed comments in Scherrer 1997: ch. 6; also Scherrer 1994: 28–35. New conflicts caused by Islamists (trained in Afghanistan with al-Qaeda in Tajikistan, Kyrgyzstan and Kazakhstan.

5. The Russian Federation is the legal successor to the Russian Soviet Socialist Republic (RSSR).

6. Moldova versus Trans-Daniestr, Georgia versus South Ossetia, Georgia versus Abkhazia, Chechnya versus Ingushetia.

7. See Scherrer 1997: 308–9.

8. The use of autonomy arrangements, economic privileges and other concessions acted as a preventive against the outbreak of ethnic violence in the Soviet Union between 1920 and 1988.

9. See note 4 above. Further examples are be found in Yugoslavia: Croatia versus Krajina and Slavonia (Serb minority) and tripartite Bosnia. Bosnia constitutes a special case in so far as there is no majority and the rules governing power-sharing and the principle of rotation in the allocation of high office were annulled in a quasi-collective way.

10. Emil Payne, 'Settlement of Ethnic Conflict in Post-Soviet Society', in Callieβ and Merkel 1994: 469–84.

11. Ingushetians versus Ossetians (North-Caucasus), Armenians versus Azeris (Nagorno-Karabakh), and Ossetians versus Georgians (South Ossetia).
12. For instance the Uzbek pogroms against the Meshketian Turks in the Ferghana valley (June 1989), other pogroms against Caucasians in Novy Usen (Kazakhstan), and the overdue repatriation of the Crimean Tatars after their demonstrations in Red Square (July 1987).
13. A collapse of the state such as occurred in the case of the USSR in 1990 would not have surprised the founding fathers of the Soviet Union. In 1914, Lenin correctly anticipated that '[only] a [genuine] recognition of the right to separation can reduce the danger of a collapse of the state'.
14. The ranks of the rebel 'Confederation of the Mountain Peoples' in North Caucasus include the confederation's founder, former Soviet general Dzhokhar Dudayev of oil-rich Chechnya, and various forces from the former Autonomous Soviet Socialist Republics of Dagestan, Abkhazia versus Georgia, and Ossetia versus Ingushetia. The Republic of Ingushetia was created in 1991.
15. The secessionists have not shrunk from acts of terror and the state has responded with annihilatory measures. In June 1995, the taking of 2000 civilian hostages by Chechnyan irregulars marked the extension, for the first time, of the war into an area of the federation populated by Russians, followed by a further extension into Dagestan at the start of 1996. In both cases, military attempts to secure the release of the hostages unharmed ended in failure, triggering internal political crises. Yeltsin and his government acted more and more repressively.
16. See Scherrer 1998*a*.
17. The conflict in Tajikistan was the bloodiest yet in the CIS. In 1992, the Islamists suffered a military and political defeat. About 50,000 people lost their lives and half a million people were driven out (refugees and IDPs). A number of armed groups withdrew to Afghanistan, where they are reputedly receiving support from radical groups. The ongoing conflict in Afghanistan will continue to have regional spillover effects in the three neighbouring CIS states and Pakistan and Iran. Pressure by the Taliban militia on the two Shiite groups in Afghanistan (the Tajiks of the northwest, led by warlord Ahmed Shah Masoud, and the Farsi-speaking Hazara in central Afghanistan, led by the Hizb-e Wahdat militia) could become dangerously acute. When the fundamentalist Sunnite Taliban overran the provinces of Parvan and Kapisa at the beginning of 1997, hundreds of thousands of Tajiks were driven out. The conflict in Afghanistan has become increasingly ethnicized in recent years. Pakistan has been more and more bare-faced in its interventions. The battle-line runs between the Pashtunisian quasi-majority and the large minorities of Tajiks, Uzbeks, Hazara, Turkmens, Beluch, Farsiwan and Nuristani. There is a vague hope that Tajikistan will avoid 'Afghanization' by having a real division of power between the ruling ex-communist apparatchiks and the Islamists, thus integrating the Islamists into the political system. However, since 1991, the political conflict over a secular constitution and the future role of Islam has been overlaid with various clan conflicts. In the period 1994–97, the rebels drew attention to themselves by repeatedly taking foreign hostages and issuing demands for money. Women and Western NGO staff were not spared in this process.
18. Numerically, the small and smallest peoples of the north make up just under 1 per cent of the population of the Russian Federation. The bewilderingly multi-ethnic population of the north falls into six linguistic groups. A large number of peoples from three language-groups with small populations (100,000 in total)

face a particularly hard task in improving their status. These are the old-established paleo-Asiatic peoples, the Inuit and Aleut in the most northerly part of the Far East, and the Tungusian linguistic group in central and eastern Siberia (not including the Evenk).

19. The Yakuts themselves make up just under half the population in their republic. But a large proportion of the population live on the plains of the rivers Lena and Vilyui. It is not at all true to say that the Yakuts are teetering 'on the edge of the abyss' (as Winifred Dallmann has claimed, blanket-fashion, for all the peoples in the north – *pogrom* 180). Between 1979 and 1989, they had a healthy yearly population growth rate of 1.4 per cent – far exceeding the average for Russia – and the overwhelming majority of them (95 per cent) continue to use their mother-tongue as their first language.

20. The indigenous Evenk, a society based on hunting and fishing, have already been driven out of Yakutia by industrial development and ecological destruction. The factors highlighted by Jablokov in this connection are: pollution of water by thallium (used in the diamond industry); the ecological disaster at the Vilyui reservoir; the plundering of coal-reserves in southern Yakutia; and radiation from nuclear explosions (*pogrom*, 180: 18–19).

21. Sakha-Yakutia is responsible for 20 per cent of world diamond production, and for a third of the Russian Federation's gold production – in other words, world economic conditions play a role here. According to Emil Payne (now Yeltsin's adviser on nationality issues), the South African firm De Beers Consolidated bought up tens of millions of dollars' worth of diamonds from Sakha-Yakutia in order to prevent a price collapse on the world market. In 1992–93, the republic sought unilaterally to raise its share in the diamond business from the 27 per cent permitted in treaties with the federal government to 40 per cent (*TA*, 24 February 1993).

22. The members of UNPO include eight republics of the Russian Federation (Chuvashia, Chechnya, Ingushetia, Komi, Mari, Tatarstan, Udmurtia and Sakha-Yakutia); the Abkhaz (Georgia), Crimean Tatars and Gagauz (Moldova), are also members of this kind of alternative UN. Four former Soviet Socialist Republics (Armenia, Georgia, Estonia and Latvia) were members of UNPO before they were recognized as sovereign states.

23. But European integration is not an automatic process – as was believed until the Danish 'no' to Maastricht. The Swiss rejection of the European Economic Area (EEA) and the Norwegian rejection of EU membership were more than compensated for by the desire of three western European states (Austria, Sweden and Finland) and a number of eastern European states (Poland, the Czech Republic, Slovakia, Hungary, Romania and Slovenia) to join. In Switzerland, the membership question provoked a government crisis and led to a split along the linguistic borders.

24. The risk of conflict is greatest in the Caucasus and in Central Asia; five armed conflicts have taken place there. See Payne 1993: 19–29.

25. In the Middle Kingdom, the distinction between *nei* and *wai* (inner/outer) was integral; it corresponded to the distinction between Han and barbarians. From the time of the Han dynasty (200 BCE–220 CE), the name Han was applied to all the rice-growers living under Han dominion in the alluvial land of the Yellow river. The colonization of 'outer' areas began even before this time.

26. Fairbanks 1968.

27. Yin 1989: 431–50; Shen Che and Lu Kiaoya, *Life among the Minority Nationalities of Northwest Yunnan* (Beijing: Foreign Language Press, 1989).

28. The FRG is the most populous state in Western Europe and in the EU.
29. The idea of a critical mass should not be confused with that of a 'strategic group'. This latter is a special quasi-group dependent on the vagaries of politics, which carries weight in conflict situations because it is made up of members of the élite but which is mainly seeking to secure its share of wealth and power at the central-state level (see Evers and Schiel 1988: 25).
30. These have no lobby and, despite their demographic weight, no critical mass. Their number is approximately equivalent to the total number of Indians in the USA.
31. The 'national question' was discussed as early as the First Congress of the Chinese Communist Party in Shanghai in 1921. At the second congress, in 1922, the creation of republics for the Mongolians, Tibetans and Turks (Uighur) was discussed. In declarations issued by the CCP to the Mongolians of Inner Mongolia (20 December 1935) and the Muslims of the north-east – notably the Uighur of Xinjiang/East Turkestan – the party leadership promised to institute regional autonomy for non-Hans. See Rosa Murphy, 'Las Minorias en China', in *IWGIA Boletín*, 1 (1993) 25–8 (27).
32. Mao took over parts of Lenin's nationality policy as early as 1930, in the Yenan period. Despite this, the structure of the Chinese state has remained unitary (rather than federal). In contrast to Japan, which Lenin (1914, 687) had already forecast would fulfil 'the preconditions for the fullest development of the production of goods' and would see 'the fastest growth of capitalism', the 'largest part of Asia', as he put it, would have first to break free from dependence and oppression.
33. Murphy, *op. cit.* 28.
34. The Uighurs are the most easterly Turkish-speaking people. The Uighurs are the native people of Eastern Turkestan, also known as Xinjiang or Uygur Autonomous Region. The latest Chinese census gives the present population of the Uyghurs as 7.2 million. Another half million are living in the FSU. Exiled organizations have their own news networks, for example the http://www.taklamakan.org/index.html or Eastern Turkestan Information Bulletin (on http://www.geocities.com/CapitolHill/1730/index.html, which is run by the Eastern Turkestani Union in Europe.
35. Both these peoples have exiled politicians representing them in international forums. Representatives of the Uighur (east Turkestan), and of six other Turkish-speaking nations and nationalities (all from the CIS), are members of UNPO (see UNPO 1994*a*). The exiled Tibetan community is a co-founder and founding member of UNPO, Tsering Jampa, an exiled Tibetan, is its deputy general secretary. The Tibetans are also running their own news network (see http://www.tibet.org/).
36. Uighurs and Tibetans are the best organized (including at the international level) chiefly on the basis of a minority religion (for census figures, see Yin 1989: 341). The urbanized and Sinicized Hui are the descendants of the Muslims who came to China as Arab seafarers, or as traders along the Silk Road, during the Tang dynasty (618–907). Yi opposition seems nowadays to be of a passive kind. Besides most of China's five million Yi the Chuxiong Yi autonomous prefecture in the border area of Yunnan with Burma has 35 nationalities living on its territory.
37. The term *yuanzu minzu* ('indigenous peoples') is to be preferred to *tuzu renmin* because, it has been claimed, *tuzu* has connotations of 'savage', 'primitive', and culturally 'low-level' (*renmin* = 'population'). See Alliance of Taiwan Aborigines, Statement by Luang-Chang Mao Panu, about the discriminative term for 'indigenous peoples' used in the Chinese version of the Draft Universal

Declaration of the Rights of Indigenous Peoples, UNWGIP 11th session, Geneva 1993 (mimeo).

38. Yunnan is situated in China's southwest frontier. Yunnan borders Guizhou Province and Guangxi Autonomous Region on the east, and reaches north to Sichuan Province and Tibetan Autonomous Region. On the west and south it borders Burma (Myanmar), Laos and Vietnam along a 4060 km international boundary. The province covers 394,000 km^2 with a population of 40 million (http://www.cnc.ynu.edu.cn/).

39. See Tina Wodiunig, 'Der ethnische Raum Yünnan', in: Müller (co-ord.) 1994: 455–78.

40. See Houmphanh Rattanavong, 'Regarding What One Calls the "Thai"', in Institute of Southeast Asian Studies 1990: 162–75.

41. Ethnic groups settling the Sino-Burmese borderland in Burma, liberated or controlled areas along, and immediately next to, the international border are occupied by (from north to south): Kachin peoples such as the Jingpo and Lisu (represented by the KIO); the Palaung (rep. PSLF); the Wa (UWSA, WNO); the Lahu (rep. LNO); Akha (rep. 461, ex-CPB); and Shan and Tai/Dai (rep. MTA, SSA, SUA, etc.). The KIA/KIO had about 12,000 guerrillas under arms and the UWSA about 15,000. Both groups were forced to conclude a ceasefire treaty with the Burmese regime under pressure from China. The KIO was part of the opposition Democratic Alliance of Burma (DAB), but had its membership suspended for 'treason' in 1993, before the treaty was signed with Burma's military junta in February 1994.

42. Shen Che, 'The Lisu People: A Merry Nationality', in: idem, *Life among the Minority Nationalities of Northwest Yunnan* (Beijing: Foreign Language Press, 1989), 121–49.

43. In the Chinese literature, the Lisu are categorized linguistically as belonging to the Yi subgroup of the Tibeto-Burmese group, which comprises Tibetan, Yi, Jingpo, Qiang, and an unidentified subgroup of Lhoba. The Yi group also includes the Naxi, Hani, Lahu, Jino and Bai, whereas the Jingpo, the largest people in the ethno-political unit known as Kachin in Burma, form a separate subgroup. See Yin 1989: 449 and for visual anthropology see: http://home.earth link.net/~jechu/index.htm.

44. American Baptist missionaries converted the Lisu on either side of the China–Burma border.

45. The Nanzhao (or Nan Chao) empire, which grew up in Yunnan from 629 (during the Tang dynasty, 618–907), was – as was fiercely debated at International Congress for Thai Studies in 1990 in Kunming – dominated either by Thai, Bai or Yi; it employed Chinese advisers. See Hu Hua Sheng, in Institute of Southeast Asian Studies 1990: i, 27–41; Huang Huikun, *ibid.* ii, 185 ff.

46. The kingdom of Dali was conquered by Genghis Khan. Dali is now the seat of the autonomous Bai government and has become a base for alternative tourism. The continuity between the Nanzhao and Dali periods has been demonstrated by, among other things, genealogies. See Zhang Xilu, 'Prominent Baima Families of Nanzhao and Dali Kingdoms', in Institute of Southeast Asian Studies 1990: i, 1–27.

47. See Jane R. Hanks, 'The Confucian Heritage among the Tribes in Chinagrai (Thailand)', in Institute of Southeast Asian Studies 1990: i, 339–47; Fairbanks 1968.

48. Its seven religions are: Chinese Confucianism; Tibetan Lamaism; South-East Asian Buddhism (Theravada); the Islam of the trader-castes (Hui); the polytheism of the minorities (Zhuang, Yi, Bai, Hani); the animism of the hill tribes

(Hmong, Yao, Achang, Bouyei, Tulung, Shui, etc.); and Christianity as introduced by white missionaries since 1880 (esp. among the Lisu, Jingpo Kachin, Nu).

49. During the Ming dynasty (1368–1644) Yunnan was a place of exile. The railway-line from Chengu to Kunming was not completed until the 1970s. Yunnan has an average altitude of 2000 m, but also has some tropical areas – the Mekong/Lancang valley – located not too far from the Hengduan mountains (foothills of the Himalayas).

50. See 'India: How to Keep a Multi-ethnic State Stable?', in Friedrich-Ebert-Stiftung, *Keeping Inter-ethnic Conflicts Non-violent* (Bonn, 1995).

51. Interview on the abysses of the Indian caste system with Yogesh Varhade, 'The Dalits of India', Toronto: Ambedkar Centre for Justice and Peace 1997 (unpubl. ECOR paper).

52. Barbara R. Joshi, 'National Identity and Development: India's Continuing Conflict', *Cultural Survival Quarterly*, 13 (1989), 2: 3–8.

53. As with Adivasi Jharkhand, there is 'no room' and no political will on the part of central government to create the Boro Land demanded by the Boro. See Sanjib Baruah, 'Indigenous Peoples, Cultural Survival and Minority Policy in Northeastern India', *Cultural Survival Quarterly*, 13 (1989) 2: 53–9. See Domonic Mardi: 'The struggle for indigenous self-governance' in ECOR 9, 1997: 172–6 (Jharkhand).

54. Names such as 'Naga', 'Zo', or 'Boro' are collective names for a number of peoples or tribes. 'Boro' means 'Tibetan' before the Thai-Ahom subjugated Assam in the sixteenth century. The Boro kings had been ruling over the peoples of Assam for over 500 years. The Zo or Chin peoples comprise more than 50 distinct ethnic entities. The Naga comprise up to 40 tribes, who cannot understand each other's languages. They therefore use Nagamese (Naga mixed with Assam). See IWGIA, Doc. 56 (Copenhagen, 1986); ECOR 9, 1997: 41–84 (Naga), 101–16 (Chin).

55. See Minority Rights Group, *The Untouchables of India* (MRG Bulletin 26; London, 1982).

56. The Santals have a population of almost 10 million and are considered the largest tribal society in India. Many Santal groups have lost their lands, their forests and their culture; nowadays they either work as day-labourers for rich farmers or live a marginalized life in the cities. See the interview on the struggle of the Santals, the role of All Santal Cultural Society (AISWACS) and the Jharkhand movement with Dr Dominic Mardi, 'Santals are one of the largest tribes in India' in ECOR 9, 1997: 169–76. See also Debjani Das, 'Frauenautonomie im Patriarchat? Die Sozialisierung der Gleichheit in der Santal-Gesellschaft', paper, University of Bremen, 1994.

57. See *pogrom*, 171 (1993) ('Adivasi: Das andere Indien'), 12–38.

58. The forests are falling victim to heavy industry, for example in Chota Nagpur (in southern Bihar), where once the Santals, Munda and Ho lived in linked forest areas. See Sharad Kulkarni, 'Adivasi und die Forstwirtschaft', *pogrom*, 171 (1993), 28.

59. Rainer Hörig, *Selbst die Götter haben sie uns geraubt: Indiens Adivasi kämpfen ums überleben*, Göttingen: GfbV 1990. Also, *Cultural Survival Quarterly*, 13 (1989) issue no. 2.

60. Frank Braßel, '*Chattisgarh Mukti Morcha*: mehr als eine Gewerkschaft', *blätter des iz3w*, 199 (1994), 14–16.

61. N. Ashirvad, 'Atrocities against Dalits', in José P. Verghese ed., *Human Rights in India Today*, 66–76. Amnesty International, *The 1993 Report on Human Rights around the World* (London, 1994), 153–5.

62. Ambekar Centre for Justice and Peace (ACJP), 'Fact Sheet: The Situation of the Dalits (Untouchables) of India' (Toronto, 1992), 2.
63. Jogesh Varhade, *ibid.*; idem statement for ACJP at UNWGIP, July 1992; idem 'The Problem of 250 Million Untouchables, the Indigenous Peoples of South Asia', statement at UN World Conference on Human Rights, Vienna, June 1993.
64. Both Adivasis and Dalits formerly suffered threefold exploitation (see Das 1994: 11): by *sahebs* (European colonial masters), *zamindar* (landowners), and *mahajans* (money-lenders). On top of this came the exploitation by the *dukus* (traders) and the civil servants who replaced the *sahebs*. Nowadays the exploitation comes from the *jotedars* (capitalist farmers), the money-lenders, the owners of craft businesses, industrialists and traders.
65. The first Backward Classes Commission of India was set up in January 1993 and submitted its report in March 1955. On the basis of its own criteria, it listed 2399 castes as socially, economically and educationally backward (SCaST). The Mandal Report still classifies 22.5 per cent of the total population as belonging to these two lowest categories. By comparison, the 'Forward Hindu Castes' account for 16.2 per cent of the total and the non-Hindu 16.2 per cent. The remaining 43.7 per cent are accounted for by 'Other Backward Castes' (OBCs).
66. The 16.2 per cent of forward castes include Brahmins with 5.5 per cent of the total population; Rajputs with 3.9 per cent; Marathas with 2.2 per cent; Jats with 1 per cent; Vaishyas-Bania with 1.9 per cent; Kayasthas with 1 per cent; and others with 2 per cent.
67. As was noted by B. P. Mandal (Chairman, Backward Classes Commission) – see Government of India, Report of the Backward Classes Commission, Pt. 1, vols i and ii (New Delhi: GOI, 1980), the reasons for this surprising phenomenon are found in habitus and costume, since 'the caste system is a great conditioner of the mind and leaves an indelible mark on a person's social consciousness and cultural mores' (p. 55). Hindu converts were acting as 'Trojan horses of the caste system' within more egalitarian religions such as Islam, Christianity and Sikhism. Only Buddhism seems to be immune. Even in the mainly Christian state of Kerala, converted Dalits continued to be treated as 'untouchables' by Syrian Christians – after generations!
68. The research was carried out between March 1979 and December 1980. The report mentions that the population figures for the most deprived sections of society, the 'depressed backward classes', are 'very arbitrary and based on pure conjecture' (Mandal 1980, § 14, page iv). Data was based on the 1961 census, notifications by various state governments, surveys and 'knowledge gained through extensive touring of the country and receipt of voluminous public evidences' (Mandal 1980: 54). 'When it comes to the ICS class one, class two bureaucratic positions where there is a real power that all people can bring the change, they only fill in 50 years about 5 to 7 percent.' (See Yogesh Varhade, 'The Dalits of India'. Toronto: Ambedkar Centre for Justice and Peace 1997. ECOR paper.)
69. For recommendations, see Mandal 1980: 58, §13.11. No previous government had dared to propose what was an almost 50 per cent job reservation quota for the under-privileged classes and castes of India. The Other Backward Classes alone number 52 per cent of India's population. In total, three-quarters of India's population are believed to be surviving near or below the poverty line, among them 150 million child labourers and bonded labourers.
70. I am indebted to Horst F. Rolly for additional information in this section. Numbers are taken from the Mandal Report. The proportion of Scheduled Castes and Scheduled Tribes among the non-Hindu populations varies greatly; it is low among

Jains, Muslims (0.02 per cent), and Buddhists (0.03 per cent), higher among Sikhs (0.22 per cent), and high among Christians (0.44 per cent or one in five).

71. Mardi in ECOR 1995*c*: 170–4.

72. Jharkhand, especially the Chota Nagpur plateau (covering southern Bihar, the southwest of West Bengal, the eastern part of Madhya Pradesh, and the north of Orissa, around the industrial city of Rourkela), and the autonomous Santal district (Santal *pargana* of West Bengal) is the site of India's heavy industry. Coal, iron ore, mica, uranium, copper and chromium are mined there. The Adivasi derive no benefit at all from their raw materials. The ecological destruction of their native area began as far back as the nineteenth century and has extended over an ever-wider area since the start of this century. See Hörig, 'Selbst die Götter', 87.

73. For a long time, there was only one armed movement fighting for Jharkhand: the MCC (Maoist Communist Centre). See Wallensteen and Axel 1993: 338. The All Jharkhand Students Union (AJSU) is said to have good contacts with the Gorkhas (GNLF: Gorkha National Liberation Front) and to be building up armed cells.

74. See interviews with I. Chish Swu and T. Muivah (NSCN), ECOR 1995*c*. The Naga elders mentioned other armed movements: 'Punjabis (Sikhs), Kashmiris, Boros, Magalayas, Miklus, Tripuris and Kapirs. All are armed, and you will hear about the Naxalites and the People's Forces fighting the Indian government in the central regions.'

75. Mardi: 'Until now the Jharkhand movement has been non-violent', ECOR 1995*c*: 171.

76. The German Gossner mission has been active among the Adivasis in the Chota Nagpur region for 150 years. See Klaus Robert, 'Inzwischen gibt es keinen Platz mehr für Weiße', *Neues Deutschland*, 9 September 1994, 11.

77. See Hörig 1990: 77–88.

78. There are on going armed hostilities with the Naga (NSCN), Meitei, Karbi, Dimasa, Boro and Tripura.

79. The UTLNF documented the human rights violations committed by the chauvinist AGP government. The UTLNF represents the Mising, Boro/Kachari (Rabha, Lalung, Mech, Sonowal, Thengal, Deuri, etc.). See United Tribal Nationalities Liberation Front, *Fate of Aboriginals under AGP Government in Assam, India* (Darrang/Assam, n.d.).

80. See Wallensteen and Axell 1993: 338.

81. According to a resolution passed by the Shiv Sena Party, the metropolis of Bombay, with its 10 million inhabitants, is to be renamed 'Mumbai' (after the local Hindu god Mumbadevi). 'Bombay' is an Anglicization of the name *bom bahia* ('beautiful bay') which the Portuguese gave to this trading centre. Bombay's history as a dynamic, multicultural metropolis and cosmopolitan port, with its urban culture and multiplicity of ethnic and religious groups (Hindus, Muslims, Parsis, Jews, Christians) living side-by-side, is thus to be erased or 'cleansed'.

82. Scherrer 1994.

83. The 1996 elections might turn out to be a turning-point in India's development: the BJP became the largest party in parliament (160 out of 537 seats: 29.8 per cent); the secular Congress Party suffered a historic defeat (136 seats: 25.3 per cent) and now holds only half the former number of seats (260). The National Front won 180 seats (33.5 per cent) and, as an alliance is the real winner of the elections. It was the BJP that was charged with forming a government, because ex-Prime Minister N. Rao allegedly neglected to inform President Shankar Dayal Sharma promptly that he was willing to support a government of the left (*Der Spiegel*, 96/21, 165–7).

84. Bernhard Imhasly about Vajpayee, 'The Outsider', in *taz*, 15 May 1996.
85. See interview with A. B. Vajpayee, 'Guru der Nationen', in *Der Spiegel*, 96/19, 160–4.
86. 'India's Challenge'; in *International Herald Tribune*, 21 April 1999, 10.
87. P. Constable: 'India's Chaotic Democracy' (*ibid.*, 3). PM Vajpayee was ousted on 17 April 1999 by a Lok Shaba vote of 270 to 269.
88. Ward Churchill, 'Crimes against Humanity', *Cultural Survival Quarterly*, 17 (1993), 4: 36–9. According to Churchill, this is an expression of 'U.S. governmental policy to bring about the "assimilation" (dissolution) of indigenous societies. In other words, Indian cultures as such were to be caused to disappear' (*ibid.* 38). Churchill, a radical Indian leader, recalls this scandal, in which no less than 40 per cent of Indians were forcibly sterilized as part of a secret programme (*ibid.* 39). Between 1880 and 1980 almost half of all Indian children were either sent under duress to far-away boarding schools (residential schools), or else were forcibly adopted – in 'blind' adoptions by white Americans.
89. The DIAND: Department of Indian Affairs and Northern Development.
90. The Hudson Bay Company (HBC) and 14 Indian nations, in what was later British Colombia, concluded the first treaties between 1850 and 1854. The agreements concluded in the Dominion of Canada between the British Crown and the Indians of northern Canada and the prairie included: five 'numbered treaties' in the period 1871–75; a sixth with the Cree in 1876 (in present-day Alberta, Saskatchewan and Manitoba); and five others in the period up to 1923.
91. 'Nunavut' in the Inuit language means 'our land'. The Inuit have been living here 'since time immemorial' (D. Samba), before the white settlers arrived in the area now known as Canada, see André Hoekema in Assies and Hoekema 1994: 181 ff.
92. See interviews with the late Howard R. Berman (professor of international law, University of San Diego) on the 'Nunavut Agreement' in ECOR 1995: 11–24, esp. 11–13, and with Kevin Knight (UNAAQ, community development corporation of the Inuit people of Canada), *ibid.* 15–19 and 56–62. Also update on Nunavut with Kevin Knight: 'Agreement between Canada and the Inuit of Nunavut may develop new regimes', ECOR 17; Moers in IRECOR 1998: 27–30.
93. See the article 'Selbstbewuβte Ureinwohner Kanadas', *NZZ*, 4 May 1994, 9.
94. See Chief Vernon Bellegarde on self-governance in ECOR 1995: 49–51.
95. Julian Burger, 'Indian Nations of the United States of America', in Burger 1987: 195.
96. The Dine reservation was marked out with a ruler, as were the boundaries of four states of the mid-southwest over which Dine land extends; right in the middle of it is the reservation for the Hopi. The Dine have ethno-linguistic links with the Dene in Canada and the Navajo (Dineh bahané) in northern Mexico. Together they form one of the largest Indian nations in North America in demographic and territorial terms – though up to now reunification has not been on their agenda. The Canadian Dine would, in any case, be excluded from this for territorial reasons.
97. Burger 1987: 199–201.
98. Center for World Indigenous Studies 1989. The ambiguity is evident from the start: the terms 'Indian nations' and 'tribal leaders' are both used.
99. The Dawes Act, also known as the General Allotment Act (which assigned 160 acres to each family head) led to mass enforced resettlements of Indian communities.
100. Similar legislation was used by the white Australians to dispossess and marginalize the indigenous peoples, on the basis of the doctrine of *terra nullius*

(revoked by the Supreme Court in 1992). A 'limit' was placed on this by the Imperial Crown Land Act of 1842 and the Australian Waste Land Act (what a title!) of 1848, see UNCHR 1995*b*: 36–41.

101. Center for World Indigenous Studies 1989.
102. Astonishingly, Canada has, on the whole, so far managed, while plundering the forests of the north, to avoid any adverse publicity. For an exception, see: Rudi Sutter: 'Kanada auf dem Holzweg', *Basler Magazin*, 10 October 1994, 1–3.
103. The Lakota Indians became members of UNPO in 1995 (the first Indian nation from North America to do so) and are seeking to internationalize their struggle. The Treaty of Fort Laramie assigned the Lakota a territory of 1.3 million acres (1 acre = 4050 m^2), but this was reduced to ever-smaller proportions. In July 1980, the US Supreme Court ruled that the Lakota had been subject to illegal expropriation, revoked the expropriations and awarded the Lakota more than US$100 million in compensation. The Lakota consider the Black Hills sacred; they refused the money, while the sum was raised to US$350 million!
104. Yin 1989.
105. Stalin's 1936 constitution cited three conditions for 'secession': the territory in question must lie on the border of the USSR; it must have a population of more than one million; and the majority of the population must belong to one nation (something that does not apply, for example, to Kazakhstan).
106. This observation applies to the first phase of the collapse. See Scherrer 1994: 28–35, 1997: 276–316.
107. §8.3: 'The congress shall have the power to regulate commerce with foreign nations, among the several states, and with the Indian tribes', and the president, 'shall have the power to make treaties' (§2.2). The 1776 declaration of independence had talked of 'merciless Indian savages' (*sic!*).
108. The Hodenosawnee Iroquois Confederation comprised the Seneca, Oneida, Mohawk, Onondaga and Tuscarora nations.
109. The BIA was created in 1824, as part of the War Department (*sic!*); its present character is traceable to the Indian Reorganization Act of 1934. Its main task is supposed to be 'to train Indians (and Inuit) to manage their own affairs under the trust relationship to the Federal Government' (*US Government Manual*, 350).
110. Ten three-year 'demonstration projects' relating to self-governance have been initiated in the USA.
111. See Ward Churchill in Center for World Indigenous Studies 1989: 59. The AIM seeks to secure control for the Indians over their own affairs, that is to deprive the tribal authorities and the BIA of their powers.
112. Joseph De La Cruz, in Center for World Indigenous Studies 1989; and Tim Coulter, *ibid.* 41: 'Indian nations are subject to practically unlimited federal powers.'
113. Lenin's stance as a champion of the right to secession for oppressed nationalities was modified with the introduction of approaches close to those of Rosa Luxemburg (mainly her work *National Question and Autonomy*, published in Berlin 1909).

6 The imperative of genocide prevention and elimination

1. Judge Baltasar Garzón of the Fifth Chamber of Spain's Audiencia Nacional, New York University Law School, Minutes of the 28 April 2000 Lecture,

cicclegal@iccnow.org. Garzón made legal history by indicting Augusto Pinochet and issuing an international arrest order against the former Chilean dictator in 1998.

2. See summary in Table 6.1. The tool box is the result of worth conducted since 1994, first published in 1998 and presented at the Stockholm Holocaust Memorial Conference in January 2000 (available www.holocaustforum.gov.se/conference/official_documents/abstracts/scherrer.htm. An edited version 'The Challenge of Genocide prevention' is available at http://preventgenocide.org/prevent/Scherrer.htm.

3. Prevent Genocide International is a US-based NGO undertaking projects such as the construction of an educational website to inform the global public about the crime of genocide, to use the world wide web to initiate dialogue about how to create an effective rapid response network and how to facilitate genocide eradication, and provide resources for persons and NGOs in over 50 countries which are not yet party to the UN Genocide Convention. See 'Mission statement and activities' on http://www.preventgenocide.org/.

4. See Scherrer 'Fundamental Human Rights must be protected', Working Paper 28, Copenhagen: COPRI 1998.

5. The report on the United Nations during the 1994 Genocide in Rwanda (Carlsson *et al.* 1999) made 14 detailed recommendations, some of which are discussed in the following text and the notes 6, 12, 20–3 and 44.

6. Ibid., VI, 1. The authors comprehensively link warning and action by recommending 'Identify situations as genocide when warranted and assume the concomitant responsibility to act.' In the future the states (specially the signatory states of the anti-genocide convention) 'must be prepared to identify situations as genocide when the criteria for that crime are met, and to assume the responsibility to act that accompanies that definition.' The authors also underline the importance of genocide prevention: 'More attention needs to be given to preventing crises from escalating or erupting into genocide.' (IV, 1.)

7. See Médecins du Monde 1999, on http://www.millenniumforum.org. The idea behind it is the same: the imperative to protect the vulnerable civilian populations in violent conflict. MM reminds us that in 1918 some 5 per cent of the victims of World War I were civilians, in 1999 95 per cent of victims of violent conflict were civilians. (MM only errs when talking about wars causing high death toll among civilians: it is not war, it is slaughter and genocidal mass violence that causes 95 per cent civilian victims.)

8. More specifically Médecins du Monde proposes that 'a special body with a mandate to collect quantitative information, evaluate situations and make recommendations be created in order that "humanitarian analyses" be taken into account and motivate political decisions. In order to confer on this humanitarian body a high degree of authority and legitimacy, it could be attached directly to the UN Security Council and should be composed of independent experts.' (Médecins du Monde 1999, *op. cit.*)

9. On the initiative of International Alert, the Forum on Early Warning and Early Response, FEWER, was launched in 1996. FEWER became a consortium of inter-governmental organizations, non-governmental organizations and academic institutions, to provide decision makers with information and analysis for early warning and options for early response to conflict. FEWER works in co-operation with regional and local NGOs and IEA – RAS (active all-over FSU) and became operational in 1998; pilot projects in the Caucasus and in the African Great Lakes

regions were started. The network was expanded in 1999 with the aim to cover (potential) spots for mass violence and emergencies world-wide.

10. 'Sharing of early warning observations and news has also matured, though not in formal systems, but through the private press. Whereas a millennium ago, it took a lifetime for news of a crisis to travel a continent, or across an ocean, today, circulation of news about emerging crises, massacres, or of humanitarian standards and views occurs almost instantly.' See *Humanitarian Times*, 29 February 2000.

11. 'For the United Nations, the priority agenda in coming years is to organize effectively for proactive conflict prevention, to develop a clear and accepted policy on humanitarian intervention and the rule of law, and to develop adequately financed legal institutions and its own volunteer police and peace keeping forces to carry out these policies.' Weiss *et al.* 2000.

12. The UN Action Plan to Prevent Genocide, as recommended by Carlsson *et al.* 1999, would 'establish networks of co-operation with humanitarian organizations, academic institutions and other non-governmental organizations with the aim of enhancing early warning and early response capacity.' An 'intensified dialogue' would not only involve the UN Secretariat and the Security Council, but also INGOs, IGOs and regional organizations such as OSCE, OAU, OAS, ASEAN and others.

13. Relating to ethnic conflict Gurr and Harff have developed indicators for the seven concepts of their theoretical model 'to explain why ethnic mobilization and conflict occur' (see: Gurr and Harff 1994, 87–92, 92). The authors aim to predict 'under what circumstances ethnic conflict will occur' (*ibid.*).

14. For the 1980s Gurr compiled 75 groups which were highly discriminated against economically and 94 groups which were highly discriminated against politically. Gurr *Minorities at Risk*, Washington: US-IPP 1993, 44 (table 2.2). In the 1980s the Minorities at Risk project identified 233 ethnopolitical groups (17.3 per cent of the world's population in 1990). The comparable figures for 1998 are 268 groups (17.4 per cent 1998 estimates; see table 1.3 in Gurr *et al.* 2000). Disadvantaged and politically active minorities are present in 116 of the world's 194 states. (Gurr 2000, ch. 1; online at www.bsos.umd.edu/ cidcm/mar).

15. The MAR project developed a scale with seven categories representing different degrees of regime repression, ranging from highest to lowest severity are genocide and politicide; 'dirty war'; pre-emptive control (for example forced assimilation); counterinsurgency; counterinsurgency and accommodation; emergency policing; and conventional policing.

16. Scherrer 1998. 'We Need a Notion of Justice as the Base for Reconciliation Policies, but Foremost We Need the Notion of Prevention' www.transnational.org/ forum/meet/scherrer_justice-reconc.html.

17. 'The critical concern today is no longer lack of early warning of impending crises, but rather the need to follow up early warning with early and effective action.' Annan 1999, § 16 (III. Responding to situations of conflict).

18. Diplomatic efforts are usually the most cost-effective and the most quickly deployed but their impact is limited. In case of genocide alert such diplomatic missions can be a waste of precious time if no operative precautions are taken.

19. In his April 1999 Africa report Annan deals with the nature of conflict in Africa and their impact on society, governance and development. After mentioning colonial conflict roots, Annan assessed 'internal factors' such as 'reliance on centralized and highly personalized forms of governance. Where there is insufficient accountability of leaders, lack of transparency in regimes, inadequate

checks and balances, non-adherence to the rule of law, absence of peaceful means to change or replace leadership, or lack of respect for human rights, political control becomes excessively important, and the stakes become dangerously high.' (Annan, Kofi/UN Secretary General 1999: § 12). The objective is peace enforcement not peacemaking, which can be done by 'facilitating dialogue, defusing tensions, promoting national reconciliation, advancing respect for human rights and institutionalizing peace' (Annan 1999, §18).

20. About the non-applicability of neutrality in the face of mass murder and genocide the UN inquiry stated that in cases of 'risk of massive killings or genocide it must be made clear in the mandate and Rules of Engagement of that operation that traditional neutrality cannot be applied in such situations' (Carlsson *et al.* 1999, IV, 1).

21. Ibid., IV, 2. No direct mentioning was made of Boutros-Ghali's idea of a UN rapid deployment force. The authors see the United Nations as 'the only organization which can bring global legitimacy to peace keeping efforts', which does not exclude initiatives taken at a regional level, but 'the United Nations must be prepared and willing to exercise the responsibility for international peace and security enshrined in its Charter, no matter where the conflict.' This can be read as a response to questions raised by Africans, such as why the UN (and the Western powers) intervened in Bosnia and Yugoslavia and why not in Rwanda? No more double standards!

22. The committee is convened by the Under-Secretary-General for Political Affairs and might acquire some additional functions.

23. Carlsson *et al.* 1999, recommend for that purpose standby arrangements to be enhanced and, 'equally importantly', such agreements shall be 'matched by the political will to allow those resources committed to be deployed in specific conflict situations'.

24. Looking at the UNAMIR disaster in Rwanda 1994 the authors rightly claimed that 'the credibility of United Nations peace keeping depends on operations being given the resources necessary to fulfil their mandates'.

25. Among others responsibilities to conduct contingency planning, to ensure that mandates fully meet the needs on the ground, to adjust the mandates of existing operations when needed, to avoid short-term financial constraints, to adjust according to the changing needs of a mission (for UN-SC), to avoid any doubt as to which Rules of Engagement apply during the mission, and to ensure that the leadership of an operation (Special Representative and Force Command) arrives in a well-planned manner.

26. Garzón is judge at the Fifth Chamber of Spain's *Audiencia Nacional* in Madrid. The Spanish authorities were not too happy about the Pinochet indictment. In Chile, contrary to some fears, the exterritorial prosecution of Pinochet has not halted the process of democratization: the socialist candidate won the presidential race early in 2000 and the rule of law is slowly being applied to the Chilean military. Pinochet's arrest in Britain showed that the top military leaders were not above the law. Chilean courts began to prosecute military leaders in 1999 and may add Pinochet to their long list. This becomes a real possibility after a court lifted Pinochet's immunity as a senator in June 2000.

27. Raphael Lemkin was an international lawyer and former League of Nations specialist; he was a member of the International Bureau for Unification of Criminal Law. 'At the Madrid Conference of 1933 Lemkin introduced the first proposal ever made to outlaw Nazism by declaring it a crime. His idea was that any Nazi who put his foot abroad should be punished by the government of the country he

entered.' In Lemkin's words: 'since the consequences of genocide are international in their implications, the repression of genocide should be internationalized. The culprit should be liable not only in the country in which the crime was committed, but in the country where he might be apprehended. The country where he is found may itself try him or extradite him.' (See Lemkin 1945, in *Free World*.)

28. The Rome Statute, general information on the ICC and other related documents, see the website of the Coalition for an International Criminal Court c/o WFM, 777 UN Plaza, 12th floor New York, www.iccnow.org. On 18 July 1998, the Rome Treaty on the Establishment of an International Criminal Court was opened for signature at the Campidoglio in Rome and 26 states signed it on that day. 'Since the end of WWI, the international community has worked for the ICC, and this achievement is to the credit of the United Nations' (see Cherif Bassiouni: 'International Court for War Crimes – a slow process', in *Chicago Tribune*, 2 May 2000). Bassiouni, DePaul University, was one of the driving forces behind the treaty to establish the ICC.

29. An international criminal court would 'end the situation where we see the Pol Pots, the Pinochets and all the dictators of the world continue to act with impunity', the British Foreign Office minister of state Peter Hain told MPs. Hain hoped Britain would be among the first of 60 states to ratify the treaty. (Press Association Newsfile, 7 November 2000.)

30. Up to 31 December 2001, 48 states have ratified the Rome Statute of the International Criminal Court. Ratifications of the Rome statute in chronological order: Senegal, 2 February 1999; Trinidad and Tobago, 6 April 1999; San Marino, 13 May 1999; Italy, 26 July 1999; Fiji, 29 November 1999; Ghana, 20 December 1999; Norway, 16 February 2000; Belize, 5 April 2000; Tajikistan, 5 May 2000; Iceland, 25 May 2000; Venezuela, 7 June 2000; France, 9 June 2000; Belgium, 28 June 2000; Canada, 7 July 2000; Mali, 16 August 2000; Lesotho, 6 September 2000; New Zealand, 7 September 2000; Botswana, 8 September 2000; Luxembourg, 8 September 2000; Sierra Leone, 15 September 2000; Gabon, 21 September 2000; Spain, 24 October 2000; South Africa, 27 November 2000; Marshall Islands, 7 December 2000; Germany, 11 December 2000; Austria, 28 December 2000; Finland, 29 December 2000; Argentina, 8 February 2001; Dominica, 12 February 2001; Andorra, 30 April 2001; Paraguay, 14 May 2001; Croatia, 21 May 2001; Costa Rica, 7 June 2001; Antigua & Barbuda, 18 June 2001; Denmark, 21 June 2001; Sweden, 28 June 2001; Netherlands, 17 July 2001; Yugoslavia, 6 September 2001; Nigeria, 27 September 2001; Liechtenstein, 2 October 2001; Central African Republic, 3 October 2001; United Kingdom, 4 October 2001; Switzerland, 12 October 2001; Peru, 10 November 2001; Nauru, 12 November 2001; Poland, 12 November 2001; Hungary, 30 November 2001; Slovenia, 31 December 2001.

31. On the last day of the year and with only hours remaining before the deadline for more rigorous procedures, Iran, the United States of America and Israel signed up. The Bush team was not happy about Clinton's decision – after a long period of attempts by the USA to obstruct the ICC.

32. Three-quarters of the world's states, the EU and several influential international organizations endorsed future ratification, such as the Commonwealth, the Francophone summit and the Parliamentary Assembly of the Council of Europe. The drafting of the court's rules of evidence and criminal procedure and the determination of the type of crimes the ICC will prosecute are in progress. On 23 October 2000, Cambodia – the country who suffered a total genocide 1975–79 with 2 million victims – became the 115th state to sign ICC statute.

33. It might be premature to state 'human rights norms have reached consensual (prescriptive) status on the international level by now' Risse *et al. The power of human rights: International norms and domestic change* (Cambridge, Melbourne: Cambridge University Press 1999); too many countries such as North Korea, Iraq, Iran, Afghanistan, Turkey, Congo, Nigeria until recently, Ethiopia and a host of other African countries defy and ignore the claimed consensus. Although, for instance torture is universally condemned and even outlawed by a convention, it is very much part of state crimes in more than 100 states, as of 1999! The convention against torture is signed by conspicuously few states.
34. The last state to become a party to the anti-genocide convention was Switzerland, on recommendation of the government in April 1999. The Swiss ministry of foreign affairs (EDA) noted that the convention outlaws genocide and obliges the signatories to prevent and punish genocide see EDA: 'Beitritt der Schweiz zur Konvention vom 9 Dezember 1948 über die Verhütung und Bestrafung des Völkermordes', Berne, 7 April 1999. EDA wrote that 'regarding the latest events, which give new actuality to this since a longer period existing convention, Switzerland to become a party to it is of particular importance.' A Swiss military court recently convicted a Rwandan *génocidaire* without reference to genocide crimes.
35. Annan gave three 'reasons' why protecting the vulnerable is not guaranteed: 'In the most extreme cases, the innocent become the principal targets of ethnic cleansers and *génocidaires*. International conventions have traditionally looked to states to protect civilians, but today this expectation is threatened in several ways. First, states are sometimes the principal perpetrators of violence against the very citizens that humanitarian law requires them to protect. Second, non-state combatants, particularly in collapsed states, are often either ignorant or contemptuous of humanitarian law. Third, international conventions do not adequately address the specific needs of vulnerable groups, such as internally displaced persons, or women and children in complex emergencies.' (Kofi A. Annan/UNDPI 2000, 46.)
36. The way the intervention was prepared for by NATO states (Rambouillet diktat), the way it was implemented (indiscriminate bombing of civilian targets for 78 days) and the results that came out of it (perpetrator and victim of the ethnic cleansing and massacres were reversed) seem in no way to justify the NATO intervention.
37. Human Rights Watch 2000, 6–8. Now the 'liberated' Albanians kill Serbs and Roma – under the eyes of NATO soldiers; common law criminality in Kosovo is also massively increasing. For the Serbs history was repeated: after the Axis powers invaded and dismembered Yugoslavia in 1941, Kosovo Albanians formed military units to fight for the Nazis, killed more than 10,000 Kosovo Serbs, drove some 100,000 out of Kosovo, and brought immigrants from Albania. Fifty-eight years later the price was again paid by the ordinary Serbs of Kosovo, who were killed in 'revenge acts' and driven out, and by the citizens of Serbia proper, whose country was bombed back to 'pre-industrial times', while their leaders remain in power; the parallels with Iraq are striking.
38. On his visit in Yugoslavia 1999, Cornelio Somaruga, head of ICRC, accused the destruction of water supply systems, electrical power stations and grid, all kinds of industrial facilities, oil refineries, heating plants, broadcast facilities, numerous bridges (including large bridges over the Danube), public buildings (including schools and hospitals); this disrupted civilian life in a way that was clearly disproportional thus 'excessive in relation to the concrete and direct military

advantage anticipated' as codified in article 57 of Protocol I to the Geneva Conventions.

39. According to FRY government estimates NATO's air war against Yugoslavia inflicted between US$20 and 30 billion worth of damage. After the change of power in Serbia, it will be chiefly the EU that will have to cover a share of this huge damage – as a form of reparation and as reintegration of Yugoslavia into the international community. The HRW and AI 1999 reports do not detail the devastation caused by NATO and the number of NATO victims was given as 300 (official numbers are around 2500). 'NATO is bound by these basic rules whenever it goes to war. Particularly when it fights in the name of human rights, it should abide by these standards scrupulously.' (Ibid., 5) HRW rightly criticized disturbing violations of international law by NATO and specially mentioned the Geneva Conventions of 1949 and their Additional Protocols of 1977 with its prohibition to target non-combatants.

40. East Timor is a former Portuguese colony, which was occupied by Indonesia in 1975, after the Portuguese revolution liberated the country. More than a quarter of the population died in the late 1970s; the death toll a result of merciless Indonesian counterinsurgency campaign against rebel FRETILIN. In 1998, Indonesia was bogged down by economic and political crisis. After the fall of dictatorship and political change in Indonesia, a referendum was allowed on 30 August 1999: 80 per cent of the East Timorese braved Indonesian threats to vote for independence. In the aftermath of the referendum, military-backed militias unleashed an orgy of destruction, driving three quarters of the population from their homes. The intervention secured their return. The chief responsible for the massacre, General Wiranto, lost all positions in January 2000 and might be brought to trial.

41. The exception is African Rights, which is an offshoot of Human Rights Watch and came into being in 1993–94, as result of HRW policy and the Rwandan disaster.

42. According to Dietrich Fischer there is an increasing interest in the Non-violent Peace Force at high levels at the UN (as expressed by UNESCO staff members who play an important role in the UN resolution and declaration on the International Year and Decade of a Culture of Peace and Nonviolence). Information on the current status of the proposal to the UN General Millennium Assembly can be found on the international peaceworkers' website www.nonviolentpeaceforce.org.

43. The UN is only one step away from the abyss of bankruptcy. An amount of some US$2 billion is outstanding shortly for armed UN peace keeping operations. If some states (chiefly the USA) are not paying their debts in time (as announced several times) it might in fact push the UN into bankruptcy.

44. The main recommendations of Carlsson *et al.* 1999 are to co-ordinate between the Secretariat, other affected agencies and INGOs, and to co-operate with regional and subregional organizations, to improve efforts to protect civilians in conflict and potential conflict situations (IV 5), to secure the UN personnel as well as the local staff, to improve the flow of information within the United Nations system (IV 8), particularly between UNHCR, UNHCHR, Special Representatives, and UN funds or programmes with the Security Council (IV 9), to improve information on human rights issues (as a base for decision-making in conflict areas), to co-ordinate national evacuation operations with UN missions on the ground (in order to avoid the retreat of an important contingent, as in the case of the Belgium contingent in UNAMIR I), and to exclude criminal states from being members of the Security Council (as Rwanda in 1994).

45. The difference was that 'Jews were to be completely annihilated. The Poles, the Slovenes, the Czechs, the Russians, and all other inferior Slav peoples were to be kept on the lowest social levels.' (Lemkin 1945).

46. Lemkin wrote with bitterness that the genocide policy begun by Germany on its own Jewish citizens in 1933 was considered as an 'internal problem' which the German state (as a sovereign power) should handle 'without interference by other states'. How can there be a principle of non-interference for crimes against humanity? Mankind needs better social and legal institutions 'to protect our civilization against the onslaught of this wanton barbarism in generations to come' (Lemkin 1945: 43).

47. 'The Committee's warning is based on the following government actions: a divide and destroy strategy of pitting ethnic groups against each other, with enormous loss of civilian life; the use of mass starvation as a weapon of destruction; toleration of the enslavement of women and children by government-allied militias; the incessant bombing of hospitals, clinics, schools and other civilian and humanitarian targets; disruption and destabilization of the communities of those who flee the war zones to other parts of Sudan; and widespread persecution on account of race, ethnicity and religion. Taken individually, each of these actions is a disaster for the victims. Taken together, they threaten the physical destruction of entire groups.' See US Holocaust Memorial Museum USHMC, 31 October 2000, online www.ushmm.org/conscience/seditorial.htm; Irving Greenberg and Jerome Shestack: 'Carnage in Sudan' in *Washington Post*, 31 October 2000, www.washingtonpost.com/wp-dyn/articles/A45149-2000Oct30.html. Sudan's dictator Bashir is quoted as saying 'Anyone who betrays this nation does not deserve the honour of living' (picture gallery on genocide and crimes against humanity in Sudan, see pictures on USHMC website www.ushmm.org/conscience/sudan.htm). The Nuba genocide alert was launched in 1991 (see Scherrer 1992); see document by Suleiman Musa Rahal: 'Genocide in the Nuba mountains committed by the NIF-Regime'. Representative of the *Nuba Mountain Solidarity Abroad* at United Nations Work Group for Indigenous Peoples (UN-WGIP), Geneva, July 1991, ECOR 17, 1998, 221–4. Regarding the Dinka see Dr Deng Akuany 'Even today the Arabs still consider Africans as slaves and as people without culture or religion'. Representative of Sudan Peoples' Liberation Movement, SPLM at UN-WGIP, Geneva: UNCHR 1993, 229–32.

48. Here, the wording needs to be more precise than to say, that 'the UN has not done enough' but the UN – and two of five permanent Security Council members – have simply done nothing at all to prevent the genocide in Rwanda, although it was in their power so to do. The UN actually acted against all those who wanted to prevent the announced mass murder, and the Security Council members France and USA did absolutely nothing to stop the ongoing genocide, although they were well informed and could initially watch it on CNN.

49. Clinton's ambassador for war crimes admitted that the United States of America could have reacted 'two or three weeks earlier', according to a personal talk with David J. Scheffer, US ambassador at large for War Crimes, and colleagues from the US State Department, at the Stockholm International Forum on the Holocaust, 27 January 2000. The Secretary of State, Ms Madeleine Albright, was one of the very few people to have refused to talk to the three-strong UN inquiry panel, possibly in an attempt to avoid disclosing her own role; Albright was US ambassador to the UN in 1994.

Bibliography

Abelsen, Emil. 1992. 'Home Rule in Greenland', UNHCR 1992: 109–16.

ABI (Arnold Bergstraesser Institut, Gerald Braun and Jakob Rösel). 1988. *Ethnische Konflikte im internationalen System*. Freiburg i.B.: ABI.

AFB (Arbeitsstelle Friedensforschung Bonn) various years. *AFB-Info*, half-yearly newsletter of the Peace Research Information Unit Bonn; *AFB-Texte*, papers on basic issues of peace and conflict research.

—— 1995. 'Fifty Years of UNESCO: the "Culture of Peace" Programme'. *AFB-Info*, 2: 1–3.

African Rights (Rakiya Omar, Alex de Waal). 1995. *Facing Genocide: The Nuba of Sudan*. London: African Rights.

—— 1994. *Rwanda: Death, Despair and Defiance*. London: AR.

—— 1994b. *Humanitarianism Unbound? Current Dilemmas Facing Multi-mandate Relief Operations in Political Emergencies*. African Rights Discussion Paper 5; London.

AGKED (Arbeitsgemeinschaft Kirchlicher Entwicklungsdienst) various years. *der überblick (du)*, quarterly.

—— 1995. *du*, 2: 'Die Herren des Krieges'.

—— 1994. *du*, 3: 'Die Vereinten Nationen auf dem Prüfstand'.

—— 1993. *du*, 3: 'Ein Volk, ein Staat? Ursachen ethnischer Konflikte'.

—— 1987. *du*, 4: 'Rüstung, Kriege, Entwicklung'.

—— 1985. *du*, 1: 'Krisenregion Zentralamerika'.

—— 1982. *du*, 3: 'Vereinte Nationen: Aufgaben und Probleme'.

—— 1981. *du*, 3: 'Militarisierung der Dritten Welt'.

AKUF (Arbeitsgruppe Konfliktursachenforschung—University of Hamburg) various years. *Das Kriegsgeschehen. Daten und Tendenzen der Kriege und bewaffneten Konflikte*. SEF: Interdependenz, no. 16, 20 and 22.

—— various years. Kriege und bewaffnete Konflikte. website http://www.sozialwiss. uni-hamburg.de/Ipw/Akuf/home.html.

—— (Thomas Rabehl ed.). 2000. *Das Kriegsgeschehen 1999. Daten und Tendenzen der Kriege und bewaffneten Konflikte*. Opladen: Leske und Budrich.

—— (Isabelle Duyvesteyn). 1995. *Wars and Military Interventions since 1945*. AKUF-Arbeitspapier 88; Hamburg: AKUF.

Albertini, Rudolf von. 1987. *Europäische Kolonialherrschaft 1880–1940*. Stuttgart: Steiner.

Amin, Samir. 1994. *L'Ethnie à l'assaut des nations: Yougoslavie, Ethiopie*. Paris: L'Harmattan.

—— 1992. *Das Reich des Chaos: Der neue Vormarsch der Ersten Welt*. Hamburg: VSA-Verlag.

—— 1992a. 'Der Kapitalismus ist eine Utopie', in Koch 1992: 158–66.

Amnesty International. various years. Annual Reports.

—— 1993. *Neues Asylrecht: Abschied vom Schutz für politisch Verfolgte*. Bonn: Amnesty International.

Anderson, Benedikt. 1991. *Imagined Communities. Reflection on the Origin and Spread of Nationalism*. Rev. edition. London and New York: Verso [orig. 1983].

—— 1991. 'Die Erschaffung der Nation durch den Kolonialstaat'. *Argument*, 2: 33, 197–212.

Anderson, Benedikt. 1988. *Die Erfindung der Nation: Zur Karriere eines erfolgreichen Konzeptes.* Frankfurt/M.: Syndikat.

Annan, Kofi. 1999. 'The Causes of Conflict and the Promotion of Durable Peace and Sustainable Development in Africa.' Report of the UN Secretary-General. New York: United Nations, 15 April.

APC–EU (Africa–Caribbean–Pacific–European Union). 1996. 'Lomé Convention'. *The Courier*, 155.

Arnold, Hans. 1995. 'Unvereinte Nationen: Die Weltorganisation und die Friedenssicherung'. *Blätter für deutsche und internationale Politik*, Bonn 10 (1995): 1191–201.

Ashworth, G. ed. 1980. *World Minorities in the 1980s.* Sunbury: Quartermain.

Asian NGO Forum at 45th Session of the UN Commission on Status of Women. 2001. 'Intersectionality of race and gender in the Asia-Pacific'. Teheran/New York, 17–21 February/6–16 March.

Asiwaju, A. I. 1985. *Partitioned Africans: Ethnic Relations across Africa's Boundaries 1884–1984.* Lagos: Lagos University Press.

Asmal, Kader. 1993. 'The Democratic Option, Ethnicity and State Power'. Paper, Grahamstown: Rhodes University.

—— 1990. *Developing a Human Rights Culture.* Durban: NADL.

Assies, Willem J. 1993. 'Self-determination and the "New Partnership"', in Assies and Hoekema 1994: 31–71.

—— and André J. Hoekema eds. 1994. *Experiences with Systems of Self-government by Indigenous Peoples.* IWGIA Document 76; Copenhagen.

Aus Politik und Zeitgeschichte. various years. Supplement to weekly *Das Parlament.*

Azar, Edward E. 1990. *The Management of Protracted Social Conflict. Theory and Cases.* Aldershot: Dartmouth.

—— and John W. Burton. 1986. *International Conflict Resolution. Theory and Practice.* Brighton: Wheatsheaf/Boulder: Rienner.

Bächler, Günther ed. 1994. *Beitreten oder Trittbrettfahren? Die Zukunft der Neutralität in Europa.* Chur: Rüegger.

—— 1993. *Umweltzerstörung: Krieg oder Kooperation? Ökologische Konflikte im internationalen System und Möglichkeiten der friedlichen Bearbeitung* Münster: agenda.

—— 1992. *Perspektiven: Friedens- und Konfliktforschung in Zeiten des Umbruchs.* Chur: Rüegger.

—— *et al.* 1992. *Das Kriegsjahr 1991: Unsere Zukunft: Friedensforscher zur Lage.* Vienna: Verlag des Verbandes der Wissenschaftlichen Gesellschaft Österreichs.

Barley, Nigel. 1986. *The Innocent Anthropologist.* New York: Viking Penguin Inc.

—— 1993. *A Plague of Caterpillars: A Return to the African Bush.* New York: Viking Penguin Inc.

Barth, Frederik ed. 1969. *Ethnic Groups and Boundaries.* Boston: Little.

Bastlund, Carina *et al.* 1994. *Rethinking Refugee Policies: Issues of Humanitarian Intervention, Relief Development and the UN Refugee Definition.* Denmark: International Development Studies, Roskilde University.

Bauman, Zygmunt. 1991. *Modernity and the Holocaust.* Cambridge: Polity Press [original 1989].

Bélanger, Sarah and Maurice Pinard. 1991. 'Ethnic Movements and the Competition Model'. *American Sociological Review*, 56: 446–57.

Bercovitch, Jacob and Jeffrey Z. Rubin eds. 1992. *Mediation in International Relations: Multiple Approaches.* London: St Martin's Press.

—— *et al.* 1991. 'Some Conceptual Issues and Empirical Trends in the Study of Successful Mediation in International Relations'. *Journal of Peace Research*, 28/1: 7–17.

—— and Theodore Anagnoson and Donette L. Wille. 1991. 'Some Conceptual Issues and Empirical Trends in the Study of Successful Mediation in International Relations'. *Journal of Peace Research*, 28/1: 7–17.

Berding, Helmut ed. 1994. *Nationales Bewußtsein und kollektive Identität.* i and ii. Frankfurt/M.: edition suhrkamp.

Berkel, R. van *et al.*/TSER Project Report. 2001. *Inclusion through Participation.* Brussels: TSER.

Bertrand, Maurice. 1995. *UNO: Geschichte und Bilanz.* Frankfurt/M.: Fischer Taschenbuch Verlag.

—— 1994. 'Une nouvelle Charte pour l'Organisation mondiale? Proposition de réponse à quelques questions', 'Réformer ou refaire l'ONU et les instituttions mondiales'. Unpublished paper.

Bienvenue, Rita M. and Jay E. Goldstein, eds. 1985. *Ethnicity and Ethnic Relations in Canada* 2nd edn. Toronto: Butterworths.

Billing, Peter. 1992. *Eskalation und Deeskalation internationaler Konflikte: Ein Konfliktmodell auf der Grundlage der empirischen Auswertung von 288 internationalen Kriege seit 1945.* Berne: Peter Lang.

Birckenbach, Hanne-Margret, Uli Jäger and Christian Wellmann eds. 1995. *Jahrbuch Frieden 1995. Konflikte—Abrüstung—Friedensarbeit.* Munich: Beck.

—— 1995a. *Jahrbuch Frieden 1994. Konflikte—Abrüstung—Friedensarbeit.* Munich: Beck.

Blätter des iz3w and Aktion dritte Welt. various years. *blätter des iz3w.* Newsletter of the Informationszentrum Dritte Welt, Freiburg i.B.

—— 1995. *blätter des iz3w:* '"Ethnopoly": Die Konjunktur von Identitätspolitik'. *Blätter für deutsche und internationale Politik*, monthly.

Blomert, Reinhard, Helmut Kuzmics and Annette Treibel. 1993. *Transformationen des Wir-Gefühls: Studien zum nationalen Habitus.* Frankfurt/M.: edition suhrkamp.

Bodley, John H. 1988. *Tribal Peoples and Development Issues. A Global Overview.* Mountain View, Cal.: Mayfield.

—— 1983. *Der Weg der Zerstörung: Stammesvölker und die industrielle Zivilisation.* Munich: Trickster.

Bondeli, Martin. 1994. '"Andererseits kann gesagt werden..." Peru: eine alternative Entwicklung?', in Judith Janoska, Martin Bondeli and Marc Hofer, *Das Methodenkapitel von Karl Marx.* Basle: Schwabe, 158–70.

Boutros-Ghali, Boutros. 1992. *An Agenda for Peace: Peacemaking and Peace-Keeping. Report of the Secretary-General Pursuant to the Statement Adopted by the Summit Meeting of the Security Council, January 31.* New York: United Nations.

Brahimi, Lakhdar *et al.*/UN Independent Panel. 2001. (see UN General Assembly/Special Committee on Peacekeeping) 2000. Report of the Panel on United Nations Peace Operations. (A/55/305-S/2000/809). New York: United Nations, 21 August. (www.un.org/peace/reports/peace_operations/).

Brass, Paul R. 1991. *Ethnicity and Nationalism: Theory and Comparison.* New Delhi: Sage.

Brock, Lothar. 1995. 'UNO und Dritte Welt: Fünf verlorene Jahrzehnte?', in Deutsches Überseeinstitut 1996: 62–80.

—— 1994. *Friedensforschung im Zeichen immer neuer Kriege.* Bonn: AFB-Texte 1.

—— and Ingomar Hauchler. 1993. *Entwicklung in Mittel- und Osteuropa: Risiken und Chancen der Transformation.* Bonn: EINE Welt 10.

Brosted, Jens and Jens Dahl eds. 1985. *Native Power: The Quest for Autonomy and Nationhood of Indigenous Peoples*. Bergen: Bergen University Press.

Brown, Michael E. and Richard N. Rosencrance eds. 1999. *The Costs of Conflict: Prevention and Cure in the Global Arena*. Oxford: Rowman & Littlefield.

Brubaker, Rogers. 1996. *Nationalism reframed. Nationhood and the national question in the New Europe*. Cambridge/New York: Cambridge University Press.

Bund Lausitzer Sorben (Zwajazk Luziskich Serbow). 1994. 'Rechtsvorschriften zum Schutz und zur Förderung des sorbischen Volkes'. *Domowina Information* (Bautzen/Budysin).

Burger, Julian. 1991. *Die Wächter der Erde*. Reinbek: Rowohlt.

—— 1987. *Report from the Frontier: The State of the World's Indigenous Peoples*. London: Zed Books.

Burns, Tom R. 2001a. Dialogue Workshop: 'Racism and Xenophobia: Key Issues, Mechanisms, and Policy Opportunities'. Brussels, 5–6 April (Programme and Papers).

—— 2001b. Dialogue Workshop: 'Preventing and Combating Racism and Xenophobia in the Enlarged European Union'. Uppsala, 8–9 June (Programme and Papers).

——Masoud Kamali and Jens Rydgren. 2001. 'The social construction of xenophobia and other-isms' Paper. Uppsala: Uppsala Theory Circle.

Burton, John W. 1996. *Conflict Resolution. Its Language and Processes*. Lanham, Md./London: Scarecrow.

—— 1990. *Conflict: Resolution and Prevention*. Basingstoke: Macmillan.

—— *et al.* eds. 1990a. *Conflict: Human Needs Theory*. Basingstoke: Macmillan.

—— and F. Dukes eds. 1990b. *Conflict: Readings in Management and Resolution*. Basingstoke: Macmillan.

—— 1990c. *Conflict: Practices in Management, Settlement and Resolution*. Basingstoke: Macmillan.

Cabral, Amilcar. 1974. *Die Revolution der Verdammten*. Berlin: Rotbuch.

Calließ, Jörg ed. 1994. *Treiben Umweltprobleme in Gewaltkonflikte? Ökologische Konflikte im internationalen System und Möglichkeiten ihrer friedlichen Bearbeitung*. Evangelische Akademie Loccum: Loccumer Protokolle 21; Loccum.

—— and Christine M. Merkel eds. 1995. *Peaceful Settlement of Conflicts as joint Task for International Organisations, Governments and Civil Society*. Evangelische Akademie Loccum: Loccumer Protokolle 24 (1 & 2); Loccum.

—— 1994. *Peaceful Settlement of Conflict: A Task for Civil Society. Third Party Intervention*. Evangelische Akademie Loccum: Loccumer Protokolle 9; Loccum.

—— 1993. *Peaceful Settlement of Conflict: A Task for Civil Society. Possibilities and Instruments for Conflict Management in Cases of Ethno-national Tension*. Evangelische Akademie Loccum: Loccumer Protokolle 7; Loccum.

—— and Bernhard Moltmann eds. 1992. *Jenseits der Bipolarität: Aufbruch in eine 'Neue Weltordnung'*. Loccumer Protokolle 4; Loccum.

Carlsson, Ingvar, Sung-Joo Han, Rufus M Kupolati and United Nations. 1999. *Report of the Independent Inquiry into the actions of the United Nations during the 1994 genocide in Rwanda*. New York: UN.

Carnegie Commission on Preventing Deadly Conflict. 1997. *Preventing Deadly Conflict: Final Report*. Washington DC: Carnegie.

Cars, Göran *et al.*/TSER Project Report. 1999. *Social Exclusion in European Neighbourhoods. Processes, Experiences and Responses*. Brussels: TSER.

Carter Center of Emory University (Conflict Resolution Program) (William Foege, ed.). 1992. *Resolving Intra-national Conflicts: A Strengthened Role for Non-governmental Actors*. Atlanta: Carter Center.

Cashmore, Ellis. 1996. *Dictionary of Race and Ethnic Relations*. Fourth Edition. London/New York: Routledge [orig. 1984].

Center for World Indigenous Studies (Carol J. Minugh, Glen T. Morris and Rudolph C. Ryster). 1989. *Indian Self-governance: Perspectives on the Political Status of Indian Nations in the USA*. Kenmore: CWIS.

Chamberlayne *et al.*/TSER Project Report. 1999. *SOSTRIS. Social Strategies in Risk Societies*. Brussels: TSER.

Chopin, Isabelle/European Network Against Racism. 1999. *Campaigning against racism and xenophobia from a legislative perspective at European level*. Brussels: ENAR.

—— and Jan Niessen/Commission for Racial Equality/Migration Policy Group. 2001. *The Starting Line and the Incorporation of the Racial Equality Directive into the National Laws of the EU Member States and Accession States*. Brussels/London: CRE-MPG, March.

—— 1998. 'Proposal for Legislative Measures to Combat Racism and to Promote Equal Rights in the European Union'. London: Starting Line Group and CRE-UK.

Chrétien, Jean Pierre. 1988. 'Les Ethnies ont une histoire', in J. P. Chrétien and G. Prunier, *Les Ethnies ont une histoire*. Paris: Karthala.

Churchill, Ward. 1991. *Critical Issues in Native North America* (ii). Copenhagen: IWGIA Document 68.

—— 1989. *Critical Issues in Native North America*. Copenhagen: IWGIA Document 62.

Clausewitz, Carl von. 1980. *Vom Kriege. Hinterlassenes Werk. Text der Erstaufl. 1832–1834*. Frankfurt/M.: Ullstein.

Clauss, Bärbel, Katja Koblitz and Detlef Richter eds. 1993. *Kriegsansichten— Friedensansichten: Vom Umgang mit Konflikten*. Münster: Lit.

Commission on Global Governance (Ingvar Carlsson and Shridath Ramphal). 1995. *Our Global Neighbourhood*. Oxford: Oxford University Press.

Confederación de los Pueblos Autóctonos de Honduras. 1993. *Ante-proyecto de decreto de la ley de creación de la reserva de la biosfera Tawahka*. Tegucigalpa.

Conflict Management Group (Harvard University). various years. *CMG Update*, quarterly newsletter.

—— 1994. *Peacekeeping, Peacemaking and Humanitarian Assistance in Areas of Conflict*. Cambridge, Mass.: CMG.

—— 1993. *Methods and Strategies in Conflict Prevention. Report of an Expert Consultation in connection with the Activities of the CSCE High Commissioner on National Minorities*. Rome: CMG.

COPRI (Copenhagen Peace Research Institute). various years. Working papers. Copenhagen: COPRI.

Corbin, Jane. 1994. *Gaza First. The Secret Norway Channel to Peace between Israel and the PLO*. London: Bloomsbury.

Cornell University Peace Studies Program (Milton Esman and Shibley Telhami). 1995. *The Role of International Organizations in Ethnic Conflict*. Ithaca, New York: Cornell University Press.

Council of Europe. 1994. *Framework Convention for the Protection of National Minorities*. Strasburg: Council of Europe.

Council of Ministers of the European Communities (CM–EC). 2000a. *Council Directive 2000/43/EC of 29 June 2000 implementing the principle of equal treatment between persons irrespective of racial or ethnic origin*. Official Journal, OJ L 180/22, 19 July.

—— 2000b. *Council Directive 2000/78/EC of 27 November 2000 establishing a general framework for equal treatment in employment and occupation*. Official Journal, OJ L 303/16, 2 December.

—— (CM–EC). 2000c. *Council Decision Establishing a Community Action Programme to Combat Discrimination*. Official Journal, L 303, 2 December.

CSCE/OSCE (Conference/Organization on Security and Co-operation in Europe). 1994. Documents/statements on or of the CSCE High Commissioner on National Minorities (1994).

—— 1994a. Documents/statements on or of the CSCE High Commissioner on National Minorities (1993).

—— 1992. 'Challenges of Change'. Summit Declaration and Decisions of the 1992 Helsinki Follow-up meeting.

DANIDA (Danish International Development Agency). 1995. *Evaluation of Emergency Assistance to Rwanda:* (1)*Terms of Reference*, (2) *Interim Report*, (3) *Final Report*. Copenhagen: DANIDA.

Debiel, Tobias. 1994. 'Kriegerische Konflikte, friedliche Streitbelegung und die Vereinten Nationen', *Aus Politik und Zeitgeschichte*, B 2.3–16, 9.

—— 1993. 'Kriege' in: SEF, *Globale Trends 1993/94*. Frankfurt/M.: Fischer: 177–97.

—— and Ingo Zander. 1992. *Die Friedensdividende der 90er Jahre*. SEF: Interdependenz 11; Bonn.

Debout, Mathieu. 1991. *Kinder der Steinzeit? Papua zwischen Militär und Mission im Hochland Neuguineas*. Moers: Aragon.

Delanty, Gerard. 2001. 'Ideas for Multicultural Citizenship In Europe'. Discussion Paper. Brussels/Liverpool.

Deng, Francis M., and I. William Zartmann eds. 1991. *Conflict Resolution in Africa*. Washington DC: Brookings Institution.

der überblick: see AGKED (Arbeitsgemeinschaft Kirchlicher Entwicklungsdienst).

Despres, Leo A. ed. 1990. *Ethnicity and Resource Competition in Plural Societies*. The Hague: Mouton.

Destexhe, Alan. 1995. *Rwanda and Genocide in the Twentieth Century*. London/East Haven: Pluto.

Deutsches Überseeinstitut (Hamburg) (Betz, Joachim, and Brüne, Stefan). various years. *Jahrbuch Dritte Welt. Daten, Übersichten, Analysen*. Munich: Beck.

DGVN (Deutsche Gesellschaft für die Vereinten Nationen) various years. Bonn: DGVN-Texte.

—— (Mahbub ul Haq). 1995. *Bericht über die menschliche Entwicklung 1995*. Bonn: UNO.

—— (Klaus Hüfner). 1995a. *Die Vereinten Nationen und ihre Sonderorganisationen: Strukturen, Aufgaben, Dokumente*. Pt. 1: *Die Haupt- und Spezialorgane*. Bonn: DGVN-Texte 40.

—— 1995b. *Die Vereinten Nationen in ihren nächsten 50 Jahren. Ein Bericht der Unabhängigen Arbeitsgruppe über die Zukunft der Vereinten Nationen*. Bonn: UNO.

—— 1992. *Die Vereinten Nationen und ihre Sonderorganisationen: Strukturen, Aufgaben, Dokumente*. Pt. 2: *Die Sonderorganisationen*. Bonn: DGVN-Texte 41.

Dinstein, Yoram. 1981. *Models of Autonomy*. New Brunswick: Transaction Books.

Duffield, Mark. 1994. 'The Political Economy of Internal War: Asset Transfer, Complex Emergencies and International Aid', in Macrae and Zwi (eds) 1994: 50–69.

Duyvesteyn, Isabelle, 1995. *Wars and Military Interventions since 1945*. WP 88/95. Hamburg: AKUF.

Eckhardt, William. 1993. 'Wars and Deaths 1945–1992', in Ruth L. Sivard (ed.) *World Military and Social Expenditures 1993*. Washington DC: World Priorities.

Eckhardt, William. 1991. 'Warfare's Toll 1500–1990', in Ruth L. Sivard (ed.), *World Military and Social Expenditures 1991*. Washington DC: World Priorities.

ECOR (Ethnic Conflicts Research Project) (Christian P. Scherrer ed.). 2001. *War in the Congo and the Role of United Nations.* Study. ECOR 26. Moers: IFEK–IRECOR.

—— 2000. *Ethno-nationalism in the World System. Conflict Management, Human Rights and Multilateral Regimes.* Study (ECOR 24). Moers: IFEK–IRECOR.

—— 1999. *Central Africa: Genocide, Crisis and Change: Peace process in Burundi – Responding to Genocide in Rwanda – Rebellion in Congo.* Study. ECOR 22. Moers: IFEK–IRECOR.

—— 1998. *Free Nagaland – NE-India's unsolved question.* Compiler of Interviews. ECOR 20. Moers: IFEK–IRECOR.

—— 1998. *Ethnicity and Mass Violence. Analysis and macro theory of most extreme contemporary problems. The quest of understanding and preventing Non-Clausewitzean mass violence.* Study. ECOR 19. Moers: IFEK–IRECOR.

—— 1998. *Ongoing Crisis in Central Africa. Conflict impact assessment and policy options.* Study. ECOR 18. Moers: IFEK–IRECOR.

—— 1998. *Struggle for Survival in the Decade of the World's Indigenous Peoples. Analysis and reports from the frontiers.* Compiler of Interviews. ECOR 17. Moers: IFEK–IRECOR.

—— 1997. *Intra-state conflicts and ethnicity: types, causes, escalation and peace strategies.* Study. ECOR 16. Moers: IFEK–IRECOR.

—— 1997. *Nicaragua's Caribbean coast regions: Recognizing multiplicity – many issues unsolved.* Study. ECOR 15. Moers: IFEK–IRECOR.

—— 1997. *Horn of Africa II: Ethiopia, Eritrea and Sudan between change and civil war.* Compiler of Interviews. ECOR 14. Moers: IFEK–IRECOR.

—— 1997. *Horn of Africa I: Ethiopia versus Oromia. 'The empire strikes back'.* Compiler of Interviews ECOR 13. Moers: IFEK–IRECOR.

—— 1997. *Ethnicity and State in Former British India: Struggle for Naga Nation, the Unification of the Chin, Civil Wars in Bangla Desh and in Burma.* ECOR 9. Moers: IFEK–IRECOR. first edition 1995.

—— 1995. *The United Nations in the Decade for the Indigenous Peoples of the World: New Challenges after 50 Years.* ECOR 12. Moers: IFEK–IRECOR.

—— 1995a. *Ethnicity and State in Rwanda 1994/95: Conflict Prevention after the Genocide. Assessment and Documents.* ECOR 11. Moers: IFEK–IRECOR.

—— 1995b. *Ethnicity and State in Burma: Ethno-nationalist Revolution and Civil War 1949–1995.* ECOR 10. Moers: IFEK–IRECOR.

—— 1994. *Ethnicity and State in the Third World: UN-WGIP 1989–94: Strengthening Indigenous Movements.* ECOR 8. Moers: IFEK–IRECOR.

—— 1994a. *Ethnicity and State in Burma 1994: Negotiations between SLORC and Rebels.* ECOR 7. Moers: IFEK–IRECOR.

—— 1993. *Ethnicity and State in Eastern Nicaragua: Autonomous Governance in Yapti Tasba.* ECOR 6. Moers: IFEK–IRECOR.

—— 1992. *Ethnicity and State in Sudan: Civil War, Politics of Famine, and Dim Prospects for Conflict Resolution.* ECOR 3. Tegelen: ECOR.

—— 1992a. *The Liberation of Eritrea.* ECOR 4. Tegelen: ECOR.

—— 1992b. *Ethnicity and State in Ethiopia: The Empire Strikes Back.* ECOR 4. Tegelen: ECOR.

—— 1991. *Ethnicity and State in Burma 1990: Ethno-nationalist Revolution Facing Massive Military Onslaught.* ECOR 2. Zurich: ECOR.

—— 1990. *Neue Weltordnung: 'Dialektik zwischen Orient und Okzident'. Ein Gespräch mit Johan Galtung.* ECOR–Papers Series, no. 3. Moers/Tegelen: ECOR, first edition (1996 second edition).

—— 1989. *Ethnicity and State in Nicaragua: Nicaragua's East Coast Minority Peoples.* ECOR 1. Zurich: ECOR.

ECRI, European Commission against Racism and Intolerance. 2000. *General Policy Recommendation No. 2 on 'Specialist bodies to combat racism, xenophobia, anti-semitism and intolerance on national level' and Appendix.*

—— 1999. *Activities of the Council of Europe with relevance to combating racism and intolerance.* CR(99) 56 final.

Eller, Jack David. 1999. *From Culture to Ethnicity to Conflict: An Anthropological Perspective on International Ethnic Conflict.* Ann Arbor: University of Michigan Press.

Elsenhans, Hartmut. 1985. 'Der periphere Staat: Zum Stand der entwicklungstheoretischen Diskussion', in Franz Nuscheler (ed.) *Dritte Welt-Forschung.* PVS-Sonderheft 16; Opladen.

Elwert, Georg. 1995. 'Gewalt, Gerüchte und das liebe Geld: Kriegsökonomie und ethnische Mobilisierung'. *blätter des iz3w,* 209: 19–21.

—— 1990. 'Nationalismus und Ethnizität'. *Kölner Zeitschrift für Soziologie und Sozialpsychologie,* 3: 404–64.

—— and Peter Waldmann eds. 1989. *Ethnizität im Wandel.* Saarbrücken: Breitenbach.

ENAR, European Network Against Racism. 2000. 'Racism is not an opinion, it is a crime'. Conference Paper. Strasburg, October www.icare.to/.

ENCOP (Environment and Conflicts Project) Volker Böge. 1992. 'Proposal for an Analytical Framework to Grasp "Environmental Conflict"', Schweizerische Friedensstiftung: Berne: ENCOP Paper 1.

—— (Stephan Libiszewski). 1992. 'What Is an Environmental Conflict?', Schweizerische Friedensstiftung: Berne: ENCOP Paper 1.

Engdahl, F. William. 1992. *Mit der Ölwaffe zur Weltmacht: Der Weg zur neuen Weltordnung.* Wiesbaden: Böttinger.

Engert, Steffi, and Uwe Gartenschläger. 1989. *Der Aufbruch: Alternative Bewegungen in der Sowjetunion. Perestroika von unten.* Hamburg: Rowohlt.

Esmann, Milton J. and Shibley Telhami eds. 1995. *International Organizations and Ethnic Conflict.* Ithaca, NY/London: Cornell University Press.

—— 1994. *Ethnic Politics.* Ithaca/London: Cornell University Press.

Estel, Bernd and Tilman Mayer. 1994. *Das Prinzip Nation in modernen Gesellschaften. Länderdiagnosen und theoretische Perspektiven.* Opladen: Westdeutscher Verlag.

Ethnopolitical Studies Centre (Emil Payne ed.) 1993. *Socio-political Situation in the Post-Soviet World.* Moscow: Foreign Policy Association.

EUMC, European Monitoring Centre on Racism and Xenophobia, by SORA/ Thalhammer, Eva *et al.* 2001. *Attitudes towards minority groups in the European Union. A special analysis of the Eurobarometer 2000 survey on behalf of EUMC.* Vienna: EUMC, March.

—— 2000. *Annual Report 1999.* Vienna: EUMC.

European Commission/Angela Liberatore. 1999. *Governance and Citizenship in Europe. Some Research Directions.* Brussels: Research DG F4, December.

European Conference Against Racism 'All different, all equal: from principle to practice'. 2000. Conclusions. Strasburg, 16 October.

European Platform for Conflict Prevention and Transformation, EPCPT/Mekenkamp *et al.* 2001. *Searching for Peace in Asia.*

—— Mekenkamp *et al.* 1999. *Searching for Peace in Africa. An Overview of Conflict Prevention and Management Activities.* Utrecht: EPCPT.

—— and PIOOM/Berghof eds. 1998. *Prevention and Management of Conflicts. An international directory.* Utrecht: EPCPT.

European Women's Lobby (EWL). 2001. 'Combating Racism and Gender Discrimination in the European Union'. A Contribution to the World Conference against Racism. Brussels: EWL.

Evans-Pritchard, Edward E. and Meyer Fortes eds. 1940. *African Political Systems*. London: Oxford University Press, esp. 272–96: 'The Nuer of the Southern Sudan'.

Evers, Hans-Dieter and Tilman Schiel. 1988. *Strategische Gruppen: Vergleichende Studien zu Staat, Bürokratie und Klassenbildung*. Berlin: Reimer.

Fairbanks, John K. 1968. *The Chinese World Order*. Cambridge, Mass: Harvard University Press.

Faulenbach, Bernd and Heinz Timmermann eds. 1993. *Nationalismus und Demokratie: Gesellschaftliche Modernisierung und nationale Idee in Mittel- und Osteuropa*. Koblenz: Klartext.

Fein, Helen ed. 1992. *Genocide Watch*. New Haven: Yale University Press.

Feith, Herb and Alan Smith. 1993. 'Self-determination in the 1990s: The Need for UN Guidelines and Machinery to Resolve Ethno-nationalist Conflicts'. Mimeograph, Canberra.

Fisher, Roger and William Ury. 1987. *Getting to Yes. Negotiating Agreement Without Giving In*. London: Arrow (orig. 1982).

Fisher, Ronald J. 1989. *The Social Psychology of Intergroup and International Conflict*. New York: Springer.

Fitzduff, Mari. 1996. *Beyond Violence: Conflict Resolution Processes in Northern Ireland*. Tokyo: United Nations University.

Forschungsstelle für Sicherheitspolitik und Konfliktanalyse (K. Haltinger, L. Bertossa and K. Spillmann). 1996. *Internationale Kooperationsbereitschaft und Neutralität*. Zurich: ETH.

Foucault, Michel. 1977. *Discipline and Punish: The Birth of the Prison*. Harmondsworth: Penguin.

—— 1973. *The Birth of the Clinic: An Archaeology of Medical Perception*. London: Tavistock.

—— 1972. *The Archaeology of Knowledge*. London: Tavistock.

Fourth World Center for the Study of Indigenous Law and Politics (Marc A. Sills and Glenn T. Morris). 1993. *Indigenous Peoples' Politics: An Introduction*, vol. i. Denver: University of Colorado Press.

Frank, Andre Gunder. 1980. *Abhängige Akkumulation und Unterentwicklung*. Frankfurt/M.: edition suhrkamp.

Freedom House. various years. *Freedom in the World: The Annual Survey of Political Rights and Civil Liberties*. New York: Freedom House.

—— various years. *Freedom Review*.

Fritsch-Oppermann, Sybille ed. 1995. *Minderheiten, Autonomie und Selbstbestimmung: Kollektiv- und Individualrechte von Minderheiten und die Menschenrechte*. Loccumer Protokolle 62; Loccum.

Fürer-Haimendorff, Christoph von. 1982. *Tribes of India: The Struggle for Survival*. London: Oxford University Press.

Furley, Oliver ed. 1995. *Conflict in Africa*. London and New York: I. B. Tauris.

Gabbert, Wolfgang. 1991. 'Ethnizität — die soziale Organisation kultureller Unterschiede', in Gabbert *Creoles — Afroamerikaner im karibischen Tiefland von Nicaragua*. Münster: Lit., 16–37.

Galtung, Johan (and Carl G. Jacobson). 2000. *Searching for Peace. The road to TRANSCEND*. London: Pluto Press.

—— 2000*b*. 'Friedensvisionen für das 21. Jahrhundert'; Schmidt, Hajo/Institut für Frieden und Demokratie: Kultur und Konflikt. Reader. Hagen:IFD.

Galtung, Johan (and Carl G. Jacobson). 1998. *After Violence: 3R, Reconstruction, Reconciliation, Resolution. Coping With Visible and Invisible Effects of War and Violence.* Downloaded from website www.transcend.org.
—— 1997a. Conflict Experience 1952–97. http://www.transcend.org/ [Concrete Proposals for Conflict Resolution in 35 Conflict Cases].
—— 1997b. *Conflict Transformation by Peaceful Means. The Transcend Method.* Manual Prepared for the UN Disaster Management Training Program. Geneva: UN (available on website www.transcend.org).
—— 1996. *Peace by Peaceful Means: Peace and Conflict, Development and Civilization.* London: Sage.
—— 1994. 'Peace and Conflict Research in the Age of Cholera: Ten Pointers to the Future'. Unpublished paper, Malta: IPRA Conference.
—— 1994a. *Menschenrechte — anders gesehen.* Frankfurt/M.: edition suhrkamp.
—— 1994b. 'Conflict Interventions', in Calließ and Merkel eds 1994: 395–417.
—— 1994c. 'Civic Approaches to Conflict', in Calließ and Merkel eds 1994: 115–22.
—— 1992. 'Konfliktformationen in der Welt von morgen', in Bächler *et al.*, eds 1992: 229–61.
—— 1992a. 'Conflict Resolution as Conflict Transformation'. *Revista del IRIPAZ*, 3/6.
—— 1977–88. *Essays in Methodology*, i–iii (1977, 1979, 1988). Copenhagen: Ejlers.
—— 1975–88. *Essays in Peace Research*, i–vi (1975, 1976, 1978, 1980, 1988). Copenhagen: Ejlers.
—— 1972. 'Eine strukturelle Theorie des Imperialismus', in Senghaas ed., 1972: 29–104.
—— 1964. 'An Editorial'. *Journal of Peace Research.* 1/1: 1–4.
Gantzel, Klaus Jürgen. 1996. *Das Kriegsgeschehen 1995. Daten und Tendenzen der Kriege und bewaffneten Konflikte im Jahre 1995.* Bonn: SEF: Interdependenz 20.
—— and Klaus Schlichte eds. various *Das Kriegsgeschehen. Daten und Tendenzen.* Hamburg: AKUF.
—— 1994. *Das Kriegsgeschehen 1993. Daten und Tendenzen der Kriege und bewaffneten Konflikte im Jahre 1993.* Bonn: SEF: Interdependenz 16.
—— Torsten Schwinghammer and Jens Siegleberg. 1992. *Kriege der Welt. Ein systematisches Register der kriegerischen Konflikte 1985–1992.* Bonn: SEF: Interdependenz 13.
—— and Jens Siegelberg. 1990. *Kriege der Welt. Ein systematisches Register der kreigerischen Konflikte 1985–1990.* Bonn: SEF: Interdependenz 4.
Garcia, Ed, Julio Macuja and Benjamin Tolosa. 1994. *Participation in Governance: The People's Right.* Manila: Ateneo University Press.
Gärtner, Heinz. 1992. *Wird Europa sicherer? Zwischen kollektiver und nationaler Sicherheit.* Vienna: Braumüller.
Gellner, Ernest. 1983. *Nation and Nationalism.* Oxford: Blackwell.
—— and Charles Micaud eds. 1972. *Arabs and Berbers.* London: Lexington Books.
GfbV (Gesellschaft für bedrohte Völker). various years. *pogrom: Zeitschrift für bedrohte Völker.*
—— 1995. *pogrom,* 180: 'Am Rande des Abgrunds: Indigene Völker in Sibirien und dem Norden Rußlands'.
—— (Wolfgang Mayr and Inge Geismar). 1994. 'Bedrohte Völker'. Pocket diary, Göttingen: GfbV.
Glasl, Friedrich. 1990. *Konfliktmanagment. Ein Handbuch.* Berne: Haupt. (Typologies 47–82, escalation model 215–87.)
Glavanis, Pandeli *et al.*/TSER Project Report. 2001. *'Muslim Voices' in the European Union: The Stranger within Community, Identity and Employment.* Brussels: TSER.
Glazer, Nathan and Daniel Moynihan eds. 1976. *Ethnicity: Theory and Experience.* Cambridge, Mass.: Harvard University Press.

Goldstone, Richard. 1995. 'Exposing the Truth'. Interview with the UN Prosecutor for the Former Yugoslavia and Rwanda in *The Courier*, 153: 2–5.

Goor, Luc van de, Kumar Rupesinghe and Paul Sciarone eds. 1996. *Between Development and Destruction. An Enquiry into the Causes of Conflict in Post-Colonial States*. The Hague, etc.: NIIR (Netherlands Institute of International Relations) Clingendael/Macmillan/St. Martin's Press.

Greive, Wolfgang ed. 1994. *Identität und Ethnizität*. Loccumer Protokolle 57; Loccum.

Grimshaw, Allen D. 1999. 'Genocide and Democide', in Kurtz and Turpin eds. 1999: Vol. 1, 53–74.

Gruiters, Jan and Efrem Tresoldi. 1994. *Sudan: A Cry for Peace*. Brussels: Pax Christi International.

Gurr, Ted Robert *et al.*/CIDCM, University of Maryland, College Park. 2001. *Peace and Conflict 2001. A Global Survey of Armed Conflicts, Self-Determination Movements, and Democracy*. College Park: CIDCM.

—— 2000. *Peoples versus States*. Washington: US Institute of Peace Press (online at Minorities at Risk site www.bsos.umd.edu/cidcm/mar.)

—— and Barbara Harff. 1996. *Early Warning of Communal Conflicts and Genocide: Linking Empirical Research to International Responses*. Tokyo: United Nations University Press.

—— 1994. 'Peoples against States: Ethnopolitical Conflict and the Changing World System'. *International Studies Quarterly*, 38: 348–77.

—— 1993. *Minorities at Risk. A Global View of Ethnopolitcal Conflict*. Washington DC: US Institute of Peace.

—— 1993a. 'Why Minorities Rebel. A Global Analysis of Communal Mobilization and Conflict since 1945'. *International Political Science Review*, 14/2: 161–201.

—— and Barbara Harff. 1992. 'Victims of the State: Genocides, Politicides and Group Repression since 1945'. *Revista del IRIPAZ*, 3/6: 96–110.

Haar, Wim De. 1995. 'Ethnic Conflict Management Theory. An Introduction to Theory and Practice: The Case of Bosnia', in Calließ and Merkel eds. 1995: 214–33.

Habermas, Jürgen. 1994. 'Annerkennungskämpfe im demokratischen Rechtsstaat'. *Revista del IRIPAZ*, 5/9: 5–25.

Harff, Barbara (with Ted R. Gurr and Alan Unger). 1999. 'Preconditions of Genocide and Politicide: 1955–1998'. Paper. State Failure Task Force.

—— (and Ted R. Gurr). 1997. *Systematic Early Warning of Humanitarian Emergencies*. Maryland: CIDCM.

—— 1992. 'Recognizing Genocides and Politicides'; in Helen Fein ed. *Genocide Watch*. New Haven: Yale University Press, 1992: 27–41.

Heinrich-Böll-Stiftung (Christian Büttner *et al.*). 1995. *Zivile Konfliktbearbeitung und Gewaltprävention: Beiträge gesellschaftlicher Akteure zur Umsetzung der Agenda for Peace*, HBS-Dokumentationen 8; Cologne.

Heintze, Hans-Joachim. 1995. *Autonomie und Völkerrecht: Verwirklichung des Selbsbestimmungsrechtes der Völker innerhalb bestehender Staaten*. Bonn: SEF: Interdependenz 19.

Heinz, Marco. 1993. *Ethnizität und ethnische Identität. Eine Begriffsgeschichte*. Bonn: Holos (diss. University of Bonn).

Héraud, Guy. 1963. *L'Europe des ethnies*. Paris: Presses d'Europe.

HIIK, Heidelberger Institut für Internationale Konfliktforschung, various years. *Conflict barometer*. Online http://www.hiik.de/

—— 2000. *KOSIMO Manual*. Online http://www.hiik.de

Hirsch, Klaus ed. 1996. *Interkulturelle Konflikte. Seminar zu Konzepten und Verfahren interkulturellen Lernens*. Protokoll 9; Bad Boll.

Hobsbawm, Eric J. 1992. *Nations and Nationalism Since 1780. Programme, Myth, Reality.* Second Edition. Cambridge: Cambridge University Press.

—— and Terence Ranger eds. 1983. *The Invention of Tradition.* Cambridge: Cambridge University Press.

Hoekema, André. 1994. *Do Joint Decision-Making Boards Enhance Chances for a New Partnership between State and Indigenous Peoples?* Amsterdam: University of Amsterdam.

Hofmann, Rainer. 1992. 'Minderheitenschutz in Europa. Überblick über die völker- und staatsrechtliche Lage'. *Zeitschrift für ausländisches öffentliches Recht und Völkerrecht,* 52/1: 1–66.

Hofmeier, Rolf and Völker Matthies eds. 1992. *Vergessene Kriege in Afrika.* Göttingen: Lamuv.

Holsti, Kalevi J. 1996. *The State, War, and the State of War.* Cambridge: Cambridge University Press.

—— 1991. 'War Issues, Attitudes, and Explanations', in Kalevi ed. *Peace and War: Armed Conflicts and International Order 1648–1989.* Cambridge: Cambridge University Press, 306–34.

Hörig, Reiner. 1990. *Selbst die Götter haben sie uns geraubt: Indiens Adivasi kämpfen ums Überleben.* Göttingen: GfbV.

Horn, Klaus. 1988. *Gewalt — Aggression — Krieg.* Baden-Baden: AFK-Schriftenreihe 13.

Horowitz, Donald L. 1992. 'Irredentas and Secession: Adjacent Phenomena, Neglected Connections', in A. D. Smith ed. *Ethnicity and Nationalism.*

—— 1985. *Ethnic Groups in Conflict.* Berkeley: University of California Press, esp. ch. 6: 229–88.

Huber, Konrad J. 1994. *The CSCE's New Role in the East: Conflict Prevention.* Radio Liberty: Research Report 3: 31.

—— 1994a. *Averting Inter-ethnic Conflict. An Analysis of the CSCE High Commissioner on National Minorities in Estonia.* Emory University, Atlanta: Conflict Resolution Program, Carter Center.

—— 1993. *The CSCE and Ethnic Conflict in the East.* Radio Liberty: Research Report 2: 31.

Human Rights Watch (Africa Watch, Americas Watch, Asia Watch, Middle East Watch, Helsinki Watch). various. *World Report.* New York: Fund for Free Expression.

—— Alison Des Forges. 1999. *Leave None to Tell the Story. Genocide in Rwanda.* New York: HRW, March (on www.hrw.org/)

Huntington, Samuel P. 1996. *The Clash of Civilizations and the Remaking of World Order.* New York: Simon & Schuster.

—— 1996a. *Kampf der Kulturen. Die Neugestaltung der Weltpolitik im 21. Jahrhundert.* München/Wien (Europaverlag).

—— 1993a. 'The clash of civilizations?' in *Foreign Affairs,* Summer 1993, 23–49.

—— 1993b 'If not civilizations, what? Paradigms of the post-cold war world'. *Foreign Affairs,* Nov./Dec. 1993, 186–94.

IA (International Alert). 1994. *Self-determination. Report of the Martin Ennals Symposium.* Saskatoon: IA.

—— (Rupesinghe, Kumar). 1994a. 'Towards a Policy Framework for Advancing Preventive Diplomacy'. Paper, Amsterdam.

—— 1993. *Conflict in the North Caucasus and Georgia.* London: IA.

ICAR (Institute for Conflict Analysis and Resolution). various years. Working Papers. Fairfax: George Mason University.

ICRA (International Commission for the Right of Aboriginal Peoples). various years. *Info-Action.*

IISS (International Institute for Strategic Studies). various years. *The Military Balance.* London: Brassey's.
—— various years. *Strategic Survey.* Oxford, London: Oxford University Press/IISS.
INEF (Institut für Entwicklung und Frieden) (Tobias Debiel). 1995. 'Die Vereinten Nationen in einer Welt des Umbruchs: Chancen und Grenzen einer kooperativen Friedenspolitik'. *Sozialwisssenschaftliche Informationen*, 24/3: 196–200.
—— 1993. *Krisen, Kriege und Konfliktbewältigung. Daten – Analysen – Schlußfolgerungen.* Duisburg: INEF.
—— 1993a. 'Kriege', in SEF, *Globale Trends 93/94. Daten zur Weltentwicklung.* Frankfurt/M.: Fischer, 177–97.
Institute of Southeast Asian Studies (Lufan Chen *et al.*). 1990. *Proceedings of the 4th International Conference on Thai Studies.* Kunming: ISAS, i–iv.
Instituto Indigenista Interamericano (Rodolfo Stavenhagen and Diego Iturralde eds). 1990. *Entre la ley y la costumbre: El derecho consuetudinario indígena en América Latina.* Mexico: Siglo XXI.
International Social Science Council (Raimo Väyrynen ed.). 1991. *New Directions in Conflict Theory: Conflict Resolution and Transformation.* London: Sage.
Isajiw, Wsevolod W. 1999. *Understanding Diversity: Ethnicity and Race in the Canadian Context.* Toronto: Thompson Educational Publishing Inc.
Ishiyama, John T. and Marijke Breuning. 1998. *Ethnopolitics in the New Europe.* Boulder/London: Lynne Rienner Publishers.
ISHR (International Service for Human Rights)/MAHR (Minnesota Advocates for Human Rights). 1992. *Orientation Manual: The UN Commission on Human Rights.* Geneva: ISHR.
IWGIA (International Work Group for Indigenous Affairs). various years. 82 Docs. 1971–94 on situation of indigenous peoples/newsletters.
—— 1995. *El Mundo indígena 1994–5.* Copenhagen: IWGIA.
—— 1993. *Yearbook 1992.* Copenhagen: Scantryk.
—— 1989. *Indigenous Self-government in the Americas.* Copenhagen: IWGIA Document 63.
JEEAR (Joint Evaluation of Emergency Assistance to Rwanda) (David Millwood, chief ed.). 1996. *The International Response to Conflict and Genocide: Lessons from the Rwanda Experience.* 5 vols. Copenhagen: JEEAR.
Jenkins, J. Craig and Bert Klandermans eds. 1995. *The Politics of Social Protest: Comparative Perspectives on States and Social Movements.* London: UCL Press.
Johann, Bernd. 1993. *GUS ohne Zukunft? Eine Region zwischen Zerfall und neuen Allianzen.* SEF: Interdependenz 15; Bonn.
Jongman, Albert J. ed. 1996. *Contemporary Genocides: Causes, Cases, Consequences.* Leiden: PIOOM.
Kadelbach, Stefan. 1992. 'Zwingende Normen des humanitären Völkerrechts', in Deutsches Rotes Kreuz, *Humanitäres Völkerrecht.* Bonn: DRK, 118–24.
Kamali, Masoud. 2001. 'Conceptualizing the "Other", Institutionalized Discrimination, and Cultural Racism' Paper. Uppsala: Dept. for Sociology.
Kawczynski, Rudko. 1997. 'The Politics of Romani Politics'; in *Transitions*, Vol. 4, No. 4, September.
Kelman, Herbert C. and V. Lee Hamilton. 1989. *Crimes of Obedience: Towards a Social Psychology of Authority and Responsibility.* New Haven: Yale University Press.
Khader, Bichara. 1997. 'L'imagination collectif occidental sur l'orient arabo-musulman' in Lehners 1997.
Kidron, Michael and Ronald Segal. 1992. *Der politische Weltatlas.* Bonn: Dietz.

Kiernan, Ben. 2000. 'Bringing the Khmer Rouge to Justice'. *Human Rights Review.* 1, 3: 92–108, April–June.

—— 1996. *The Pol Pot Regime. Race, Power, and Genocide in Cambodia under the Khmer Rouge, 1975–79.* New Haven and London: Yale University Press.

Klute, Georg. 1995. 'Der Tuaregkonflikt in Mali und Niger', in Deutsches Überseeinstitut 1996: 146–61.

Koch, Christine ed. 1992. *Schöne neue Weltordnung.* Zurich: Rotpunkt.

Koppe, Karlheinz. 1995. *Der unerreichbare Friede: Überlegungen zu einem komplexen Begriff und seinen forschungspolitischen Konsequenzen.* Bonn: AFB-Texte 1.

Kößtler Reinhart and Tilman Schiel. 1995. 'Ethnizität und Ethno-nationalismus'. *Widerspruch,* 30: 47–59.

Kramer, Fritz and Christian Sigrist eds. 1978. *Gesellschaften ohne Staat.* 2 vols. Frankfurt/M.: Syndikat.

Kriesi, Hanspeter. 1995. 'The Political Opportunity Structure of New Social Movements: Its Impact on Their Mobilization', Jenkins and Klandermans eds. 1995: 167–98.

Kritz, Neil J. ed. 1995. *Transitional Justice: How Emerging Democracies Reckon with Former Regimes.* Washington DC: US Institute for Peace Press.

Kühne, Winrich. 1992. 'Demokratisierung in Vielvölkerstaaten'. *Nord-Süd aktuell,* 2/VI: 290–300.

Kurtz, Lester and Jennifer Turpin eds. 1999. *Encyclopedia of Violence, Peace, and Conflict.* 3 vols. San Diego: Academic Press.

Kymlicka, Will. 1996. *Multicultural Citizenship. A Liberal Theory of Minority Rights.* Oxford: Oxford University Press.

Laely, Thomas. 1994. 'Ethnien à la burundaise', in Müller co-ord.: 207–47.

Lederach, John Paul. 1998. *Preparing For Peace: Conflict Transformation across Cultures.* Syracuse: Syracuse University Press.

—— 1994. 'Building Peace: Sustainable Reconciliation in Divided Societies'. Draft paper, Tokyo: United Nations University.

Lehners, Jean Paul ed. 1997. *L'Islam et l'espace euro-méditerranéen.* Luxembourg: CUL.

Lemarchand, René. 1994. 'The Apocalypse in Rwanda'. *Cultural Survival Quarterly,* 18/2–3: 29–33.

Lenin, Vladimir Ilyich. 1988. 'Zur Frage der Nationalitäten', in *Lenins Vermächtnis.* Moscow: APN.

—— 1961. 'Über das Selbstbestimmungsrecht der Nationen', in *Lenins·Werke,* xx. Berlin: Dietz.

—— 1961a. '§14: Die nationale Frage: Die Aufgaben des Proletariats in unserer Revolution', in *Werke,* xxiv. Berlin: Dietz.

Lentz, Carola. 1995. 'Joker im Spiel. Ethnizität: Moralische Gemeinschaft oder politische Strategie?'. *blätter des iz3w,* 209: 14–17.

Leuzinger, Elsy ed. 1985. *Kunst der Naturvölker.* Frankfurt am M./Berlin/Vienna: Propyläen Kunstgeschichte 22.

Lijphart, Arend. 1984. *Democracies: Patterns of Majoritarian and Consensus Government.* New Haven: Yale University Press.

—— 1977. *Democracy in Plural Societies. A Comparative Exploration.* New Haven and London: Yale University Press.

Lyons, Gene M. and Michael Mastanduno eds. 1995. *Beyond Westphalia? State Sovereignty and International Intervention.* Baltimore: The Johns Hopkins University Press.

Lyons, Oren R. and John Mohawk eds. 1992. *Exiled in the Land of the Free: Democracy, Indian Nations, and the US Constitution.* Santa Fe, New Mexico: Clear Light Publishers.

Macrae, Joanna and Anthony Zwi eds. 1994. *War and Hunger: Rethinking International Responses to Complex Emergencies.* London: Zed.

Mader, Gerald, Wolf-Dieter Eberwein and Wolfgang R. Vogt/ÖSFK eds. 1997. *Europa im Umbruch: Chancen und Risiken der Friedensentwicklung nach dem Ende der Systemkonfrontation.* ÖSFK-Studien für europäische Friedenspolitik, Band 2. Münster (agenda).
—— 1996. *Frieden durch Zivilisierung? Probleme – Ansätze – Perspektiven.* Band 1. Münster (agenda).
Mall, Hugh. 1998. *The Peacemakers: Peaceful Settlements of Disputes Since 1945.* Basingstoke: Macmillan Press.
Mandal, B. P., Chairman, Backward Classes Commission/Government of India. 1980. *Report of the Backward Classes Commission. First Part. Volumes I & II.* New Delhi: GOI 31/12/80.
Mann, Michael ed. 1990. *The Rise and Decline of the Nation State.* Oxford: Blackwell.
Mannens, Wolf. 1994. 'Cultural Rights: A Bridge between Individual and Collective Rights'. Mimeograph, The Hague.
Martinelli, Marta. 1998. *Mediation Activities by non-State Actors: an Account of Sant'Egidio's Initiatives.* Working Paper 9. Copenhagen: COPRI.
Martiniello, Marco. 2001. 'Affirmative Action and Racism'. Paper for the Workshop Racism and Xenophobia. Brussels, 5–6 April.
Matthies, Volker ed. 1995. *Vom Krieg zum Frieden: Kriegsbeendigung und Friedenskonsolidierung.* Bremen: Temmen.
—— 1993. *Frieden durch Einmischung?* Bonn: Dietz.
—— 1992. 'Kriege in der Dritten Welt', in Nohlen and Nuscheler eds.: 359–73.
Mazrui, Ali. 1994. 'Global Apartheid: Structural and Overt'. *Alternatives,* 19, 195–3.
Mbaya, Etienne Richard. 1992. 'Relations between Individual and Collective Human Rights', in Hohnholz *et al.* eds. *Law and State.* Tübingen: Institut für wissenschaftliche Zusammenarbeit, 7–23.
McDonald, John W. and Diane B. Bendahmane. 1987. *Conflict resolution: Track two diplomacy.* Washington DC: US Government Printing.
McDowall, David. 1991. *The Kurds.* London: MRG.
Medecins Sans Frontieres/Doctors Without Borders. 1997. *World in Crisis. The Politics of Survival at the End of the Twentieth Century.* London and New York: Routledge.
Meillassoux, Claude. 1976. *'Die wilden Früchte der Frau' – Über häusliche Produktion und kapitalistische Wirtschaft.* Frankfurt/M.: Syndikat. (Orig. 1975. *Femmes, greniers et capitaux* Paris: Maspero.)
Memorial Human Right Center, Moscow. 1992. *Annual Report.* Moscow: HRC.
Merkel, Christine M. 1995. *Zivile Konflikttransformation. Gutachten: Zivile Gewaltreduzierung und Streitbeilegung in ethno-nationalen Spannungsfeldern. Aufgaben, Konzepte, Instrumente und Institutionen.* Loccum: Evangelische Akademie Loccum.
MFS (Militärische Führungsschule Zurich) (Karl W. Haltinger). 1995. *Sicherheit '95: Sicherheits- und verteidigungspolitische Meinungsbildung im Trend.* Zurich: Militärische Führungsschule.
Midlarsky, Manus I. ed. 1992. *The Internationalization of Communal Strife.* New York: Routledge.
Mietzsch, Oliver. 1993. 'Der Beitrag von internationalen Regimen zur Lösung von Konflikten', in Clauss, Koblitz and Richter eds. 1993: 165–80.
—— 'Die KSZE als regionale Institution zur Konfliktverhütung', in Staack ed. 1992: 91–117.
Mitchell, Christopher R. 1997. *Intractable Conflicts: Keys to Treatment.* Work Paper no. 10. Gernika: Gernika Gogoratuz
—— 1995. *Cutting Losses: Reflections on Appropriate Timing.* Working Paper no. 9. Fairfax: George Mason University, Institute for Conflict Analysis and Resolution (ICAR).

—— and Michael Banks eds. 1996. *Handbook of Conflict Resolution. The Analytical Problem-Solving Approach.* London and New York: Pinter.

Modood, Tariq and Werbner Pnina eds. 1997. *The Politics of Multiculturalism in the New Europe: Racism, Identity and Community.* London: Zed.

Moser, Rupert ed. 2000. *Die Bedeutung des Ethnischen im Zeitalter der Globalisierung.* Bern: Haupt.

—— 1989. 'Kulturelle und interethnische Dissonanzen als Ursache von Migrationen', in W. Kälin and Rupert Moser eds. *Migrationen aus der Dritten Welt.* Berne: Haupt.

Moynihan, Daniel P. 1993. *Pandaemonium: Ethnicity in International Politics.* Oxford: Oxford University Press.

MRG (Minority Rights Group). See *ad loc.* for reports and papers.

Müller, Hans-Peter co-ord. 1994. *Ethnische Dynamik in der außereuropäischen Welt.* Zürcher Arbeitspapiere zur Ethnologie 4; Zurich.

—— et al. eds. 1992. *Kulturelles Erbe und Entwicklung: Indikatoren zur Bewertung des soziokulturellen Entwicklungsstandes.* BMZ-Forschungsberichte 98; Munich.

Nabudere, Dani W. 1994. 'The African Challenge'. *Alternatives,* 19: 163–71.

Nagel, Joane and Matthew C. Snipp. 1993. 'Ethnic Reorganization: American Indian Social, Economic, Political and Cultural Strategies for Survival'. *Ethnic and Racial Studies,* 16/2: 201–35.

NCDO (National Committee for Sustainable Development, NL). 1997. *The Amsterdam Appeal 1997. Enhancing European Union conflict prevention. An action plan for European leaders and civil society.* Amsterdam: NCDO.

—— 1997. *Background papers to the European conference on conflict prevention.* Den Haag: RAI.

—— 1996. *Genocide is not a natural catastrophe. Background paper for the conference.* Amsterdam: NCDO.

NCIV (Nederlands Center voor Inhemse Volken/Dutch Centre for Indigenous Peoples). 1993. *Outline of the Congress 'Voices of the Earth': Indigenous Peoples, New Partners and the Right of Self-determination in Practice.* Amsterdam: NCIV.

NGO Working Group on Migration and Xenophobia. 2001. Preparatory Committee Inter-sessional open-ended Working Group. Geneva: UNHCHR, 6–9 March. www.migrantwatch.org

Nickel, Rainer. 2000. 'The promises of Equality and Recognition' in *Equality and Difference in Multiethnic Societies – Legal Protection against Discrimination as a Safeguard for Recognition.* Articles written on the official topics of the European Conference Against Racism. www.icare.to/

Nietschmann, Bernard. 1997. 'Areas of inquiry dealing with extreme problems in the world: State-Nation-Conflicts – A prevented debate'. Interview with Bernard Nietschmann; in: ECOR 17: 37–58.

—— 1987. 'Militarization and Indigenous Peoples'. *Cultural Survival Quarterly,* 11/3: 1–16.

Nispen, Patricia van. 1994. 'International Conflict Prevention and Resolution: Communication Process Agreement'. Unpublished paper.

Nohlen, Dieter and Franz Nuscheler eds. 1992–93. *Handbuch der Dritten Welt.* 3rd edn. 8 vols. Bonn: Dietz. And in this, i. 14–30: 'Ende der Dritten Welt?'

Nuscheler, Franz. 1994. *Internationale Migration: Ein Hauptproblem für Global Governance.* INEF–Report 9; Duisburg.

—— 1992. 'Menschenrechte und Entwicklung', in Nohlen and Nuscheler eds.: i. 269–86.

OECD, Organization for Economic Co-operation and Development – Development Assistance Committee (OECD-DAC). 1997. *DAC Guidelines on Conflict, Peace and Development Co-operation*. Paris: OECD/OCDE.

Olzak, Susan and Joane Nagel eds. 1986. *Competitive Ethnic Relations*. New York: Academic Press.

OSCE, Organization for Security and Co-operation in Europe. various years. OSCE Decisions. Reference Manual. Prague: OSCE.

—— 1999. OCSE Handbook. Vienna: OSCE.

Ottaway, Marina. 1999. *Africa's New Leaders: Democracy or State Reconstruction?* New York: Carnegie Institution for International Peace.

Paffenholz, Thania. 1995. 'Vermittlung: Kriegsbeendigung und Konfliktregelung durch Einmischung', in Matthies ed.: 39–56.

Palley, C. *et al.* 1991. *Minorities and Autonomy in Western Europe*. London: MRG.

Payne, Emil. 1994. 'Settlement of Ethnic Conflict in Post-Soviet Society', in Calließ and Merkel, eds.

—— ed. (Ethnopolitical Studies Centre). 1993. *Socio-political Situation in the Post-Soviet World*. Moscow: Foreign Policy Association.

PCA (Permanent Court of Arbitration). 1993. *Optional Rules for Arbitrating Disputes between Two Parties of which Only One is a State*. The Hague: International Bureau of the PCA.

—— 1993a. *First Conference of the Members of the Court*. The Hague: PCA/Foundation Asser Institute.

—— 1992. *Optional Rules for Arbitrating Disputes between Two States*. The Hague: International Bureau of the PCA.

Pfetsch, Frank R., ed. 1996. *Globales Konfliktpanorama 1990–95*. Münster: Lit.

—— 1991. *Konflikte seit 1945*. 5 vols. (Europe, Arab world/Islam, black Africa, America, Asia), Freiburg: Ploetz.

Philip, George, ed. 1993. Weltatlas. Hamburg: Xenos.

Phillips, Alan and Allan Rosas eds. 1993. *The UN Minority Rights Declaration*. Turku/Åbo: Åbo Academic Printing and London: MRG.

PIOOM (Projecten Interdisciplinair Onderzoek naar de Oorzaken van Mensenrechtenschendigen/Interdisciplinary Research Program on Root Causes of Human Rights Violations: Center for the Study of Social Conflicts) (Albert Jongman and Alex Schmid). various years. *World Conflict Map*. Leiden: PIOOM.

—— 1994. 'Contemporary Armed Conflicts. A Global Inventory'. *PIOOM Newsletter*, 6/1: 17–21.

—— (Nico J. Schermers and Alex Schmid). 1994a. *Prospects for Soviet Successor States based on a Consociational Analysis*. PIOOM Paper 3; Leiden.

Plant, Roger. 1994. *Land Rights and Minorities*. London: MRG.

pogrom: see GfbV.

Prunier, Gerard. 1995. *The Rwanda Crisis 1959–94. History of a Genocide*. London: Hurst.

Puxon, Grattan. 1987. *Europe's Gypsies*. London: Minority Rights Group.

Rabehl, Thomas and Stefan Trines eds. 1997. *Das Kriegsgeschehan 1996*. IWP-Arbeitspapier 6. Hamburg: AKUF.

Reiterer, Albert F. 1988. *Die unvermeidbare Nation: Ethnizität, Nation und nachnationale Gesellschaft*. Frankfurt/M.: Campus.

Rémond, Bruno. 2001. 'How Regions are Governed', in *Le Monde diplomatique*, May, www.en.monde-diplomatique.fr/2001/05/14europe

Reporter ohne Grenzen (Salgado, Sebastião). 1996. *Die Würde des Menschen. 100 Fotos für die Pressefreiheit*. Frankfurt/M.: Reporter ohne Grenzen.

República de Nicaragua. 1987. Estatuto de la autonomía de las regiones de la Costa Atlántica, Ley No. 28. *La Gaceta, Diario Oficial*, XCI/238: 2833–8.

Reyneri, Emilio *et al*./TSER Project Report. 1999. Migrant Insertion in the Informal Economy Deviant Behavior and the Impact on Receiving Societies. Final Report ERB, SOE 2 CT95-3005. Brussels: TSER.

Roberts, Adam. 1994. 'The Crisis in UN Peacekeeping'. *Survival*, 36/3: 93–120.

Ropers, Norbert. 1998. 'Towards a Hippocratic Oath of Conflict Management?' in EPCP, PIOOM, Berghof *et al*. 27–33.

—— 1995. *Peaceful Intervention: Structures, Processes and Strategies for the Constructive Regulation of Ethnopolitical Conflicts*. Berghof Report 1; Berlin.

—— 1995a. *Die Bearbeitung ethno-politischer Konflikte in der Staten- und Gesellschaftswelt: Siebenbürgen 1990–95*. Berlin: Berghof Forschungszentrum für konstruktive Konfliktbearbeitung.

—— and Tobias Debiel. eds. 1995. *Friedliche Konfliktbearbeitung in der Staaten- und Gesellschaftwelt*. Bonn: EINE Welt 13.

—— 1993. 'Weltordnung und Weltinnenpolitik', in SEF 1993: 21 ff.

—— and Peter Schlotter. 1993. 'Minderheitenschutz und Staatszerfall'. *Blätter für deutsche und internationale Politik*, 38/3: 859–71.

—— 1992. *Die KSZE: Multilaterales Konfliktmanagement im weltpolitischen Umbruch*. Bonn: SEF.

—— 1992. *Transnationale Konfliktmanagement als Beitrag zu einer weltweiten Zivilkultur*. Duisburg: INEF.

—— 1989. 'Regimeanalyse und KSZE-Prozeß' in B. Kohler-Koch ed., *Regime in den internationalen Beziehungen*. Baden-Baden: Nomos, 315–42.

Rosenberg, Tina. 1995. 'Overcoming the Legacies of Dictatorships'. *Foreign Affairs*, 74/3: 134–52.

Rothchild, Donald. 1991. 'An Interactive Model for State–Ethnic Relations', in Deng and Zartmann eds. 1991: 190–215.

—— and Victor A. Olorunsola eds. 1983. *State versus Ethnic Claims: African Policy Dilemmas*. Boulder, Col.: Westview Press.

Rothman, Jay. 1997. *Resolving Identity-Based Conflict in Nations, Organizations, and Communities*. San Francisco: Jossey-Bass Publishers.

—— 1992. *From Confrontation to Cooperation: Resolving Ethnic and Regional Conflict*. London: Sage.

Rothschild, Joseph. 1981. *Ethnopolitics. A Conceptual Framework*. New York: Columbia.

Rummel, Rudolph J. 1997. *Statistics of Democide: Genocide and Mass Murder since 1900*. New Brunswick, NJ: Transaction.

—— 1994. *Death by Government: Genocide and Mass Murder*. New Brunswick, NJ: Transaction.

—— 1994a. 'Power, Genocide and Mass Murder'. *Journal of Peace Research*, 31/1: 1–10.

Rupesinghe, Kumar. 1992. *Early Warning and Conflict Resolution*. Basingstoke: Macmillan Press and New York: St. Martin's Press.

—— 1992a. *Internal Conflict and Governance*. Basingstoke: Macmillan Press and New York: St Martin's Press.

—— 1992b. *Ethnicity and Conflict in a Post-Communist World: The Soviet Union, Eastern Europe and China*. Basingstoke: Macmillan Press and New York: St Martin's Press.

—— and Khawar Mumtaz eds. 1996. *Internal Conflicts in South Asia*. Oslo/ London: PRIO/Sage.

—— and Valery A. Tishkov eds. 1996. *Ethnicity and Power in the Contemporary World*. Tokyo: United Nations University Press.

Ruzza, Carlo. 1999. 'Anti-racism and EU institutions'. Article prepared for presentation at the 1999 ESA Conference Social Movements Network, Essex University.

Ryan, Stephen. 1993. 'Grass-roots Peacebuilding in Violent Ethnic Conflict', in Calließ and Merkel eds. 1993: 313–42.

—— 1990. *Ethnic Conflict and International Relations*. Aldershot: Dartmouth.

Samad, Yunas. 2001. 'Emergence of Islam as Identity rather than Fundamentalism'. Paper. Dialogue Workshop 'Racism and Xenophobia'. Brussels, April.

Sandole, Dennis J. D. 1992. *Conflict Resolution in the Post-Cold War Era: Dealing with Ethnic Violence in the New Europe*. Working Paper No. 6, October 1992. Fairfax: George Mason University, Institute for Conflict Analysis and Resolution (ICAR).

Satha-Anand, Chaiwat. 1985. *Of Imagination and the State*. Thammasat University Paper 6; Bangkok.

Scherrer, Christian P. 2003. *Responses to Genocide*. Forthcoming.

—— 2002a. *Ethnicity, Nationalism and Conflict*. Forthcoming.

—— 2002b. *Genocide and Crisis in Central Africa: Conflict Roots, Mass Violence, and Regional War*. Westport CT/London: Praeger.

—— 2001a. *Ethnizität, Krieg und Staat in der Dritten Welt: Zentralamerika, Burma, Horn of Afrika. Fallbeispiele und Vergleich*. IFEK-Reports 3–5. Moers: IFEK-IRECOR.

—— 2000. *Indigene Völker und Staat: Von Krieg und äußerer Einmischung zum Frieden durch Autonomie. Der Fall Nicaragua*. IFEK Report 3. Moers: IKEK-IRECOR.

—— 2000a. 'Genocide and Genocide Prevention: General Outlines Exemplified with the Cataclysm in Rwanda'. Copenhagen: Vandkunsten (Rev. of http://www.copri.dk/copri/downloads/14–1999.doc).

—— 2000b. 'Ethno-Nationalismus als globales Phänomen' in Moser ed. 17–90.

—— and Håkan Wiberg eds. 1999. *Ethnicity and Intra-state Conflict: Types, Causes and Peace Strategies*. Aldershot: Ashgate.

—— and Jan Oberg 1999. *Peace Education for Burundi*. Lund: TFF.

—— 1999. 'Structural Prevention and Conflict Management, Imperatives of' in Lester Kurtz ed. in chief *Encyclopedia of Violence*, Vol. 3. San Diego, London: Academic Press 1999, 381–429.

—— 1999a. 'Towards a theory of modern genocide. Comparative genocide research: definitions, criteria, typologies, cases, key elements, patterns and voids'; in: *Journal of Genocide Research*, 1(1): 13–23, Basingstoke: Carfax Publ.

—— 1999b. 'Ethnisierung und Völkermord in Zentralafrika: Rwanda und Burundi – Länder der Tausend Massengräber' in Stig Förster and Georg Hirschfeld eds. *Der Genozid in der modernen Gesellschaft*. Münster (Jahrbuch für Historische Friedensforschung 7): 101–29.

—— 1999c. 'Feindbild Islam und "Kampf der Kulturen"? – Kritik an Huntington und Bemerkungen zur aktuellen Entwicklung in der Türkei' in Jean-Paul Lehners ed. *L'Islam et l'espace euro-méditerranéen*. Luxembourg: Centre Universitaire.

—— 1999d. 'Towards a comprehensive analysis of ethnicity and mass violence: Types, dynamics, characteristics and trends' in H. Wiberg and C. P. Scherrer eds. 52–88.

—— 1999e. *The Impact of Aid on the Genocide and the Ongoing Crisis in the Great Lakes Region. Review of First Draft*. Paris: OECD-DAC.

—— 1999f. 'Genocide and Genocide prevention: The case of Rwanda' in Jensen SørenBuus ed. *Genocide and mass traumatization*. Glostrup: UH-PI.

Working Paper 18 – 1999. Copenhagen: COPRI (http://www.copri.dk/copri/downloads/18-1999.doc)

—— 1998. *Ethnicity and Mass Violence*. Moers: IFEK-IRECOR.

Working Paper 18 – 1998a. *Towards a theory of modern full-scale genocide.* COPRI: Working Paper 22 – 1998.

—— 1998b. *The United Nations and World's Indigenous Peoples.* COPRI: Working Paper 19–98.

—— 1998c. *Resolving the Crisis in Central Africa I and II.* COPRI: Working Papers 16/31.

—— 1998d. *Africa torn by Violent Intra-state Conflict.* Copenhagen: COPRI: Working Paper 12/98.

—— 1998e. *The First Indian Government in the Americas: Caught up in Neglect, Confusion and Disunity – Ways out?.* Copenhagen: COPRI: Working Paper 7/98.

—— 1998f. *CONF Research Plan 1997–2000.* Copenhagen: COPRI: Working Paper 5/98.

—— 1998g. 'We need a notion of justice as the base for reconciliation policies, but foremost we need the notion of prevention'. Lund: TFF www.transnational.org/forum/meet/scherrer_justice-reconc.html

—— 1997. *Ethno-Nationalismus im Zeitalter der Globalisierung: Ursachen, Strukturmerkmale und Dynamik ethnisch-nationaler Gewaltkonflikte. (Handbuch zu Ethnizität und Staat, ii).* Münster: agenda.

—— 1997a. *Ethnisierung und Völkermord in Zentralafrika: Genozid in Rwanda, Bürgerkrieg in Burundi und die Rolle der Weltgemeinschaft.* Frankfurt/M. and New York: Campus.

—— 1997b. *Intra-state Conflict, Ethnicity and Mass Violence.* Copenhagen: COPRI: Working Paper 22/97.

—— 1997c. 'Mehrheiten versus Minderheiten: Zur Kritik erklärungswürdiger Konzepte', *Wissenschaft und Frieden*, 15, 1: 8–13.

—— 1997d. *Central Africa: Conflict Impact Assessment and Policy Options.* Copenhagen: COPRI: Working Paper 25/97.

—— 1996. *Ethno-Nationalismus im Weltsystem: Prävention, Konfliktbearbeitung und die Rolle der internationalen Gemeinschaft. (Handbuch zu Ethnizität und Staat, i).* Münster: agenda.

—— 1996a. 'Ursachen und Wahrnehmung von inter-ethnischen und ethno-nationalen Konflikten' in Hirsch 1996: 53–70.

—— 1996b. 'Der Diktatur den Hahn zudrehen: Föderalismus für Nigeria'. *pogrom*, 187, 46–8.

—— 1996c. 'Ethnisierung und Völkermord in Rwanda 1994'. *Widerspruch*, 30: 61–86.

—— 1996d. 'Der apokalyptische Völkermord in Rwanda: Ein Verbrechen des Gehorsams' in Sareika Kinkelbur and Schmidt eds, *Peace is a Revolutionary Idea.* Iserlohn: EAI, 29–56.

—— 1996e. 'Nunavut-Autonomie macht's möglich: Die Inuit setzen auf Partnerschaften mit indigenen Völkern weltweit', *pogrom*, 189, 42–44.

—— 1996f. 'Krieg der Zivilisationen? Zur Huntington-Debatte'. *Widerspruch.* 32: 99–107.

—— 1996g. 'Ethno-Nationalismus als globale Herausforderung' in Deutsches Überseeinstitut 1997. Munich: Beck, 35–55.

—— 1996h. *Überlegungen zur Neuorientierung der Friedens- und Konfliktforschung angesichts der ethno-nationalistischen Herausforderung.* Bonn: AFB-Texte 1.

—— 1995. 'Justice and Conflict Prevention after the Genocide: A Primary Task for Rwanda' in Calließ and Merkel eds.: i. 351–90.

—— 1995a. 'Selbstbestimmung statt Fremdherrschaft: Sezessions- und Autonomie-regelungen als Wege zur konstruktiven Bearbeitung ethno-nationaler Konflikte' in Ropers and Debiel eds.: 257–83.

—— 1995b. 'Burma: Ethno-nationalistische Guerrilla und die letzten großen Teakwälder', in Calließ and Merkel eds.: 173–206.

Working Paper 18 – 1995*c*. 'Gruppenkonflikte als Krisenherde' in Fritsch-Oppermann ed.: 63–101.

—— 1995*d*. 'Korrelation der Kolonialpolitiken mit der postkolonialen ethno-nationalistischen Konflikthaftigkeit. Register der 101 Kriege 1985–1994', in Fritsch-Oppermann ed.: 151–7.

—— 1994. *Ethno-nationalismus als globales Phänomen*. Duisburg: INEF-Report 6.

—— 1994*a*. 'Ethnische Strukturierung und politische Mobilisierung in Äthiopien', in Müller co-ord.: 133–205.

—— 1994*b*. 'Ethno-Nationalismus als Interventionsfall?' in Bächler ed.: 149–64.

—— 1994*c*. 'Regional Autonomy in Eastern Nicaragua (1990–94): Four Years of Self-government Experience in Yapti Tasba' in Assies and Hoekema eds.: 109–48.

—— 1994*d*. 'The UNPO: Another Type of NGO', Tegelen: ECOR.

—— 1994*e*. 'Ethnizität und Krise des Staates in der Dritten Welt' in Greive ed.: 37–62.

—— 1993. 'Recognizing Multiplicity: Conflict Resolution in Eastern Nicaragua', in Calließ and Merkel eds.: 209–80.

—— 1993*a*. 'Der Dritte Weltkrieg'. *Überblick*, 3: 29–33.

—— 1993*b*. 'A Model Process for Indigenous Peoples'. Interview with Howard R. Berman, Amsterdam (mimeo).

—— 1991. 'Dialektik zwischen Orient und Okzident: Thesen von Johan Galtung'. *Dritte Welt*, 4: 101–12.

—— 1991*a*. 'Selbstbestimmung für indigene Nationalitäten'. *Widerspruch*, 22: 41–50.

—— 1989. 'Ethnizität und Staat in der Dritten Welt. Projektbericht'. Unpublished paper.

—— 1988. *Tourismus und Selbstbestimmung – ein Widerspruch. Das Fallbeipiel Tanzania*. Berlin: Reimer.

—— (Hans Petter Buvollen). 1994. 'Nicaragua: Indians and New Alliances'. *Indigenous Affairs*, 1: 22–35.

Schiemann Rittri, Catherine *et al.* 1995. *Friedensbericht 1995: Tod durch Bomben. Wider den Mythos vom ethnischen Konflikt*. Chur: Rüegger.

Schlichte, Klaus. 1994. 'Is Ethnicity a Cause of War?'. *Peace Review*, 6/1: 59–65.

SEF (Stiftung Entwicklung und Frieden/Development and Peace Foundation). various years. EINE Welt: Texte der Stiftung Entwicklung und Frieden and Interdependenz (listed *ad loc.*).

—— various years. *Globale Trends. Fakten Analysen Prognosen*. Frankfurt/M.: Fischer.

—— various years. *Policy Papers*. Bonn.

—— 1996. *Entwicklung Kulturen Frieden. Visionen für eine neue Weltordnung*. Bonn

—— 1995. *Mit der WTO ins nächste Jahrhundert*. Bonn: SEF Policy Paper 1.

—— 1991. *Gemeinsame Verantwortung in den 90er Jahren: Die Stockholmer Initiative zu globaler Sicherheit und Weltordnung*. Bonn: EINE Welt 5.

—— 1991*a*. *Menschen auf der Flucht: Fluchtbewegungen und ihre Ursachen*. Bonn: SEF: Interdependenz 8.

Senghaas, Dieter. 1997. 'Die fixe Idee vom Kampf der Kulturen' in Blätter. Bonn 2/: 213–21.

—— 'Bibliographische Notizen zum zivilisatorischen Hexanon'; in Jörg Calließ ed.: *Wodurch und wie konstituiert sich Frieden? Das zivilisatorische Hexanon auf dem Prüfstand*. Papers. Loccum: EAL.

—— 1996. 'Religion – Nation – Europa: Erkenntnisse über gelungene Vergemeinschaftungsprozesse' in Mader *et al*: 55–66.

—— 1995. 'Treiben Umweltkonflikte in Gewaltkonflikte? Überlegungen' in Calließ: 301–10.

Senghaas, Dieter. 1995a. 'Frieden als Zivilisierungsprojekt', in Vogt ed.: 37–54.

—— 1993. 'Einheimische Konflikte oder die Wiederkehr der Nationalismus', in Calließ and Merkel eds: 61–81.

—— 1993a. 'Global Governance: How Could This Be Conceived', in Jörg Calließ ed. *Auf dem Weg zur Weltinnenpolitik.* Evangelische Akademie Loccum: Loccumer Protokolle, 21/93: 103–25.

—— 1992. 'Therapeutische Konfliktintervention in ethnonationalistischen Konflikten', in Senghaas *Friedensprojekt Europa.* Frankfurt/M.: edition suhrkamp, 116–40.

—— 1992a. *Die Zukunft der internationalen Politik nach dem Ende des Ost-West-Konfliktes.* Unpublished conference paper.

—— 1990. *Europa 2000: Ein Friedensplan.* Frankfurt: edition suhrkamp.

—— 1989. *Regionalkonflikte in der Dritten Welt: Autonomie und Fremdbestimmung.* Baden-Baden: Nomos.

—— 1988. *Konfliktformationen im internationalen System.* Frankfurt/M.: edition suhrkamp.

—— ed. 1978. *Weltwirtschaftordnung und Entwicklungspolitik: Plädoyer für Dissoziation.* Frankfurt/M.: edition suhrkamp.

—— ed. 1974. *Periphere Kapitalismus. Amalysen über Abhängigkeit und Unterentwicklung.* Frankfurt/M.: edition suhrkamp.

—— ed. 1972. *Imperialismus und strukturelle Gewalt. Analysen über abhängige Reproduktion.* Frankfurt/M.: edition suhrkamp.

—— and Michael Zürn. 1992. 'Kernfragen für die Friedensforschung der neunziger Jahre' in *Politische Vierteljahreszeitschrift*, 33: 455–62.

Seton-Watson, Said, ed. 1977. *Nation and States: An Enquiry into the Origins of Nations and the Politics of Nationalism.* Boulder, Col.: Westview Press.

SFS (Schweizerische Friedensstiftung) (Klingenburg, Konrad and Mietzsch, Oliver). 1992. *Herausforderung im Wandel: Die KSZE.* Berne: Arbeitspapiere der SFS 15.

Shearer, David. 1998. *Private Armies and Military Intervention.* IISS Adelphi Paper 316. London: Oxford University Press.

Sheehy, Ann and Bohdan Nahaylo. 1980. *The Crimean Tatars, Volga Germans and Meskhetians: Soviet Treatment of Some National Minorities.* London: MRG Report 6.

Shiels, Frederick ed. 1984. *Ethnic Separatism and World Politics.* Lanham: University Press of America.

Siebold, Thomas. 1995. *Die soziale Dimension der Strukturanpassung – eine Zwischenbilanz.* Duisburg: INEF-Report 13.

Siedschlag, Alexander. 1995. 'Konfliktmanagment in der post-bipolaren Welt: Möglichkeiten und Grenzen–Konzepte–Konfliktmodelle', in Calließ and Merkel eds. (2): 447–85.

Siegelberg, Jens. 1995. 'Umweltprobleme und Gewaltkonflikte aus Sicht der Kriegsursachenforschung', in Calließ ed.: 67–71.

Siim, Birte et al./TSER Project Report. 2000. *Gender and Citizenship: Social Integration and Social Exclusion in European Welfare States.* Brussels: TSER.

Singer, J. David and Melvin Small. 1984. *The Wages of War 1816–1980. A Statistical Handbook, with Disputes and Civil War Data.* Ann Arbor: CoW.

SIPRI (Stockholm International Peace Research Institute). various years. *SIPRI Yearbooks. Armaments, Disarmament and International Security.* Oxford: Oxford University Press/SIPRI.

—— 2000. SIPRI Yearbook 2000. http://editors.sipri.se/pubs/yearb.html

Sisk, Timothy D./USIP. 1996. *Power Sharing and International Mediation in Ethnic Conflicts.* Washington DC: United States Institute of Peace Press.

Smith, Anthony David. 1992. 'Ethnicity and Nationalism', in Smith ed. *Ethnicity and Nationalism.* Leiden: Brill.

—— 1991. *National Identity*. London: Penguin Books, esp. 'The Ethnic Basis of National Identity', 19–42.

Smith, Paul ed. 1991. *Ethnic Groups in International Relations. Comparative Studies on Governments and Non-dominant Ethnic Groups in Europe, 1850–1940*. Aldershot: Dartmouth.

Sollenberg, Margareta and Peter Wallensteen. various years. 'Major armed conflicts'. SIPRI Yearbooks.

Soyinka, Wole. 1995. 'Nacht über Nigeria'. Interview with Wole Soyinka. *Tages-Anzeiger Magazin*, 45: 56–63.

Staack, Michael. ed. 1992. *Aufbruch nach Gesamteuropa: Die KSZE nach der Wende im Osten*. Münster: Lit.

Staub, Ervin. 1992. *The Roots of Evil. The origins of Genocide and Other Group Violence*. Cambridge: Cambridge University Press (original 1989).

Stavenhagen, Rodolfo. 1996. *Ethnic Conflict and the Nation-State*. Basingstoke and London: Macmillan.

—— 1994. 'Indigenous Rights: Some Conceptual Problems'. Amsterdam: Seminar paper.

—— 1990. *The Ethnic Question: Conflicts, Development and Human Rights*. Tokyo: UN University Press.

Strazzari, Francesco. 1998. *Security-building in Protracted Ethnopolitical Conflict. Third Parties along Southeast European Peripheries*. Unpublished paper. Florence: EUI.

STT (Survie Touarègue – Temoust). 1994. *Issalan n Temoust*, first issue of newsletter of SST.

Stüben, Peter E. ed. 1988. *Die neuen 'Wilden': Umweltschützer unterstützen Stammesvölker: Theorie und Praxis der Ethno-Ökologie*. Ökozid 4; Gießen.

—— and Valentin Thurn eds. 1991. *WüstenErde: Der Kampf gegen Durst, Dürre und Desertifikation*. Gießen: Ökozid 7.

Summer Institute of Linguistics/Barbara F. Grimes, chief ed., R. S. Pittman and J. E. Grimes, eds. 1996. *Ethnologue. Languages of the World*. 13th edition. Dallas: SIL. (Catalogue of some 6700 languages spoken in 228 countries) http://www.sil.org/ethnologue/

Suny, Ronald. 1991. 'Sozialismus und Nationalitätenkonflikt in Transkaukasien', *Argument*, 186: 213–26.

Survival (quarterly of the International Institute for Strategic Studies). 1993. 35/1: 'Ethnic Conflict and International Security'.

Sutter, Alex. 1995. 'Die Fremden und Wir'. Mimeograph.

Swedish Ministry for Foreign Affairs. 1997. *Preventing Violent Conflict. A Study. Executive Summary and Recommendations*. Stockholm: UM.

Terkessidis, Mark. 2001. 'Das rassistische Wissen. Wie Wissenschaft und soziale Praxis "Minderwertigkeit" produzieren'; iz3w, no. 253: 38–41.

—— 2000. *Migranten*. Berlin: Rotbuch.

—— 1998. *Psychologie des Rassismus*. Darmstadt: Westdeutscher Verlag.

Tetzlaff, Rainer. 1993. *Menschenrechte und Entwicklung*. EINE Welt 11; Bonn. (Pub. in English as: *Human Rights and Development*, EINE Welt 12).

—— et al. 1992. 'Politicized Ethnicity: An Underestimated Reality in Post-colonial Africa', in *Law and State*, 24–53. Tübingen: IWZ.

Thompson, Dennis and Dov Ronen eds. 1986. *Ethnicity, Politics and Development*. Boulder: Lynne Rienner.

Tierra Nuestra – Visiones Latinoamericanas/Agencia de Prensa Internacional Alternativa. 1995. 'El retorno de los caudillos'. *Tierra Nuestra* 11: 1–21.

Tishkov, Valery. 1997. *Ethnicity, Nationalism and Conflict in and after the Soviet Union. The Mind Aflame*. London: Sage

Trenin, Dimitri. 1994. 'Russians as Peacemakers'. *Internationale Politik und Gesellschaft*, 257–66.

Trimikliniotis, Nicos. 2001. 'The Role of State Processes in the Production of "Ethnic" Conflict: The Nation-State Dialectic, *Europeanisation* and Globalisation'. Workshop Paper. Limasol/Brussels.

Tungavik (Inuit of Nunavut), and Canadian Ministry of Indian Affairs and Northern Development. 1993. Agreement between the Inuit of the Nunavut Settlement Area and Her Majesty the Queen in Right of Canada. Ottawa.

UN General Assembly. 1992. Declaration on the rights of persons belonging to national or ethnic, religious and linguistic minorities. (General Assembly, 47th session, 1 December. 1992).

UNCHR (United Nations Commission on Human Rights)/ECOSOC. various years. Reports of the Working Group on Indigenous Populations. Annual sessions, July/August in Geneva.

—— 2000. Establishment of a Permanent Forum on Indigenous Issues. Decision of UNCHR. E/2000/87. Geneva 27 April.

—— (Petter Wille). 2000. Indigenous Issues. Report of the open-ended intersessional *ad hoc* working group on a permanent forum for indigenous people. E/CN.4/2000.86. Geneva 18 March.

—— (Luis-Enrique Chávez). 1999. Indigenous Issues. Report of the working group established in accordance with CHR resolution 1995/32. E/CN.4/2000/84. Geneva 6 December.

—— (Erica-Irene Daes). 1999. Indigenous people and their relationship to land. Second progress report. E/CN.4/1999/20. Geneva 22 June.

—— 1999. Report on the Fifty-fifth Session. E/CN.4/1999/167. Geneva.

—— (Miguel Alfonso Martínez). 1999. Study on treaties, agreements and other constructive arrangements between states and indigenous peoples. Final Report. E/CN.4/Sub.2/1999/20. Geneva 22 June.

—— 1995. Considerations of a permanent forum for indigenous people (E/CN.4/Sub.2/AC.4/1995/7).

—— 1995a. International decade of the world's indigenous people (E/CN.4/Sub.2/AC.4/1995/5).

—— (Miguel Alfonso Martínez). 1995b. Study on treaties, agreements and other constructive arrangements between states and indigenous peoples. Second progress report (E/CN.4/Sub.2/AC.4/1995/27).

—— 1994. Technical review of the UN draft declaration on the rights of indigenous peoples (E/CN.4/Sub.2/AC.4/1994/2/Add.1).

—— 1993. Draft declaration on the rights of indigenous peoples (E/CN.4/Sub.2/1993/26).

—— 1980. The right to self-determination. (CHR/SC-PDPM: rapporteur Héctor Gros Espinel).

—— (L. E. Johansen, *et al.*). 1992. Report of the meeting of experts to review the experience of countries in the operation of schemes of internal self-government for indigenous peoples, Nuuk, Greenland, September 1991. Statements and background papers: (E/CN.4/1992/42/Add.1).

—— (Miguel Alfonso Martínez). 1992a. Discrimination against indigenous peoples: study on treaties. (E/CN.4/Sub.2/1992/32).

—— 1991. Preliminary report. (E/CN.4/Sub.2/AC.4/1991/Misc.2).

UNDHA (United Nations Department of Humanitarian Affairs). various years. *DHA News.*

—— 1995. *DHA News Special: 1994 in Review.*

UNDP (United Nations Development Programme). various years. *Human Development Report.* New York: UNDP. Online www.undp.org

UNDPI (United Nations Department of Public Information). 2000. (Kofi A. Annan). *'WE, the Peoples'. The role of the United Nations in the 21st Century. New Century, new challenges.* Doc E.00.I.16. New York: UNDPI.

—— 1996. *The United Nations and Somalia, 1992–1996.* New York: UNDPI. (The United Nations Blue Book Series, Vol. VIII).

UNESCO (United Nations Educational, Scientific and Cultural Organization). 1994. First consultative meeting of the Culture of Peace programme, final report (CPP-94/CONF.601/3). Paris: UNESCO.

—— 1994a. *'The Culture of Peace programme: From national programmes to a project of global scope'.* Paris: UNESCO.

—— 1994b. First international forum on the Culture of Peace in San Salvador, 16–18 February, final report. Paris: UNESCO.

—— 1994c. 'Toward a Culture of Peace', Focus in UNESCO Sources, 62: 7–16.

—— 1993. Action programme to promote a Culture of Peace. Summary. Paris: UNESCO.

UNICEF (United Nations Children's Fund)/Mine Awareness Project. 1993. The UNICEF Mine Awareness Project in El Salvador. San Salvador: UNICEF.

United Nations. 1994. *Seeds of a New Partnership: Indigenous Pepoles and the United Nations.* New York.

—— (José R. Martínez Cobo) 1986. *Study of the Problem of Discrimination against Indigenous Populations,* i–iv. New York: United Nations. Doc. E/CN.4/Sub.2/1986/7 and Add. 1–4; vol. v, *Conclusions, Proposals and Recommendations,* was issued as a separate publication.

UNPD, United Nations Population Division. 1999. *World Population Prospects: The 1998 Revision* (http://www.popin.org/pop1998/)

UNPO (Unrepresented Nations and Peoples Organization). various years. Member factsheets and reports on members' human rights situations.

—— 1995. *General Assembly IV. Summary Report and Documentation.* The Hague.

—— 1994. *The First Three Years. 1991–1994. Report.* The Hague.

—— 1994a. UNPO Members 1994. The Hague.

—— 1994b. *Conflict Prevention: The Post-Cold War Challenge.* i: Report CSCE. ii: Project. The Hague.

—— 1993. *Self-determination in Relation to Human Rights, Democracy and the Protection of the Environment.* The Hague.

—— (David Goldberg). 1992. *Human Rights Dimensions of Population Transfer.* The Hague.

—— 1992a. *Preventing the Use of Force by States against Peoples under their Rule.* Conference report. The Hague.

—— 1992b. *Summary of the UNPO.* The Hague.

—— (Lord Ennals). 1992c. *Report of an UNPO Mission to Abkkhazia, Georgia and the Northern Caucasus.* The Hague.

—— 1991. *Covenant of the UNPO* (incl. amendments of August 1991). The Hague.

UNRISD (United Nations Research Institute for Social Development). various. years. UNRISD Discussion Papers (DP).

—— various years. UNRISD Occasional Papers (OP).

—— 1995. *Ethnic Violence, Conflict Resolution and Cultural Pluralism. Report.*

—— (Jeff Haynes). 1995a. *Religion, Fundamentalism and Ethnicity. A Global Perspective.* Geneva: UNRISD DP 65.

—— (WSP: War-torn Societies Project). 1995b. *The Challenge of Peace: An Interactive Newsletter,* vol. 1.

—— 1995c. *Rebuilding War-Torn Societies: An Action-Research Project on Problems of International Assistance in Post-conflict Situations.* Geneva: UNRISD.

—— (Yusuf Bangura). 1994. *The Search for Identity: Ethnicity, Religion and Political Violence.* Geneva: UNRISD OP 6.

—— (Valery Tischkov). 1994a. *Nationalities and Conflicting Ethnicity in Post-communist Russia.* Geneva: UNRISD DP 50.

—— (Crawford Young). 1994b. *Ethnic Diversity and Public Policy: An Overview.* Geneva: UNRISD OP 8.

—— (Ralph R. Premdas) 1993. *Ethnicity and Development: The Case of Fiji.* Geneva: UNRISD DO 46.

—— (Abbas Rashid and Farina Shaheed). 1993a. *Pakistan: Ethno-politics and Contending Elites.* Geneva: UNRISD DP 45.

Unser, Günther. 1988. *Die UNO: Aufgaben und Strukturen der Vereinigten Nationen.* 4th edn. Munich: Beck/dtv.

Uppsala Conflict Data Project, Uppsala University. various years. 'Major Armed Conflicts', in SIPRI Year-books.

—— (Taylor B. Seybolt) 2000. 'Major Armed Conflicts', in *SIPRI Yearbook 2000.* Oxford: Oxford University Press.

Väyrynen, Raimo ed. 1991. *New Directions in Conflict Theory: Conflict Resolution and Conflict Transformation.* London: Sage.

Villagrán de Leon, Francisco. 1994. 'The OAS and the Democratic Development'. *Revista del IRIPAZ,* 5/9: 145–52.

Vogt, Wolfgang R., ed. 1995. *Frieden als Zivilisierungsprojekt: Neue Herausforderungen an die Friedensund Konfliktforschung.* Baden-Baden: AFK-Schriftenreihe 21.

—— 1990. 'Positiven Frieden wagen', in Vogt. ed. *Mut zum Frieden.* Darmstadt: Wissenschaftliche Buchgesellschaft.

Volger, Helmut. 1995. 'Die vergessenen Völker'. *Blätter für deutsche und internationale Politik,* 11: 1358–66.

Waldmann, Peter. 1988. *Ethnischer Radikalismus: Ursachen und Folgen gewaltsamer Minderheitenkonflikte.* Baden-Baden: Nomos.

Walker, Jenonne. 1993. 'International Mediation of Ethnic Conflicts'. *Survival,* 35/1: 102–17.

Wallensteen, Peter and Margareta Sollenberg. 1998. 'Armed conflict and regional conflict complexes, 1989–97' in *Journal of Peace Research,* 35/5: 621–34.

—— 1997.'Armed conflicts, conflict termination and peace agreements, 1989–96' in *Journal of Peace Research,* 34/3: 339–58.

—— and Karin Axell. 1993. 'Armed Conflict at the End of the Cold War, 1989–92' in *Journal of Peace Research,* 30/3: 331–46.

Wallensteen, Peter et al./Uppsala Conflict Data Project. various years. 'Major armed conflict' in *SIPRI yearbook.*

Wallerstein, Immanuel. 1995. *Die Sozialwissenschaft 'kaputtdenken': Die Grenzen der paradigmen des 19. Jahrhunderts.* Weinheim: Beltz Athenäum.

Walt van Praag, Michael C. van. 1997. 'The Struggle for Self-determination and the Role of UNPO' in *ECOR* 9: 197–203.

—— 1994. 'UNPO Was Created and Is Run by the Nations and People that Are not Represented in the UN and in International Fora'. *ECOR* 12: 49–55.

—— 1993. 'The Political Rights of Indigenous Peoples and the Political Need for Change'. Unpublished paper.

War Annuals (John Laffin ed.) 1985–87. *War Annual: A Guide to Contemporary Wars and Conflicts.* London: Brassey's.

—— 1989–93. *The World in Conflict: War Annuals. Contemporary Warfare Analysed.* London: Brassey's.

Wasmuht, Ulrike C. 1992. *Friedensforschung als Konfliktforschung: Zur Notwendigkeit einer Rückbesinnung auf den Konflikt als zentrale Kategorie.* Bonn: AFB-Texte 1.

Wearne, Phillip/MRG. 1994. *The Maya of Guatemala.* London: MRG.

Weeks, Dudley. 1994. *The Eight Essential Steps to Conflict Resolution. Preserving Relationships at Work, at Home, and in the Community.* New York: Tarcher/ Putnam.

Wegemund, Regina. 1991. *Politisierte Ethnizität in Mauretanien und Senegal.* Arbeiten IAK 79; Hamburg.

Weiss, Cora J. Dean and V. Nichols/Millennium Forum. Peace, Security and Disarmament Group. 2000. *The Priority Actions for Civil Society, Governments and the United Nations.* (www.millenniumforum.org)

Westad, Odd A. 1992. 'Rethinking Revolutions: The Cold War in the Third World'. *Journal of Peace Research,* 29: 455–64.

Wiberg, Håkan. 1997. 'Kriegsursachenforschung: wie dürftig ist sie?'; in: EuS, 8: 3, pp. 308–12.

—— and Christian P. Scherrer eds. 1999. *Ethnicity and Intra-state Conflict: Types, Causes and Peace Strategies.* Aldershot: Ashgate 1999.

Widerspruch, half-yearly periodical. 1995: 'Ethnische Politik, Krieg und Völkermord' (30); 1991: 'Neo-Kolonialismus' (22).

Wimmer, Andreas. 1994. 'Der Kampf um den Staat: Zur vergleichenden Analyse ethnischer Konflikte' in Müller co-ord.: 511–38.

Winkler, August and Hartmut Kaelble eds. 1993. *Nationalismus, Nationalitäten, Supranationalität: Europa nach 1945.* Stuttgart: Klett-Cotta.

Wittfogel, Karl A. 1977. *Die Orientalische Despotie: Eine vergleichende Untersuchung totaler Macht.* Frankfurt/M.: Ullstein.

World Conference of Indigenous Peoples on Territory, Environment and Development (Kari-Oca). 1992. 'Kari-Oca Declaration and Indigenous Peoples Earth Charter', Kari-Oca (Brazil).

Worldwatch Institute (Michael Renner). 1990. *Konversion zur Friedensökonomie.* Schwalbach: Worldwatch Paper 3.

Wulf, Herbert. 1991. *Waffenexport aus Deutschland: Geschäfte mit dem fernen Tod.* Reinbek bei Hamburg: Rowohlt.

WWC (WoodrowWilson Center) (John Stone). 1995. *Problems in Advanced Industrial Societies: Ethnic Conflict in the Post-Cold War Era.* Washington DC: Workshop Paper.

—— (Charles Tripp ed.) 1995a. *Sectarianism and the Secular State: Ethnic Conflict in the Post-Cold War Era.* Conference report. Washington DC: WWC.

Yamskov, Anatoly N. 1994. 'The "New Minorities" in Post-Soviet States'. *Cultural Survival Quarterly,* 18/2–13: 58–61.

Yin, Ma. 1989. *China's Minority Nationalities.* Beijing: Foreign Language Press.

Young, Crawford. 1993. *The Rising Tide of Cultural Pluralism: The Nation State at Bay?* Madison, Wisc./London: University of Wisconsin Press.

Zartmann, I. William, ed. 1997. *Governance as Conflict Management: Politics and Violence in West Africa.* Washington DC: Brookings Institution.

—— ed. 1995. *Elusive Peace. Negotiating an End to Civil Wars.* Washington DC: Brookings Institution.

—— 1992. *Resolving Regional Conflicts. International Perspectives.* London: Sage.

—— ed. 1989. *Ripe for Revolution: Conflict and Intervention in Africa.* Oxford: Oxford University Press.

—— and Francis M. Deng eds. 1991. *Conflict resolution in Africa.* Washington DC: Brookings Institution.

Zimmermann, Klaus. 1992. *Sprachkontakt, ethnische Identität und Identitätsbeschädigung.* Frankfurt/M.: Vervuert.

Journals of Interest

AfricAsia; Blätter des iz3W; The Courier (Brussels: EU-ACP); *Cultural Survival; The Economist; Indigenous Affairs* (Copenhagen: IWGIA); *Journal of Peace Research* (Oslo: PRIO/Sage); *Le Monde diplomatique; Peace Review; pogrom; South; Der Spiegel; Sü dwind; Survival; Die Wochenzeitung.*

Index